Terrorist Profiling and Law Enforcement

This book analyses the usefulness of terrorist profiling utilised by law enforcement officers as a pre-emptive means to assist them in the detection, prevention and deterrence of terrorism and/or its preparatory activities.

It explores two main themes arising from the phenomenon of terrorist profiling: the lawfulness of terrorist profiling and the utility of profiling. These two themes are explored in three separate parts. Firstly, the book begins by drawing upon human rights concerns arising from the use of terrorist profiling by law enforcement officers. Secondly, an analytical framework capable of making determinations on the usefulness of terrorist profiling. This framework develops a profiling spectrum that ranges from formal and informal manifestations of terrorist profiling that forms the basis for evaluating its usefulness. Finally, the book presents an examination of various manifestations of terrorist profiling by separating the analysis of the 'construction' of profiles on the one hand, from their 'application,' on the other, so as to be able to identify and examine profiling's usefulness as a technique to assist law enforcement officers make predictions about likely offender characteristics.

This book ultimately concludes that terrorist profiling should only be conducted by undertaking a systematic assessment of the construction of profiles separate from the application of profiles whilst simultaneously taking into account fundamental human rights concerns with the practice of terrorist profiling.

The work will be an essential resource for academics, law enforcement officers and lawyers in the disciplines of law, criminology, human rights, criminal justice and policing. As the book engages with terrorist profiling, it will also be of interest to those engaged in the psychology of terrorism.

Noel McGuirk is a Lecturer in Law specialising in terrorism law at Lancaster University Law School. Previously, Noel was a judicial research assistant at the Courts Service (Ireland) based in the Court of Appeal and worked on various research projects during his tenure. Noel's research interests broadly focus on the relationship between terrorism, counterterrorism and human rights law. He is particularly interested in analysing legal responses to terrorism that have been adopted by various states to assist in preventing, detecting and deterring terrorism threats.

Terrorist Profiling and Law Enforcement

Detection, Prevention, Deterrence

Noel McGuirk

Routledge
Taylor & Francis Group
LONDON AND NEW YORK

First published 2021
by Routledge
2 Park Square, Milton Park, Abingdon, Oxon OX14 4RN

and by Routledge
52 Vanderbilt Avenue, New York, NY 10017

Routledge is an imprint of the Taylor & Francis Group, an informa business

© 2021 Noel McGuirk

The right of Noel McGuirk to be identified as author of this work has been asserted by them in accordance with sections 77 and 78 of the Copyright, Designs and Patents Act 1988.

All rights reserved. No part of this book may be reprinted or reproduced or utilised in any form or by any electronic, mechanical, or other means, now known or hereafter invented, including photocopying and recording, or in any information storage or retrieval system, without permission in writing from the publishers.

Trademark notice: Product or corporate names may be trademarks or registered trademarks, and are used only for identification and explanation without intent to infringe.

British Library Cataloguing-in-Publication Data
A catalogue record for this book is available from the British Library

Library of Congress Cataloging-in-Publication Data
Names: McGuirk, Noel, author.
Title: Terrorist profiling and law enforcement : detection, prevention, deterrence / Noel McGuirk.
Description: Abingdon, Oxon ; New York, NY : Routledge, 2021. | Includes bibliographical references and index.
Identifiers: LCCN 2020039033 (print) | LCCN 2020039034 (ebook) | ISBN 9780367437763 (hardback) | ISBN 9781003005711 (ebook)
Subjects: LCSH: Terrorism–Prevention. | Criminal behavior, Prediction of. | Law enforcement.
Classification: LCC HV6431 .M4255 2021 (print) | LCC HV6431 (ebook) | DDC 363.325/16–dc23
LC record available at https://lccn.loc.gov/2020039033
LC ebook record available at https://lccn.loc.gov/2020039034

ISBN: 978-0-367-43776-3 (hbk)
ISBN: 978-1-003-00571-1 (ebk)

Typeset in Galliard
by KnowledgeWorks Global Ltd.

In memory of a loving Dad. Ar dheis Dé go raibh a h'anam.

And to a loving mother for always being there for me.

Contents

Table of cases

Table of statutes

Figures and tables

Figures

Tables

Acknowledgements

The research and writing of this book was substantially undertaken as part of my PhD at the University of Birmingham. I am very grateful to my PhD supervisor, Dr Adrian Hunt, for his dedication, diligence, expert wisdom, support, patience, encouragement and not least his honesty over the course of my PhD studies. I am also grateful to the College of Arts and Law and Birmingham Law School for funding my PhD as it would never have been possible to complete this work without this funding. I would also like to thank Dr Lawrence McNamara for encouraging me and instilling in me the confidence to undertake a PhD research project. I would also like to thank the chapter reviewers by Routledge. Although they are anonymous, I am very grateful for their very helpful comments that developed the chapters. I would also like to thank the staff at Routledge, especially Alison Kirk and Emily Summers who I worked closely on this project. Finally, I would like to thank my family and especially Ian who has supported me without question.

Preface

This book has been written with the primary readership in mind being academics, students at undergraduate and postgraduate (taught and research) levels, practitioners and law enforcement officers. A key trend in law and policy aimed at combatting terrorism is the increasing use of policing strategies that allow law enforcement officers anticipate risk so that they can engage in preventing, interrupting and prosecuting those suspected of terrorism offences before their commission. One such pre-emptive policing strategy is the use of terrorist profiling. The rationale underpinning terrorist profiling is to allow law enforcement officers identify those likely to involved in terrorism or its associated activities so that law enforcement officers can prevent, interrupt and prosecute suspects before an act of terrorism. The use of terrorist profiling is highly controversial given that its use has been perceived as being unlawful. Previous attempts at analysing terrorist profiling has tended to rely solely on human rights law as the analytical lens to evaluate the usefulness and lawfulness of terrorist profiling.

The discussion in this book argues that the effectiveness and usefulness of terrorist profiling should only be undertaken by deconstructing the profiling process so as to allow a thorough examination of the phenomenon of terrorist profiling. As a result, the discussion in this book establishes two analytical lenses as the basis to systematically examine terrorist profiling. Firstly, the discussion develops an effectiveness framework that examines the construction of terrorist profiles separately from the application of terrorist profiles. Secondly, the discussion also draws upon criminal profiling methodologies and approaches as the basis to evaluate different manifestations of terrorist profiling. These analytical lenses are used to conduct a taxonomy on different manifestations of terrorist profiling so as to systematically evaluate their usefulness as a law enforcement tool to predict likely terrorist characteristics.

1 Introduction

1.1 Introduction

This book examines whether law enforcement officers are able to rely on profiling methods or approaches as a pre-emptive means to assist them in the detection, prevention and deterrence of terrorism and/or its preparatory activities by assisting them to identify those engaged or likely to be involved in acts of terrorism. Although the phenomenon of terrorist profiling has been examined previously, this book poses a number of new questions about terrorist profiling (outlined later in the chapter) in order to analyse its usefulness as a law enforcement tool to assist in managing the risks arising from the enduring war on terror.

The politics at the international level over the past decade and beyond has been primarily focused on creating laws and policies to ensure the protection of citizens and institutions of democracies against those countries, groups and individuals wishing to use violence as a means to demonstrate their objection and hostility towards the norms of democracy, liberty and freedom.[1]

Enders and Sandler identify 'that states have a positive duty towards ensuring the safety of its national culture, identity and democracy from the arbitrary interference of terrorism.'[2] This duty can be identified as comprising at least two strands. Firstly, the duty to protect against threats of terrorism and secondly the duty to uphold fundamental human rights and freedoms. In isolation, these duties are not contentious, but the means adopted by governments to discharge these duties often create controversy. Specifically, laws and policies aimed at managing the threat of terrorism regularly come into direct conflict with the duty to protect and uphold fundamental rights and freedoms.

These issues generally involve focusing on the question: to what extent it can be considered legitimate for a state to interfere with fundamental rights and freedoms so as to protect against the threat of terrorism? This often creates a conundrum for governments as to how to balance their duty to protect against the threat of terrorism versus their duty to uphold fundament rights and freedoms.

Over the course of the past few decades, various governments have sought to conduct this balancing exercise by relying on risk management strategies through the creation of counterterrorism frameworks. A recurrent theme in counterterrorism law and policy is that they provide law enforcement officers with an array of special police powers aimed at assisting in the prevention, detection and prosecution of those engaged in terrorism and/or terrorism preparatory activities.

The justification in favour of creating special police powers is due to the serious nature of the threat posed by terrorism to human life and the difficulty for law enforcement officers using more traditional police powers to detect, deter and prosecute terrorism suspects. Counterterrorism frameworks frequently represent 'a fusion of national security and criminal justice policies in an attempt to move towards pre-emptive strategies of "prevention and control" of terrorism threats.'[3]

The counterterrorism 'strategies of prevention and control have resulted in a shift towards' a reliance on 'anticipatory risk' practices in policing policy 'which aims to allow law enforcement officers to identify, interrupt and prosecute those suspected of terrorism offences before their commission.'[4] One such policing policy is the use of a profiling method or approach that is aimed at assisting law enforcement officers identify those likely to be engaged in terrorism or its preparatory activities.

1.2 Terrorism and profiling a definitional problem

At this stage, it is necessary to define profiling in a general sense and further to consider the definition of terrorism for the purposes of this book.

Profiling may be considered as being a process that allows the profiler to identify a sequence of commonalities from different sets of data so as to predict likely offender characteristics.[5] There is a lack of consensus in the literature as to the precise definition of profiling which sways between a narrow and a broad definitional approach. For the purposes of this book, a broad definition of profiling is adopted so as to ensure that a significant array of profiling methods and approaches can be included for analysis. As a result, profiling is defined as being any technique or process that seeks to allow law enforcement officers to identify probable offender characteristics.[6]

The term profiling has become interchangeable with the terms 'offender profiling, criminal profiling, criminal personality profiling and psychological profiling' as a label for profiling techniques.[7] Many methods use the same structure such as the analysis of crime scene evidence, victim reports and/or previous criminal records to identify common offender characteristics. The core differences lie in the abilities and the characteristics of the profiler and the use of the information by profilers to make predictions on likely offender characteristics.[8] For example, some profiling methods may rely on forensic evidence to make predictions of likely characteristics, whilst other methods may use previous offending records to engage in statistical reasoning to identify commonalities to make predictions as to likely offender characteristics. Doughlas *et al* identify that there are commonly three phases of profiling in criminal justice including: 'firstly, criminal investigation, secondly apprehension and thirdly prosecution.'[9]

Consequently, the use of any data by a profiler so as to make predictions about 'likely offender characteristics can be considered some form of profiling' that may occur during criminal investigation, apprehension or prosecution of offenders.[10]

The definition of terrorism is similarly problematic as there is no consensus in law or academia about its scope.[11] The absence of consensus may be attributable to the broad range of views and differences of opinion about the use of violence to further objectives.[12] Despite this lack of an agreed consensus, it is possible to develop a definition of terrorism in two ways. Firstly, there have been various attempts at the international and domestic levels to criminalise acts of violence. Secondly, it is also possible to draw upon academic literature to support a definition of terrorism for the purposes of analysis in this book.

Internationally, the United Nations General Assembly has condemned various uses of violence as acts of terrorism in the following terms:

> criminal acts intended or calculated to provoke a state of terror in a general public, a group of persons or particular persons for political purposes are in any circumstances unjustifiable, whatever the considerations of a political, philosophical, ideological, racial, ethnic, religious or any other nature that may be invoked to justify them.[13]

Additionally, terrorism is described in the 'International Convention for the Suppression of the Financing of Terrorism' as being

> [a]ny other act intended to cause death or serious bodily injury to a civilian, or to any other person not taking an active part in the hostilities in a situation of armed conflict, when the purpose of such act, by its nature or context, is to intimidate a population, or to compel a government or an international organization to do or to abstain from doing any act.[14]

At the domestic level in countries, such as the United Kingdom (UK), there is a statutory definition of terrorism that allows us to capture a formal definition of terrorism. Section 1 of Terrorism Act 2000(TA) provides a broad definition of terrorism as being:

1 In this Act 'terrorism' means the use or threat of action where—

  a the action falls within subsection (2),
  b the use or threat is designed to influence the government [or an international governmental organisation] or to intimidate the public or a section of the public, and
  c the use or threat is made for the purpose of advancing a political, religious [racial] or ideological cause.

2 Action falls within this subsection if it—

  a involves serious violence against a person,
  b involves serious damage to property,

c endangers a person's life, other than that of the person committing the action,

d creates a serious risk to the health or safety of the public or a section of the public, or

e is designed seriously to interfere with or seriously to disrupt an electronic system.

3 The use or threat of action falling within subsection (2) which involves the use of firearms or explosives is terrorism whether or not subsection (1)(b) is satisfied.[15].

The definition of terrorism has also provoked considerable debate in the literature where a survey by Schmid and Jongman across over 100 definitions of terrorism led them to conclude that terrorism should be defined as being:

> …an anxiety-inspiring method of repeated violent action, employed by a (semi-) clandestine individual, group or state actors, for idiosyncratic, criminal or political reasons, whereby – in contrast to assassination – the direct targets of violence are not the main targets.[16]

Although the international, domestic and academic discussion on the definition of terrorism shows considerable variation in approach, for the purposes of analysis throughout this book, it is necessary to identify a working definition of the term. There are at least two aspects that can be identified as being common denominators across the differing definitions. Firstly, the 'use of violence or threat of violence' and secondly the motives and objectives of the organisers/perpetrators of terrorism. As a result, terrorism for the purposes of analysis in this book shall be defined as being any 'use or threat of violence with the purpose of advancing a political, religious, racial or [any] cause.'[17] It is contended that this definition reflects most of the legal and academic definitions that law enforcement officers will employ when performing their duties.

1.3 Central analytical aim

The primary aim of this book is to assess the usefulness of terrorist profiling as a counterterrorism tool. This aim is pursued by asking: to what extent (if at all), and in what ways (if any) terrorist profiling may be useful as part of the law enforcement process of identifying individuals engaged in acts of terrorism and associated preparatory activities?

In order to answer this question, three sub-questions emerge:

- What is terrorist profiling?
- How should the usefulness of terrorist profiling be examined?
- Can terrorist profiling ever be considered a useful counterterrorism tool?

The approach adopted in this book to assess the usefulness of terrorist profiling so as to determine the likely utility of various manifestations of terrorist profiling. The assessment of the usefulness of any counterterrorism tool can be conducted in a variety of different ways depending on the context of the analysis being pursued. For example, the discussion later in the book will highlight that past approaches examining terrorist profiling tend to navigate between a human rights assessment and a utilitarian assessment. A human rights assessment tends to focus on the compatibility of terrorist profiling with fundamental human rights standards. Alternatively, a utilitarian assessment tends to focus on the assistive value of terrorist profiling regardless of the compatibility of human rights standards. A core argument advanced in this book is that viewing both of these assessments as being mutually exclusive fails to conduct a systematic assessment of the theory and the practice of terrorist profiling.

Profiling by its very nature exists in a variety of forms which means that there is no one model that can be drawn upon to examine the usefulness of terrorist profiling. It is a flexible concept that can apply to almost any method or approach aimed at discerning likely offender characteristics. This means that the usefulness of terrorist profiling is best examined by undertaking an examination of its core processes by separating the analysis of the 'construction' of profiles on the one hand, from their 'application,' on the other, so as to be able to examine the usefulness of profiling as a technique to assist law enforcement officers make predictions about likely offender characteristics. This separation of the profiling process allows a systematic assessment of the phenomenon of terrorist profiling by breaking it down into its constituent parts.

The examination of the usefulness of terrorist profiling is conducted by examining the likely 'effectiveness' of different manifestations of terrorist profiling. The framework for analysing effectiveness is set out later in this chapter at 1.7. This effectiveness framework analyses terrorist profiling by separating the construction and application of terrorist profiling so as to question, whether there are any circumstances in which this practice may be considered capable of achieving its aim of assisting law enforcement officers to identify those likely to be involved in terrorist activities or its preparatory activities. The argument advanced in this book is that if a manifestation of terrorist profiling can satisfy the effectiveness framework, then it may be possible to draw a conclusion that specific manifestations of terrorist profiling could be considered useful as it is likely to deliver on its aim of assisting law enforcement officers identify those engaged in terrorism or its preparatory activities.

However, this measure of usefulness fails to appreciate the human rights concerns that might arise from the reliance on terrorist profiling by law enforcement officers. Any assessment of the usefulness of terrorist profiling must engage with a complex array of human rights issues that may impact any conclusion drawn on the usefulness of terrorist profiling. This book does not seek to position the usefulness of terrorist profiling above human rights norms and proceeds on the basis of engaging in chapter two with the complex array of human rights issues raised by the very practice of terrorist profiling. The objective of this discussion early in the book is to consider from a legal perspective whether any form of profiling can be considered compatible with human rights norms, as this is viewed as being a precursor to analysing the usefulness of terrorist profiling. This assessment is primarily undertaken by considering the human rights norms and standards that are most relevant from a law enforcement officer's perspective operating in the field and those affecting the assessment of the utility of the manifestations of terrorist profiling examined in chapters four to six.

This book develops a taxonomy of terrorist profiling by examining available evidence on different manifestations of terrorist profiling. In developing this taxonomy, it is contended that an analysis of terrorist profiling is best conducted where profiling is examined as occurring along a spectrum. At one end of this spectrum a form of profiling exists that is best classified as being examples of 'formal terrorist' profiling. Formal terrorist profiling can be defined as the systematic and official use of any profiling method or approach by law enforcement officers that is aimed at identifying likely terrorist characteristics. There are at least three defining features of formal terrorist profiling: an official and systematic process to construct a profile, the application of a profile by law enforcement officers and the ability to review the operation and practice of formal terrorist profiling. Formal manifestations of profiling may in some instances be characterised as being an assistive tool to help law enforcement officers identify individuals that are engaged in acts of terrorism or preparatory activities.

At the opposite end of the spectrum there are other manifestations of terrorist profiling that are best classifiable as being examples of 'informal' terrorist profiling. Informal terrorist profiling exhibits at least two common characteristics. Firstly, it is common for states to refuse to acknowledge the existence of manifestations of informal terrorist profiling as being a form of profiling. Secondly, manifestations of informal terrorist profiling do not exhibit the same level of a systematic process, approach or structure in direct contrast to those manifestations of formal terrorist profiling. Informal manifestations of terrorist profiling are unlikely to be a tool capable of assisting law enforcement officers to identify suspects likely to be engaged in terrorism and/or preparatory activities.

1.4 Book outline

Following this introductory chapter, the discussion begins in chapter two by examining the human rights concerns arising from the discussion on the usefulness of terrorist profiling in chapters three to five. The human rights concerns are examined first as a preliminary issue to determine the likely circumstances (if any) that profiling may be considered compatible with fundamental rights. In this chapter, it is argued that there are two precursory issues in any assessment on the usefulness of terrorist profiling that may have an impact on the conclusion drawn on usefulness in chapters four to six. Firstly, whether it can ever be justified to include sensitive characteristics in terrorist profiling and secondly, if so, in what circumstances can sensitive characteristics be justified in the construction and application of terrorist profiles. The argument advanced in this chapter is that there is no single answer to either of these questions from the perspective of law enforcement officers but rather there are at least two sets of arguments that need to be taken into account in assessing the justification of including sensitive characteristics in the profiling process.

Firstly, there are positive arguments which involve focusing on the lawfulness of including sensitive characteristics in the terrorist profiling process. Secondly, there are normative arguments which involve assessing whether the inclusion of sensitive characteristics is something that the state ought to avoid in light of the risk that particular individuals or groups of individuals may become the focal point of enhanced law enforcement scrutiny. The discussion in chapter two concentrates on identifying, explaining and evaluating the positive arguments concerning the justification question. The normative arguments are considered individually in chapters four to six when the discussion turns to assessing the impact of terrorist profiling.

In resolving the positive or lawfulness issue of including sensitive characteristics, the discussion in chapter two contends that there appears to be a basis to argue that formal manifestations of terrorist profiling may be considered justified and hence lawful for at least two reasons. Firstly, the systematic nature of manifestations of formal terrorist profiling means that it is possible to review, alter and adapt profiling so that the risk of relying solely on sensitive characteristics is minimised. Secondly, the sensitive characteristics are included with non-sensitive characteristics to reduce or manage the risk of sensitive characteristics becoming the main or sole criteria to identify individuals for enhanced levels of review by law enforcement officers.

The discussion in chapter two also argues that manifestations of informal terrorist profiling can *never* be justified on the grounds that these profiling processes are not subject to review and lack transparency in assessing their usefulness. Additionally, manifestations of informal terrorist profiling carry a risk that particular individuals exhibiting the sensitive characteristics become the concentration for law enforcement officers in the detection, prevention and prosecution of acts of terrorism and preparatory activities.

After assessing the positive/lawfulness issue in favour of including sensitive characteristics, the key issue in this book is then to consider the normative argument related to classifying and evaluating manifestations of formal and informal terrorist profiling. However, in order to begin conducting a normative assessment of terrorist profiling, it is necessary to create an analytical lens to evaluate the likely usefulness of terrorist profiling being able to fulfil its core objective of being assistive to law enforcement officers in the detection, prevention and prosecution of acts of terrorism and preparatory activities.

In starting to resolve this issue, the discussion in chapter three progresses by conducting an examination of different profiling methods and approaches that can be adopted in criminal profiling. This chapter examines criminal profiling as a basis to critique the likely usefulness of manifestations of terrorist profiling examined in subsequent chapters. This discussion identifies that there are two types of profiling: deductive and inductive profiling.

Deductive profiling is where law enforcement officers use profiling methods to react to crimes already committed and deduce offender characteristics by using forensic crime evidence and victim reports. The use of deductive profiling to identify likely offender characteristics is supported by offenders exhibiting particular pathologies in their commission of crime. For example, pathological crimes such as murder, rape and arson tend to be committed in a particular way, where the defendant may leave clues about their likely characteristics that may assist the profiler to construct an accurate profile. The discussion in chapter three suggests that this type of profiling is not suitable in the context terrorism given that terrorists are unlikely to exhibit the pathologies necessary to allow the profiler to accurately predict likely offender characteristics. Further, this type of profiling is about trying to apprehend an offender still at large but in some instances of contemporary terrorism, the use of suicide bombers results in the death of the actual bomber. As a result, a deductive profiling method or approach may not be considered capable of assisting law enforcement officer predict likely terrorist characteristics.

Alternatively, inductive profiling is where the law enforcement officer relies on proactive profiling methods as a tool to predict likely offender characteristics to prevent future criminality. The discussion in chapter three argues that this type of profiling may be considered as being more suitable in the context of terrorism so long as the profiler takes into account at least four issues. This includes the changing nature of information on terrorists, the availability of terrorism information/data, the accuracy of available data and not all suspects exhibiting the characteristics will necessarily be terrorists.

In light of the deductive/inductive analytical lens, the discussions in chapters four to six examine various manifestations of terrorist profiling so as to consider their potential usefulness to assist law enforcement officers detect, deter and prosecute those likely to be engaged in terrorism and/or preparatory activities. Each of these different manifestations of profiling is assessed in terms of its 'effectiveness.' The approach adopted to measure and evaluate 'effectiveness' is explained in section 1.7 of this chapter below.

Chapter four examines manifestations of formal terrorist profiling by focusing on various approaches adopted in Germany and the United States (US). This chapter separately examines the construction and application of profiles that draw upon knowledge discovery processes and data mining approaches. Knowledge discovery processes is where a profiler engages in a systematic extraction of information from various data sources so as to construct a profile of likely offender characteristics. Data mining is one step within a knowledge discovery process that assists the profiler make sense of the data that they have extracted.

A key theme evident in this discussion is that manifestations of formal terrorist profiling, as considered in this chapter, tend to adopt a highly systematic and formalised process to construct and apply profiles that follow an inductive profiling method/approach. Specifically, the construction of profiles is premised upon a broad range of data and their application in the field is subject to continuous testing so that the accuracy of these profiles can be reviewed and as a result they may have the potential to improve through iterative development.

It is acknowledged that the discussion cannot prove in absolute terms that the examined manifestations of formal terrorist profiling may capable of assisting law enforcement officers identify those likely to be engaged in acts of terrorism in practice. Nevertheless, from a theoretical perspective the approaches adopted in these manifestations of terrorist profiling provide a basis to control the data used in the construction of profiles and to further monitor the use of profiles in the field. As a result, it may be argued that there is a reasonable degree of probability that these manifestations of formal terrorist profiling may have the potential to assist law enforcement officers in preventing, detecting and deterring acts of terrorism over time. However, the discussion in this chapter questions whether the usefulness of this type of terrorist profiling is overshadowed by its impact on society as a whole. Nevertheless, it is argued that although manifestations of formal terrorist profiling are problematic, they are more capable of being controlled given their open and transparent nature.

Chapter five examines behavioural terrorist profiling as a further manifestation of terrorist profiling. This chapter argues that behavioural terrorist profiling cannot accurately be classified as being an example of formal terrorist profiling in comparable terms with those manifestations of formal terrorist profiling examined in chapter four. This is due to the fact that the manifestation of behavioural terrorist profiling examined in this chapter did not appear to exhibit the same level of a systematic process in the construction/application of profiles. However, the manifestation of behavioural terrorist profiling considered in this chapter tends to exhibit more of a formalised process that partially relied on inductive profiling methods/approaches in contrast to manifestations of informal terrorist profiling examined in chapter six. Consequently, the discussion in chapter five argues that the manifestation of behavioural terrorist profiling examined is on the profiling spectrum and can be positioned between formal and informal terrorist profiling.

Chapter six examines manifestations of profiling which may be classifiable as being closer towards manifestations of informal terrorist profiling on the profiling spectrum. In order to examine manifestations of informal terrorist profiling, the discussion in this chapter assesses the exercise of police powers so as to demonstrate to quite a high degree of probability that some uses of police powers may be classifiable as an example of informal terrorist profiling. These police powers include police-initiated stop and searches, the use of powers of arrest and the power to engage in identity checking and the raiding of premises. This classification rests on two core arguments. Firstly, the exercise of these powers is not officially recognised as being a form of profiling. Secondly, they do not appear to exhibit a comparable systematic process, approach or structure in the construction and application of profiles as those manifestations of formal terrorist profiling examined in chapter three. The selection of countries in this chapter may appear ad hoc from a methodological perspective but the evidence presented in this chapter is entirely based on available evidence.

The assessment of stop and search powers begins by examining the structure of this power established in various statutes so as to discern the types of data and the treatment of this data that can be drawn upon in the construction of profiles. The discussion of the application of the various stop and search powers in practice argues that there is a strong likelihood, that these powers may be considered as showing the hallmarks of a profiling process that is far short of the processes evidence in manifestations of formal profiling examined in chapter four.

The discussion also considers qualitative studies on peoples' experiences of other uses of police powers including the use of targeted identity checking, the use of arrest powers and the targeted raiding of premises in France and Germany. This discussion argues that these studies further support the contention that some uses of police powers may be considered as resembling a hallmark of informal profiling. Although, these qualitative studies may expose potential abuses of police powers, they combine to show a strong possibility that law enforcement officers in some instances may be using these powers in an almost crude way to profile those suspected of being involved in terrorism.

The discussion in chapter six ultimately concludes that the use of these manifestations of informal terrorist profiling poses three grave concerns that questions the usefulness of this form of profiling. This includes the lack of an acknowledgment that these powers may in some instances be considered as being a form of profiling, which seriously impacts the reviewability of profiling. Additionally, the apparent absence of a process to construct profiles possess significant risks to the accuracy of the profile by being able to minimise the limitations of deductive and inductive profiling methods that is discussed in chapter three. Finally, the apparent application of these police powers on specific ethnicities raises serious concerns related to the lawfulness of each application of these powers. As a result, the discussion in this chapter concludes these manifestations of informal terrorist profiling are unlikely to assist any law enforcement officer prevent, detect or deter acts of terrorism by assisting in the identification of likely terrorist characteristics.

1.5 Contribution to knowledge

Although there is much analysis and discussion in the literature on the subject of profiling and terrorist profiling, this book makes at least three core contributions to existing knowledge.

Firstly, one of the core themes that the discussion in this book explores is whether law enforcement officers can use profiling methodologies to assist with preventing, detecting and deterring terrorism by affording law enforcement officers the ability to identify likely terrorist characteristics. The book draws upon established criminal profiling methodologies as the basis to engage in an analytical assessment of terrorist profiling. As a result, this book claims to be one of the first attempts to engage in identifying, explaining and evaluating manifestations of terrorist profiling by reference to core established profiling methodologies. This adds to the previous knowledge by extending the reach of criminal profiling methodologies as one basis to evaluate manifestations of terrorist profiling.

Secondly, this book also argues that the usefulness of terrorist profiling is best examined by adopting a three-tiered evaluative approach so as to ensure that each constitute part of terrorist profiling is thoroughly examined. This means that any examination of profiling should be analysed by reference to the input assessment, output assessment and the impact assessment. The input assessment provides the basis to analyse the types of data that can be used to construct profiles whilst the output assessment focuses on the application of that profile in practice. However, a further layer of assessment involves considering the broader impact of the use of profiling in practice so as question its usefulness to identify those likely to be involved in terrorism and/or preparatory activities.

Thirdly, in light of the identification and explanation of criminal profiling methodologies and the effectiveness framework, this book is able to classify different manifestations of profiling by creating a profiling spectrum. The profiling spectrum ranges from formal terrorist profiling to informal terrorist profiling. This spectrum provides a systematic basis to examine the usefulness of terrorist profiling as an assistive tool for law enforcement officers by separating the process to construct and apply profiles.

This approach is not undertaken in existing research. The assessment of the usefulness of terrorist profiling in the literature raises a dichotomy between portraying profiling as an essential tool to assist law enforcement officers detect and prevent acts of terrorism and an unnecessary and unlawful practice capable of creating and perpetuating stereotypes which disproportionately affect ethnic and racial minorities in addition to stigmatising individuals who may have been previously involved in criminality.[18]

For example, De Schutter and Ringleheim,[19] Moeckli,[20] Goldson,[21] Parmar,[22] Ojanen[23] and Edley[24] all consider the use of terrorist profiling by law enforcement officers by conducting a legal assessment of the compatibility of terrorist profiling in light of human rights standards and norms. Although human rights standards and fundamental norms may provide a basis to assess/measure the effectiveness of terrorist profiling, an inherent limitation of this approach is that it frequently characterises terrorist profiling as being ineffective primarily on the basis of human rights norms and standards without undertaking a systematic identification, explanation or evaluation of the different profiling methods used to construct profiles. Further this literature does not specifically focus on the effectiveness of these methodologies as a tool to assist law enforcement officers in identifying individuals engaged in terrorism or preparatory activities.

Alternatively, terrorist profiling has also been evaluated by conducting a utilitarian assessment of its capacity to assist law enforcement officers in detecting and preventing acts of terrorism.[25] This approach commonly characterises terrorist profiling as being effective on the basis of its necessity as part of counterterrorism policy to assist law enforcement officers to foil and intercept serious terrorist attacks prior to their commission.[26] For example, a terrorist attack intercepted by law enforcement officers includes the attempted truck bombings in Singapore thought to have been targeting Singapore's airport, financial and embassy districts.[27]

However, this approach fails to identify the specific role fulfilled by terrorist profiling in comparison to other counterterrorist measures in assisting law enforcement officers preventing and detecting terrorism. Any assessment of terrorist profiling which fails to identify its role within counterterrorism may be subject to the criticism that the assistive value of terrorist profiling may be over or under inflated in the prevention and detection of terrorism and as a result is unable to determine a realistic assessment/measurement of effectiveness.

The effectiveness of terrorist profiling has also been assessed/measured on the strength of moral arguments. This approach commonly characterises terrorist profiling as being ineffective on basis of empirical evidence, which demonstrates a negative impact of terrorist profiling on ethnic minority communities. For example, Swiney demonstrates the negative impact of terrorist profiling on Arab and Muslim communities by drawing on empirical research conducted on a selection of Arab and Muslim communities across the US since the September 11 attacks.[28] This involved analysing empirical data collected from a range of Arab and Muslim community support centres across the US to identify common concerns in Arab and Muslim communities stemming from the use of terrorist profiling by law enforcement officers. This approach can also be considered limited as the assessment of effectiveness is largely conducted on the basis of opinion canvassed from various communities as opposed to an enhanced investigation of the processes involved in constructing and applying terrorist profiles.

The problem with these previous assessments of terrorist profiling is that they tend to either support or reject terrorist profiling without undertaking a systematic assessment of the profiling methodologies that distinguishes between the construction and application of profiles. This approach may be considered problematic, as it tends to concentrate on manifestations of profiling that are not accurately classifiable as being examples of profiling. Specifically, the discussion throughout this book will show that most of the previous examinations on profiling tend to concentrate on manifestations of profiling that are classifiable as being manifestations of informal terrorist profiling which are examined in chapter six. The discussion in chapter six argues that manifestations of informal terrorist profiling are off the profiling spectrum given that they exhibit an apparent absence of a systematic process to construct and/or apply terrorist profiles in contrast to manifestations of formal terrorist profiling.

There is a distinct lack of debate, discussion and analysis in the literature that provides an analytical framework to assess/measure the effectiveness of terrorist profiling which is capable of characterising terrorist profiling as being effective, ineffective or harmful on the basis of analysing the process of constructing terrorist profiles separate from the application of terrorist profiles. It is contended that the characterisation of terrorist profiling as being effective, ineffective or harmful can only be done by developing an analytical framework that is capable of assessing/measuring the effectiveness of the profiling methods used in the construction of terrorist profiles separately from the application of terrorist profiles by law enforcement officers, as this provides a basis for a methodical and systematic investigation of the effectiveness of terrorist profiling.

Therefore, the examination of profiling in this book extends beyond previous attempts by examining the construction and application of profiles separately within a systematic framework capable of drawing conclusions on the usefulness of terrorist profiling to identify likely terrorist characteristics. It should be noted here that the purpose of this approach is *not* to advance or support the use of terrorist profiling but rather to deconstruct the profiling process from construction to application of profiles so that any evaluation of profiling is more advanced than previous efforts by conducting a more in-depth assessment of terrorist profiling.

1.6 Research limitations

It is acknowledged that there are methodological challenges in the study of terrorist profiling that are common in any research. Specifically, in this book, there are challenges that relate to the limited availability of evidence to allow an affirmative conclusion to be drawn on the classification of profiling and the assessment of the usefulness of the different manifestations of terrorist profiling examined. However, the discussion throughout this book argues that there is sufficient evidence presented to support the various evaluations made on the different manifestations of terrorist profiling on the basis of a high degree of probability.

It is argued that the use of established criminal profiling methods as an analytical lens to evaluate the evidence on terrorist profiling and further the classification of terrorist profiling along a spectrum ranging from formal to informal terrorist profiling begins to address the methodological challenges. It should be noted here that at various points throughout this book, the selection of countries examined may appear somewhat random or *ad hoc* but the selection is primarily based on available evidence to support the research aim of this book. The very nature of the examination of terrorist profiling in this book is about deconstructing the profiling process so as to create an analytical lens that is capable of examining the usefulness of different manifestations of profiling. As a result, it will be necessary to examine different countries and manifestations of profiling based on available evidence so as to develop the profiling spectrum and to some degree test the framework established in the next section to assess the effectiveness of terrorist profiling.

1.7 An analytical framework to assess/measure the effectiveness of terrorist profiling

As identified and explained above an overarching concern of this book involves assessing the usefulness of terrorist profiling. The usefulness assessment is undertaken by questioning the effectiveness of profiling methods as the means to help law enforcement officers identify likely terrorist characteristics so as to determine whether terrorist profiling may be able to help identify those likely to be engaged in terrorism or its preparatory activities. The central aim of this section is to identify an analytical framework capable of assessing/measuring the effectiveness of terrorist profiling which can be drawn upon in subsequent chapters when examining different manifestations of terrorist profiling.

In previous research, I set out a framework to measure/assess the utility of profiling as a counterterrorism tool, which I adopt in this book to conduct the assessment of the likely effectiveness of different manifestations of terrorist profiling.[29] In this research, the core argument advanced was that terrorist profiling is best examined by adopting a three-tiered assessment framework as the basis to create a systematic framework capable of deconstructing the profiling process into an 'input,' 'output' and 'impact' assessment.

The first step involves conducting an 'input' assessment of terrorist profiling that focuses entirely on the construction of terrorist profiling. This part of the assessment entirely concentrates on the raw source data for profiles as well as the methods and approaches that can be used to construct a profile. This can be considered a fundamental starting point for the assessment of any profiling process as it considers how profiles are constructed by focusing on the methods/approaches used in the construction of profiles. This part of the evaluation of terrorist profiling involves drawing upon established criminal profiling methods as the basis to evaluate the processes and approaches adopted to construct a profile.

The second step involves conducting an 'output' assessment of terrorist profiling that focuses entirely on the application of terrorist profiling. This part of the assessment involves examining the use of profiles by law enforcement officers on the basis of discernible evidence of their application. It can involve relying on data such arrests or prosecutions, or any other available data on the application of terrorist profiling.

The third step involves conducting an 'impact' assessment of terrorist profiling that focuses entirely on the discernible evidence of the wider implications of using this counterterrorism tool. A core argument advanced in this book is that any assessment of the process to construct and apply profiles must go beyond this assessment by considering the impact of adopting such a measure. This forms an important basis to understand whether the costs associated with terrorist profiling may be considered as being too high, even if it can be considered capable of theoretically aiding law enforcement officers distil likely terrorist characteristics.

Therefore, the analytical framework adopted in this book to advance the assessment of the utility or usefulness of terrorist profiling is a twin-step process. The first step involves conducting an input assessment focused on the construction of profiles, the output assessment focused on the application of profiles as well as the broader impact of profiles. The second step involves relying on the assessment conducted at the first step to classify terrorist profiling by reference to the profiling spectrum that ranges from formal to informal. This classification is aimed at assisting in understanding the very types of profiling that are likely to be useful in assisting law enforcement officers in the detection, prosecution and deterrence of terrorism and/or its preparatory activities.

Notes

1. M. Elliott, 'The "war on terror", UK Style: the detention and deportation of suspected terrorists' (2010) 8(1) International Journal of Constitutional Law 131, 131.
2. W. Enders and T. Sandler, 'The effectiveness of anti-terrorism policies: a vector-autoregression-intervention analysis' (1993) 87(4) American Political Science Review 829, 830.
3. Elliott, 'The "war on terror", UK Style: the detention and deportation of suspected terrorists' (n1), 131.
4. ibid.
5. B. Snook, J. Eastwood, P. Gendreau, C. Goggin and R. Cullen, 'Taking stock of criminal profiling: a narrative review and meta-analysis' (2007) 34(4) Criminal Science and Behaviour 437, 437–438.
6. M. Horvath, 'Offender Profiling' in S. Tong, R. Bryant and M. Horvath, *Understanding Criminal Investigation* (John Wiley & Sons Publishing, 2009), 69.
7. J. Douglas, R. Ressler, A. Burgess and C. Hartman, 'Criminal profiling from crime scene analysis' (1986) 4 Behavioural Science and Law 401, 405.
8. P. Gendreau, C. Goggin, E. Cullen and M. Paparozzi, 'The Common Sense Revolution and Correctional Policy' in J. Maguire, (ed) *Offender Rehabilitation and Treatment: Effective Programmes and Policies to Reduce Reoffending* (John Wiley & Sons Publishing, 2002), 359–365.
9. Doughlas, Ressler, Burgess and Hartman, 'Criminal profiling from crime scene analysis' (n7) 401–405. See also: B. Turvey, *Criminal Profiling: An Introduction to Behavioural Evidence Analysis* (Academic Press, 1999), chp 1.
10. Doughlas, Ressler, Burgess and Hartman, 'Criminal profiling from crime scene analysis' (n7), 404.
11. A. Robertson, *Global Issues: Terrorism and Global Security* (Infobase Publishing, 2007), 3–4.
12. A. Schmid, 'The Definition of Terrorism' in A. Schmid (ed) *The Routledge Handbook of Terrorism Research* (Routledge, 2011), 40.
13. UN General Assembly, Measures to eliminate international terrorism: resolution/ adopted by the General Assembly, 17 February 1995, A/RES/49/60, available at: http://www.refworld.org/docid/3b00f3171c.html (accessed 30th July 2020), para 3.
14. UN General Assembly, *International Convention for the Suppression of the Financing of Terrorism*, 9 December 1999, No. 38349, available at: http://www.refworld.org/docid/3dda0b867.html (accessed 30th July 2020), Article 2(b).
15. Terrorism Act 2000, section 1(1) and (2).
16. A. Schmid and A. Jongman, *Political Terrorism: A New Guide to Actors, Authors, Concepts, Data Bases, Theories, and Literatures* (Transaction Publishers, 1988), 6.
17. Crown Prosecution Service, *Guidance in Relation to the Prosecution of Offences Relating to Daesh and the Conflict in Syria, Iraq and Libya (revised December 2016)* (Crown Prosecution Service, 2016), para 6.
18. J. Rosen, *The Naked Crowd: Reclaiming Security and Freedom in an Anxious Age* (Random House, 2004), 24–29.
19. O. De Schutter and J. Ringelheim, 'Ethnic profiling: a rising challenge for European human rights law' (2008) 71(3) Modern Law Review 358.
20. D. Moeckli, 'Discriminatory profiles: law enforcement after 9/11' (2005) 5 European Human Rights Law Review 517. See also: D. Moeckli, 'Anti-Terrorism Laws, Terrorist Profiling and the Right to Non-Discrimination' in A. Salinas De Frias, K. Samuel and N. White (eds), *Counter-Terrorism: International Law and Practice* (Oxford University Press, 2012).

21. J. Goldson, *Ethnic Profiling and Counter-Terrorism: Trends, Dangers and Alternatives*, 6th June 2006, available from: http://www.soros.org/initiatives/justice/articles_publications/articles/counterterrorism_20060606/goldston_20060606.pdf (accessed 03rd July 2020).
22. A. Parmar, 'Policing and Ethnic Profiling' in K. Pall Sveinsson (ed), *Ethnic Profiling: The Use of Race in UK Law Enforcement* (Runnymede, 2010).
23. T. Ojanen, 'Terrorist profiling and human rights concerns' (2010) 3(2) Critical Studies in Terrorism 295. See also: T. Ojanen, 'Human Rights Dilemmas in Terrorist Profiling' in M. Scheinin (ed), *Law and Security – Facing the Dilemmas* (EUI Law, 2009), available at: ≪http://cadmus.eui.eu/bitstream/handle/1814/12233/LAW_2009_11.pdf?sequence=3≫ (accessed 03rd July 2020).
24. C. Edley, 'The New American Dilemma: Racial Profiling Post 9/11' in R. Leone and G. Anrig (eds), *The War on Our Freedoms* (Public Affairs Publishing, 2003).
25. T. Coke, 'Racial Profiling Post 9/11: Old Story, New Debate' in C. Brown (ed), *Lost Liberties: Ashcroft and the Assault on Personal Freedoms* (New York Press, 2003), 13–32.
26. R. Reddick, 'Point: the case for profiling' (2004) 79 International Social Science Review 154, 154–157.
27. P. Rogers, 'The War on Terrorism: Winning or Losing' (2003) *ORG Briefing Paper*, available at: http://www.oxfordresearchgroup.org.uk/publications/briefings/winningorlosing.htm (accessed 2nd July 2020).
28. C. Swiney, 'Racial profiling of Arabs and Muslims in the US: historical, empirical and legal analysis applied to the war on terrorism' (2006) 3(1) Muslim World Journal of Human Rights 1.
29. N. McGuirk 'A framework to measure/assess the utility of profiling as a counter-terrorism tool' (2019) Policing: A Journal of Policy and Practice, *Advance Access*, paz056, https://doi.org/10.1093/police/paz056 (accessed 2nd July 2020).

Bibliography

Coke, T., 'Racial Profiling Post 9/11: Old Story, New Debate' in C. Brown (ed), *Lost Liberties: Ashcroft and the Assault on Personal Freedoms* (New York Press, 2003).

Crown Prosecution Service, *Guidance in Relation to the Prosecution of Offences Relating to Daesh and the Conflict in Syria, Iraq and Libya (revised December 2016)* (Crown Prosecution Service, 2016).

de Schutter, O. and Ringelheim, J., 'Ethnic profiling: a rising challenge for European human rights law' (2008) 71(3) *Modern Law Review* 358.

Douglas, J., Ressler, R., Burgess, A. and Hartman, C., 'Criminal profiling from crime scene analysis' (1986) 4 *Behavioural Science and Law* 401.

Edley, C., 'The New American Dilemma: Racial Profiling Post 9/11' in R. Leone and G. Anrig (eds), *The War on Our Freedoms* (Public Affairs Publishing, 2003).

Elliott, M., 'The "war on terror", UK Style: the detention and deportation of suspected terrorists' (2010) 8(1) *International Journal of Constitutional Law* 131.

Enders, W. and Sandler, T., 'The effectiveness of anti-terrorism policies: a vector-autoregression-intervention analysis' (1993) 87(4) *American Political Science Review* 829.

Gendreau, P., Goggin, C., Cullen, E. and Paparozzi, M., 'The Common Sense Revolution and Correctional Policy' in J. Maguire, (ed), *Offender Rehabilitation and Treatment: Effective Programmes and Policies to Reduce Reoffending* (John Wiley & Sons Publishing, 2002).

Goldson, J., *Ethnic Profiling and Counter-Terrorism: Trends, Dangers and Alternatives*, 6th June 2006, available at: http://www.soros.org/initiatives/justice/articles_publications/articles/counterterrorism_20060606/goldston_20060606.pdf</seurld (accessed 03rd July 2020).

Horvath, M., 'Offender Profiling' in *S. Tong, R. Bryant and M. Horvath (eds), Understanding Criminal Investigation* (John Wiley & Sons Publishing, 2009).

McGuirk, N., 'A framework to measure/assess the utility of profiling as a counterterrorism tool' (2019) Policing: A Journal of Policy and Practice, *Advance Access, paz056*, available at: https://doi.org/10.1093/police/paz056 (accessed 2nd July 2020).

Moeckli, D., 'Anti-Terrorism Laws, Terrorist Profiling and the Right to Non-Discrimination' in A. Salinas De Frias, K. Samuel and N. White (eds), *Counter-Terrorism: International Law and Practice* (Oxford University Press, 2012).

Moeckli, D., 'Discriminatory profiles: law enforcement after 9/11' (2005) 5 *European Human Rights Law Review* 517.

Ojanen, T., 'Terrorist profiling and human rights concerns' (2010) 3(2) Critical Studies in Terrorism 295. See also: T. Ojanen, 'Human Rights Dilemmas in Terrorist Profiling' in M. Scheinin (ed), *Law and Security – Facing the Dilemmas* (EUI Law, 2009), available at: ≪seurld>http://cadmus.eui.eu/bitstream/handle/1814/12233/LAW_2009_11.pdf?sequence=3</seurld>≫ (accessed 03rd July 2020).

Parmar, A., 'Policing and Ethnic Profiling' in K. Pall Sveinsson (ed), *Ethnic Profiling: The Use of Race in UK Law Enforcement* (Runnymede, 2010).

Reddick, R., 'Point: the case for profiling' (2004) *79 International Social Science Review* 154.

Robertson, A., *Global Issues: Terrorism and Global Security* (Infobase Publishing, 2007).

Rogers, P., 'The War on Terrorism: Winning or Losing' (2003) *ORG Briefing Paper*, available at: http://www.oxfordresearchgroup.org.uk/publications/briefings/winningorlosing.htm (accessed 2nd July 2020).

Rosen, J., *The Naked Crowd: Reclaiming Security and Freedom in an Anxious Age* (Random House, 2004).

Schmid, A., 'The Definition of Terrorism' in A. Schmid (ed), *The Routledge Handbook of Terrorism Research* (Routledge, 2011).

Schmid, A. *and Jongman, A., Political Terrorism: A New Guide to Actors, Authors, Concepts, Data Bases, Theories, and Literatures* (Transaction Publishers, 1988).

Snook, B., Eastwood, J., Gendreau, P., Goggin, C. and Cullen, R., 'Taking stock of criminal profiling: a narrative review and meta-analysis' (2007) 34(4) *Criminal Science and Behaviour* 437.

Swiney, C., 'Racial profiling of Arabs and Muslims in the US: historical, empirical and legal analysis applied to the war on terrorism' (2006) 3(1) *Muslim World Journal of Human Rights* 1.

Turvey, B., *Criminal Profiling: An Introduction to Behavioural Evidence Analysis* (Academic Press, 1999).

UN General Assembly, *International Convention for the Suppression of the Financing of Terrorism, 9 December 1999*, No. 38349, available at: http://www.refworld.org/docid/3dda0b867.html (accessed 30th July 2020).

UN General Assembly, *Measures to Eliminate International Terrorism: Resolution/Adopted by the General Assembly, 17 February 1995*, A/RES/49/60, available at: http://www.refworld.org/docid/3b00f3171c.html (accessed 30th July 2020).

2 The compatibility of terrorist profiling with fundamental rights

2.1 Introduction

The assessment and examination of the usefulness of terrorist profiling raises significant issues pertaining to the compatibility of terrorist profiling with fundamental rights. This issue overshadows any assessment of the usefulness or the utility of terrorist profiling and as a result, this chapter deals with the fundamental rights question at this early stage. The primary aim of this chapter is to determine whether terrorist profiling, as examined in this book, may be considered compatible with fundamental rights.

It is contended that the compatibility of terrorist profiling with fundamental rights raises a particular concern relating to the inclusion of certain types of data, such as those classifiable as being 'sensitive characteristics,' as part of the process of constructing and applying terrorist profiles. In the previous chapter, sensitive characteristics was defined as including race, ethnicity, age, gender, country of origin etc. If terrorist profiling is aimed at assisting law enforcement officers to make distinctions 'between those likely to be involved in terrorism and/or it preparatory activities, the general population of law breaking and the general population at large,' then the inclusion of sensitive characteristics may be considered as being an important data source.[1] However, the inclusion of sensitive characteristics in the terrorist profiling process may lead to law enforcement officers over relying on these characteristics in the construction and/or application of profiles, especially as they will be the most visible characteristics to the officer using the profile in the field.

The over reliance on sensitive characteristics may result in particular individuals or groups becoming subjected to enhanced levels of scrutiny and suspicion without any justification other than the individuals exhibiting some of the sensitive characteristics. The potential for over reliance on sensitive characteristics creates an inevitable tension in any terrorist profiling process. This tension relates to the identification of the point at which the inclusion of sensitive characteristics can be considered an important part of the profiling process versus the point at which their inclusion can become unjustifiable, unlawful and perhaps harmful.

It is contended that there are at least two core questions requiring attention to determine the compatibility of terrorist profiling with fundamental rights.

Firstly, whether it can ever be justified to include sensitive characteristics in terrorist profiling and secondly, if so, in what circumstances may sensitive characteristics be included in the construction and/or application of terrorist profiling.

In order to address these questions, this chapter begins by drawing upon at least three different theoretical approaches including a utilitarian assessment, a human rights assessment and a combination of these two approaches. The chapter then proceeds by examining the definition of profiling where sensitive characteristics are included to ensure that forms of profiling such as 'racial' or 'ethnic' profiling can be distinguished for analytical purposes. The final part of the chapter proceeds to engage with each of the theoretical approaches set out above to address the compatibility of terrorist profiling with fundamental rights by reference to international human rights law.

2.2 Theoretical approaches to assess the compatibility of terrorist profiling with fundamental rights

The assessment of the compatibility of any counterterrorism measure, such as terrorist profiling, with fundamental rights often invokes a debate that is presented as being a choice between human rights or security without evaluating whether and to what extent, if at all, human rights and security can be accommodative of each other. In order to address this conundrum, the starting point in assessing the compatibility of terrorist profiling with fundamental rights is to examine the previous attempts aimed at analysing the inclusion of sensitive characteristics in terrorist profiling. On the basis of this literature, it is possible to identify three possible theoretical positions to address the compatibility of terrorist profiling with terrorist profiling.

The first approach is that adopted by those such as American Civil Liberties Union,[2] Cuellar,[3] Harcourt,[4] Harris,[5] Roach[6] and Moeckli[7] who argue that the inclusion of some sensitive characteristics, such as race or ethnicity, in the construction and/or application of profiling will always pose an unjustifiable risk that particular individuals or groups of individuals resembling the sensitive characteristics will become subject to official scrutiny and suspicion by law enforcement officers. Due to this risk, they commonly argue that all forms of profiling involving the inclusion of sensitive characteristics such as race, ethnicity and country of origin should be prohibited regardless of any assistive value to law enforcement officers. Ashworth suggests that this view of terrorist profiling can be classified as being a 'human rights absolutists' approach given that it refuses to accept any compatibility between fundamental rights and the inclusion of sensitive characteristics in terrorist profiling.[8]

A difficulty with this approach is that it tends to obscure the analysis and the assessment of the inclusion of sensitive characteristics, such as race/ethnicity, by concentrating on manifestations of profiling where race/ethnicity are either the sole characteristic or part of a wider range of characteristics used by law enforcement officers. Frequently, these manifestations of profiling may be classifiable as being examples of low visibility manifestations of profiling where law enforcement officers exercise considerable degrees of informal discretion in the selection of individuals for enhanced levels of scrutiny or investigation, such as those manifestations of informal terrorist profiling that are examined in chapter six. As a result, the analysis which characterises profiling as being unlawful commonly fails to analyse different manifestations of profiling where sensitive characteristics are included in combination with other non-sensitive characteristics. It is contended that any assessment of sensitive characteristics in the construction and/or application of profiles must undertake an examination of different manifestations of profiling where sensitive characteristics are not necessarily the sole criteria so as to provide a full examination and determination of the justification question.

The second approach is that adopted by those such as Ramierz *et al*,[9] Schuck[10] and Turley[11] who contend that including sensitive characteristics forms an important part of the profiling process so as to assist law enforcement officers narrow and filter their search for likely terrorists in the prevention and detection of acts of terrorism. For example, the Chief Constable of the British Transport Police commented in response to the London Bombings in 2005 that:

> [w]e should not waste time searching old white ladies. It is going to be disproportionate. It is going to be young men, not exclusively, but it may be disproportionate when it comes to ethnic groups.[12]

This approach tends to accept, without question, the justification of including sensitive characteristics, even if sensitive characteristics form the sole criteria for selecting individuals for enhanced investigation by law enforcement officers. This view on the inclusion of sensitive characteristics in terrorist profiling can be classified as being closer towards a utilitarian approach that places significant importance on order or security above the value of human rights.[13] This approach may more accurately be labelled a 'security absolutist' approach.

A difficulty with this approach is that it tends to overestimate the importance of sensitive characteristics in the profiling process without assessing whether sensitive characteristics can justifiably be included as part of the profiling process. The 'security absolutists' approach tends to focus on the end goal of attaining security which may adversely impact the assessment of the usefulness of terrorist profiling as a counterterrorism tool. Furthermore, any argument categorically supporting the inclusion of sensitive characteristics in any circumstance may be tainted by the 'emergency' posed by the threat of terrorism. This means that the 'emergency', all too frequently surrounding counterterrorism, may limit a full analysis of the justification of including sensitive characteristics in terrorism profiling. As a result, any argument founded entirely on the threat of terrorism must be viewed with caution, as it may fail to provide a full assessment of the justification for including sensitive characteristics in terrorist profiling.

The third approach is that adopted by those such as Amar,[14] Banks,[15] Derbyshire,[16] Ellmann,[17] Kinsley[18] and Risee and Zeckhauser[19] who offer a qualified acknowledgement of the potential assistive value of including sensitive characteristics in the construction and/or application of terrorist profiling but express some doubt on its widespread application. In particular, they commonly argue that including sensitive characteristics, such as race and ethnicity, in the construction and/or application of profiles may only be justified where sensitive characteristics do not become the sole criterion in the selection of individuals for enhanced levels of investigation. This view on the inclusion of sensitive characteristics in terrorist profiling may be classified as being more of a 'balanced approach' as it refrains from adopting a trenchant security or human rights absolutist approach.

This balanced approach has been criticised by some, such as Ashworth, who noted that the very concept of 'balance' might only be theoretical with little evidence in practice.[20] The weakness of this approach is that it views the pursuit of security through counterterrorism law and human rights as being something of a trade-off where human rights must sometimes be sacrificed to achieve security. The acceptance of any trade-off between security and human rights is criticised by some, such as Luban[21] and Thomas,[22] as being a false dichotomy. However, it is argued that to advance a steadfast 'human rights absolutists' approach or a steadfast 'security absolutists' approach fails to conduct a broad review and scrutiny of the arguments for the justification of including sensitive characteristics in the profiling process, as they are polarised by being categorically against or in favour of including sensitive characteristics.

This balanced approach may present a way to assess the justification for including sensitive characteristics in the construction and/or application of profiles, but it is important to acknowledge at least two core weaknesses that may undermine this approach. Firstly, there is a need to ensure that any argument advanced in favour of including sensitive characteristics is not overshadowed or tainted by manifestations of profiling where sensitive characteristics become the sole criteria in selecting individuals for enhanced investigation. Secondly, the assessment on the inclusion of sensitive characteristics must not become tainted by the 'emergency' posed by a threat of terrorism. This means that any individual assessment of a manifestation of terrorist profiling needs to remain alive to these two risks as they may impact any conclusion drawn on any manifestation of terrorist profiling.

These two limitations may be managed by drawing an analytical distinction between different manifestations of terrorist profiling to assess the justification question. It was explained in the introductory chapter that a distinction should be drawn between different manifestations of terrorist profiling by reference to a profiling spectrum ranging from formal to informal manifestations of terrorist profiling. This profiling spectrum is presented in more detail in chapters four to six, but it is critical to note here that it represents an important means to assess the justification question. Those manifestations of profiling classifiable as being on the formal end of the profiling spectrum tend to rely upon a mix of sensitive and non-sensitive characteristics and draw upon a range of systematic profiling methods and approaches in the construction and/or application of terrorist profiling. Alternatively, those profiling manifestations that exist on the informal side of the profiling spectrum appear to rely significantly on sensitive characteristics and do not appear to draw upon methods/approaches as systematic as those in manifestations of formal terrorist profiling in the construction and/or application of terrorist profiling.

Therefore, the ability to draw distinctions between different manifestations of terrorist profiling may allow for greater analysis on a case-by-case basis of each profiling manifestation as opposed to drawing pejorative views on all forms of profiling without a systematic means to assess each manifestation.

2.3 The definition of profiling when sensitive characteristics are used in the profiling process

It is now necessary to draw a further distinction between profiling manifestations that generally draw upon a range of sensitive and non-sensitive data sources, *versus* manifestations of profiling that rely significantly on sensitive characteristics. This distinction affects the assessment of the justification of including sensitive characteristics in manifestations of terrorist profiling. As a starting point, it is acknowledged that not all manifestations of terrorist profiling will inevitably involve the inclusion of sensitive characteristics.

Barovick suggests that 'profiling refers to the police practice of viewing certain characteristics as indicators of criminal behaviour.'[23] From a theoretical perspective, profiling should assist law enforcement officers to separate

> a subsection of the population from the larger whole on the basis of specific criteria that purportedly correlate to risk and subjecting the subgroup to special scrutiny for the purposes of preventing violence, crime or some other undesirable activity.[24]

However, a key issue in all forms of profiling is determining which characteristics, if any, are more or less indicative of criminality or terrorism. Where sensitive characteristics become the predominant characteristics over all other characteristics, this has been characterised in the literature as being manifestations of 'racial profiling,' 'religious profiling' or 'ethnic profiling.'[25] If the inclusion of sensitive characteristics, such as race, religion, ethnicity, country of origin etc. imply that individuals or groups of individuals are more likely to be engaged in criminality or terrorism without justification, then it may be argued that sensitive characteristics can never be justified as relevant characteristics in the construction and/or application of terrorist profiles. It is important to emphasise that this book is not making the argument that the inclusion of sensitive characteristics may be justifiable in every manifestation of profiling. Rather, manifestations of terrorist profiling must be assessed on a case-by-case basis to consider the circumstances, if any, that sensitive characteristics may be justifiably included in the profiling process. The assessment of the justification of including sensitive characteristics is about creating an impartial and evaluative process that allows each constituent part of the profiling process to be examined systematically or as far as it is possible to be examined systematically.

Racial profiling is debated at length throughout the literature with many commentators setting forward differing definitions.[26] The term 'racial profiling' can be first traced to a description appearing in the New York Times of a police traffic stop in the US undertaken as part of 'Operation Pipeline' by the 'Drugs Enforcement Agency' (DEA) which was aimed at identifying individuals likely to be engaged in drug couriering in the US.[27] Racial profiling emerged during the 1980s and 1990s as a label to criticise police operations in the 'wars on crime and drugs' where police officers relied substantially on sensitive characteristics as indicators of crime without any justification.[28]

The use of the term 'racial profiling' as a label to describe those manifestations of terrorist profiling where sensitive characteristics are included in the profiling process may limit any impartial evaluative analysis of the usefulness of terrorist profiling. Specifically, the origins of the label 'racial profiling' is that of a pejorative term to criticise those manifestations of profiling where police practice have relied unjustifiably on sensitive characteristics as an indicator of criminality or terrorism. It is difficult to see how any argument could be substantiated to support these manifestations of profiling. The analytical problem is that the association of the 'racial profiling' label with all manifestations of terrorist profiling that may rely on sensitive characteristics, even to a limited extent, may unhelpfully brand all forms of profiling drawing on sensitive characteristics as being a form of profiling which unjustifiably targets those resembling the sensitive characteristics.

Risse and Zeckhauser argue that the term 'racial profiling' used to broadly analyse the inclusion of race and/or ethnicity in profiling is problematic as it is commonly conflated with three issues: 'the use of race as an information-carrier for investigative purposes'; 'police abuse'; 'the disproportionate use of race in profiling.'[29]

This conflation has tended to shape and overshadow the debate on assessing 'justification' and it is compounded by many of the criticisms of the inclusion of sensitive characteristics drawing inspiration from evidence of police abuse of their powers where law enforcement practice appear to be over relying on sensitive characteristics. This makes the assessment of the justification for including sensitive characteristics profoundly difficult. In any objective assessment of the circumstances where sensitive characteristics may justifiably be included as relevant characteristics, our interest is solely on the value of sensitive characteristics as being 'an information-carrier for investigative purposes' with 'police abuse' and 'overreliance' being classifiable as being downstream issues affecting justification.[30]

A consequence of the criticism of the inclusion of sensitive characteristics is that the debate is polarised by being either fervently in favour or against the inclusion of sensitive characteristics. As a consequence of this polarisation, it may be difficult to separate these three issues so as to evaluate the value of sensitive characteristics 'as an information-carrier' to determine whether they can be considered capable of assisting law enforcement officers identify potential suspects. Specifically, 'police abuse' and their 'over-reliance' on sensitive characteristics may overshadow any potential analysis of the justification of sensitive characteristics. However, whilst it may be difficult, it does not invalidate the assessment and evaluation of the circumstances where the inclusion of sensitive characteristics may be justifiable. This difficulty may be unravelled by defining profiling where sensitive characteristics have been included so we can identify the subject of analysis of this chapter, the justification of sensitive characteristics in terrorist profiling.

The problem of conflation is apparent in many of the common definitions of racial profiling found in the literature. For example, Ramirez *et al* define profiling as being

> any police initiated action that relies on the race, ethnicity or national origin, rather than the behaviour of an individual or information that leads the police to a particular individual who has been identified as being, or having been engaged in criminal activity.[31]

A key problem with this definitional approach is that profiling, as understood by Ramirez *et al*, is defined by contrasting 'race, ethnicity or national origin' with 'the behaviour of an individual or [police] information that leads the police to a particular individual who has been identified as being, or having been engaged in criminal activity.'[32] This definition suggests that profiling will commonly rest on 'race, ethnicity or national origin' instead of an assessment of an individual's behaviour or a combination of both.[33] It fails to evaluate the circumstance where sensitive characteristics may only be one of a range of characteristics included in the construction and/or application of profiles. Arguably, it assists those who seek to characterise any manifestation of profiling as being substantially reliant on sensitive characteristics without appreciating whether sensitive characteristics can be included as part of a range of other non-sensitive characteristics.

According to Risse and Zeckhauser, this definitional approach suggests 'profiling serves purposes other than apprehending criminals, imparting an aura of illegitimacy to profiling by definition.'[34] Specifically, this definition of this type of racial profiling carries the risk that certain sensitive characteristics are indicative of terrorism as opposed to evaluating the inclusion of other non-sensitive characteristics such as an individual's behaviour. The definition is constructed in such a way that suggests sensitive characteristics must be included in the profiling process. Additionally, it is also arguable by adopting this dual approach to defining racial profiling it suggests that law enforcement officers will use either the sensitive characteristics such as race, ethnicity, country of origin, etc. or 'specific information on suspicious activity.' As a result, the definition fails to appreciate the circumstance where sensitive characteristics are included in combination with other non-sensitive characteristics.

Risse and Zeckhauser propose an alternative definition to avoid the previous problematic approaches towards defining profiling where sensitive characteristics are included. They suggest that profiling where sensitive 'characteristics such as race, ethnicity' are used can be defined as being 'any police-initiated action that relies on race, ethnicity or national origin and not merely on the behaviour of an individual.'[35] This approach avoids the problems identified with the other definitional attempts by refraining from constructing a definition that suggests that profiling rests on the inclusion of sensitive characteristics. This approach allows an assessment of whether the inclusion of sensitive characteristic are justifiable and, if so, in what circumstances by being able to appreciate the value of sensitive characteristics 'as an information carrier for investigative purposes.'

A further definition of racial profiling can be found in a defunct US statute 'End Racial Profiling Act, 2001' which may be considered as being capable of resolving the difficulties in the academic literature on how to define profiling that includes sensitive characteristics. Section 989 of the 2001 Act stated:

> [t]he practice of a law enforcement agent relying, to any degree, on race, ethnicity, or national origin in selecting which individuals to subject to routine investigatory activities, or in deciding upon the scope and substance of law enforcement activity following the initial routine investigatory activity, except that racial profiling does not include reliance on such criteria in combination with other identifying factors when the law enforcement agent is seeking to apprehend a specific suspect whose race, ethnicity, or national origin is part of the description of the suspect.[36]

On the basis of this statutory definition, there are at least two ways to define racial profiling.

Firstly, there is a narrow definition that assumes race/ethnicity, or sensitive characteristics, are the only relevant factors to be used to construct profiles. In the literature this is commonly referred to as 'hard definitions of racial profiling.'[37] This form of profiling can occur where law enforcement officers identify individuals for enhanced levels of scrutiny solely on the basis of sensitive characteristics. It is contended that manifestations of hard racial profiling are inevitably likely to be classified as being unlawful and even harmful. This is due to the fact that they depart from the fundamental principle of the rule of law which advocates that 'law enforcement determinations should be based on individual conduct, not on membership in an ethnic, racial, national or religious group.'[38]

Secondly, there is also an alternative way to define racial profiling where race/ethnicity, or sensitive characteristics, are used in combination with other non-sensitive characteristics in the construction of profiles. This is commonly referred to in the literature as being 'soft definitions of racial profiling.'[39] This form of profiling can occur whenever sensitive characteristics are 'part of the calculus of suspicion which may include other factors such as … behaviour.'[40]

The distinction between hard and soft forms of racial profiling can be considered as being fundamental to assess the justification of including sensitive characteristics in the construction and/or application of terrorist profiles. However, it is necessary to determine whether the division between hard and soft forms of profiling represents a way to justify the inclusion of sensitive characteristics in terrorist profiling. It is argued that the justification for including sensitive characteristics in the construction and/or application of profiles can be explored by firstly considering whether their inclusion may be justified in the context of the philosophical foundations of the right to non-discrimination and secondly the content of the right to non-discrimination as a result of its development in international, regional and domestic law.

2.4 The lawfulness of including sensitive characteristics in terrorist profiling

As noted in the introductory section of this chapter, the assessment on the compatibility of including sensitive characteristics ultimately requires a lawfulness assessment. The framework that this section uses to assess the lawfulness of including sensitive characteristics in the construction and/or application of terrorist profiling is drawn from international, regional and domestic legal standards which focus substantially on the right to non-discrimination. The content of the right to non-discrimination as protected in numerous international, regional and domestic legal standards provides a basis to explore whether the inclusion of sensitive characteristics may ever be considered justified. This is due to the fact that the compatibility of including sensitive characteristics in manifestations of terrorist profiling with fundamental rights often raise substantial issues of equality and discrimination.

There were two key distinctions drawn in the earlier part of this chapter between different manifestations of profiling: formal and informal manifestations of terrorist profiling and hard and soft manifestations of racial profiling. These distinctions will form an imperative basis in this section to assess the lawfulness of including sensitive characteristics in manifestations of terrorist profiling.

There are at least two considerations relevant to the assessment of the justification of including sensitive characteristics in terrorist profiling. Firstly, whether any manifestation of terrorist profiling may be considered as being lawful. Secondly, even if some manifestations may be considered as being technically lawful, it will be necessary to further consider whether there are additional reasons, which may suggest that it should be unlawful.

In order to address both of these questions it is necessary to reflect on philosophical underpinning of the right to non-discrimination before examining its content and scope.

2.4.1 Philosophical underpinnings of the right to non-discrimination

A starting point in understanding the content and scope of the right to non-discrimination is to consider its foundation in the works of Aristotle who advanced a principle of equality.[41] The central plank of Aristotle's equality principle was the belief that equals be treated equally and those unequal be treated unequally. A flaw with Aristotle's equality principle was its failure to define the equals and to determine distinctions in conduct. As Westen contends a principle of equality can only have meaning if it has values to define 'individuals' and the 'conduct' capable of being alike so as to be able understand equality.[42]

However, the contemporary development of the principle of equality originates in the works of Hobbes[43] and Locke[44] suggested that those in ownership of property acquired the same 'natural rights' so that they are 'equal and independent.' In a similar vein, Kant suggested that due to our individual humanity we are all equal with equality stemming from our general humanity. Rawls[45] and Dworkin[46] have made more recent contributions to the concept of equality. According to Rawls

> [e]ach person is to have an equal right to the most extensive total system of equal basic liberties compatible with a similar system of liberty for all.[47]

This contention suggests that equality is derived from the premise of 'equal liberty' and any interference with this premise can only be justified if the advantage to be achieved through interference serves the interests of everyone in society.[48] Additionally, Moeckli suggested that in Dworkin's theory, the foundation of society requires that all individuals have an innate right to be treated equally which requires governments to respect this right through the development and establishment of principles and laws.[49] The connection between equality and the state made by Dworkin suggests that the state can only derive its legitimacy through the development of principles and laws protecting equality.[50]

This discussion reveals that there are a number of philosophical foundations supporting a residual right to equality encompassing a freedom from discrimination that extends beyond the concept of 'equality' formulated in laws and legal standards. These foundations of equality are more fluid than those found in legal standards and it may be argued that those manifestations of terrorist profiling classifiable as being on the 'formal' side of the profiling spectrum and are tantamount to soft manifestations of racial profiling could in theory be compatible with this standard of equality. This is on the basis that in this type of profiling no individual is selected for a distinction in treatment solely on the basis of any one criteria used in the construction and/or application of terrorist profiles. However, those manifestations of terrorist profiling on the informal side of the profiling spectrum and are tantamount to hard manifestations of racial profiling may conflict or at least create considerable tension with these philosophical foundations of the principle of equality, as there is a risk that law enforcement officers select individuals for enhanced levels of scrutiny without any justification other than portraying a particular characteristic.

2.4.2 *The content and scope of the legal right to non-discrimination*

Beyond the philosophical debate, international, regional and domestic courts have developed the content of the right to equality and non-discrimination by distinguishing between conduct that is permissible and impermissible. The starting point in this analysis and discussion can be to consider the definition of discrimination so as to begin to identify the boundary between permissible and impermissible conduct in the context of manifestations of soft racial profiling. The right to non-discrimination is expressed in a number of key international legal standards including:

Article 1(3) of the United Nations (UN) Charter expresses that all states aim

> to achieve international co-operation in ... promoting and encouraging respect for human rights and for fundamental freedoms for all without distinction as to race, sex, language or religion.[51]

The importance of protecting equality and non-discrimination is also expressly stated in the Preamble and Articles 13(1)(b), 55(c) and 76(c) requiring states to abide by 'human rights and fundamental freedoms without distinction based on race, religion or language.'[52]

The Universal Declaration on Human Rights (UDHR) specifically protects equality and non-discrimination in Articles 1, 2(1) and 7. Article 2(1) of the ICCPR obliges member states to

> ensure that all individuals within its territory enjoy the rights recognised in the Covenant without discrimination of any kind including grounds of race, ... religion, national or social origin....[53]

Additionally, Article 26 of the ICCPR provides that

> all people are entitled to the equal protection of the law free from discrimination, guaranteeing all people equal and effective protection against discrimination on any ground including race, ... religion, ... national or social origin...[54]

Article 1 of CERD defines racial discrimination as being

> any distinction, exclusion, restriction or preference based on race ... or national or ethnic origin which has the purpose or effect of nullifying or impairing the recognition, enjoyment, exercise on an equal footing of human rights ....[55]

Article 2 of CERD also obligates states to refrain from engaging in acts or practices that can result in racial discrimination. Additionally, Article 5 expressly obligates states to 'prohibit and eliminate racial discrimination in all its forms' and to guarantee citizens equal treatment before the law. Additional measures are found in Article 3 of the Convention Relating to the Status of Refugees (Refugee Convention) which ensures that refugees are free from discrimination concerning 'race, religion or country of origin.'[56] Other international laws advocating the protection of equality and non-discrimination include the International Covenant on Economic, Social and Cultural Rights[57] (ICESCR) and the Convention on the Rights of the Child[58] (CRC).

According to the UN Human Rights Committee discrimination in the context of the ICCPR can be defined as being

> any distinction, exclusion, restriction or preference which is based on any ground such as race, colour, sex, language, religion, political or other opinion, national or social origin, property, birth or other status and which has the purpose or effect of nullifying or impairing the recognition, enjoyment or exercise by all persons, on an equal footing, of all rights and freedoms.[59]

The construction of the right to equality and non-discrimination in international law is commonly characterised in the literature as either 'subordinate [or] autonomous provisions.' 'Subordinate' provisions are those that allow individuals a right to non-discrimination in conjunction with their enjoyment of human rights as set out in international law. For example, Article 2(1) of the UDHR and Article 2(1) of the ICCPR protect against discrimination so far as to the content of these provisions is concerned but there is no general right against discrimination.

Alternatively, autonomous provisions provide a general right against discrimination with examples being found in Article 26 of the ICCPR and Articles 2 and 5 CERD advancing a general protection from discrimination. The content of the general protection from discrimination has been subject to discussion. For example, according to the Human Rights Committee's General Comment XVIII concerning non-discrimination, opined that a difference in treatment would not be considered as being discriminatory

> if the criteria for such differentiation are reasonable and objective and the aim is to achieve a purpose which is legitimate under the Covenant.[60]

Additionally, CERD in its General Recommendation XIV[61] opined that it will assess the legality of a measure against 'the objectives and purposes of the Convention.'[62]

These international standards are supported by two 'soft law' standards including the UN Code of Conduct for Law Enforcement Officials[63] ('Code') and the Programme of Action adopted by the UN World Conference against Racism 2000[64] ('Programme'). Both the Code and the Programme call on states to eliminate discrimination in law enforcement.[65] Other international soft law standards prohibiting discrimination include the Declaration on the Human Rights of Individuals Who are Not Nationals of the Country in which They Live[66] and the UN Body of Principles for the Protection of All Persons under Any Form of Detention or Imprisonment.[67]

In order to conduct an assessment of the justification for including sensitive characteristics in terrorist profiling it is necessary to consider the interpretation of these standards. According to Moeckli it is possible to distil the content of the right to non-discrimination into at least five key considerations including (a) no need for discriminatory intent to be established, (b) the need for a comparator, (c) the pursuit of a legitimate aim, (d) the proportionality of the measure and (e) the standard of review applicable.[68] The assessment of the lawfulness of manifestations of terrorist profiling and in particular on the inclusion of sensitive characteristics in the construction and/or application of terrorist profiling involves concentrating on assessing the legitimate aim, the proportionality and the standard of review. The other key considerations are not necessarily relevant to assessing the lawfulness question at issue in this chapter. Specifically, there is no contention that the inclusion of sensitive characteristics is necessarily evidence of a discriminatory intent and it is presumed there is a comparator in individual cases.

2.4.2.1 Legitimate aim

If it can be accepted that the inclusion of sensitive characteristics in the construction and/or application of terrorist profiles results in individuals in analogous situations being treated differently, then the focus of analysis shifts to objectively assessing whether the difference in treatment can be regarded as being 'in pursuit of a legitimate aim.' In light of some academic literature,[69] it may be argued that the legitimate aim test has become a redundant test, especially in the context of terrorism. In particular, the very nature of the threat of terrorism posed to a state's national security is likely to easily meet this requirement.[70]

As a result, it is contended that so long as sensitive characteristics are included to assist in managing the threat of terrorism, it is highly likely to satisfy the requirement of being 'in pursuit of a legitimate aim.'

2.4.2.2 The proportionality of the measure

The assessment of the proportionality of measure, or in our case the inclusion of sensitive characteristics in profiles, requires that there must be proportionality between the distinction in treatment and the legitimate aim being realised. The existence of proportionality has been evident in the jurisprudence of the European Convention on Human Rights (ECHR) in the *Belgium Linguistics Case*,[71] *the UK courts in interpreting the* Human Rights Act 1998[72] and in the jurisprudence of the German Constitutional Court.[73] The assessment of proportionality commonly involves a three-stage test.

The first consideration involves assessing the suitability of the measure so as to determine whether the measure is suitable to achieve the aim of the policy.[74] Secondly, the measure must be least restrictive measure available to achieve the stated policy so as to be considered necessary.[75] Thirdly, there is a balancing exercise to be undertaken so as to assess the rights and interests of the disadvantaged individual against the broader societal interests in the pursuit of the aim to determine proportionality.[76] During the third stage, a court may be influenced by whether there is a sufficient basis within the measure adopted to protect against its abuse or potential abuse.[77] This simply means that if the adopted measure is capable of protecting against its abuse or potential abuse, then it may be considered as being more acceptable from a human rights perspective.

In examining the first assessment, 'suitability,' Panaccio identifies that there are two common ways human rights courts approach this part of this test.[78] Firstly, there is a 'less taxing' assessment where the court checks whether the measure under scrutiny is 'causally able to achieve the stated aim.'[79] Secondly, there is a 'more demanding form' where the courts will determine whether the measure at issue is 'irrational/unreasonable because it generates a disproportionate degree of [harmful] effects.'[80]

In applying these standards to the assessment of the lawfulness and justification for the inclusion of sensitive characteristics, it is necessary to reconsider the analytical distinction drawn between formal and informal manifestations and hard and soft manifestations of racial profiling.

The discussion in chapter six examines manifestations of terrorist profiling classifiable as being examples of informal terrorist profiling. It is contended that informal manifestations of terrorist profiling cannot be considered as being suitable to permit sensitive characteristics to be included. This is due to the fact that the discussion in chapter six demonstrates to a high degree of probability these manifestations of terrorist profiling are very unlikely to be 'causally able to achieve the stated aim' of assisting law enforcement officers with the identification, detection and prosecution of terrorists or potential terrorists. Furthermore, the 'more demanding' test would also be unlikely to be satisfied given the discussion in chapter six on the likely harmful effects arising from the use of this form of profiling.

It would also seem probable that those manifestations of terrorist profiling that move towards the informal side of the profiling spectrum, such as those discussed in chapter five would not satisfy either of these tests for the very same reasons as those manifestations of informal terrorist profiling.

In the context of formal manifestations of terrorist profiling and soft manifestations of racial profiling, it may be argued from a theoretical perspective that the suitability is something that may be asserted. Specifically, this type of profiling (if properly conducted) may at least be considered as being 'causally able' to assist law enforcement officers identify those individuals likely to be engaged in terrorism and/or preparatory activities in light of the input and output assessment that is conducted in chapter three. However, if the court applied the 'more demanding' test then it may be argued that formal manifestations could only be capable of satisfying this test if the harmful effects arising from the use of formal terrorist profiling could be addressed.

In considering the second part of the test, the least restrictive measure available, terrorist profiling will often form part of much broader range of counterterrorism initiatives that vary greatly in intrusiveness. Sweet and Mathews identify that this part of the test common asks whether 'there is any alternative measure that is less restrictive of rights while being equally effective in attaining the stated' aim or goal of the measure in question.[81] The inclusion of sensitive characteristics in informal manifestations of terrorist profiling (such as those manifestations that are examined in chapter six) would unlikely be considered as being the least restrictive measure given that law enforcement officers could easily alter the profiling process by adding other non-sensitive characteristics. However, the inclusion of sensitive characteristics in manifestations of formal terrorist profiling may be considered capable of being the least intrusive measure for law enforcement officers to select individuals for investigation in contrast to other forms of counterterrorism policing powers, such as powers of arrest, and given that formal manifestations rely on a mix of sensitive and non-sensitive characteristics.

In considering the last part of the test, the balancing exercise between the impact and aim of the measure, it is likely that manifestations of informal terrorist profiling that are examined in chapter six would not satisfy this part of the test. This assessment is advanced on the basis that those manifestations of informal terrorist profiling examined chapter six tended to commonly highlight a negative impact of this type of profiling on Muslim communities. The likely harmful impact arising from the use of manifestations of informal terrorist profiling may well be considered as outweighing any legitimate aim even in the context of a prevailing threat of terrorism. Furthermore, in light of the examination of informal terrorist profiling manifestations in chapter six, it is arguable that there are little or no mechanisms to protect against potential abuses of these examples of terrorist profiling. As a result, it seems that informal manifestations of terrorist profiling would not likely satisfy the test.

In considering manifestations of formal terrorist profiling, such as those examined in chapter four, this latter part of the test may be satisfied given these manifestations of terrorist profiling have significant systematic processes to construct and apply profiles, which are open to review and are capable of being challenged. Furthermore, if these manifestations of terrorist profiling are properly conducted then it may be capable of managing the limitations that are identified in chapter four that commonly arise in manifestations of formal terrorist profiling. As a result, this may mean that formal terrorist profiling could be considered as having a broader societal interest by assisting in counterterrorism over the rights and interests of those disadvantaged individuals subjected to profiling so as to satisfy this part of the test.

In summary, the proportionality of including sensitive characteristics can only be assessed in each individual manifestation of terrorist profiling. Although the assessment in this section has been primarily concerned with manifestations of soft racial profiling, it is impossible to brand soft racial profiling as being proportional in every circumstance. Rather, the conclusion to be drawn here is that the assessment of proportionality will require an individual assessment in each manifestation of profiling in terms of suitability, its necessity to achieve the aim and its proportionality in achieving the aim.

2.4.2.3 The standard of review

The standard of review commonly adopted by the courts to assess discrimination varies according to a number of factors present in each case. In *Handyside*[82] the European Court of Human Rights (ECtHR) developed the concept of a 'margin of appreciation' which allows states some latitude between the human rights obligation in law and realising these obligations in practice. Although, the 'margin of appreciation' concept has been criticised as being a vague test lacking a practical substance, at minimum the application of the right to non-discrimination in common with other rights requires an element of flexibility in applying the law in practice.[83] The standard of review in the context of sensitive characteristics is going to be an enhanced level of review as sensitive characteristics are by their very nature classifiable as being suspect grounds of discrimination, which require particular justification for any differential in treatment.

The prohibition of discrimination on the grounds of race is considered a core part of customary international law. In addition to customary law, international and regional law also prohibit distinctions in treatment on the basis of race. For example, the ECtHR held that 'a special importance should be attached to discrimination based on race.'[84] Similarly, in the US the Supreme Court in *Hirabayashi v United States*[85] and *Korematsu v United States*[86] developed a strict scrutiny test for any measure capable of creating a distinction in treatment on the grounds of race. In *Ghaidan v Godin-Mendoza*[87] the House of Lords in the UK held that any distinctions in treatment on the basis of race 'are properly stigmatised as discriminatory' 'unless some good reason exists.'[88]

Similarly, any distinction on the grounds of religion is clearly prohibited as part of human rights law. In *Hoffmann v Austria*[89] the ECtHR stated 'notwithstanding any possible arguments to the contrary, a distinction based essentially in religion alone is not acceptable.'[90] In the UK, the House of Lords in Ghaidan[91] stated distinctions in treatment on the grounds of religion would not be considered 'acceptable, without more, as a basis for different legal treatment.'[92]

Finally, there has been some case law to demonstrate that distinctions based on citizenship or country of origin also attract a heightened level of review. For example, in *Gaygusuz v Austria*[93] the ECtHR applied a strict review of distinctions based on religion where it stated

> very weighted reasons would have to be put forward before the Court could regard a difference of treatment based exclusively on the ground of nationality as compatible with the Convention.[94]

2.4.2.4 *Further observations*

In light of the discussion thus far, it is evident that any distinction in treatment on any of the suspect grounds, which include sensitive characteristics, will be difficult to justify as it attracts a heightened level of review. For example, in *Rosalind Williams Lecraft v Spain*[95] the complainant, who was a US born black naturalised Spanish citizen, was subjected to an enhanced identity check at a Spanish border as her appearance was not common with the appearance more frequently associated with Spanish nationality. The complainant contended that she was only subjected to an enhanced identity check because of the colour of her skin and her ethnicity which she alleged breached Article 2 of the ICCPR.

Amongst other arguments, Spain sought to reject the complaint's allegation on two key grounds.

Firstly, Spain argued that checking immigration documents was simply a measure adopted to deal with illegal immigration across all Spanish borders.[96] Spain also contended that its national law, 'Organisation Act No 7/1985 on the Rights and Freedoms of Foreigners in Spain' placed an explicit obligation on all foreigners to carry appropriate identity documents when entering Spain so as to allow border officials to validate identity. Other domestic laws including the 'Public Security (Organisation) Act' and the 'Decree on the National Identity Document' provided Spanish domestic authorities with the power to check identity documents.

A key concern of the Spanish authorities was that there were relatively few ethnic minorities in Spain being black born and this ethnicity group was a significant source of concern as many illegal immigrants have notoriously sought to enter Spain from sub-Saharan Africa. Therefore, Spain sought to justify the interference with the complainant's ICCPR rights by arguing that the measure adopted was no more than necessary to deal with the problem of illegal immigration and that the complainant was only selected so as to rule her out from illegal immigrants. The evidence provided supporting this contention was the fact that the complainant had not been subjected to any further enhanced identity checks in the 15 years from the commencement of the complaint.

Secondly, Spain also argued that the manner in which the enhanced security check was carried out was in a 'respectful manner and at a time and place where it is normal for people to be carrying identity papers.'[97] Therefore, the action undertaken by the law enforcement officers was no more than necessary to validate the complainant's identity for lawful purposes.

In determining the complaint, the Human Rights Committee held that

> not every differentiation of treatment will constitute discrimination, if the criteria for such differentiation are reasonable and objective and if the aim is to achieve a purpose which is legitimate under the Covenant.[98]

However, in this particular instance as the complainant was not given any information concerning the reasons for her enhanced identity check, the Committee concluded that the complainant

> was singled out for the identity check in question solely on the ground of her racial characteristics and that these characteristics were the decisive factor in her being suspected of unlawful conduct.[99]

Consequently, the subjection of the complainant to an enhanced identity check could not be considered reasonable and objective.

This case can be classified as being an example of a manifestation of hard racial profiling where sensitive characteristics, such as race and ethnicity, appeared to be the sole criteria used by the state to identify the complainant for an enhanced security check. The inclusion of sensitive characteristics in profiling may be justifiable if the state can substantiate an explanation that is 'reasonable and objective.' In this case the protection of the state's perceived threat from inward bound illegal immigrants at Spanish borders was insufficient to be considered 'reasonable and objective.' It is evident from the Committee's determination that they appeared to be particularly influenced by the inability of the law enforcement officers to rely on other non-sensitive characteristics in selecting individuals for enhanced scrutiny.

The significance of this case is that it may support the argument advanced in this chapter that it is in theory at least possible to argue that where sensitive characteristics are included alongside or in addition to non-sensitive characteristics, it may be justifiable to include sensitive characteristics. This justification would rest on sufficient evidence being available to substantiate the investigative value of terrorist profiling in the context of preventing, detecting or deterring acts of terrorism or preparatory activities. The assessment of whether this evidence is 'reasonable and objective' must be by reference to the content of the affected human right. Additionally, the threshold for this test is justifiably high given the risks posed by terrorist profiling and in particular the inclusion of sensitive characteristics in any form of profiling.

As a result of this discussion, informal manifestations of terrorist profiling and hard manifestations of racial profiling can never be justified and are almost always likely to be considered as being unlawful and even may be classified as being harmful as individuals or groups of individuals are subjected to enhanced levels of scrutiny by law enforcement officers without any reasonable justification. It is the reliance on sensitive characteristics as being the sole criteria or the risk of being the sole criteria for identifying individuals or groups of individuals that makes informal manifestations of terrorist profiling and manifestation of hard racial profiling unlawful and arguably harmful. Furthermore, the apparent inability to place sufficient controls against potential abuses of these informal manifestations of terrorist profiling further support the argument that these examples of terrorist profiling cannot be considered lawful. Consequently, it is argued that these manifestations of terrorist profiling are harmful as they carry an innate potential to alienate individuals or groups of individuals from ethnic, racial, national or religious groups that become the focal point for law enforcement without any justification other than being part of that ethnic, racial, national or religious group.

In the early part of this chapter some academic literature, such as American Civil Liberties Union,[100] Cuellar,[101] Harcourt,[102] Harris,[103] Moeckli[104] and Roach[105] determined that the inclusion of any sensitive characteristics in profiling posed an unjustifiable risk that particular individuals or groups of individuals exhibiting the sensitive characteristics may become subjected to official scrutiny and suspicion by law enforcement officers. In light of the discussion above, it seems probable that this determination may be characterised as being a form of 'hard racial profiling.' Consequently, the use of sensitive characteristics where they become or risk becoming the sole criteria used in the construction and/or application of profiles are unquestionably unjustifiable as this manifestation of profiling will always pose an indefensible risk that particular individuals or groups of individuals betraying the sensitive characteristics will become subject to official scrutiny and suspicion by law enforcement officers.

However, a further analytical distinction was drawn relating to formal manifestations of terrorist profiling and manifestations of soft racial profiling. These manifestations may be considered as being lawful and therefore 'justifiable' as suspects are not selected for enhanced levels of investigation by law enforcement officers solely on the grounds of sensitive characteristics. Rather a suspect's selection is based on a combination of different characteristics that compromise sensitive and non-sensitive characteristics. Furthermore, manifestations of formal terrorist profiling also exhibit a systematic process in the construction and/or application of profiles. This systematic process serves as a means to keep the profile under constant review so as to safeguard against, amongst other things, the danger of overreliance on sensitive characteristics at the construction and/or application of profile stages. Other literature was drawn upon in the early stages of this chapter, such as Amar,[106] Banks,[107] Derbyshire,[108] Ellmann,[109] Kinsley[110] and Risee and Zeckhauser[111] suggest that the inclusion of sensitive characteristics in the profiling process may be justifiable so long as they are included with other non-sensitive characteristics and that the sensitive characteristics do not become the sole criteria in identifying and selecting individuals for enhanced investigation by law enforcement officers.

Consequently, the inclusion of sensitive characteristics in addition to non-sensitive characteristics in formal manifestations of terrorist profiling can be considered justified as the risk of the sensitive characteristics becoming the sole criteria is lessened due to the reviewability of manifestations of formal terrorist profiling. This means that manifestations of formal terrorist profiling may be considered as being lawful so long as these manifestations of terrorist profiling are properly conducted and any interferences with human rights are justifiable by reference to human rights standards.

2.5 Conclusion

The primary aim of this chapter was to determine whether terrorist profiling, as examined in this book, may be considered compatible with fundamental rights. This was to allow consideration of the human rights issues arising from the examination of the usefulness of terrorist profiling which could overshadow the conclusions that will be drawn on the usefulness of terrorist profiling in the subsequent chapters. This aim was pursued by asking whether the inclusion of sensitive characteristics can ever be justified and, if so, in what circumstances? The argument advanced in this chapter was that there is no singular answer to address these questions but rather it involves considering a sequence of arguments to assess the justification question.

These sequence of arguments require first a legal determination as to whether the inclusion of sensitive characteristics can be considered lawful, and then secondly even if lawful, whether there may well be other reasons to suggest it should be unlawful and therefore unjustifiable.

In light of the discussion throughout this chapter, it is argued that so long as manifestations of formal terrorist profiling and manifestations of soft racial profiling are properly conducted, they may be considered lawful. This contention rests on at least two core arguments.

Firstly, the formal and systematic nature of the profiling process in these manifestations of terrorist profiling mean it is possible to review, alter and adapt profiling so that the risk of relying solely on sensitive characteristics is minimised on a continuous basis. For example, the examination of formal manifestations of terrorist profiling in chapter four identifies that some terrorist profiling schemes, such as the German *Rasterfahndung* scheme, were entirely reviewable and as a consequence of this they could be curtailed so as ensure minimum human rights are attained.

Secondly, the sensitive characteristics are included with non-sensitive characteristics to reduce the risk of sensitive characteristics becoming the main or sole criteria to identify individuals for enhanced levels of review by law enforcement officers. For example, in manifestations of formal terrorist profiling examined in chapter three such as the German *Rasterfahndung* scheme and the US terrorist profiling adopted at ports relied on a range of data in the construction and application of profiles.

However, turning to address the second part of the justification question, whether there are other reasons to suggest formal terrorist profiling should be unlawful and therefore unjustifiable. This question is essentially a 'values' issue and the discussion in chapter three questions whether the cost of the manifestations of formal terrorist profiling is so high that it begins to undermine the democratic legitimacy of the state's authority to govern. The danger posed by these manifestations of terrorist profiling is that they effectively require the state to engage in exercises tantamount to mass snooping exercises on its citizens. The requirement of vast arrays of personal data to feed into the construction and/or application of formal manifestations of terrorist profiling undermines these examples of profiling. Nevertheless, it is argued that manifestations of formal terrorist profiling (if properly conducted) remain capable of being considered lawful in contrast to manifestations of informal terrorist profiling given the fact that formal terrorist profiling is reviewable and controllable.

Those manifestations of informal terrorist profiling and manifestations of hard racial profiling can never be justifiable on the grounds that these profiling process are not subject to review or transparency so as to assess whether these manifestations of terrorist profiling can be considered unjustifiably targeting individuals or groups of individuals simply on the grounds of exhibiting the selected sensitive characteristic.

Additionally, manifestations of informal terrorist profiling and hard racial profiling carry a risk that particular individuals exhibiting the sensitive characteristics become the concentration for law enforcement officers in the detection, prevention and prosecution of acts of terrorism and preparatory activities. For example, in manifestations of informal terrorist profiling that are examined in chapter six, there is considerable evidence to demonstrate to a high degree of probability that some uses of the powers to stop and search in addition to other discretionary police powers may have been deployed to engage in the racial profiling of individuals that belong to Muslim communities. Furthermore, even if some of the evidence that is examined in chapter six could be considered examples of police abuse of their discretionary powers, then it may serve to demonstrate the inability of the statutory frameworks advancing these discretionary police powers to protect against the potential abuses of these powers.

To sum up, the inclusion of sensitive characteristics in manifestations of formal terrorist profiling may in some circumstances be considered lawful and therefore justifiable. However, the inclusion of sensitive characteristics in manifestations of informal terrorist profiling are likely unlawful and therefore are very likely to be unjustifiable.

Notes

1. N. McGuirk, 'A framework to measure/assess the utility of profiling as a counter-terrorism tool' (2019) Policing: A Journal of Policy and Practice 1, 2.
2. American Civil Liberties Union, *Sanctioned Bias: Racial Profiling* (American Civil Liberties Union, 2004), 3.
3. M. Cuellar, 'Choosing anti-terror targets by national origin and race' (2003) 6(1) Harvard Latino Law Review 9, 11.
4. B. Harcourt, 'Rethinking racial profiling: a critique of the economics, civil liberties and constitutional literature and of criminal profiling more generally' (2004) 71(4) The University of Chicago Law Review 1275, 1345. See also: B. Harcourt, 'Muslim Profiles Post 9/11: Is Racial Profiling an Effective Counter-terrorist Measure and Does It Violate the Right to be Free from Discrimination?' in B. Goold and L. Lazarus (eds), *Security and Human Rights* (Hart Publishing, 2007), 73–76.
5. D. Harris, 'Racial profiling revisited: "just common sense" in the fight against terror?' (2002) 17 Criminal Justice 36, 37.
6. K. Roach, 'Making progress on understanding and remedying racial profiling' (2004) 41 Alberta Law Review 895.
7. D. Moeckli, 'Discriminatory profiles: law enforcement after 9/11 and 7/7' (2005) 5 European Human Rights Law Review 517.
8. A. Ashworth, 'Security, Terrorism and the Value of Human Rights' in B. Goold and L. Lazarus (eds), *Security and Human Rights* (Hart Publishing, 2007), 205.
9. D. Ramirez, J. Hoopes and T. Quinlan, 'Defining racial profiling in a post-September 11th world' (2003) 40 American Criminal Law Review 1195, 1207–1207.
10. P. Schuck, 'Context is everything with racial profiling', LA Times, 27th January 2002.
11. J. Turley, 'Use profiling judiciously' LA Times, 4th January 2002.
12. V. Dodd, 'Asian men targeted in stop and search', The Guardian 17th August 2005.
13. F. Teson, 'Liberty Security' in R. Wilson (ed), *Human Rights in the 'War on Terror'* (Cambridge University Press, 2005), 59–61.

14. V. Amar, 'Life after 9/11: the golden rule of racial profiling', LA Times, 22nd September 2002.
15. R. Banks, 'Essay: racial profiling and anti-terrorism efforts' (2004) 89 Cornell Law Review 1201.
16. J. Derbyshire, 'A (potentially) useful tool' (2002) Responsive Community 67, 67–70.
17. J. Ellmann, 'Racial profiling and terrorism' (2003) 19 New York Law School Journal of Human Rights 305, 314–347.
18. M. Kinsley, 'Discrimination we're afraid to be against' (2002) Responsive Community 64, 64–66.
19. M. Risse and R. Zeckhauser, 'Racial profiling' (2004) 32(2) Philosophy and Public Affairs 131.
20. Ashworth, 'Security, Terrorism and the Value of Human Rights' (n8), 209–210.
21. D. Luban, 'Eight Fallacies About Liberty and Security' in R. Wilson (ed), *Human Rights in the 'War in Terrorism'* (Cambridge University Press, 2005), 245–246.
22. P. Thomas, 'Emergency and anti-terrorist powers 9/11: USA and UK' (2003) 26 Fordham International Law Journal 1193, 1206.
23. H. Barovick, 'Driving while black', Time, 15th June 1998, 35.
24. S. Choudry, 'Protecting Equality in the Face of Terror: Ethnic and Racial Profiling and s. 15 of the Charter' in R. Daniels, P. Macklem and K. Roach (eds), *The Security of Freedom: Essays on Canada's Anti-Terrorism Bill* (University of Toronto Press, 2001), 369.
25. S. Han, 'The long shadow of racial profiling' (2012) 1 British Journal of American Legal Studies 77, 82–86.
26. See: S. Gross and D. Livingston, 'Racial profiling under attack' (2002) 102 Columbia Law Review 1413, 1415; D. Harris, 'Flying while Arab: lessons from the racial profiling controversy' (2002) 6 Civil Rights Journal 8, 8 and Ramirez, Hoopes and Quinlan, 'Defining racial profiling in a post September 11th world' (n9), 1205.
27. D. Harris, 'Racial profiling redux' (2003) 22 Saint Louis University Public Law Review 73, 77.
28. D. Johnston, D. Brazier, K. Forrest, C. Ketelhut, D. Mason and M. Mitchell, 'Attitudes toward the use of racial/ethnic profiling to prevent crime and terrorism' (2011) 22(4) Criminal Justice Policy Review 422, 423.
29. Risse and Zeckhauser, 'Racial profiling' (n19), 135.
30. M. Risse, 'Racial profiling: a reply to two critics' (2007) Criminal Justice Ethics 4, 4.
31. D. Ramierz, J. McDevitt and A. Farrell, *A Resource Guide on Racial Profiling Data Collection Systems: Promising Practices and Lessons Learned* (Northeast University, 2000), 4–6. For other very similar formulations see: R. Banks, 'Race-based suspect selection and colorblind equal protection doctrine and discourse' (2001) 48 UCLA Law Review 1077. Gross and Livingston 'Racial profiling under attack' (n26), 1415.
32. E. Hedican, *Ipperwash: The Tragic Failure of Canada's Aboriginal Policy* (University of Toronto Press, 2013), 233.
33. ibid.
34. Risse and Zeckhauser, 'Racial profiling' (n19), 136.
35. ibid, 137.
36. End Racial Profiling Act, 2001, s. 989.
37. I. Fiala, 'Anything new? The racial profiling of terrorists' (2003) 16(1) Criminal Justice Studies 53, 54.
38. Open Society Justice Initiative, *Ethnic Profiling in the European Union: Pervasive, Ineffective and Discriminatory* (Open Justice Institute, 2009), 19.
39. Fiala, 'Anything new? The racial profiling of terrorists' (n37), 54.

40. A. Jones, 'The corrective use of lawsuit data in policing: reconstructing the vocabulary of racial profiling' (2013) 5 Widener Journal of Law, Economics and Race 1, 7.
41. S. Fredman, *Discrimination Law* (Clarendon Press, 2011), 1–8.
42. P. Westen, 'The empty idea of equality' (1982) 95 Harvard Law Review 537, 547–548.
43. T. Hobbes, *Leviathan* (CreateSpace Independent Publishing Platform, 2011), 75–78.
44. J. Locke, *Two Treaties of Government* (Book Jungle, 2009).
45. J. Rawls, *A Theory of Justice* (Harvard University Press, 1999).
46. R. Dworkin, *Taking Rights Seriously* (Harvard University Press, 1977).
47. Rawls, 'A Theory of Justice' (n45), 266.
48. D. Moeckli, *Human Rights and Non-Discrimination in the War on Terror* (Oxford University Press, 2008), 60.
49. ibid, 61.
50. ibid.
51. United Nations, *Charter of the United Nations*, 24 October 1945, 1 UNTS XVI, available at: http://www.refworld.org/docid/3ae6b3930.html (accessed 29th September 2019), Article 1(3).
52. B. Ganor and A. Conte, 'Legal and policy issues in establishing a framework for human rights compliance when countering terrorism' (2005) International Policy Institute for Countering Terrorism 1, 38.
53. UN General Assembly, *International Covenant on Civil and Political Rights*, 16 December 1966, United Nations, Treaty Series, vol. 999, p. 171, available at: http://www.refworld.org/docid/3ae6b3aa0.html (accessed 29th September 2019), Article 2(1).
54. ibid, Article 26.
55. UN General Assembly, International Convention on the Elimination of All Forms of Racial Discrimination, 21 December 1965, United Nations, Treaty Series, vol. 660, p. 195, available at: http://www.refworld.org/docid/3ae6b3940.html (accessed 29th September 2019), Article 1(1).
56. UN General Assembly, *Convention Relating to the Status of Refugees*, 28 July 1951, United Nations, Treaty Series, vol. 189, p. 137, available at: http://www.refworld.org/docid/3be01b964.html (accessed 29th September 2019), Article 3.
57. UN General Assembly, *International Covenant on Economic, Social and Cultural Rights*, 16 December 1966, United Nations, Treaty Series, vol. 993, p. 3, available at: http://www.refworld.org/docid/3ae6b36c0.html (accessed 29th September 2019).
58. UN General Assembly, *Convention on the Rights of the Child*, 20 November 1989, United Nations, Treaty Series, vol. 1577, p. 3, available at: http://www.refworld.org/docid/3ae6b38f0.html (accessed 29th September 2019).
59. Human Rights Committee, *General Comment 18, Non-discrimination (Thirty-seventh session, 1989), Compilation of General Comments and General Recommendations Adopted by Human Rights Treaty Bodies*, U.N. Doc. HRI/GEN/1/Rev.1 at 26 (1994), para 6.
60. Human Rights Committee, *General Comment 18, Non-discrimination (Thirty-seventh session, 1989), Compilation of General Comments and General Recommendations Adopted by Human Rights Treaty Bodies*, U.N. Doc. HRI/GEN/1/Rev.1 at 26 (1994). para 13.
61. UN Committee on the Elimination of Racial Discrimination, *General Recommendation XIV(42), on art. 1, para. 1 of the Convention*, U.N. GAOR, 48th Sess., Supp. No. 18, U.N. Doc. A/48/18 (1993).
62. ibid, para 2.

63. UN General Assembly, *Code of conduct for law enforcement officials*, 5 February 1980, A/RES/34/169, available at: http://www.refworld.org/docid/48abd572e.html (accessed 29th September 2019).
64. United Nations, Durban Declaration and Plan of Action, Adopted at the World Conference Against Racism, Racial Discrimination, Xenophobia and Related Violence, 8 September 2001, available at: http://www.refworld.org/docid/3db573314.html (accessed 29th September 2019).
65. Code of Conduct for Law Enforcement Officials, Article 2 and UN World Conference Against Racism 2000, paragraph 2.
66. UN General Assembly, *Declaration on the Human Rights of Individuals Who Are Not Nationals of the Country in Which They Live: resolution / adopted by the General Assembly, 13 December 1985*, A/RES/40/144, available at: http://www.refworld.org/docid/3b00f00864.html (accessed 29th September 2019).
67. UN Commission on Human Rights, *Body of principles for the protection of all persons under any form of detention or imprisonment*, 7 March 1978, E/CN.4/RES/19(XXXIV), available at: http://www.refworld.org/docid/3b00f0846c.html (accessed 29th September 2019).
68. Moeckli, 'Human Rights and Non-Discrimination in the War on Terror' (n47), 60.
69. O. Arnadottir, *Equality and Non-Discrimination under the European Convention on Human Rights* (Martinus Nijhoff, 2012), 49–51 and K. Partsch, 'Discrimination' in R. Macdonald, F. Matscher and H. Petzold (eds), *The European System for the Protection of Human Rights* (Kluwer Law, 2008).
70. *Klass v Germany* (1978) 2 EHRR 214, para 46.
71. (1968) 1 EHRR 252.
72. The Human Rights Act 1998 incorporates the European Convention on Human Rights into UK domestic law. *R (Daly) v Secretary of State for the Home Department* (2001) UKHL 26. See also: J. Jowell, 'Beyond the rule of law: towards constitutional judicial review' (2000) Public Law 671 and D. Feldman, 'Proportionality and the Human Rights Act 1998' in E. Ellis (ed), *The Principle of Proportionality in the Laws of Europe* (Hart Publishing, 1999), 117–121.
73. BVerfGE 19, 342 (1965) *Wencker.*
74. *Observer and Guardian v United Kingdom* (1991) 14 EHRR 153.
75. *Informationsverenin Lentia and others v Austria* (1993) 17 EHRR 93.
76. *National Union of Belgian Police v Belgium* (1975) 1 EHRR 578.
77. Y. Arai-Takahashi, 'Proportionality' in D. Shelton (ed), *The Oxford Handbook of International Human Rights Law* (Oxford University Press, 2013), 452.
78. C. Panaccio, 'In defence of two-step balancing and proportionality in rights adjudication' (2011) 24 Canadian Journal of Law & Jurisprudence 109, 112.
79. Arai-Takahashi, 'Proportionality' (n 77), 451.
80. ibid.
81. A. Sweet and J. Mathews, 'Proportionality balancing and global constitutionalism' (2008) 47 Columbia Journal of Transnational Law 72, 75.
82. *Handyside v United Kingdom* (1976) 1 EHRR 737.
83. J. Schokkenbroek, 'The prohibition of discrimination in Article 14 of the convention and the margin of appreciation' (1998) 19 Human Rights Law Review 20.
84. *East African Asians v United Kingdom* (1973) 3 EHRR 76, para 207.
85. 320 US 81 (1943).
86. 323 US 214 (1944).
87. (2004) UKHL 30.
88. ibid, para 9.
89. (1993) 17 EHRR 293.
90. ibid, para 9.
91. *Ghaidan v Godin-Mendoza* (n87).

92. ibid, para 9.
93. (1996) 23 EHRR 364.
94. ibid, para 42.
95. *Rosalind Williams Lecraft v Spain* Comm No. 1493/2006, 30 July 2009.
96. ibid, para 4.2.
97. ibid, para 4.4.
98. ibid, para 7.4.
99. ibid.
100. *American Civil Liberties Union*, 'Sanctioned Bias: Racial Profiling' (n2).
101. *Cuellar*, 'Choosing anti-terror targets by national origin and race' (n3).
102. *Harcourt*, 'Rethinking racial profiling: a critique of the economics, civil liberties and constitutional literature and of criminal profiling more generally' (n4).
103. *Harris*, 'Racial profiling revisited: "just common sense" in the fight against terror?' (n5).
104. *Moeckli*, 'Discriminatory profiles: law enforcement after 9/11 and 7/7' (n7).
105. *Roach*, 'Making progress on understanding and remedying racial profiling' (n6).
106. *Amar*, 'Life after 9/11: the golden rule of racial profiling' (n14).
107. *Banks*, 'Essay: Racial profiling and anti-terrorism efforts' (n15).
108. *Derbyshire*, 'A (potentially) useful tool' (n16).
109. *Ellmann*, 'Racial profiling and terrorism' (n17).
110. *Kinsley*, 'Discrimination we're afraid to be against' (n18).
111. *Risse* and *Zeckhauser*, 'Racial profiling' (n19).

Bibliography

American Civil Liberties Union, *Sanctioned Bias: Racial Profiling* (American Civil Liberties Union, 2004).

Amar, V., 'Life after 9/11: the golden rule of racial profiling', LA Times, 22nd September 2002.

Arai-Takahashi, Y., 'Proportionality' in D. Shelton (ed.), *The Oxford Handbook of International Human Rights Law* (Oxford University Press, 2013).

Arnadottir, O., *Equality and Non-Discrimination under the European Convention on Human Rights* (Martinus Nijhoff, 2012).

Ashworth, A., 'Security, Terrorism and the Value of Human Rights' in B. Goold and L. Lazarus (eds), *Security and Human Rights* (Hart Publishing, 2007).

Banks, R., 'Essay: racial profiling and anti-terrorism efforts' (2004) 89 *Cornell Law Review* 1201.

Banks, R., 'Race-based suspect selection and colorblind equal protection doctrine and discourse' (2001) 48 *UCLA Law Review* 1077.

Barovick, H., 'Driving while black', *Time*, 15th June 1998, 35.

Choudry, S., 'Protecting Equality in the Face of Terror: Ethnic and Racial Profiling and s. 15 of the Charter' in R. Daniels, P. Macklem and K. Roach (eds), *The Security of Freedom: Essays on Canada's Anti-Terrorism Bill* (University of Toronto Press, 2001).

Cuellar, M., 'Choosing anti-terror targets by national origin and race' (2003) 6(1) *Harvard Latino Law Review* 9.

Derbyshire, J., 'A (potentially) useful tool' (2002) *Responsive Community* 67.

Dodd, V., 'Asian men targeted in stop and search', The Guardian 17th August 2005.

Dworkin, R., *Taking Rights Seriously* (Harvard University Press, 1977).

Ellmann, J., 'Racial profiling and terrorism' (2003) 19 *New York Law School Journal of Human Rights* 305.

Feldman, D., 'Proportionality and the Human Rights Act 1998' in E. Ellis (ed), *The Principle of Proportionality in the Laws of Europe* (Hart Publishing, 1999).

Fiala, I., 'Anything New? The racial profiling of terrorists' (2003) 16(1) *Criminal Justice Studies* 53.

Fredman, S., *Discrimination Law* (Clarendon Press, 2011).

Ganor, B. and Conte, A., 'Legal and policy issues in establishing a framework for human rights compliance when countering terrorism' (2005) *International Policy Institute for Countering Terrorism* 1.

Gross, S. and Livingston, D., 'Racial profiling under attack' (2002) 102 *Columbia Law Review* 1413.

Han, S., 'The long shadow of racial profiling' (2012) 1 *British Journal of American Legal Studies* 77.

Harcourt, B., 'Muslim Profiles Post 9/11: Is Racial Profiling an Effective Counter-Terrorist Measure and Does It Violate the Right to Be Free from Discrimination?' in B. Goold and L. Lazarus, *Security and Human Rights* (Hart Publishing, 2007).

Harcourt, B., 'Rethinking racial profiling: a critique of the economics, civil liberties and constitutional literature and of criminal profiling more generally' (2004) 71(4) *The University of Chicago Law Review* 1275.

Harris, D., 'Flying while Arab: lessons from the racial profiling controversy' (2002) 6 *Civil Rights Journal* 8.

Harris, D., 'Racial profiling redux' (2003) 22 *Saint Louis University Public Law Review* 73.

Harris, D., 'Racial profiling revisited: "just common sense" in the fight against terror?' (2002) 17 *Criminal Justice* 36.

Hedican, E., *Ipperwash: The Tragic Failure of Canada's Aboriginal Policy* (University of Toronto Press, 2013).

Hobbes, T., *Leviathan* (CreateSpace Independent Publishing Platform, 2011).

Johnston, D., Brazier, D., Forrest, K., Ketelhut, C., Mason, D. and Mitchell, M., 'Attitudes toward the use of racial/ethnic profiling to prevent crime and terrorism' (2011) 22(4) *Criminal Justice Policy Review* 422.

Jones, A., 'The corrective use of lawsuit data in policing: reconstructing the vocabulary of racial profiling' (2013) 5 *Widener Journal of Law, Economics and Race* 1.

Jowell, J., 'Beyond the rule of law: towards constitutional judicial review' [2000] *Public Law* 671.

Kinsley, M., 'Discrimination we're afraid to be against' (2002) *Responsive Community* 64.

Locke, J., *Two Treaties of Government* (Book Jungle, 2009).

Luban, D., 'Eight Fallacies About Liberty and Security' in R. Wilson (ed), *Human Rights in the 'War in Terrorism'* (Cambridge University Press, 2005).

McGuirk, N., 'A framework to measure/assess the utility of profiling as a counterterrorism tool' (2019) *Policing: A Journal of Policy and Practice* 1.

Moeckli, D., 'Discriminatory profiles: law enforcement after 9/11 and 7/7' (2005) 5 *European Human Rights Law Review* 517.

Moeckli, D., *Human Rights and Non-Discrimination in the War on Terror* (Oxford University Press, 2008).

Open Society Justice Initiative, *Ethnic Profiling in the European Union: Pervasive, Ineffective and Discriminatory* (Open Justice Institute, 2009).

Panaccio, C., 'In defence of two-step balancing and proportionality in rights adjudication' (2011) 24 *Canadian Journal of Law & Jurisprudence* 109.

Partsch, K., 'Discrimination' in R. Macdonald, F.Matscher and H. Petzold (eds), *The European System for the Protection of Human Rights* (Kluwer Law, 2008).

Ramirez, D., Hoopes, J. and Quinlan, T., 'Defining racial profiling in a post-September 11th world' (2003) 40 *American Criminal Law Review* 1195.

Ramierz, D., McDevitt, J. and Farrell, A., *A Resource Guide on Racial Profiling Data Collection Systems: Promising Practices and Lessons Learned* (Northeast University, 2000).

Rawls, J., *A Theory of Justice* (Harvard University Press, 1999).

Risse, M., 'Racial profiling: a reply to two critics' (2007) *Criminal Justice Ethics* 4.

Risse, M. and Zeckhauser, R., 'Racial profiling' (2004) 32(2) *Philosophy and Public Affairs* 131.

Roach, K., 'Making progress on understanding and remedying racial profiling' (2004) 41 *Alberta Law Review* 895.

Schokkenbroek, J., 'The prohibition of discrimination in Article 14 of the convention and the margin of appreciation' (1998) 19 *Human Rights Law Review* 20.

Schuck, P., 'Context is everything with racial profiling', LA Times, 27th January 2002.

Sweet, A. and Mathews, J., 'Proportionality balancing and global constitutionalism' (2008) 47 *Columbia Journal of Transnational Law* 72.

Teson, F., 'Liberty Security' in R. Wilson (ed), *Human Rights in the 'War on Terror'* (Cambridge University Press, 2005).

Thomas, P., 'Emergency and anti-terrorist powers 9/11: USA and UK' (2003) 26 *Fordham International Law Journal* 1193.

Turley, J., 'Use profiling judiciously' LA Times, 4th January 2002.

Westen, P., 'The empty idea of equality' (1982) 95 *Harvard Law Review* 537.

3 Criminal profiling and its applicability to terrorist profiling

3.1 Introduction

A substantive issue with the use of any profiling method or approach in the context of terrorism is how, if at all, profiling may be utilised by law enforcement officers to assist in the detection and identification of those likely to be engaged in terrorism and/or its preparatory activities. The natural starting point to assess the applicability of profiling to terrorism is to examine criminal profiling as this provides an established analytical lens to assess the applicability of profiling more generally to terrorism.

Criminal profiling can be described as being an investigative process that has been subjected to an increasing degree of interest over the past four decades from both academics and mainstream popular media.[1] This interest in criminal profiling can be classified as being conflicting in nature. For instance, it has been praised as a key investigative tool[2] and also criticised for being tedious and of little investigative value.[3]

Criminal profiling at its most basic is a method/approach that may assist law enforcement officers identify likely offender characteristics and traits of unknown offenders from information gleaned from the crime scene and/or previous criminal records.[4] As noted in the introductory chapter above, criminal profiling is a process allowing the profiler to identify a sequence of commonalities from the crime scene and/or previous criminal records to predict likely offender characteristics.[5] For the purposes of the discussion, profiling is defined broadly as being any technique or process which is likely to allow law enforcement officers to identify likely 'offender characteristics can be considered some form of profiling.'[6]

The primary aim of this chapter is to identify, explain and evaluate the various different methodologies that can be adopted within criminal profiling. The objective of this discussion is to use this analysis in later chapters as an analytical tool to evaluate whether counterterrorism strategies can use profiling methods and processes to identify likely terrorist characteristics.

It is evident from the literature that law enforcement officers can use criminal profiling in at least two ways: deductively and inductively.[7]

Deductive profiling is where law enforcement officers use profiling methods to react to crimes already committed and deduce offender characteristics by using forensic crime evidence and victim reports. The methods used within deductive profiling follow a reactive methodology where the profile purports to be rationally or logically deduced following a thorough analysis of the crime scene and the victim.

In contrast, inductive profiling occurs when law enforcement officers use proactive profiling methods as a tool to detect and prevent crime. This is a profiling method where police officers use analytical methods to predict likely offender characters so as to prevent future criminality. The distinguishing feature of inductive profiling methods is its dependence upon a statistical analysis of previous offending records to identify the common characteristics of known offenders so as to allow the profiler to make predictions about likely offender characteristics.[8]

The distinction between deductive and inductive profiling will become important in subsequent chapters when the discussion turns to concentrate on analysing different manifestations of terrorist profiling. Specifically, this distinction will assist in analysing whether law enforcement officers can rely on criminal profiling methodologies in a reactionary way to assist in the identification of terrorist characteristics and/or in a preventative way to predict likely terrorist characteristics.

There are three main parts to this chapter. In the first part, the discussion concentrates on evaluating deductive profiling methods in order to determine whether there are any methods within deductive profiling that can be used within counterterrorism in assisting with the identification of likely terrorist characteristics. In the second part, the discussion progresses by examining inductive profiling so as to identify and evaluate whether these profiling methods/approaches can be used within the counterterrorism context. The discussion in the final part of the chapter ultimately concludes that only inductive profiling methods/approach may be of some use in assisting law enforcement officers identify likely terrorist characteristics if the profiling process takes into account at least four critical issues analysed below.

3.2 Deductive profiling

As noted above, deductive profiling is the practice where law enforcement officers use crime scene evidence to deduce likely offender characteristics. It involves a profiler using deductive profiling methods to extract key information from the crime scene to establish likely offender characteristics. Essentially it is the behavioural analysis of specific crimes scenes, crimes and victims which is drawn from the forensic evidence relating to a specific offender.[9] Deductive profiling concentrates primarily on using forensic evidence to rationally and logically deduce likely offender characteristics.

On the basis of the literature, it can be argued that deductive profiling reflects two approaches: non-scientific approaches and scientific approaches. Both of these approaches draw upon various methodologies including 'behavioural analysis, [psychological] analysis, crime scene analysis, police officer investigative experience and empirical studies conducted with [known] offenders.'[10]

The 'scientific' profiling approaches in this chapter are considered scientific because they tend to rely on investigative psychology to test, validate and replicate the accuracy of the profiles. Additionally, scientific approaches generally aim to develop a wide range of literature, knowledge and practice so as to allow an entire profiling process to be enhanced and developed with each case profiled.

The 'non-scientific' profiling approaches are considered non-scientific because they do not attempt to test, validate or replicate any of the profiles constructed. Additionally, non-scientific profiling approaches do not use any scientific discipline to enhance the reliability of the profiles constructed. In essence, each profile constructed using a non-scientific approach is only a standalone example or manifestation of profiling. It does not seek to build a growing body of literature, knowledge or practice.

For the purposes of analysis, an approach or method will be considered scientific if it exhibits certain features including: the ability to test its application by replication, the publication and validation of its results and its ability to draw upon one or more scientific disciplines.

3.2.1 The origins of profiling

The 'origins of profiling can be traced to fictional literature of the nineteenth century when various characters were given specific roles of catching' serial murderers and rapists.[11] 'Modern profiling can be attributed to the works of psychiatrist James Brussel who successfully profiled a bomber in New York City in the late 1960s.'[12] The methods employed by Brussel involved a two-step process: firstly he studied all known information about the bomber which included an analysis of the letters and demands made to the police by the bomber.[13] Secondly, he also examined the methods used by the bomber to carry out his attacks on New York City.[14]

Brussel was assisted in constructing the profile by using 'previous personality traits constructed by Ernst Kretchmer which allowed Brussel to compartmentalise the likely offender characteristics of the bomber.'[15] The profile produced by Brussel 'allowed the police to focus [and target] their investigation' on the likely characteristics and personality traits of the unknown offender.[16] It was the success of Brussel's work which elevated the use of profiling into the media spotlight as his profile resembled almost the identical characteristics of the actual bomber.

The effect of Brussel's work was to spotlight the potential of using profiling to identify unknown offenders when traditional investigative techniques failed. Although, it should be acknowledged that police investigate work has long involved elements of profiling, even prior to Brussel where law enforcement officers have used crimes schemes to assist them identify likely offenders.

The specific focus of this chapter now turns to investigate the non-scientific and scientific profiling approaches so as to examine whether any deductive profiling methods can be used in the context of terrorism.

3.2.2 Non-scientific deductive profiling approaches

Whilst there is much academic literature on criminal profiling, there are at least five non-scientific profiling approaches capable of being classified as examples of deductive profiling:

1 'Douglas, Ressler, Burgess and Hartman' approach
2 'Holmes and Holmes' approach
3 'Keppel and Walter' approach
4 'Turco' approach
5 'Turvey' approach[17]

The 'Douglas, Resseler, Burgess and Hartman' approach 'was primarily used for the identification of unknown offenders which employed a categorisation process to assimilate information from the crime scene.'[18] Douglas *et al*'s approach is the closest approach to a law enforcement officer using their own investigative experience and intuition so as to identify potential offender characteristics by using evidence from the crime scene which may exhibit personality and behavioural traits of an unknown offender.[19]

Typically, this approach would involve six stages. Firstly, a field officer would gather vital information including: crime scene evidence, a victimology report, any available 'forensic information, the preliminary police reports and any photographs of the [crime] scene.'[20] The profiling officer would use this information to make certain decisions to predict likely offender characteristics, which is known as the secondary decision process stage. The third stage is where the field officer would make a crime assessment. This involves a reconstruction of the crime scene to focus attention on how the offender committed the crime. The fourth stage involves the construction of the offender profile by using all the information the officer has collected and analysed. The fifth stage is where the actual investigation of crime takes place with the help of the profile constructed from the fourth stage. The final stage involves the successful apprehension of the offender based upon all the evidence gathered and the constructed profile.

The typical example of the use of the Douglas *et al* approach is where the police officer goes out to a crime scene and firstly collects all available evidence, secondly analyses the evidence with a view to identifying likely offender characteristics and thirdly uses all information collected to create an offender profile. It may be characterised as being 'unscientific' as it does not use any process which is capable of being tested, replicated or validated for the accuracy of profiling predictions. As a result, it would seem that this profiling approach is focused on drawing upon a law enforcement officer's intuition so as to interpret specific crime scene information.

The 'Holmes and Holmes' approach develops the Douglas *et al*'s approach. It not only uses all the stages of collecting, analysing and constructing the profile but goes further by being more selective in the information it uses to construct the profile.[21] Whilst the Holmes and Holmes approach uses the Douglas *et al* six-step approach, it differs somewhat 'by matching evidence and information from the crime scene to various criminal typologies with an additional focus on the geography of the area in which the crime occurs.'[22]

The 'Holmes and Holmes' approach significantly draws upon behavioural analysis professionals: Kolko and Kazdin,[23] Sakheim *et al*,[24] Rider,[25] Groth *et al*,[26] Knight and Prently[27] and Burgess *et al*.[28] The practical difference between the Holmes and Holmes approach and the Douglas *et al* approach is that under Holmes and Holmes, the field officer still goes out to the crime scene to collect all available evidence but the key distinction is how that information and evidence is used to construct the profile. Unlike the Douglas *et al* method it does not solely allow the police officer to construct the profile upon their own intuition and experience, but rather it uses typologies to aid the connection between the crime scene evidence and the profile. For example, the typologies advanced within the Holmes and Holmes approach focuses on the crime scene evidence which would indicate whether the offender was organised or disorganised.[29] This typology would allow certain probabilities to be included in the profile, for instance, if the crime scene evidence suggested a disorganised offender then it could be true that they are disorganised in 'appearance, psychological state, domestic situation and criminal activity.'[30] Essentially, this would allow more characteristics to be predicted which could lead to a closer identification of the offender. Additionally, it may be considered a more intelligent use of available information to identify more defined characteristics of the offender.

The third approach, advocated by 'Keppel and Walter,'[31] further develops the profiling approaches in Holmes and Holmes and Douglas *et al*. In particular, the authors critique the Holmes and Holmes approach 'as being too wide ranging and being of little investigative value as it is largely unsupported by empirical data.'[32] Keppel and Walter's approach is similar in many respects to the Holmes and Holmes approach in that they draw heavily upon academic literature to support their profiling approach.

Similar to Holmes and Holmes they use the Douglas *et al* approach as the template for the collection of evidence from the crime scene.[33] The key difference between Holmes and Holmes and Keppel and Walter is that the latter uses academic literature which has an empirical basis to validate some of the typologies used. In particular, Keppel and Walter focus exclusively on the crimes of murder and rape and use academic literature which present empirical studies to validate the typologies used. The empirical literature used by Keppel and Walter is produced by Hazelwood and Burgess[34] who interviewed 33 suspects in the Michigan State Penitentiary who were prosecuted for crimes of rape and murder.

The fourth method, advocated by 'Turco,'[35] 'focuses on developing a psychological theory' as a profiling hypothesis 'which draws heavily upon the work of Liebert' who was a specialist psychiatrist in the context of identifying common traits found in convicted serial murders.[36] Turco's approach is somewhat different to the previous three approaches as it is the first real attempt at bringing some scientific elements within the non-scientific profiling approaches. The primary focus of Turco's approach is to identify the psychological problems the offender exhibited at the crime scene and to discern the likely characteristics by using psychological theories to explain why an offender committed the violent crime.[37]

The particular approach adopted by Turco develops profiles along three dimensions: firstly, the profiler considers all crime scene evidence. Secondly, the profiler engages in an assessment of this evidence in the context of neurological behavioural disorders in order to develop the profile. Turco's approach integrates the crime scene evidence with contemporary medical science on neurological disorders, as he argued 'that between 20% and 90% of violent offenders suffered from brain impairment or structural abnormalities' which were relevant to understanding the destructive behaviour of killers in violent crimes.[38] The third stage in Turco's approach creates the profile of the offender with an understanding of the impact of neurological disorders upon the likely characteristics of the offender. Turco's approach employs a differential method to the previous three approaches because it only focuses on violent crimes by using an understanding of neurological disorders to distil likely offender characteristics.

The fifth and most recently developed approach is that developed by 'Turvey' which primarily uses behavioural analysis as a basis to predict potential characteristics of an unknown offender.[39] Turvey's approach relies exclusively upon physical and behavioural evidence from the crime scene. It typically involves two stages, firstly actually gathering evidence from the crime scene and then secondly using this evidence to deduct a profile of likely characteristics.[40] In practice Turvey's methodology seeks to marry together much of the previous work on gathering information from the crime scene with already known information from previous crimes focusing exclusively on utilising behavioural science to distil the likely characteristics of the offender.[41] Turvey distinguishes his approach by referring to inductive profiling as 'a process reliant upon subjective expertise involving broad generalisations or statistical reasoning.'[42] Turvey places his method of profiling within deductive profiling referring to it as 'a forensic-evidence based process-orientated, method of investigative reasoning about the behavioural patterns of a particular offender.'[43]

In essence the Turvey approach brings together a range of physical and behavioural evidence to draw a specific conclusion. In particular, Turvey draws upon Groth *et al*'s[44] behaviour-motivational typologies for rape offenders which are common to some of the other non-scientific approaches including Douglas *et al*, Holmes and Holmes and Turco.

Although Groth *et al*'s typologies only relate to rapists, Turvey's approach uses the rapist typologies for a broader range of criminal behaviour including 'kidnapping, child molestation, terrorism, sexual assault homicide and arson.'[45] Turvey argues that the typologies developed by Groth *et al* remained constant across a range of offences and focused only on classifying behaviours as opposed to offenders.[46] The key distinction between Turvey and the other methods of profiling is that, this method focuses exclusively on classifying behavioural traits and characteristics as opposed to offenders.

3.2.3 Non-scientific deductive profiling approaches a critique

There are six principal criticisms that can be made of the non-scientific profiling methods/approaches, including the absence of standardised methods and approaches, the poor consistency in the use of language, the misapplication of typologies, the high dependence on law enforcement instinct and prior investigative experience, the absence of clear procedures and for being of little investigative value.

3.2.3.1 An absence of standardised methods and approaches

Across each of the approaches there is no well-defined method or 'standard for profiling but rather each departs upon different routes to construct a profile of offender characteristics.'[47] It can be argued that having standardised methods and approaches within profiling is vital to the success of developing a coherent method in the construction of a profile.[48] Additionally, the setting of 'goals should form a core aspect' in the construction 'of a profile because they represent the guidance necessary to standardise the development of profiles across a range of offences.'[49]

Across the non-scientific methods/approaches, it is possible to identify that there are at least ten different common goals for profiling.[50] For example, Douglas *et al*'s approach places primary importance upon analysing the crime scene, providing offender characteristics, providing police leads and evaluating suspect belongings left at the crime scene. Whereas Holmes and Holmes's approach primarily focuses on providing offender characteristics and evaluating suspect belongings left at the crime scene.

Therefore, all of the profiling approaches use the crime scene evidence in different ways to achieve different goals but ultimately are aimed at providing unknown offender characteristics. The central problem is that none of the methods sufficiently address the question of consistency of methodology and they do not offer any consensus on the issue.[51]

Those crimes which allow the profiler to garner particular information from the crime scene allow the profiler identify commonalities between crimes so as to enable the construction of a profile.[52] This may suggest that crimes, such as murder or rape, have identifiably similar patterns including – 'where they were committed, how they are committed and who they are committed against.'[53] For example, the Doughlas *et al*'s approach deals with rape, murder, arson and threats to life. Whereas Holmes and Holmes approach only deals with rape, paedophilia, murder and arson. There is no available evidence capable of demonstrating any of the approaches actually work outside of these offences. It is clear that the offences profiled using the non-scientific methods are pathological in nature which allows the profiler to identify possible patterns and trends not only from the crime scene but also from previous offences.

3.2.3.2 Poor consistency in the use of language

The use of vocabulary throughout each of the approaches varies author by author 'which contributes to a problematic [coherent] application of the principles' in the construction of a profile.[54] The primary problem with using different vocabulary throughout each approach is that at each vital stage in the construction of a profile, from collecting to analysing crime scene evidence, each author describes the process differently despite essential commonalities existing. For example, all of the non-scientific approaches rely, to varying degrees, upon physical evidence from the crime scene although each of the methods describe the process of collecting evidence by using different vocabulary. There are two main criticisms that can be made of the language used by the authors:

i There is a lack of consistency in many of the profiling approaches in the language used to explain the profiling techniques and processes.[55] For example, serial killers are described as being those individuals with a minimum of three victims with a cooling off period between killings in the Douglas *et al* approach.[56] Whereas, in the Holmes and Holmes approach serial killers do not have a cooling off period between killings.[57] Additionally, Douglas *et al*'s approach argues that an offender's behaviour is likely to change and adjust over a number of offences whereas in the Holmes and Holmes approach they argue that offending behaviour across an offence will remain constant throughout.

ii There is a lack of evolution towards a standardised vocabulary within the non-scientific methods. Whilst it can be argued that each method is entitled to use its own terminology as long as the methods are moving towards a consolidation of vocabulary. Unfortunately, each of the approaches are deficient in developing a core vocabulary for profiling. For example, some of the methods use terminology without actually explaining its context or its definition. Turco uses terms such as 'dyscontrol syndrome' and 'pre-Odeipal matrix' without dealing with what the terms mean or how they connect to profiling.

3.2.3.3 Misapplication of typologies

The main focus of the non-scientific methods (except for Turco) is principally focused on the use of typologies where the authors try to match the offender to particular typologies largely developed by the academic literature.[58] The use of typologies throughout the non-scientific approaches creates three specific problems:

i The non-scientific approaches attempt to cluster offences according to general similarities identifiable from a crime scene analysis so as to create a general overview and picture of an unknown offender. This creates a conceptual belief of accuracy by establishing similar patterns of behaviour which can be supported by academic study.[59] However, it can be argued that not every individual will match the criterion of a profile constructed from general similarities as not every offender will be the same. The non-scientific methods do not make clear what a profiler should do when an offender does not match all or any of the criterions from the general similarities of other crimes. This creates a conceptual weakness within the non-scientific methods in that they do not appear to factor in changes within each crime under investigation and the impact this may have on the identification of offenders.[60]

ii There are considerable inconsistencies within the typologies used by the various authors of the non-scientific approaches. For example, some approaches such as Holmes and Holmes begin with the geographical importance of the offence and progress to deal with offender motives without making the linkages between motives and the geographical significance of the criminal act. Additionally, in Holmes and Holmes when linking the geographical significance to motives the authors use typologies which are based upon a study of 100 inmates in one penitentiary in America. Although the study of 100 inmates does provide an empirical insight into the offences committed and does attempt to offer explanation as to why those convicted offenders committed their offences, it fails methodologically when the authors seek to use one study to form a representation of those offences nationally or globally.[61] It cannot be legitimate to use one study as the basis of predicting crimes nationally as it fails to reflect different cultures, attitudes to crime and propensity to commit crime.

iii The non-scientific approaches do not sufficiently address the issue of when offenders can be categorised across a range of profiles because they exhibit a number of the traits and characteristics of a range of profiles. This situation would arise when there is an overlap between the various typologies; the non-scientific methods do not make it sufficiently clear or present a justification for which particular typology should apply.

3.2.3.4 The high dependence on law enforcement instinct and prior investigative experience

It is evident from all of the non-scientific methods that they are heavily influenced by the intuition of the profiler which is relative to the experience that the profiler has gained in investigating or profiling the offence under examination. This can create a difficulty where a profiler may become influenced by their previous experience of those offences when constructing a profile. Canter suggests that all profiling has an element of intuition in the choices and selections made by the profiler.[62] However, in non-scientific profiling the core basis for constructing the profile is the intuition of the profiler. This presents two core problems: firstly the more reliant a process is upon the intuition of another human being the more it reduces the reliability of that process. This inherently weakens the reliability and legitimacy of profiling. Secondly, none of the non-scientific methods validate their recommendations; there is no evidence to suggest that they actually work in the identification of offenders.[63] This carries an inherent danger that investigations may or at least run a high risk, of being misdirected by a wrongly constructed profile.

3.2.3.5 An absence of clear procedures

The inherent problem with all the non-scientific approaches is that they do not specify clear procedures for constructing a profile.[64] If the primary goal of a profile can be accepted as being the identification of the offender then it must correspond that a profiling technique should at least inform the profiler how crime scene evidence should correlate to offender characteristics.[65] The central problem in the non-scientific methods is that they identify particular characteristics such as an offender's physical characteristics but they do not show how these characteristics can be gleaned from the crime scene evidence. Therefore, one of the primary failures of the non-scientific approaches is that it fails to provide proper analysis and explanations on how to distil the likely offender characteristics from an examination and interpretation of crime scene evidence.

The second fundamental problem from having unclear procedures is that whilst four of the methods advocate the use of typologies to support their arguments, they fail to explain how to use an actual typology to aid the construction of a profile. The final problem with unclear procedures is that fact that none of the methods are sufficiently clear on how to deal with offences that have overlap between the different categorises of profiles. It is unclear how a profiler should select a profile when an offender can potentially fall within more than one profile.

3.2.3.6 Little investigative value?

An important aspect in evaluating the non-scientific methods is to determine whether they actually work. None of the methods provide evidence to support their use. Therefore, all of the attempts to draw out a procedure for constructing profiles are conducted on the basis of a hypothesis. As none of the methods are validated, they present severe credibility issues as to their accuracy and actual use.

3.2.4 Scientific deductive profiling approaches

A common theme evident across many authors of the non-scientific profiling methods and approaches is their usage of scientific terminology when making the linkages between crime scene evidence and the various typologies used in the construction of potential offender characteristic profiles. However, none of these methods and approaches claim to represent a completely scientific approach to deduct potential offender characteristics.[66]

A scientific method for the purposes of this chapter will be considered 'scientific' when that method or approach exhibits certain features including the ability to replicate the results, test the results and validate the results of the profiles constructed. Additionally, it must be possible to assess the process used to construct the profile in order to ascertain whether it remains constant across a range of profiles. Further, it should also be possible to identify the areas where the profile fails and the areas where the profile succeeds in identifying offender characteristics. Each of the authors in the non-scientific approaches directly or indirectly accentuates the importance of investigative experience and professional judgement as a key component in the process of profile construction.

The first attempt to inject elements of scientific methodologies into profiling was undertaken in the work of David Canter.[67] Much of the Canter's work grew out of an impetus to criticise the non-scientific methods of profiling. Canter's principal criticisms of the non-scientific methods revolve around the lack of research conducted by the proponents of the non-scientific methods.[68]

From a scientific perspective there are two key differences between Canter's work and the previous non-scientific profiling approaches. Firstly, Canter places profiling within investigative psychology in an attempt to validate his profiles. Secondly he publishes all of his results, both successes and failures in an attempt to identify a process that works. In essence the Canter profiling process becomes more scientific than the other non-scientific approaches, as it uses investigative psychology to develop processes to test, replicate and validate the profiles constructed.

Investigative psychology (IP) uses a collection of psychological techniques developed principally by Canter which are a mix of inductive and deductive techniques which is subject to the quality and the amount of data accumulated and available.[69] The deductive elements use current crime scene evidence whilst the inductive elements seek to use previous criminal records to draw comparisons to the current offence under investigation and past criminality.

IP adopts a five-step approach to offender profiling which includes an analysis of an offender's interpersonal coherence at the crime scene, the significance of time and place of the criminal act, any criminal characteristics exhibited by the offender, the potential of the offender having a criminal career and a forensic awareness of all the crime scene evidence.[70]

It is explained by Canter that interpersonal coherence involves examining the behaviour of individuals when they interact with other people.[71] It refers to examining the consistency between offending and non-offending behaviour. Canter argues that the same characteristics exhibited during a criminal offence are exhibited during the offender's everyday life.[72]

The significance of the time and place of a criminal act draws on typological models employed in environmental criminology.[73] The offence may occur at a time and/or a place that holds some personal significance that may indicate to the profiler something about the offender's likely characteristics. The example that Canter uses here is where a criminal act occurs along a major road route, which he suggests that this may demonstrate that the offender is a courier or truck driver because the criminal act took place close to a major road route.[74] The underlying significance of considering the time and place of a criminal act is the suggestion that offenders will most likely commit serious crime in an area they are familiar with.[75] This area will more commonly be close to the offender's personal life, or at minimum may have significance to the offender.[76]

The consideration of the likely criminal characteristics of other convicted offenders who engage in similar crimes can assist investigators in establishing typical and common characteristics of that offence.[77] Canter identifies that the aim here is to see whether the nature of the crime and the way it is committed can lead to some classification which can assist the profiler in leading to likely offender characteristics.[78] This involves drawing parallels between past criminality and current criminality.

It is also argued by Canter that the consideration of whether the unknown offender may have a criminal career may assist the profiler in establishing the potential offender characteristics.[79] An example provided by Canter is the offender who is a rapist and is able to enter a premises undetected may indicate that they have committed prior offences in burglary where they utilised those skills of entering a premises.

The final facet of Canter's profiling approach is being forensically aware of all available evidence which is closely related to the previous criminal career dynamic. This is where the offender has an awareness of the evidence likely to be used by the police to assist in their detection. For example, a rapist who uses a condom and takes the condom with them after a crime may have an arrest history in rape. Additionally, a murderer who takes the spent gun cartridges with them is likely to be aware that they could be used by the police to link offences.

From compiling this information, there are five characteristics or clusters of information that are important within Canter's approach of profiling in assisting the profiler to construct the likely offender characteristics.[80] These include (1) the location of the criminal act, (2) the criminal bibliography of likely the offender, (3) the domestic/social characteristics of the crime, (4) the likely personal characteristics of the offender and (5) the occupational and educational history of the offender.

Canter's profiling approach draws upon both deductive and inductive elements of profiling. The inductive element of Canter's approach uses previous criminal information to identify commonalities between convicted offender characteristics and particular offences. For example, Canter's approach makes linkages between those convicted of murder and those crimes of murder being investigated in an attempt to correlate some of the particular similarities between crimes so as to distil likely offender characteristics. The process used by Canter to draw out these similarities and commonalities is primarily through using investigative psychology techniques to distil likely offender characteristics. The deductive element of Canter's profiling approach lies in the fact that this approach is primarily used to investigate crimes that have already been committed.

3.2.5 Scientific deductive profiling approaches a critique

There are two key criticisms that can be made of Canter's IP approach in constructing profiles.

Firstly, the inductive element of Canter's approach relies heavily upon linking a sample of past criminal records to a current crime under investigation so as to predict the likely offender characteristics.[81] For example, one of the core components of Canter's work is the ability to use past criminal records and information as a basis to predict likely offender characteristics for a particular crime being investigated. The main criticism of this practice is the fact that the size of the sample criminal records to predict commonalties between the crime being investigated and the previous occurrence of that crime may simply be too small to allow accurate and creditable predictions of the likely offender characteristics.[82] In essence, Canter's work is subjected to a relatively small sample of past criminal records which questions the legitimacy of making connections between past criminality and current criminality.[83] However, as time passes and the more Canter conducts his profiling techniques this flaw may be corrected, as with the more crimes profiled by Canter the greater the body of literature will become.

Secondly, many of the statistical procedures used in making linkages between past criminality and the current criminality will take a single behaviour and interpret it outside of its context in which it occurs.[84] For example if a rapist bites the breast of a victim during an assault, this behaviour may have for all intents and purposes the same meaning regardless of its motivation.[85] It may be the case that an offender is trying to correct resistance presented by the victim in reaction to the assault or alternatively it may be an offender who is biting out of sadistic impulses. The two motivations here and subsequent meaning of the behaviour are different but may be treated as being the same by an applying the IP analysis.

In conclusion on scientific approaches of profiling, it can be identified that at minimum there are clearer processes to use in constructing profiles.[86] These processes may be considered more 'scientific' than the non-scientific approaches as they at least allow the possibility of replication, testing and validation in future profiling.

This discussion will now turn to examine the deductive profiling approaches in the context of terrorism in order to identify if there are any processes that can be used in the identification of likely terrorist characteristics.

3.2.6 *The applicability of deductive profiling approaches to terrorism*

In dealing with the non-scientific profiling approaches first, it is evident that many of the non-scientific methods and approaches discussed above primarily draw upon a profiler's experience, their intuition and the use of typologies to compare and contrast offences under investigation.[87] The lack of standardised methods and approaches, the poor consistency in the use language, the misapplication of typologies coupled with the heavy reliance upon intuition all form together to question the legitimacy and accuracy of predicting offender characteristics. There is a severe lack of evidence to assess whether this design of profiling actually works at either assisting or helping the investigation and the detection of criminal offenders.[88] The principal problem with the non-scientific methods is that they fail to incorporate principles, approaches and methods that can be validated by replication which would increase the likelihood of accuracy in processes and methodologies in the construction of profiles.

In the context of terrorism, it is important to consider how the non-scientific approaches might be used to identify unknown terrorist characteristics. On the basis of the discussion above there are two core problems in using non-scientific methods to identify terrorists:

1. Non-scientific profiling methods all deal with crimes that may be considered pathological in nature where offenders exhibit core traits across a range of offences.[89] For example, murder, rape, arson etc., all these offences carry specific characteristics and tendencies which other offenders are likely to exhibit in the commission of that offence.[90] It is possible to map out these characteristics and tendencies of convicted offenders. However, it may be considered that terrorism offences do not necessarily exhibit the same or similar pathology.[91]
2. The use of typologies forms a central function in the development of profiles within non-scientific profiling approaches.[92] For example, the typologies used in the Holmes and Holmes approach demonstrates that profiling in general may only be suitable for particular crimes which are serial in nature. The four crimes that Holmes and Holmes provide typologies for are murder, rape, arson and paedophilia – all of these crimes are serial in nature which allow for the identification of patterns and trends to detect the behavioural and personality characteristics from the crime scene analysis. It is questionable whether terrorism offences can use typologies for constructing profiles as terrorism represents a very dynamic threat changeable country by country which varies considerably over time.

In conclusion, it may be argued that non-scientific profiling approaches do not exhibit any practical or logical processes which can be used in the context of identifying likely terrorist characteristics.

In dealing with scientific profiling approaches it can be argued that there are two core weaknesses which question the viability of using scientific approaches in the context of terrorism.

Firstly, the scientific approach is highly contingent upon making linkages between the crime scene evidence and past criminality. The problem presented by this dynamic is that it may be considered difficult to link each terrorism crime scene when in fact it has been essentially destroyed. Additionally, this issue can become further complicated as information on terrorist offences and convictions may differ greatly from country to country.

Secondly, the core aim and focus of the scientific profiling approach is to identify characteristics of an offender who is at large and so far undetected. In contemporary terrorism, the use of suicide bombers have formed a central strategy in successfully executing acts of terrorism. Therefore, using scientific profiling approaches would be contrary to its overall objective as the offender being profiled will already be dead with the act of terrorism.

For these reasons it may be argued that the deductive profiling methods and approaches are not generally suited to form a basis for identifying likely offender characteristics in the context of contemporary terrorism.

The discussion will now turn to analyse whether there are any methods within inductive profiling which can be used within the context of terrorism to identify likely offender characteristics.

3.3 Inductive profiling

3.3.1 Introduction

As noted above, inductive profiling is the practice where law enforcement officers use past criminal records to predict future crimes and likely offender characteristics to detect future trends in criminal activity. It involves a profiler extracting key information from previous criminal records and establishing commonalities between that information. Essentially, the inductive profiling process becomes an inferential process whereby the profiler makes a sequence of rational judgments about the information gleaned from previous criminal records which leads to an overall conclusion of likely offender characteristics.

The statistical information used for predicting probability is drawn from at least two sources: firstly, previous criminality and/or secondly police officer investigative experience.[93] If the profiler can identify patterns in the characteristics of offenders from previous criminal records or previous officer investigative experience, then correlations of future criminal behaviour may become possible. Inductive profiling can be used for specific crimes such as drug trafficking or in specific geographical areas which are known for high crime rates as a basis for identifying potential offenders. It holds the potential for being an important tool in allowing police officers to target their policing policies in practice.

A core foundation in inductive profiling is the assumption that the higher the probability of matching an individual to a profile constructed from past criminality, the greater the likelihood that person will be engaged in crime.[94]

Therefore, the distinction between deductive and inductive profiling is that deductive profiling is reactive to a particular crime and seeks to assist police officers to solve crimes that are already committed. In contrast, inductive profiling is intended to interfere with or foil crimes which have not yet been committed. The core basis of inductive profiling is the ability to predict likely crime with the likely offender characteristics. It is aimed at assisting police officers in predicting criminality based upon previous occurrences and patterns of crime.

There is a considerable imbalance in the coverage in the literature between inductive and deductive profiling. There is substantial coverage of deductive profiling whilst inductive profiling is covered somewhat less. It may be argued that there is a substantial coverage of deductive profiling as it has evolved essentially from police officer investigative experience, whereas inductive profiling has tended to evolve as an attempt to correct methodological weaknesses within deductive profiling and as a way to predict patterns of future criminality.

The discussion of inductive profiling is divided into five parts. The discussion in the first part provides a general background to inductive profiling by examining the wider issue of the increasing use of probability and prediction within criminal justice more generally. It is important to consider this aspect because it highlights the fact that inductive profiling forms part of a much wider general theme which demonstrates a trend towards actuarial science and methods of prediction within criminal justice. The discussion in the second part concentrates on analysing the actual methods used within inductive profiling so as to consider how profiles are actually constructed using inductive methods. The discussion in the third part provides a critique and an evaluation of the inductive profiling methods. The discussion in the fourth section concentrates on the relevance and applicability of using inductive profiling methods to identify likely terrorist characteristics.

3.3.2 Actuarial prediction and criminal justice

Kaufmann argues that during the 1980s and 1990s there has been an increasing trend in the criminal justice system towards using risk-assessment instruments, algorithms and profiling.[95] Harcourt explains that selective incapacitation policies, parole prediction, predictions of future dangerousness and 'three strike' laws are examples of these increasing actuarial procedures.[96]

The use of prediction and probability for crime can be traced to the first half of the 1920s when parole boards made predictions about offender recidivism rates. This early approach involving the prediction of offending modelled its approach on the same scientific approach used by insurance companies to estimate the probable cost of insuring new applicants.[97] Over time the acknowledgement of correlations between criminality and an offender's personal circumstances, physical traits, genetic makeup and the environment of the offender changed the decisive elements of predictability. Parole boards used group traits, individual traits and their record in prison to predict the likelihood of an individual reoffending if released early on parole.[98]

The increasing emphasis over the past century towards the individualisation of punishment of offenders has fuelled an actuarial rise in law enforcement policy that desires to identify correlations between crime patterns and offender characteristics.[99] This method of crime prediction involves the mechanical combination of information so as to classify crime with the ultimate objective of discerning the probability or a likelihood of a criminal act.[100] In the context of decision-making in law enforcement, the core aspect of prediction involves probabilistic reasoning by analysing any identified correlations between crime, criminal patterns and offenders.[101]

The general goals of actuarial methods in criminal justice, and more specifically policing, are deterrence and efficiency. Both of these goals combine to form a utilitarian model for police action – the deterrent effect on the offender increases proportionally with the 'cost factor' of catching offenders. Therefore, if actuarial policing methods can increase the likelihood of identifying and catching offenders there is a correlation between deterring future offences and identifying potential offenders which may result in a general cost reduction for policing. The inductive profiling approach rests on a simple premise; if different people with similar characteristics commit similar crimes, other unknown offenders will share these common personality and general traits.[102]

Furthermore, if actuarial methods of policing can be used within the context of terrorism then this may have significant advantages in managing the threat of terrorism and its preparatory activities. As terrorists have used everyday objects, such as planes and trains, to successfully execute mass terrorism killings, it has become increasingly difficult for police officers to identify potential terrorists. The ability of current terrorists to operate under the guise of normality and turn everyday items into weapons capable of mass destruction requires a unique counterterrorism strategy to manage the risk and threat of terrorism as it evolves over time. The advantage of using actuarial methods and approaches to predict the likely characteristics of terrorists so as to allow police pre-emption would not only bring financial benefits but also, and more importantly, it would prevent the needless loss of life caused by acts of terrorism by allowing the police to pre-empt planned attacks.

This section will now turn to investigate the inductive profiling methods to identify how inductive profiling actually works in practice.

3.3.3 *Inductive profiling methods the computation of an inductive argument*

Inductive arguments and profiles involve the development of a hypothesis which can draw upon a variety of methodologies and processes.[103] As Burch explains:

> [t]here are several common types of inductive arguments, including predictions about the future, arguments from analogy, inductive generalisations, (many) arguments from authority, arguments based on signs and causal inference.[104]

On the basis of the literature, it is possible to identify two common and prevalent types of inductive profiling methods. The first is *inductive generalisation* which creates inductive profiles that argue from a specific point to a grand generalised theme.[105] For example, this would involve drawing conclusions formed about offender 'characteristics from observations of a single [criminal] event or [convicted offender] or a small number of criminal events' or convicted offenders.[106] After these observations, the profiler would draw generalisations to suggest or predict similar criminal events or potential offender characteristics which are likely to be encountered by the police in future crime.

The second discernible method of inductive method is *statistical argument*.[107] This is where a collection of previous conviction records is used to identify a statistical correlation and pattern between previous convictions and offender characteristics. For example, it would typically involve a police officer sifting through a sample of previous conviction records to draw out and match offending characteristics with particular types of crimes. The accuracy of the statistical argument is a matter of probability and ultimately can only be considered a matter of 'likelihood.'[108]

Most inductive profiles will combine inductive generalisations from the profiler's experience and secondly statistical argument from previous criminal records.

The actual inductive profiling process relies solely on statistical and/or correlational reasoning to identify likely offender characteristics – it essentially revolves around the construction of a sequence of probabilities.[109] For example, inductive profiling involves a profiler making a sequence of inferences from criminal records which allows them to make generalisations, known as a premise which becomes the working assumption for the police officer in the field.[110] The specific observations made from previous cases and instances of offending allow differences and similarities to emerge within particular categories of crime. For example, this may involve a police officer sifting through previous crime records to identify patterns and commonalities. In order for commonalities to be identified it would involve the profiler researching through past witness statements, criminal records and any information on past crimes to identify similarities within particular crimes such as murder, rape, drug related crimes, etc. It is argued by Kocsis that the core skill required by the profiler is the ability to calculate statistics from previous criminal records and pre-existing crime information.[111]

3.3.4 *Inductive profiling a critique*

Inductive profiling is arguably a much simpler method in contrast to deductive profiling because it solely uses past offending records and/or police officer investigative experience for the prediction of future crime and likely offender characteristics.

Aside from the main critique that inductive profiling is only a prediction of 'likelihoods' and as such can never be considered as definitively accurate, there are four key criticisms of the legitimacy and the creditability of using inductive methods for identifying likely offender characteristics: firstly, the size of the criminal record sample, secondly the accuracy of criminal records, thirdly the variance in practice and finally the profiler training.

3.3.4.1 *The size of the criminal record samples*

Popper argues that samples of past cases will not always allow for the drawing of accurate conclusions and generalisations about criminality and offender characteristics.[112] The key task for any profiler using inductive methods is to decide which records to use and how many samples of records to include as the raw source of information. The accuracy of any prediction will be contingent upon the ability of the profiler to select not only relevant records but also an appropriate number of records to build a statistical base of common information. For example, as it was shown in the discussion on deductive profiling, Holmes and Holmes failed to demonstrate that the inclusion of interviews with 100 convicted offenders in a US penitentiary added any accuracy to their profiling methodology. Rather, the interviews only served to identify commonalities between the 100 interviewees which could not be taken as representative of the crimes profiled by Holmes and Holmes.

The particular issue with the selection of records concerns the ability to identify which records are most representative of crime and how many records to include. For example, is it better for the profiler to select records on a chronological basis or on a random basis? How many records make a good statistical basis to extract the key information? The particular danger with having no set procedures for selecting records and for setting a minimum number of samples is that it may lead to the profiler towards selecting particular types of criminal records.

It can be argued that the random selection of previous crime records for the purposes of predicting future crimes is problematic in ensuring accuracy in the prediction. Ultimately the reliability of using past criminal records as a core source of statistical data to predict future criminal trends, patterns and offending characteristics will depend heavily upon the volume of the sample and the accuracy of the information contained within those records.

3.3.4.2 The accuracy of criminal records

There are at least two critical issues in using previous criminal records as the key source for the future predictability of crime and likely offender characteristics.

Firstly, a study conducted by Farrington and Lambert into the prediction of likely burglar offender characteristics from past criminal records of violent crimes demonstrates serious accuracy issues within the recording of criminal information.[113] The research presented by Farrington *et al* sets out to test whether inductive profiling can actually assist field officers in the prediction of offender's characteristics likely to be involved in burglary or violent crime. They used existing police records and compared a vast array of criminal offences to form predictions; in total they used 665 criminal records. They found that there were common correlations between height, weight, build, gender, ethnicity, facial hair, tattoos and hair colour towards the types of crimes committed.[114] Their research demonstrated that there were a number of commonalities which could allow a process to identify potential offender characteristics. In particular, they found that 'offender's features, offence features, victim features, victim reports of the offender and witness reports of the offender' should always be included in an inductive profile to attempt to provide a full profile of prediction.[115]

However, the research found that the accuracy of police records was deficient and in particular the methods used by the police to record data varied leading to inaccuracies in the actual recording of key information. The lack of systematic and consistent inclusion of all important information within criminal records lead to many predictions being subjected to substantial assumptions to compensate for any missing information.[116] Although commonalities were identifiable from the records the authors found that many generalisations were required to compensate for the lack of consistent information in order to build predictive offender characteristics.[117] Ultimately in this particular example, it can be argued that due to the poor recording of criminal information and the assumptive nature of inductive profiling, many profiles only serve as a useful tool amongst many other policing practices to assist field officers in the detection of crime.

Secondly, there are further issues with using particular types and categories of crime for the prediction of future crime and offender characteristics.[118] Turvey argues that there are at least four central issues which may affect the creditability and the reliability of certain recorded crimes for use as a statistical output.[119]

In Turvey's first argument, he identifies that an anger retaliatory offender who commits a crime in response to an angered situation who does not possess any psychological illnesses does not represent a good statistical source for predicting future offending probability. As a result, those offenders who commit crimes as a 'one off' criminal act who were angered by a situation are not likely to be a good source for probability of future crime.

In Turvey's second argument, he identifies that domestic violence-related offences cannot be predictive of other similar crimes. He argues that domestic violence crimes are a particular type of crime that exhibit specific characteristics and traits which are often unique to their individual circumstances. In Turvey's third argument, he identifies that those convictions that are a direct result of police intelligence are also not likely to be a good statistical source. In cases where crimes are detected by police intelligence, it is unclear as to whether the police would have been able to detect that crime without the aid of specific intelligence. The inclusion of these types of criminal records may interfere with the accuracy of a profile when using records that have not resulted from police intelligence.

In Turvey's final, he argues that offences involving controlled substances such as drugs and narcotics are too varied and too unpredictable to allow future crimes to be predicted on their basis. For example, Turvey suggests that when offenders have consumed controlled substances their rationality and ability to commit crime is highly subjective to the individual offender.

On the basis of Turvey's arguments, it can be contended that the ability to predict offending on past occurrences of crime becomes entangled with issues of credibility and reliability surrounding the source information used as the basis for predicting offender characteristics. If police officers use past offending records to build the likely identity of future offender characteristics and patterns, it is likely the whole basis of prediction is at best only probable.

3.3.4.3 The variance in practice

There are two central issues involving the variance in practice within inductive profiling. Firstly, there is a variance in practice in constructing the profile and secondly, there is a variance in practice in the application of the profile in practice.

In dealing with the first issue, there is no national co-ordinated procedure for ensuring consistency in the construction of profiles.[120] This means that profiling officers construct profiles without any specific guidelines. The particular danger with profilers operating without specific guidelines is that profilers can decide which factors they should include in constructing the profile.[121] The profiler can use factors such 'as age, gender, race and ethnicity of the offender' from the criminal records to identify commonalities between particular crimes and particular genres of offenders.[122] For example, a profiler may find that a particular age range, gender and race are common amongst criminal records which are associated with particular categories of crimes.[123] This can become problematic if any one of the factors takes precedence in the construction of the profile.

In dealing with the second issue, when a profile is used in practice a police officer can use the race, gender, age and ethnicity factors amongst other factors to apply the profile to identify potential offenders and criminality.[124] Over time the police officer can become tainted by a repetitious use of profiles constructed from experience and/or past criminal records using the same factors to extract offender characteristics.[125] If the same or similar factors continually re-emerge, law enforcement officers can become targeted at specific individuals or groups of individuals who fit this profile.[126]

The practice of police officers using inductive profiling may be justifiable in so far as it allows policing resources to be concentrated on identifying and locating unknown offenders on the basis of an identified likelihood of offending characteristics from a profile.[127] The practice of profiling becomes similar in nature to sampling:[128] when police officers use profiled characteristics derived from inductive processes, they are essentially attempting to sample more members of the predicted higher offending groups.[129] Instead of the alternative random sampling, which would be the only way to achieve a proportional cross-section of the population, the police are in principle sampling greater numbers from within the predictive higher-offending groups which attempts to skew the sampling results in favour of frequent offender types.[130]

However, the problem becomes apparent if particular groups of individuals become the focus as a result of inductive profiling methods.[131] For example, if particular races or age groups become the subject content of profiles then these groups of individuals will become more likely to be disproportionately subjected to law enforcement policies and police checks in comparison to other members of society.[132] The basis of the identification of these groups of people may be solely based on an imperfect collection of historical criminal records.[133] In essence inductive profiling methodologies allow profiles to be repeatedly used which may or may not be fully accurate.[134]

There are two critical questions which arise out of a method and process which allow the identification of a group of individuals to become subject to greater police scrutiny without any actual evidence of criminality. Firstly, does the concentrated sampling by the police actually result in crime detection? Secondly, how does the law become concentrated on particular types of characteristics?

In considering the first question, it is not evident that inductive profiling methods can actually result in crime detection as the methods do not facilitate profilers to validate the accuracy of their profiles. There is no mechanism to identify the success in detecting criminality using inductive profiling.

Additionally, in considering the second question, the real danger of inductive profiling methods is that it may facilitates the potential that numerous individuals may become subject to continual suspicion by police officers simply because they fit a particular characteristic or trait.[135] Whilst 'Code A of the Police and Criminal Evidence Act 1984'[136] specifies the factors a police officer may take into account in forming reasonable suspicion of criminality, it only specifies the range of factors and arguably does not ensure that particular marginalised communities are not demonised because they exhibit particular characteristics within an inductive profile.

3.3.4.4 Profiler training

The standards applied to the training of profilers differ greatly not only from country to country but from police force to police force.[137] There is no consistency in profiler training, with sometimes profiles being constructed by police officers with investigative experience and sometimes profiles being constructed by personnel trained in investigative psychology.[138] The net effect of using different personnel for creating profiles is that there can be a mismatch between the skills of the profiler and the skills required to build an accurate profile.[139]

Traditionally, inductive profiles were qualified with phrases such as 'normally, likely, often, many, rarely, most, some, probably, usually, always, never' etc. to indicate to the profile user that the information contained within the profile is only at best probable and its accuracy is contingent upon certain factors relevant to the crime and the offender.[140] In more recent times, research conducted by Turvey indicates that profilers are no longer using these qualifiers in inductive profiles which may have a consequential effect on the accuracy of profiling in practice creating the distinct potential to sway police attention in a particular direction which may or may not be accurate.[141]

The training of the profiler presents a critical issue for ensuring consistency and accuracy in the development of inductive profiles. Ultimately without effective training, guidelines and frameworks for profilers, the inductive profiling process becomes subject to criticism for being ineffective.

3.3.4.5 Summary conclusions

Before moving on to examining inductive profiling methods within the context of terrorism it is important to point out that within criminal law there are a number of imperfections within inductive profiling methods. Firstly, there are a number of problems surrounding the size of the sample used by the profiler and how best to select these records. Secondly, there are difficulties surrounding the accuracy of the criminal records as a raw source of information for the statistical calculation of future criminality and offender characteristics. Thirdly, there are significant issues with the variance in practice of profiling which affect not only the construction of the profile but also its application in practice. Finally, there are further issues surrounding the training of profilers and the skills training required to ensure consistency in profiling methods and techniques.

The critique of inductive profiling methods demonstrates that inductive profiling at best only provides the field officer with an indication of characteristics which may or may not be accurate in detecting and identifying potential offenders.

This section will now turn to evaluate whether the inductive methods of profiling can be used within the terrorism context to identify potential unknown terrorists.

3.3.5 Inductive profiling and its applicability to terrorism

As noted above, the starting point for inductive profiling methods within criminal law is the identification of criminal records and then to draw out from these records commonalities using probabilistic reasoning to identify likely offender characteristics. Therefore, in applying these profiling methods within the counterterrorism context to assist law enforcement officers with the identification of likely terrorist characteristics, the starting point must be focused on considering what information is available on convicted terrorist.

Early behavioural research conceptualised terrorism as 'psychological and behavioural deviance.'[142] The early behavioural studies conducted on known terrorists sought to place the origin of the deviance within disturbances from the terrorist's childhood.[143] However, with greater advances in science in the understanding of psychology, the general consensus amongst modern experts is that terrorists are not psychologically abnormal nor do they exhibit any characteristics which could be considered abnormal – in fact they are more than often 'normal' everyday citizens.[144]

As a result of their normality, it is challenging to construct a precise general profile which will reflect current terrorist types or at least the identity of those individuals likely to be associated with contemporary terrorism.[145] For example, it might be considered that in the aftermath of September 11 and the London Bombings on 7/7 that the current 'face' of terrorism originates from individuals with an appearance from Asia/South-East Asia. Although numerous terrorist organisations exist globally, one of the current biggest threats faced by the UK, Europe and the USA is found within the al Qaeda terrorist organisation. A survey documented by Gunarantna highlights that al Qaeda recruits from more than 74 countries worldwide with more than 40 different nationalities.[146] This evidence suggests that it is particularly difficult to locate physical traits, ethnicity, gender, common characteristics etc. as uniquely or commonly associated with the current 'face' of terrorism.[147]

Therefore, using inductive profiling methods to identify potential terrorist characteristics requires an examination of past convicted terrorists or known terrorists to distil the commonalities to use as a statistical basis for the prediction of likely future terrorist characteristics. As terrorism and the threat of terrorism remains a global phenomenon, it can be argued that the best inductive profile would be constructed from an array of terrorism offences and terrorism records across a number of countries so as to allow a full statistical basis to construct inductive profiles. Before considering the actual methods used within inductive profiling, it is possible to identify four fundamental challenges within counterterrorism laws and terrorism records which combine to present some difficulties and challenges in ensuring the reliability of using inductive profiles within a counterterrorism context.

Firstly, there are issues surrounding the classification of terrorist offences arising out of the changing nature of terrorism laws and frameworks which criminalise terrorism that affect the identification and selection of terrorism records for inductive purposes. Secondly, there are issues with the overlapping nature of the prosecution of terrorism crimes under ordinary criminal law in addition to specific terrorism laws. Thirdly, in comparison to ordinary criminal law, there are significantly lower successful prosecutions under terrorism laws which mean that there are very few individuals actually convicted of terrorism offences. Finally, there are likely to be issues of accuracy in the actual content of the terrorism records which may affect the validity of using these records as a basis to distil likely terrorist characteristics. This chapter will now turn to examine each of these issues in turn below before considering the general challenges of using inductive profiling methods within a counterterrorism context.

3.3.5.1 Inductive profiling and terrorism records

It is not evident that all the information available on convicted terrorists will be relevant for predicting current contemporary terrorist characteristics. Terrorism has changed radically over the past century and in particular in the last two decades which continues to evolve on a global scale. It is argued by Rapoport that terrorism has occurred in a sequence of four waves each lasting approximately forty years each starting from the 1870s.[148] He argues that the first wave began in Russia in 1870 and was a direct result of a slow democratisation process. He further argues that the second wave of terrorism began with the dissident's efforts in colonised countries to secure European withdrawal from overseas territories. Rapoport identifies the third wave of terrorism as the principal terrorist threats throughout the twentieth century. Examples provided by Rapoport are tactical assassinations with the hi-jacking of airplanes and public office buildings in addition to lucrative kidnappings.[149] The final wave of terrorism is the current manifestation of terrorism and is a religious orientated form of terrorism which originally centred upon Islam.[150]

If Rapoport's arguments can be accepted as being accurate, then the individual convictions of terrorist offenders within each of these waves are likely to be drastically different. Additionally, the laws criminalising terrorism will differ greatly in each period of history to match the threat of terrorism faced by particular countries. The difference will not necessarily be within the laws prohibiting terrorism acts but rather in their application in practice in targeting the prevalent contemporary threat. As a result, terrorism records are likely to be reflective the laws in operation and their application to individual instances of terrorism.

The laws criminalising terrorism have evolved from at least two things: firstly, the threat faced by a particular country and secondly, the ability of legal frameworks to facilitate prosecutions.[151] For example in the UK the changing nature of the terrorism threat over the past seven decades has seen a continuous development of specific terrorism laws which have resulted in a differential array of terrorism convictions.[152] In the UK's more recent history, an attempt to criminalise terrorism was taken in response to the Northern Ireland troubles in the 1970s with the enactment of the 'Prevention of Terrorism Act 1974.' The Northern Ireland troubles presented a unique threat which saw the introduction of a number of Prevention of Terrorism Acts (PTA) from 1974 until 1989 which were initially designed to deal with specific threats within Northern Ireland but subsequently were widened out to cover the UK wide terrorism threats not only emanating from Northern Ireland but also international terrorism.[153]

These laws facilitated the prosecution of those individuals or groups of individuals suspected of terrorism. As the threat of terrorism faced by the UK changed direction at the end of twentieth century the criminalisation of terrorism became more permanent with the introduction of the 'Terrorism Act 2000' (TA). Other Acts of Parliament such as the 'Crime and Security Act 2001,' 'Prevention of Terrorism Act 2005,' 'Terrorism Act 2006,' 'Terrorism (Northern Ireland) Act 2006' and the 'Justice and Security (Northern Ireland) Act 2007' and the 'Counter Terrorism Act 2008' have attempted to fine tune the counterterrorism framework in step with the gravity and changing nature of the threat faced by the UK from contemporary terrorism.

Therefore, during the 1970s in the UK it is possible to identify the laws designed to criminalise terrorism changing from a narrow Northern Ireland specific focus to wider international terrorist focus to the current focus of radical, fundamental and international terrorism threats coupled with some outstanding threats from Northern Ireland 'republicans.' The issue that stems from this is the fact that the successful prosecutions taken on foot of these laws will result in a specific terrorism record corresponding to the specific instance of terrorism. For example, the early PTA criminalisation of terrorism will be dominated with the Northern Ireland troubles whilst the more recent successful prosecutions will be dominated by the contemporary terrorism threat. It is inevitable that due to the nature of terrorism evolving and shifting in focus, there will be categorises of terrorism records which will be similar, less similar and those that will be completely different.

In order to manage the issue of how best to categorise terrorism records, there must be a process within the identification, selection and collation of terrorism records which allows a profiler to separate and streamline those terrorism records which belong to each category of terrorism. For example, if the police are profiling current threats, each individual threat will require a separate statistical base of terrorism records to make those predictions more accurate and tailored to meet the specific threat under investigation.

In summary, if inductive profiling methods are to be used in the context of terrorism the question now becomes whether it is possible to identify conviction records within each type or category of terrorism? And whether there are any commonalities or similarities between each of these convictions that will allow a profiler to employ statistical and probabilistic reasoning to identify likely terrorist characteristics? The next section will examine the issues and challenges even when terrorism records can be identified.

3.3.5.2 Inductive profiling and the overlapping nature of terrorist crimes

It is important to consider that not all convictions of terrorism are prosecuted on the basis of terrorism specific offences but rather some are convicted on ordinary criminal law. Some terrorists are convicted of ordinary criminal offences whilst others are convicted of specialist counterterrorism offences depending upon the available evidence. For example, in England and Wales in 2018 there were 380 individuals charged with ordinary criminal offences which were connected to terrorism activities.[154]

3.3.5.3 Inductive profiling and the size of terrorism record samples

The strongest collection of records to engage in inductive profiling to discern probable terrorist characteristics will likely be from a range of prosecution records from countries which have been the subject of contemporary terrorism. Prosecution records can be selected as being a strong source of raw data as the content and accuracy of the data can be considered as being tested through the courts in a legal system resulting in the conviction of a terrorist. The selection of countries would ideally need to be based on those who have experienced contemporary terrorism such as the USA, the UK, France, Belgium, Spain etc. and beyond as this would provide a wider perspective for any profiler to build a statistical basis for predicting probable terrorist characteristics of those individuals likely to be engaged in acts of contemporary terrorism.

This need for a wide range of terrorism records may be a significant impediment for inductive profiling as the sharing of this type of information between different countries may be considered sensitive to national security. However, even if countries share information on terrorism prosecutions, a further issue relates to the fact that the criminalisation of terrorism and its preparatory acts tends to be very specific to individual legal systems which is often influenced by the gravity of the threat faced on a country specific perspective. This would mean that even if it were possible to identify a suitable range of terrorism records, there would be substantial practical challenges arising out of how best to classify a terrorist conviction for the purposes of future probability and prediction. Additionally, there is the further problem of very few individuals actually being convicted of terrorism offences which creates the specific difficulty of having a poor array of raw source data to base the prediction of terrorist characteristics.

For instance, if the UK is taken as example again, the Home Office national statistics on terrorism offences illustrate that there were 259 terrorism arrests in the year ended September 2019 which subsequently resulted in 49 of these individuals (comprising 19% of those arrested) being charged with terrorism offences with only 15 of these individuals resulting in a conviction.[155] Although there were initially 49 charges, 23 of these were not proceeded with which may indicate these records are very likely insufficient for inductive profiling purposes, if they were not sufficient to support a prosecution. A further six of these cases were dealt with by 'alternative means' such as a caution or a return to prison from licence. Therefore, in the year ended September 2019 only 15 conviction records *may* be considered useful in the computation of an inductive profile. The problem of few conviction records is symptomatic of similar difficulties with records from previous years. For example, in considering the year ended September 2018 there were 325 terrorism-related arrests, which subsequently resulted in only 71 of these individuals being charged and out of these 51 defendants were prosecuted with 49 of these being convicted.[156] This highlights that only 49 records in the ended September 2018 *may* be considered useful to rely upon in the construction of an inductive profile to discern probable terrorist characteristics. It seems plausible to suggest that there is likely to be at least theoretical correlation between the number of terrorism records and the accuracy of an inductive profile. If there are really only 49 and 15 raw datasets in respect of 2018 and 2019, it seems likely this gives rise to a concern in the ability of profilers to develop accurate inductive profiles. Furthermore, even considering all available information since the terrorist attacks on September 11, 2001, there is a similar problem with the size of the records as well as shifts in the occurrence of terrorism. This means that even if all of the terrorism records from September 11, 2001 are relied upon in England and Wales, there remains a specific problem around the size of the records as well as the changes in the occurrence and manifestation terrorism over this timeframe that would inevitably impact the inductive profile of probable terrorist characteristics. For example, the 2019 statistics also reveal that since September 11, 2001 there have been 708 terrorism-specific prosecutions which resulted in 600 convictions.[157] This would mean that over a period of almost two decades, there would only be 600 terrorism records to discern probable terrorist characteristics. The consideration of the Home Office national statistics illustrates some of the key difficulties faced when using terrorism records which may arguably be less useful than what is currently available for criminal profiling.

3.3.5.4 Terrorism records and the accurate recording of information

A further issue is that there are likely to be significant accuracy issues in the recording of important information within records relating to terrorist offences. As within criminal inductive profiling there are a number of significant difficulties in ensuring that law enforcement officers record relevant information consistently within each criminal record. This may mean that terrorism conviction records are likely to encounter the same or similar difficulties in ensuring consistently and accuracy in the recording of key information between the records. This difficulty is further complicated by the fact that terrorism is international in scale and using records from different legal systems will have completely different sets of information. The central concern for a profiler would be to determine how best to use the terrorist record to extract data which will allow a statistical reasoning of the likely offender characteristics. With so many different legal systems and so many different laws for terrorism this task becomes extremely difficult and complex.

In considering the points discussed above, the use of terrorism records as a raw source of information for probabilistic reasoning of likely future terrorist characteristics becomes entangled in specific difficulties of actual terrorism offences, counterterrorism regimes and terrorism records. The root of the difficulties is twofold: firstly, the actual accuracy of the recording of information within the terrorism record and secondly, the vast array of offences an individual could be convicted of within counterterrorism.

3.3.5.5 Conclusion: inductive terrorist profiling and other issues

Aside from the critical issues concerning the raw source data in inductive profiling of terrorists, there are also some additional potential flaws in adopting this approach to identify probable terrorist characteristics. As noted above, the first common type of method in inductive profiling is *inductive generalisation* which involves developing a hypothesis that argues from a specific point to a general theme. Applying this methodology to terrorism is highly questionable from a creditability perspective. In particular, each occurrence of contemporary terrorism tends to be very sporadic and does not occur often or at least in a pattern. It may be considered difficult to create an inductive profile which can take specific terrorist characteristics from individual occurrences of terrorism to create a generalised theme applicable on a global scale. Any generalisations made are likely to be very broad with little relevance to establishing accurate likely terrorist characteristics.

In conclusion, inductive profiling presents a number of core issues, including the raw source information for probabilistic prediction, the selection of information for use in prediction and the profiler training which create specific challenges for the use of inductive profiling methods to identify likely terrorist characteristics. In particular, the accuracy of probability from scant and deficient information leads directly to question the legitimacy of using inductive profiling methods for identifying likely terrorist characteristics. The central problem is whether inductive profiling methods can actually lead to the identity of terrorist characteristics? Many countries, including the UK, will face difficulties in ensuring the information is consistent and constant across a common range of cases. There are significant credibility issues surrounding the use of inductive profiling methods to arrive at the identity of terrorist characteristics, but ultimately countries use inductive profiling as an inexpensive and quick method to assist in managing terrorism threats.

However, its use can come at the expense of wasted resources, misguided investigations and unnecessary harassment to particular groups of society under suspicion.

3.4 Conclusion

The primary aim of this chapter was to evaluate whether criminal profiling methods and approaches can be used in the context of counterterrorism in assisting law enforcement officers to identify likely terrorist characteristics. There are a number of advantages and disadvantages in using the various profiling methods discussed above to distil probable terrorist characteristics.

The profiling approaches identified in deductive profiling do not appear to present a basis to allow law enforcement officers to predict likely terrorist characteristics. In particular, there are two core issues within deductive profiling approaches which support the argument that these approaches are generally not appropriate to profile the likely terrorist characteristics of individuals likely to be engaged in the current threat of terrorism.

Firstly, deductive profiling approaches have been primarily used for crimes that can be considered pathological in nature, such as murder, rape, arson etc. The offenders who commit these types of crimes tend to exhibit behaviours that are considered serial in nature, which allow direct comparisons to be made between particular crime scenes and past offenders. However, in the context of terrorism it was noted that terrorism offences do not tend to exhibit the same or similar pathology. Therefore, this creates the specific difficultly with using methods and processes which are contingent upon identifying the sequential pathology between offenders and crime scenes.

Secondly, it was also noted above that the whole purpose and aim of deductive profiling was to identify an unknown offender still undetected by the police. Some instances of contemporary terrorism have tended to use suicide bombers which have resulted in the death of the actual bomber. Therefore, using deductive methods and approaches to identify these types of terrorists who are already dead as a result of the terrorist act is going to be completely contrary to the aims and purpose of deductive profiling.

In the final conclusion on using deductive profiling methods and approaches in the context of terrorism, it can be argued that they do not form the basis to identify likely terrorist characteristics as the methods do not appear to apply within the sphere of contemporary terrorism.

In considering inductive profiling methods, it can be argued that these profiling methods may be of some use in assisting law enforcement officers to identify likely terrorist characteristics if it is performed in a way that takes into account a number of issues. In particular, it was identified above that there are four critical issues which challenge the use of inductive profiling in the context of terrorism.

Firstly, it is not evident that all terrorism information will be relevant for predicting current contemporary terrorist characteristics. The changing nature of terrorism over the past century there are likely to be significant issues with changes in counterterrorism laws criminalising terrorism and the terrorism records which flow from the counterterrorism laws. As the laws which criminalise terrorism will differ not only country by country but also individually year on year within each country, inductive profiling methods will require a categorisation of criminal records so as to allow a reliable and accurate raw dataset to emerge for constructing inductive profiles.

Secondly, there are issues relating to the actual terrorism record. It can be argued that as the current threat of terrorism is global in nature, the best collection of terrorism records to use as a statistical basis to predict likely terrorist characteristics will be those terrorism records from across the globe. It is not evident whether countries will actually share information freely amongst the international community as the information may be considered sensitive to national security. Even where countries do share information and terrorism records, there will be issues around how best to categorise terrorism records. For instance, some terrorists will be prosecuted under ordinary criminal offences whilst others will be prosecuted under terrorism specific offences.

Thirdly, as noted within criminal inductive profiling there sometimes can be difficulties in ensuring that all relevant information is actually recorded correctly and accurately within each criminal record. It is highly likely that similar problems will be present within terrorist records. As there is no nationally, or internationally, co-ordinated approach to the collection of information within criminal records, it is likely that when key information is missing from terrorism records, its absence may become subject to compensation by weighty assumptions on the part of the profiler.

Finally, it is important to consider that not all terrorism arrests actually become subject to prosecution through the courts. Current terrorism frameworks provide for direct deportation of individuals. Therefore, not all of the information on terrorism will be found within terrorism records.

In order to manage the issues raised by these weaknesses, inductive profiling methods require that there must be a way to filter the terrorism records so as to allow:

a A categorisation of the record so that it can be identified that terrorism-specific offences and ordinary criminal law can be identified. This will allow that a full statistical database where the profiler can attain the correct information when profiling particular terrorism threats.

b A further categorisation and filtering of terrorism records beyond the terrorism law and ordinary law distinction discussed above, which will allow the profiler to identify the types of terrorism records. For example, in the UK a profiler would need to access a database that allows them to distinguish between Northern Ireland-related terrorism records and those relating to radical and fundamental terrorism. Therefore, it must be possible for the profiler to distinguish between the types of terrorism faced by the country profiling for likely terrorist characteristics.

Additionally, there are four other issues which need to be addressed to further manage the challenges presented by inductive profiling in the context of terrorism:

- i The size of the terrorism record samples is likely to create difficulties in producing a statistical prediction on likely terrorist characteristics. As the current threat of radical terrorism is in essence only ten years old since the September 11, 2001 attacks, it was noted above that only 418 individuals have been successfully prosecuted in the UK relating to terrorism specific offences.[158] Although this is likely to improve with time as more and more individuals are prosecuted. However, it is something that any profiler would need to take into account when profiling by using inductive methods. A profiler could take this into account by alerting the user of the profile that only a limited number of terrorism records were used in the calculation of the profile. This would allow the law enforcement officer in the field to use the profile with caution.
- ii The accuracy of the information recorded in the terrorism record samples is likely to create some difficulties in ensuring the predictability of likely terrorist characteristics. Inductive profiling methods would become significantly more coherent if a consistent approach was developed for the recording of key information. This weakness could be corrected by drawing up standard codes of practice for the collection of terrorism data which individual countries could implement.
- iii The variance in practice, firstly in constructing the profile and secondly the variance in practice in the application of the profile by the law enforcement officer can combine to create a significant issue in using inductive profiles in the context of terrorism. In dealing with the first issue, inductive profiling would benefit from the development of specific national and international guidelines to assist profilers identify which factors they should take into account in constructing profiles. In dealing with the second issue law enforcement officers require further training in the application of profiles in practice. Additionally, a policy should be developed which only allows inductive profiles to be used within a range of other counterterrorism strategies.
- iv The final issue of using inductive profiling methods in the context of terrorism is interlinked to the previous point. In order to increase the accuracy of the profiles, there must be consistent training for all profilers. The practice of profiling varies not only from country to country but also from police force to police force. Therefore, a national training qualification should be developed to allow all profilers gain and develop the skills set necessary for consistent profiling.

In consideration of the above, it is arguable that inductive profiling as part of a broader counterterrorism strategy may assist law enforcement officers in the identification of likely terrorist characteristics.

Therefore, on the basis of the discussion in this chapter it is possible to argue a working hypothesis for the use of criminal profiling methods and approaches in the context of terrorism. Firstly, deductive profiling is almost devoid of all value for the profiling of likely terrorist characteristics. Secondly, inductive profiling, provided it is conducted within defined and controlled circumstances, is likely to assist law enforcement officers in the identification of potential terrorist characteristics.

Notes

1. W. Petherwick, 'What's in a name? Comparing applied profiling methodologies' (2003) 5 Journal of Law and Social Challenges 173, 173. See also: G. Copson, *Coals to Newcastle? Part 1: A Study of Offender Profiling* (Home Office Policy Research Group, 1995). S. Egger, 'Psychological profiling: past present and future'(1999) 15 Journal of Contemporary Criminal Justice 242. P. Wilson, R. Lincoln and R. Kocsis 'Validity, utility and ethics of profiling for serial violent and sexual offenders' (1997) 4 Psychiatry, Psychology and the Law 1.
2. J. Doughlas and A. Burgess, 'Criminal profiling: a viable investigative tool against crime' (1986) 55 FBI Law Enforcement Bulletin 9, 9–13.
3. J. Goodwin, *Murder USA: The Ways We Kill Each Other* (Ballantine Publishing, 1978), 274–279.
4. A. Pinizotto, 'Forensic psychology: criminal personality profiling' (1984) 12 Journal of Police Science and Administration Section 1, 32–40.
5. B. Snook, J. Eastwood, P. Gendreau, C. Goggin and R. Cullen, 'Taking stock of criminal profiling: a narrative review and meta-analysis' (2007) 34(4) Criminal Science and Behaviour 437, 437–438.
6. M. Horvath, 'Offender Profiling' in S. Tong, R. Bryant and M. Horvath (eds), *Understanding Criminal Investigation* (John Wiley & Sons Publishing, 2009), 69.
7. J. Bumgarner, *Profiling and Criminal Justice in America* (ABC-Clio Publications, 2004), 28–29.
8. W. Neuman and B. Wiegand, *Criminal Justice Research Methods: Qualitative and Quantitative Approaches* (Allyn and Bacon Publishing, 2000), 45.
9. Horvath, 'Offender Profiling' (n6), 73.
10. ibid.
11. S. Hicks and B. Sales, *Criminal Profiling* (American Psychological Association, 2006), 4–5.
12. J. Douglas, *Mindhunter: Inside the FBI's Elite Serial Crime Unit* (Scriber Publishing, 1995), 34.
13. ibid.
14. ibid.
15. J. Brussel, *Casebook of a Crime Psychiatrist* (Bernard Geis Associates, 1968), 17–22.
16. ibid, 32–33.
17. For example: R. Holmes and J. DeBurger, 'Profiles in terror: the serial murderer' (1985) 49(3) Federal Probation 29. R. Holmes and S. Holmes, 'Understanding mass murder: a starting point' (1992) 56(1) Federal Probation 53. R. Homant and D. Kennedy, 'Psychological aspects of crime scene profiling: validity research' (1998) 25 Criminal Justice and Behaviour 319.
18. J. Douglas, A. Burgess and R. Ressler, *Crime Classification Manual* (Lexington Publishing, 1992). See also: J. Douglas, R. Ressler, A. Burgess and C. Hartman, 'Criminal profiling from crime scene analysis' (1986) 4 Behavioural Sciences and the Law 401, 401–405.

19. P. Cook and D. Hinman, 'Criminal profiling: science and art' (1999) 15(3) Journal of Contemporary Criminal Justice 230, 231.
20. ibid.
21. R. Holmes and S. Homes, *Profiling Violent Crimes: An Investigative Tool* (Thousand Oaks, 1996).
22. ibid, 49.
23. D. Kolko and A. Kazdin, 'The emergence and recurrence of child firesetting: a one-year prospective study' (1992) 20 Journal of Abnormal Child Psychology 17.
24. G. Sakheim, M. Vigdor, M. Gordon and L. Helprin, 'A psychological profile of juvenile firesetters in residential treatment' (1985) 64 Child Welfare 453.
25. A. Rider, 'The firesetter: a psychological profile (Part 1)' (1980) 49(6) FBI Law Enforcement Bulletin 6.
26. A. Groth, A. Burgess and L. Holmstrom, 'Rape: power, anger and sexuality' (1977) 134 American Journal of Psychiatry 1239.
27. R. Knight and R. Prently, 'The development antecedents and adult adaptations of rapist subject subtypes' (1987) 14 Criminal Justice and Behaviour 403.
28. A. Burgess, A. Groth and L. Holmstrom, *Sexual Assault of Children and Adolescents* (Lexington Publishing, 1978).
29. Holmes and Homes, 'Profiling Violent Crimes: An Investigative Tool' (n21), 49.
30. ibid.
31. R. Keppel and R. Walter, 'Profiling killers: a revised classification model for understanding sexual murder' (1999) 43 International Journal of Offender Therapy and Comparative Criminology 417.
32. ibid, 418.
33. ibid, 436.
34. R. Hazelwood and A. Burgess, *Practical Aspects of Rape Investigation: A Multidisciplinary Approach* (CRC Press, 1987).
35. R. Turco, 'Psychological profiling' (1990) 34 International Journal of Offender Therapy and Comparative Criminology 147.
36. J. Libert, 'Contributions of psychiatric consultation in the investigation of serial murder' (1986) 29 International Journal of Offender Therapy and Comparative Criminology 187.
37. Turco, 'Psychological profiling' (n35), 149.
38. Ibid, 151.
39. B. Turvey, *Criminal Profiling: An Introduction to Behavioural Evidence Analysis* (Academic Press, 1999).
40. ibid, 14.
41. ibid, 16.
42. ibid, 15–16.
43. ibid.
44. Groth, Burgess and Holmstrom, 'Rape: power, anger and sexuality' (n26).
45. Turvey, 'Criminal Profiling: An Introduction to Behavioural Evidence Analysis' (n39), 170.
46. ibid.
47. J. Jackson, *Offender Profiling; Theory, Research and Practice* (Wiley Publications, 1995), 16–18.
48. D. Muller, 'Criminal profiling. Real science or just wishful thinking?' (2000) 4(3) Homicide Studies 234, 246–247.
49. D. Canter and L. Alison, *Offender Profiling series II: Profiling in Policy and Practice* (Ashgate Publishing, 1999), 23.
50. Hicks and Sales, 'Criminal Profiling' (n11), 68.
51. J. Annon, 'Investigative profiling: a behavioural analysis of the crime scene' (1995) 13(4) American Journal of Forensic Psychology 67, 68–71.

52. D. Grubbin, 'Offender profiling' (1995) 6 Journal of Forensic Psychiatry 259, 259–262.
53. ibid.
54. ibid.
55. Hicks and Sales, 'Criminal Profiling' (n11), 72.
56. ibid.
57. ibid, 73.
58. Hicks and Sales, 'Criminal Profiling' (n11), 72.
59. Grubbin, 'Offender Profiling' (n52), 260.
60. ibid.
61. D. Canter and N. Wentink, 'An empirical test of Holmes and Holmes serial murder typology' (2004) 31 Criminal Justice Behaviour 489, 510–515.
62. D. Canter, 'Offender profiling and criminal differentiation' (2000) 5 Legal and Criminological Psychology 23.
63. Hicks and Sales, 'Criminal Profiling' (n11), 76.
64. B. Snook, R. Cullen, C. Bennell, P. Taylor and P. Gendreau, 'The criminal profiling illusion: what's behind the smoke and mirrors?' (2008) 35(10) Criminal Justice and Behaviour 1257, 1259–1260.
65. J. Jackson and D. Bekerian, *Offender Profiling: Theory, Research and Practice* (John Wiley & Sons Publishing, 1997), 159–162.
66. Canter and L. Alison, 'Offender Profiling Series II: Profiling in Policy and Practice' (n49), 6.
67. D. Canter, 'To catch a rapist' (1988) New Society 14.
68. D. Canter, *Criminal Shadows* (Harper Collins, 1995), 82–83.
69. M. McGrath, 'Criminal profiling: is there a role for the forensic psychiatrist?' (2000) 28 Journal of the American Academy of Psychiatry and Law 319, 320–325.
70. D. Canter and D. Youngs, *Investigative Psychology: Offender Profiling and the Analysis of Criminal Action* (John Wiley & Sons Publishing, 2009), 79–85.
71. Canter, 'Criminal shadows' (n67), 89–92.
72. P. Ainsworth, *Offender Profiling and Crime Analysis* (Willan Publishing, 2001), 30–35.
73. Canter, 'Criminal shadows' (n68), 89–92.
74. ibid.
75. Ainsworth, 'Offender Profiling and Crime Analysis' (n72), 199.
76. J. Boon, 'The contribution of personality theories to psychological profiling' in J. Jackson and D. Bekarian (eds), *Offender Profiling: Theory, Research and Practice* (John Wiley & Sons Publishing, 1997), 43–49.
77. Canter, 'Criminal shadows' (n67), 91–92.
78. D. Canter, 'Offender profiles' (1989) 2(1) The Psychologist 14, 15–16.
79. Canter, 'Criminal shadows' (n67), 91–92.
80. ibid.
81. Ainsworth, 'Offender Profiling and Crime Analysis' (n72), 78–80.
82. ibid.
83. R. Kocsis, 'Validities and abilities in criminal profiling: the dilemma for David Canter's investigative psychology' (2006) 50(4) International Journal of Offender Therapy and Comparative Criminology 458, 460–461.
84. Petherwick, 'What's in a name? Comparing applied profiling methodologies' (n1), 182.
85. ibid, 182–183.
86. D. Hindman and P. Cook, 'Profiling and Criminal Investigative Analysis of Violent Crimes with Multiple Offenders' in H. Hall and L. Whitaker (eds), *Collective Violence: Effective Strategies for Assessing and Intervening in Fatal Group and Institutional Aggression* (CRC Press, 1999).
87. C. Bartol, 'Police psychology: then, now and beyond' (1996) 23 Criminal Justice and Behaviour 70, 75–89.

88. N. Poythress, R. Otto, J. Darkes and L. Starr, 'APA's expert panel in the congressional review of the USS Iowa incident' (1993) 48 American Psychologists 8, 14–15.
89. Cook and Hindman, 'Criminal profiling: science and art' (n19), 235. See also: J. Douglas and M. Olshaker, *Unabomber: On the Trail of American's Most Wanted Serial Killer* (Pocket Books, 1996).
90. ibid, 235–236.
91. G. Dean, 'Criminal Profiling in a Terrorism Context' in R. Kocsis (ed), *Criminal Profiling: International Theory, Research and Practice* (Humana Press, 2010), 169–170.
92. Cook and Hindman, 'Criminal profiling: science and art' (n19), 239–241.
93. W. Petherick and B. Turvey, 'Behavioural Evidence Analysis: An Ideal Deductive Method of Criminal Profiling' in B. Turvey (ed), *Criminal Profiling: An Introduction* (Academic Press, 2008).
94. D. Harris, *Profiles in Injustice* (The New Line Press, 2002), 16–17.
95. M. Kaufmann, *Ethnic Profiling and Counter-Terrorism* (Lit Verlag, 2009), 8–15.
96. B. Harcourt, *Against Prediction. Profiling, Policing and Punishing in an Actuarial Age* (University of Chicago Press, 2007), 16.
97. H. Hart, 'Predicting parole success' (1923) 41(3) Journal of American Institute of Criminal Law and Criminology 405, 411.
98. H. Borden, 'Factors for predicting parole success' (1928) 19 Journal of Criminal Law and Criminology 328, 328–329. See also: L. Brown, 'The development of a parolee classification system using discriminate analysis' (1978) 15 Journal of Research in Crime and Delinquency 92.
99. Harcourt, 'Against Prediction. Profiling, Policing and Punishing in an Actuarial Age' (n96), 44.
100. P. Meel, *Clinical versus Statistical Prevention: A Theoretical Analysis and a Review of the Evidence* (Jason Aronson Publishing, 1954), 3.
101. Harcourt, 'Against Prediction. Profiling, Policing and Punishing in an Actuarial Age' (n96), 18.
102. Holmes and Holmes, 'Profiling Violent Crimes: An Investigative Tool' (n21), 5–10.
103. H. Lee and R. Gaensslen, *Forensic Science: An Introduction to Criminalistics* (McGraw-Hill, 1983), 2.
104. R. Burch, *Study Guide for Hurley's a Concise Introduction into Logic* (Thompson-Wadsworth, 2003), 7.
105. Turvey, 'Criminal Profiling: An Introduction to Behavioural Evidence Analysis' (n39), 54.
106. D. Walton, *Informal Logic: A Handbook for Critical Argumentation* (Cambridge University Press, 1989), 198.
107. Turvey, 'Criminal Profiling: An Introduction to Behavioural Evidence Analysis' (n39), 54.
108. Walton, 'Informal Logic: A Handbook for Critical Argumentation' (n106), 199.
109. W. Petherick and B. Turvey, 'Behavioural Evidence Analysis: An Ideo-deductive Method of Criminal Profiling' in B. Turvey (ed), *Criminal Profiling: An Introduction* (Academic Press, 2008).
110. J. Thornton, 'The General Assumptions and Rationale of Forensic Identification' in D. Faigman, D. Kaye, M. Saks and J. Sanders (eds), *Modern Scientific Evidence: The Law and Expert Testimony* (West Publications, 2008).
111. R. Kocsis, *Criminal Profiling: Principles and Practice* (Humana Press, 2006), 36.
112. K. Popper, 'On the sources of knowledge and of ignorance' (1960) Proceedings of the British Academy of Sciences 39, 39–41.
113. D. Farrington and S. Lambert, 'Predicting Offender Profiles from Victim and Witness Descriptions' in J. Jackson and D. Bekerian (eds), *Offender Profiling – Theory, Research and Practice* (John Wiley & Sons Publishing, 2001), 133.

114. ibid, 139.
115. ibid, 155.
116. ibid, 156.
117. ibid.
118. R. Kocsis, 'An empirical assessment of content in criminal psychological profiles' (2003) 47(1) International Journal of Offender Therapy and Comparative Criminology 37, 42–44.
119. B. Turvey, 'Serial Crime' in B. Turvey (ed), *Criminal Profiling: An Introduction to Behavioural Evidence Analysis* (Academic Press, 2008), 51–54.
120. Kocsis, 'An empirical assessment of content in criminal psychological profiles' (n118), 138.
121. Farrington and Lambert, 'Predicting Offender Profiles from Victim and Witness Descriptions' (n113), 138.
122. ibid.
123. V. Borooah, 'Racial bias in police stops and searches: an economic analysis' (2001) 17 European Journal of Political Economy 17, 18–22. See also: V. Borooah, 'Economic analysis of police stops and searches: a reply' (2002) 18 European Journal of Political Economy 607. S. Chakravarty, 'Economic analysis of police stops and searches: a critique' (2002) 18 European Journal of Political Economy 597.
124. Holmes and Holmes, 'Profiling Violent Crimes: An Investigative Tool' (n21), 38–39.
125. Harris, 'Profiles in Injustice' (n94), 24–25.
126. ibid.
127. Harcourt, 'Against Prediction. Profiling, Policing and Punishing in an Actuarial Age', (n96), 23.
128. Sampling is referring to when police officers use their discretionary powers to 'stop and search' individuals in public places randomly to detect criminality.
129. Harcourt, 'Against Prediction. Profiling, Policing and Punishing in an Actuarial Age', (n96), 24–25.
130. ibid.
131. D. Roberts, 'Race, vagueness and the social meaning of order-maintenance policing' (1999) 89 British Journal of Criminology 775, 775–779.
132. ibid.
133. ibid.
134. C. Dowden, C. Bennell and S. Bloomfield, 'Advances in offender profiling: a systematic review of the profiling literature published over the past 30 years' (2007) 22 Journal of Police and Criminal Psychology 44, 50–51.
135. Harris, 'Profiles in Injustice' (n94), 41–42.
136. Home Office, *Code of Practice for the Exercise by Police Officers of Statutory Powers of Stop and Search, Code A* (Home Office/TSO, 2015), 6.
137. Turvey, 'Serial Crime' (n119), 51–54.
138. Kocsis, 'An empirical assessment of content in criminal psychological profiles' (n118), 41–42. See also: C. Bennell, N. Jones, P. Taylor and B. Snook, 'Validities and abilities in criminal profiling: a critique of the studies conducted by Richard Kocsis and his colleagues' (2006) 50(3) International Journal of Offender Therapy and Comparative Criminology 344.
139. N. Daeid, 'Differences in offender profiling in the United States of America and the United Kingdom' (1997) Forensic Science International 25, 29–31.
140. Turvey, 'Serial Crime' (n119), 56–57.
141. ibid.
142. F. Hacker, *Crusaders, Criminals, Crazies: Terror and Terrorism in Our Time* (Norton Publishing, 1976), 33–36.
143. ibid.

144. J. Madsen, 'The rationale of suicide terrorism' (2004) Review of International Social Questions 8.
145. R. Borum, *Psychology of Terrorism* (University of South Florida, 2004), chp 2.
146. R. Gunaratna, *Inside al Qaeda: Global Network of Terror* (Columbia University Press, 2002), chp 3.
147. J. McCulloch and S. Pickering, 'Pre-crime and counter-terrorism: impacting future crime in the "war on terror"' (2009) 49(5) British Journal of Criminology 628, 629.
148. D. Rapoport, 'Modern Terror: The Four Waves' in A. Cronin and J. Ludes (eds), *Attacking Terrorism: Elements of a Grand Strategy* (Georgetown University Press, 2004), 46–59.
149. ibid, 55–60.
150. ibid, 61.
151. C. Walker, *Terrorism and the Law* (Oxford University Press, 2011), 3–4.
152. C. Walker, *The Anti-Terrorism Legislation* (Oxford University Press, 2009), 34–36.
153. ibid, chp 11.
154. Home Office, *Operation of Police Powers under the Terrorism Act 2000 and Subsequent Legislation: Arrests, Outcomes and Stops & Search, Great Britain, Year Ending September 2019* (Home Office, 2019), 5.
155. ibid, 7.
156. ibid.
157. ibid, 8.
158. ibid.

Bibliography

Ainsworth, P., *Offender Profiling and Crime Analysis* (Willan Publishing, 2001).

Annon, J., 'Investigative profiling: a behavioural analysis of the crime scene' (1995) 13(4) *American Journal of Forensic Psychology* 67.

Bartol, C., 'Police psychology: then, now and beyond' (1996) 23 *Criminal Justice and Behaviour* 70.

Bennell, C., Jones, N., Taylor, P. and Snook, B., 'Validities and abilities in criminal profiling: a critique of the studies conducted by Richard Kocsis and his colleagues' (2006) 50(3) *International Journal of Offender Therapy and Comparative Criminology* 344.

Boon, J., 'The Contribution of Personality Theories to Psychological Profiling' in J. Jackson and D. Bekarian (eds), *Offender Profiling: Theory, Research and Practice* (John Wiley & Sons Publishing, 1997).

Borden, H., 'Factors for predicting parole success' (1928) 19 *Journal of Criminal Law and Criminology* 328.

Borooah, V., 'Economic analysis of police stops and searches: a reply' (2002) 18 *European Journal of Political Economy* 607.

Borooah, V., 'Racial bias in police stops and searches: an economic analysis' (2001) 17 *European Journal of Political Economy* 17.

Borum, R., *Psychology of Terrorism* (University of South Florida, 2004).

Brown, L., 'The development of a parolee classification system using discriminate analysis' (1978) 15 *Journal of Research in Crime and Delinquency* 92.

Brussel, J., *Casebook of a Crime Psychiatrist* (Bernard Geis Associates, 1968).

Bumgarner, J., *Profiling and Criminal Justice in America* (ABC-Clio Publications, 2004).

Burch, R., *Study Guide for Hurley's a Concise Introduction into Logic* (Thompson-Wadsworth, 2003).

Burgess, A., Groth, A. and Holmstrom, L., *Sexual Assault of Children and Adolescents* (Lexington Publishing, 1978).

Canter, D., 'To catch a rapist' (1988) *New Society* 14.

Canter, D., *Criminal Shadows* (Harper Collins, 1995).

Canter, D. and Alison, L., *Offender Profiling Series II: Profiling in Policy and Practice* (Ashgate Publishing, 1999).

Canter, D., 'Offender profiles' (1989) 2(1) *The Psychologist* 14.

Canter, D. and Wentink, N., 'An empirical test of Holmes and Holmes serial murder typology' (2004) 31 *Criminal Justice Behaviour* 489.

Canter, D. and Youngs, D., *Investigative Psychology: Offender Profiling and the Analysis of Criminal Action* (John Wiley & Sons Publishing, 2009).

Chakravarty, S., 'Economic analysis of police stops and searches: a critique' (2002) 18 *European Journal of Political Economy* 597.

Cook, P. and Hinman, D., 'Criminal profiling: science and art' (1999) 15(3) *Journal of Contemporary Criminal Justice* 230.

Copson, G., *Coals to Newcastle? Part 1: A Study of Offender Profiling* (Home Office Policy Research Group, 1995).

Daeid, N., 'Differences in offender profiling in the United States of America and the United Kingdom' (1997) *Forensic Science International* 25.

Dean, G., 'Criminal Profiling in a Terrorism Context' in R. Kocsis (ed), *Criminal Profiling: International Theory, Research and Practice* (Humana Press, 2010).

Douglas, J., *Mindhunter: Inside the FBI's Elite Serial Crime Unit* (Scriber Publishing, 1995).

Douglas, J. and Burgess, A., 'Criminal profiling: a viable investigative tool against crime' (1986) 55 *FBI Law Enforcement Bulletin* 9.

Douglas, J., Burgess, A. and Ressler, R., *Crime Classification Manual* (Lexington Publishing, 1992).

Douglas, J. and Olshaker, M., *Unabomber: On the Trail of American's Most Wanted Serial Killer* (Pocket Books, 1996).

Douglas, J., Ressler, R., Burgess, A. and Hartman, C., 'Criminal profiling from crime scene analysis' (1986) 4 *Behavioural Sciences and the Law* 401.

Dowden, C., Bennell, C. and Bloomfield, S., 'Advances in offender profiling: a systematic review of the profiling literature published over the past 30 years' (2007) 22 *Journal of Police and Criminal Psychology* 44.

Egger, S., 'Psychological profiling: past present and future' (1999) 15 *Journal of Contemporary Criminal Justice* 242.

Farrington, D. and Lambert, S., 'Predicting Offender Profiles from Victim and Witness Descriptions' in J. Jackson and D. Bekerian (eds), *Offender Profiling Theory, Research and Practice* (John Wiley & Sons Publishing, 2001).

Goodwin, J., *Murder USA: The Ways We Kill Each Other* (Ballantine Publishing, 1978).

Groth, A., Burgess, A. and Holmstrom, L., 'Rape: power, anger and sexuality' (1977) 134 *American Journal of Psychiatry* 1239.

Grubbin, D., 'Offender profiling' (1995) 6 *Journal of Forensic Psychiatry* 259.

Gunaratna, R., *Inside al Qaeda: Global Network of Terror* (Columbia University Press, 2002).

Hacker, F., *Crusaders, Criminals, Crazies: Terror and Terrorism in Our Time* (Norton Publishing, 1976).

Harcourt, B., *Against Prediction. Profiling, Policing and Punishing in an Actuarial Age* (University of Chicago Press, 2007).

Harris, D., *Profiles in Injustice* (The New Line Press, 2002).

Hart, H., 'Predicting parole success' (1923) 41(3) *Journal of American Institute of Criminal Law and Criminology* 405.

Hazelwood, R. and Burgess, A., *Practical Aspects of Rape Investigation: A Multi-Disciplinary Approach* (CRC Press, 1987).

Hicks, S. and Sales, B., *Criminal Profiling* (American Psychological Association, 2006).

Hindman, D. and Cook, P., 'Profiling and Criminal Investigative Analysis of Violent Crimes With Multiple Offenders' in H. Hall and L. Whitaker (eds), *Collective Violence: Effective Strategies for Assessing and Intervening in Fatal Group and Institutional Aggression* (CRC Press, 1999).

Holmes, R. and de Burger, J., 'Profiles in terror: the serial murderer' (1985) 49(3) *Federal Probation* 29.

Holmes, R. and Holmes, S., 'Understanding mass murder: a starting point' (1992) 56(1) *Federal Probation* 53.

Holmes, R. and Homes, S., *Profiling Violent Crimes: An Investigative Tool* (Thousand Oaks, 1996).

Homant, R. and Kennedy, D., 'Psychological aspects of crime scene profiling: validity research' (1998) 25 *Criminal Justice and Behaviour* 319.

Home Office, *Code of Practice for the Exercise by Police Officers of Statutory Powers of Stop and Search*, Code A (Home Office/TSO, 2015).

Horvath, M., 'Offender Profiling' in S. Tong, R. Bryant and M. Horvath (eds), *Understanding Criminal Investigation* (John Wiley & Sons Publishing, 2009).

Jackson, J., *Offender Profiling; Theory, Research and Practice* (Wiley Publications, 1995).

Jackson, J. and Bekerian, D., *Offender Profiling: Theory, Research and Practice* (John Wiley & Sons Publishing, 1997).

Kaufmann, M., *Ethnic Profiling and Counter-Terrorism* (Lit Verlag, 2009).

Keppel, R. and Walter, R., 'Profiling killers: a revised classification model for understanding sexual murder' (1999) 43 *International Journal of Offender Therapy and Comparative Criminology* 417.

Knight, R. and Prently, R., 'The development antecedents and adult adaptations of rapist subject subtypes' (1987) 14 *Criminal Justice and Behaviour* 403.

Kocsis, R., 'An empirical assessment of content in criminal psychological profiles' (2003) 47(1) *International Journal of Offender Therapy and Comparative Criminology* 37.

Kocsis, R., 'Validities and abilities in criminal profiling: the dilemma for David Canter's investigative psychology' (2006) 50(4) *International Journal of Offender Therapy and Comparative Criminology* 458.

Kocsis, R., *Criminal Profiling: Principles and Practice* (Humana Press, 2006).

Kolko, D. and Kazdin, A., 'The emergence and recurrence of child firesetting: a one-year prospective study' (1992) 20 *Journal of Abnormal Child Psychology* 17.

Lee, H. and Gaensslen, R., *Forensic Science: An Introduction to Criminalistics* (McGraw-Hill, 1983).

Libert, J., 'Contributions of psychiatric consultation in the investigation of serial murder' (1986) 29 *International Journal of Offender Therapy and Comparative Criminology* 187.

Madsen, J., 'The rationale of suicide terrorism' (2004) *Review of International Social Questions* 8.

McCulloch, J. and Pickering, S., 'Pre-crime and counter-terrorism: impacting future crime in the "war on terror"' (2009) 49(5) *British Journal of Criminology* 628.

McGrath, M., 'Criminal profiling: is there a role for the forensic psychiatrist?' (2000) 28 *Journal of the American Academy of Psychiatry and Law* 319.

Meel, P., *Clinical versus Statistical Prevention: A Theoretical Analysis and a Review of the Evidence* (Jason Aronson Publishing, 1954).

Muller, D., 'Criminal profiling. Real science or just wishful thinking?' (2000) 4(3) *Homicide Studies* 234.

Neuman, W. and Wiegand, B., *Criminal Justice Research Methods: Qualitative and Quantitative Approaches* (Allyn and Bacon Publishing, 2000).

Petherick, W. and Turvey, B., 'Behavioural Evidence Analysis: An Ideal Deductive Method of Criminal Profiling' in B. Turvey (ed), *Criminal Profiling: An Introduction* (Academic Press, 2008).

Petherwick, W., 'What's in a name? Comparing applied profiling methodologies' (2003) 5 *Journal of Law and Social Challenges* 173.

Pinizotto, A., 'Forensic psychology: criminal personality profiling' (1984) 12 *Journal of Police Science and Administration Section* 1.

Popper, K., 'On the sources of knowledge and of ignorance' (1960) Proceedings of the British Academy of Sciences 39.

Poythress, N., Otto, R., Darkes, J. and Starr, L., 'APA's expert panel in the congressional review of the USS Iowa incident' (1993) 48 *American Psychologists* 8.

Rapoport, D., 'Modern Terror: The Four Waves' in A. Cronin and J. Ludes (eds), *Attacking Terrorism: Elements of a Grand Strategy* (Georgetown University Press, 2004).

Rider, A., 'The firesetter: a psychological profile (Part 1)' (1980) 49(6) *FBI Law Enforcement Bulletin* 6.

Roberts, D., 'Race, vagueness and the social meaning of order-maintenance policing' (1999) 89 *British Journal of Criminology* 775.

Sakheim, G., Vigdor, M., Gordon, M. and Helprin, L., 'A psychological profile of juvenile firesetters in residential treatment' (1985) 64 *Child Welfare* 453.

Snook, B., Cullen, R., Bennell, C., Taylor, P. and Gendreau, P., 'The criminal profiling illusion: what's behind the smoke and mirrors?' (2008) 35(10) *Criminal Justice and Behaviour* 1257.

Snook, B., Eastwood, J., Gendreau, P., Goggin, C. and Cullen, R., 'Taking stock of criminal profiling: a narrative review and meta-analysis' (2007) 34(4) *Criminal Science and Behaviour* 437.

Thornton, J., 'The General Assumptions and Rationale of Forensic Identification' in D. Faigman, D. Kaye, M. Saks and J. Sanders (eds), *Modern Scientific Evidence: The Law and Expert Testimony* (West Publications, 2008).

Turco, R., 'Psychological profiling' (1990) 34 *International Journal of Offender Therapy and Comparative Criminology* 147.

Turvey, B., 'Serial Crime' in B. Turvey (ed), *Criminal Profiling: An Introduction to Behavioural Evidence Analysis* (Academic Press, 2008).

Turvey, B., *Criminal Profiling: An Introduction to Behavioural Evidence Analysis* (Academic Press, 1999).

Walker, C., *Terrorism and the Law* (Oxford University Press, 2011).

Walker, C., *The Anti-Terrorism Legislation* (Oxford University Press, 2009).

Walton, D., *Informal Logic: A Handbook for Critical Argumentation* (Cambridge University Press, 1989).

Wilson, P., Lincoln, R. and Kocsis, R., 'Validity, utility and ethics of profiling for serial violent and sexual offenders' (1997) 4 *Psychiatry, Psychology and the Law* 1.

4 Formal terrorist profiling

The construction and application of terrorist profiles

4.1 Introduction

The primary aim of this chapter is to begin analysing the usefulness of different manifestations of terrorist profiling. This aim is pursued by relying on the effectiveness framework established in chapter one and the deductive/inductive analytical lens established in chapter three.

The discussion throughout this chapter argues that by relying on the effectiveness framework, it is possible to deconstruct the profiling process so as to analyse the construction and application of terrorist profiling separately. This deconstruction allows the deductive/inductive analytical lens established in chapter three to evaluate the potential usefulness of terrorist profiling. A core argument advanced in this chapter is that there are a variety of indicators of usefulness that are not simply fixed on whether terrorist profiling can be considered as capable of working or even likely to work in assisting law enforcement officers. This variety of indicators take into account utility or usefulness as well as considering other factors such as the impact of profiling on society. This involves questioning whether the cost associated with using terrorist profiling outweighs its potential usefulness as a counterterrorism tool assisting in the prevention, detection and prosecution of those likely to be involved in terrorism and/or its preparatory activities.

At its most elementary level, the use of profiling methods/approaches in countering terrorism with the aim of discerning likely terrorist characteristics can be described as being a form of terrorist profiling. In a similar way to criminal profiling, terrorist profiling may exist deductively where law enforcement officers deduce likely terrorist characteristics based on available crime scene evidence in response to a particular attack, a foiled attack or a preparatory attack. Or alternatively, terrorist profiling may exist inductively where law enforcement officers draw upon an array of data aimed at predicting likely terrorist characteristics.

Terrorist profiling exists in a variety of different manifestations. As a result, there is no one type of profiling synonymous with the label 'terrorist profiling.' It is contended that in order to analyse terrorist profiling an analytical distinction needs to be made between different manifestations of terrorist profiling. This analytical approach is a departure from previous evaluations conducted on the usefulness of profiling methods/approaches in the context of terrorism. Nevertheless, it is maintained that this distinction forms an important and necessary part of analysing profiling methods/approaches in the context of terrorism so as to evaluate whether these methods/approaches may be considered useful to law enforcement officers in discerning likely terrorist characteristics.

This chapter begins by drawing upon the profiling spectrum established in chapter one. It was explained in chapter one that a form of profiling exists at one end of the profiling spectrum that is best described as being formal terrorist profiling. Formal terrorist profiling can be defined as the systematic and official use of any profiling method or approach by law enforcement officers which is aimed at identifying likely terrorist characteristics. The discussion in this chapter argues that there are at least three defining features of formal terrorist profiling: an official and systematic process to construct a profile, the application of a profile by law enforcement officers and the ability to review the operation and practice of formal terrorist profiling. Additionally, in this chapter it will be shown that those manifestations of terrorist profiling accurately classifiable as being on the 'formal' side of the profiling spectrum draw significantly on the inductive profiling methods/approaches analysed in chapter three.

The aim is pursued in four sections.

Firstly, the chapter begins by considering the use of knowledge discovery processes and data mining as a formal terrorist profiling method. This approach allows for an identification, explanation and evaluation of 'knowledge discovery processes' and 'data mining' approaches used in the construction of formal terrorist profiles.

Secondly, the chapter progresses by examining different manifestations of formal terrorist profiling in Germany and the US. This discussion provides a useful basis to evaluate the application of formal terrorist profiling methods used by law enforcement officers to assist in the identification of individuals likely to be engaged in terrorism or its associated preparatory activities. This discussion draws upon the inductive profiling methods/approaches set out in chapter three as the basis to classify the systematic nature of the manifestations of profiling examined in this chapter.

Thirdly, the chapter progresses further by assessing/measuring the effectiveness of formal terrorist profiling in light of the discussion of the methods used in the construction of terrorist profiles and the application of terrorist profiles by law enforcement officers and the effectiveness framework established in chapter one.

Finally, the conclusion considers to what extent (if at all), and in what ways (if any) terrorist profiling may be useful as part of the law enforcement process of identifying individuals engaged in acts of terrorism and associated preparatory activities. It is argued that by examining the construction and application of terrorist profiling separately, it is arguable that over time these manifestations of profiling may be assistive to law enforcement officers.

4.2 Knowledge discovery processes and data mining

4.2.1 Introduction

Over the course of the last half century there has been considerable growth in the capabilities of not only creating data but also, and more importantly, collecting, storing, transmitting and searching data including highly sensitive personal information.[1] In an era of digitalisation, previously inaccessible personal information involving the 'individual' is now commonly created, collected, stored and transmitted in personal, public, private and governmental databases which is capable of exhibiting trends and patterns that may be a significant indicator of future behaviour.

In a law enforcement context, the access to different datasets containing personal and public information which can be connected together into a 'meaningful' form holds an innate potential to allow law enforcement officers predict future trends and patterns in behaviour. This prediction in human behaviour may assist law enforcement officers to identify likely offending trends and patterns including likely offender characteristics. Similarly, in the context of terrorism, access to vast arrays of information contained in a variety of databases holds an innate potential to identify significant knowledge which can be used as a basis to identify trends and patterns which may be considered significant.[2]

The discovery of 'knowledge' from data can be considered a knowledge discovery process which either involves the extraction of explicit information from single databases, or alternatively it can involve 'the non-trivial extraction of implicit, previously unknown and potentially useful information from more than one database.'[3] The discovery of explicit knowledge from data usually involves traditional information retrieval searches that rely upon linking explicit data within the same database.[4] For example, a driving licensing database will typically contain information such as driver's name, address, data of birth, licence type, etc. and any search of a driver licensing database will reveal the explicit knowledge in the database. This type of knowledge discovery is akin to information retrieval in response to a specific query or 'search.'

Alternatively, the discovery of implicit knowledge from data will usually involve more complex knowledge discovery processes involving the use of 'data mining techniques' and methods to reveal relationships and repetitions in data from different databases. Data mining, therefore, can be considered one step in the broader 'process of knowledge discovery' which assists in revealing patterns and trends from different databases.[5]

4.2.2 The construction of profiles using knowledge discovery processes and data mining

There are typically five phases in the use of knowledge discovery processes and data mining in the construction of profiles.[6] The first phase is called 'selection' which involves the identification of the different sources of databases. Roiger explains that this involves identifying different databases which contain information that merit further analysis.[7] The second phase is called 'pre-processing' which involves eliminating information that can be considered irrelevant or is considered what is common termed 'noise.' 'Noise' refers to information that is likely to either mislead the knowledge discovery process or obscure the value in the identified patterns.[8]

The third phase is 'transformation' which involves converting the pre-processed information into 'searchable' datasets. In essence, transformation creates a 'master database' which is commonly referred to as the 'data warehouse or data mart.'[9] Typically data warehouses will contain four types of data which can 'be used in the knowledge discovery process.'[10] Firstly, 'integrated data' can be considered data which has been pre-examined so as to identify common patterns and trends. Secondly, 'detailed and summarised data' can be considered data that is 'raw' or 'granular' data which is the most elementary and basic form of data available. Thirdly, 'historical data' is the inclusion of any data that has been previously used in a knowledge discovery process. Fourthly, 'metadata' which is data that provides the contextual background to particular types of data. The inclusion of metadata in data warehouses is important to help appreciate the significance of patterns and trends associated with particular types of data. It is only through the careful pre-processing of detailed and summarised data with historical data and metadata that a workable and effective dataset emerges which may be capable of identifying trends and patterns of significance. This form of pre-processing allows the profiler to appreciate the significance of the reoccurrence of particular patterns and trends in the data.

The fourth phase is 'the data mining' phase where various methods and 'techniques are applied [to all] the data in the data' warehouse in an attempt to identify common trends and patterns of significance in the data.[11] The definition of data mining is discussed and debated in a vast array of different academic literature; however, there is a lack of consensus on a specific and unified definition.[12] For example, Taipale broadly defines data mining 'as the non-trivial process of identifying valid, novel, potentially useful and ultimately understandable patters in data.'[13] Whilst Thursaingham argues that 'at the core of the data mining process is the application of data analysis and discovery algorithms' to identify patterns and trends in vast quantities of information.[14] In essence, data mining refers to the process that allows 'the analysis of data by automatic means in order to discover previously unknown knowledge in data.'[15] More generally, data mining is the ability to apply algorithms to different categories of data so that it can be organised to reveal previously unknown relationships between the data which signifies some value to the pattern identified.[16] It is the discovery of previously unknown patterns, trends and connections between different categories of data that is significant which allows the prediction of other similar patterns, trends and connections into the future.

Data mining can be conducted in at least two ways.

Firstly, it can be conducted by relying on a previously known profile or model so as to find the occurrence of a pattern within a dataset.[17] This is commonly referred to in the literature as 'subject based' searches or 'goal oriented' searches.[18] The profiler in this type of data mining develops a theory or a hypothesis about a particular subject or pattern and then seeks to find the frequency of that theory within a range of datasets. Subject-based searches develop what is commonly referred to as 'statistical models' which use algorithms to discover the closest match or the frequency of that model or profile within the searchable dataset.[19] This data mining approach commonly uses 'machine learning methods'[20] to improve the accuracy of relationship between the different types of information in the databases. This data mining approach is considered a 'supervised method' as it starts with 'strong suspicions or clues concerning a specific event, person or small groups of events and/or persons.'[21] The use of subject-based searches by law enforcement officers are aimed at being a temporary mechanism to enhance the operation of the law by providing law enforcement officers with greater knowledge on particular occurrences.

Secondly, data mining can also be conducted in a less formalised way to identify previously unrecognised patterns and trends in information within an array of different databases.[22] This approach is commonly identified in the literature as 'pattern-based' searches or 'global-based' searches. Pattern-based searches are considered 'fishing expeditions' where law enforcement officers aim to 'fish' for unknown patterns in vast arrays of data as they usually operate in an unstructured and unsupervised way. The results yielded from these fishing expeditions can be used in future data mining exercises as relevant search criteria.[23] This data mining approach can be considered more permanent in character as it is primarily aimed at enhancing law enforcement officer's general knowledge.

The final phase in 'the knowledge discovery process is the interpretation and evaluation of the results' yielded from 'the data mining' phase.[24] After the data has been 'mined' for patterns and trends the profiler will firstly interpret the results and then evaluate them for their usefulness. Patterns and trends that can be considered useful will be retained for further analysis or adjustment so as to repeat the knowledge discovery process to improve the quality of the results yielded. Therefore, it is evident that knowledge discovery processes are by their nature 'incremental and iterative' that need to be conducted repeatedly so as to identify the significance of 'patterns and trends' gleaned from different forms of data.[25]

It is noteworthy that all knowledge discovery processes involving the use of data mining approaches involve a significant reliance on the use of mathematical algorithms in connecting the data together so as to identify patterns and trends of significance.[26] As identified in the five phases above, the use of algorithms is employed at two key stages in the construction of terrorist profiles. Firstly, in the pre-processing of data phase where algorithms assist in eliminating irrelevant information from the datasets and thereby assist in creating meaningful datasets and secondly at the data mining phase where a further algorithm is required to elicit key trends and patterns from the newly constructed pre-processed dataset.

A particular concern is the reliance on 'individuals' to create specific algorithms capable of pre-processing an array of different forms of data into one significant and meaningful dataset, and further creating a secondary algorithm which is capable of identifying the patterns and trends in the newly created dataset. In at least two stages in the construction of a profile, this process is contingent upon an individual creating multiple algorithms so as to correctly attach the appropriate weight and significance to individual pieces of information contained within the array of different databases. It is arguable that where an algorithm fails to correctly attach the appropriate weight to particular pieces of information, any profiles constructed will be highly defective and deficient in being able to assist law enforcement officers identify individuals likely to be engaged in terrorist acts or preparatory activities.

The use of knowledge discovery processes and data mining methods and techniques in criminal justice has emerged in a variety of different types of applications. For example, Dahbur and Muscarollo found that data mining methods could reveal as much as ten times more connections between different data concerning armed robbery cases than in comparison to human law enforcement officers' trawls of the same databases.[27] Similarly Blokland *et al* and De Bruin *et al* have found that data mining methods could reveal useful relationships from a collection of datasets containing information such as marital status, previous criminal history and previous intoxicating substance abuse history so as to develop a typical profile containing likely characteristics of repeat offenders.[28] Furthermore, data mining has also been used by Adderley and Musgrove to identify common characteristics of sex offenders by drawing upon a range of databases of the convicted sex offenders.[29] These examples illustrate that data mining becomes a process of connecting pre-existing known information together into significant and meaningful knowledge that may be capable of assisting law enforcement officers in the prevention and detection of crime.

4.2.3 Knowledge discovery processes and data mining summary

It is evident that the use of data mining methods and approaches form part of a broader knowledge discovery process to identify implicit knowledge contained within vast arrays of databases. The first three phases of the knowledge discovery process are aimed at identifying, enhancing and pre-processing the available information into searchable datasets which data mining methods and approaches can be applied so as to identify implicit patterns and trends contained within the searchable data.

The final phase of the knowledge discovery process is primarily aimed as being an interpretative and evaluative exercise of the newly discovered knowledge where the profiler seeks to identify the significance of the new implicit knowledge identified from the information in the databases. These data mining approaches are contingent upon the access to vast arrays of information which is held in both public and private databases.

4.2.4 *The evaluation of knowledge discovery processes and data mining approaches in light of established profiling methods*

It was identified and explained in chapter three that the construction of profiles generally can occur either deductively or inductively. The construction of profiles created using deductive profiling approaches essentially react to crimes already committed as the profiles are constructed by using forensic evidence and victim reports. This profiling approach adopts a reactive methodology where the profile purports to be rationally or logically deducted following a thorough analysis of the available and relevant information.

It is arguable that there are at least three significant similarities between the use of deductive profiling methods and the use of knowledge discovery processes which adopt subject-based data mining approaches in the construction of profiles. Firstly, deductive profiling methods adopt a reactive methodology on the basis of pre-existing known information. Similarly, knowledge discovery processes adopting subject-based data mining approaches can be considered primarily reactive to a specific event or group of events. Secondly, deductive profiling methods rely exclusively on pre-existing known information as the basis to logically deduce the profile of the likely characteristics of the offender. Similarly, knowledge discovery processes adopting a subject-based data mining approach relies exclusively on pre-existing known information. Finally, deductive profiling approaches seek to develop typologies as a way to identify likely offender characteristics. Similarly, knowledge discovery processes adopting subject-based data mining approaches seek to develop a hypothesis and find the replication of that hypothesis within the databases. Therefore, it is evident that there are close similarities between deductive profiling methods and knowledge discovery processes that adopt subject-based data mining approaches in the construction of profiles.

Additionally, in chapter three a distinction was drawn between scientific and non-scientific deductive profiling approaches. This distinction rested upon the fact that scientific deductive profiling sought to test, validate and replicate the accuracy of the profiles through the adoption of elements of science disciplines such as investigative psychology. It is arguable that knowledge discovery processes which adopt pattern-based data mining approaches can be considered a form of scientific deductive profiling. The core feature of knowledge discovery processes which adopt pattern-based data mining approaches that makes this process 'scientific' is that fact that the process embraces the ability to test the replication and validation of the yielded results at the 'interpretation and evaluation' phase of the knowledge discovery process.

In contrast to deductive profiling, it was also identified and explained in chapter two that the construction of profiles can also be created by using inductive profiling methods. The construction of profiles using inductive profiling methods uses analytical methods to prevent crimes which have not already occurred. The defining feature of inductive profiling is its dependence upon a statistical analysis of previous offending records to identify the common characteristics of known offenders so as to allow the profiler to make predictions about likely offender characteristics.

On the basis of this analysis, it seems that there are at least three significant similarities between inductive profiling approaches and knowledge discovery processes which adopt pattern-based data mining approaches. Firstly, inductive profiling approaches are contingent upon a vast array of information in different databases. Similarly, knowledge discovery processes adopting pattern-based data mining approaches rely upon a vast array of different databases as the basis to identify patterns and trends from the information. Secondly, inductive profiling approaches can be considered an inferential process whereby the profiler makes a sequence of rational judgements about the information gleaned from previous criminal records and databases which lead to an overall conclusion of likely offender characteristics. Similarly, knowledge discovery processes adopting pattern-based data mining approaches become an inferential process whereby the profiler has to make a sequence of rational judgements about the information identified from the databases. Finally, inductive profiling approaches rely substantially on probabilities and statistics as the basis to identify patterns and trends in the information. Similarly, knowledge discovery processes adopting pattern-based data mining approaches also rely upon probabilities and statistics in identifying trends and patterns in the data at the interpretation and evaluation phase in the knowledge discovery process. Therefore, it is evident that knowledge discovery processes adopting a pattern-based data mining approach can be considered an inductive profiling approach.

In summary, knowledge discovery processes can embrace both deductive and inductive profiling approaches. It is evident that the distinction between deductive and inductive approaches in the context of knowledge discovery processes is largely contingent upon the type of data mining approach employed.

4.3 The application of knowledge discovery processes and data mining by law enforcement officers

As noted above, this chapter aims to evaluate formal terrorist profiling by conducting an analysis of different forms and manifestations of formal terrorist profiling practices in Germany and the US. Additionally, it has been noted above that the evidence of formal terrorist profiling can be difficult to find as countries commonly remain silent on its use within counterterrorism policy. However, Germany and the US, to varying degrees, have acknowledged the use of knowledge discovery processes which embrace data mining methods in their counterterrorism policy.

The discussion in this section will now turn to examine the application of data mining methods and approaches by Germany and the US. The use of knowledge discovery processes within German law enforcement policy can be considered a knowledge discovery process which has adopted a subject-based data mining approach. This application of formal terrorist profiling can be characterised a form of deductive profiling.

Alternatively, the use of knowledge discovery processes within the US can be considered a form of pattern-based data mining and therefore be characterised as being an inductive form of profiling.

The distinction between these two types of terrorist profiling methods can be considered significant for the purposes of evaluating terrorist profiling methods. In particular, it was argued in chapter two that deductive profiling methods could be classified as being ineffective in the context of terrorism. The comparisons between the German and the US application of formal terrorist profiling provides an opportunity to re-examine and re-evaluate the effectiveness of these individual profiling methods in the context of terrorism with a view to testing and measuring the extent to which terrorist profiling may be considered useful as part of the process of identifying individuals engaged in acts of terrorism or preparatory activities.

4.3.1 The application of knowledge discovery processes and data mining approaches in Germany

The application of knowledge discovery processes and data mining approaches in Germany is manifested through a 'special method of profiling using data screening' which is commonly referred to as '*Rasterfahndung*.'[30] 'Rasterfahndung' cannot be easily translated into English, however, it has been defined as the automatic processing and screening of an array of public and/or private databases in an attempt to assist law enforcement officers identify likely terrorists and terrorist characteristics.[31] Additionally, '*Rasterfahndung*' schemes have been characterised in the literature as being 'dragnet' 'fishing' investigations where law enforcement officers 'fish' for individuals likely to engaged in terrorism through a trawl of private and public databases.[32] Therefore, *Rasterfahndung* schemes can be considered knowledge discovery processes that adopt subject-based data mining approaches as they most commonly start with known information and seek to identify the frequency of that known information in different collections of databases.

The application of *Rasterfahndung* profiling schemes in Germany in a counterterrorism context has emerged in two separate periods in recent history.

The first *Rasterfahndung* scheme emerged during the course of the 1970s and 1980s which related to the development of a knowledge discovery process using data mining to assist law enforcement officers in identifying individuals who were likely to be members of the 'Red Army Fraction' (RAF). The RAF emerged as a domestic terrorist group that engaged in a number of bomb and shooting attacks throughout Germany which primarily focused on US military basis in opposition to western capitalism.[33] Whilst there were three generations of RAF terrorists, it was the latter generation which created considerable difficulty for German law enforcement officers to detect.[34] The threat of terrorism from the first two generations of the RAF was managed by German law enforcement officers infiltrating the RAF and utilising intelligence to counteract their presence within Germany.[35] However, the third generation of the RAF lived covertly within Germany which challenged traditional policing methods to detect and trace their presence. As a result, law enforcement officers developed alternative counterterrorism approaches, such as *Rasterfahndung* schemes, to assist in identifying individuals who were likely to be members of the RAF.

The legal basis for proactive *Rasterfahndung* schemes in Germany in the 1970s and 1980s was originally attributable to the decision in *B v F*.[36] The Constitutional Court held that Article 2, Sec 3 Sen 1 of the German Constitution placed a positive obligation 'on the state' to proactively safeguard 'the right to life' within Germany.[37] Additionally, as a result of counterterrorism domestic laws enacted during the 1970s and 1980s, law enforcement officers were given increasing levels of flexibility in managing the threat of terrorism through preventative measures.[38]

As a result of increasing violence and an increasing threat of violence emanating from the RAF during the 1970s and 1980s, law enforcement officers sought to develop *Rasterfahndung* schemes to assist in identifying individuals likely to be engaged in terrorism. The development of *Rasterfahndung* as part of counterterrorism policy was commonly viewed by the German government as being essential in securing its 'obligation to protect the right to life of the' German people as guaranteed by the German Constitution.[39] In effect, the right to life case allowed the German government to construct a basic right to security which necessitated specific policies to discharge their obligation to protect the right to security.[40] The use of *Rasterfahndung* schemes was presented in the German media as necessary to manage the threat of terrorism.[41]

The application of the RAF *Rasterfahndung* profiling approach involved starting with the hypothesis that members of the RAF rented their apartments under a pseudonym.[42] Additionally, it was commonly believed that RAF members routinely paid for their goods and services in cash including essential services such as electricity.[43] As a result, the first phase in the knowledge discovery process involved law enforcement officers 'selecting' databases which could be used to assist in the identification of individuals living in Germany paying for essential services and goods in cash. This involved law enforcement officers gaining access to utility company records so as to identify the reoccurrence of the generated hypothesis.

The second phase in the knowledge discovery process involved the preprocessing of this information into databases which only contained relevant information by removing information that could mislead the knowledge discovery process. This involved removing individuals who paid for their services by way of credit transfer, direct debit and cheques as the inclusion of this information was considered likely to obscure the identification of the repetition of the hypothesis.

The third phase in the knowledge discovery process involved the transformation of this information into searchable datasets through the creation of a data warehouse which contained a master database of all individuals paying for goods and services in cash. The fourth phase involved the actual data mining which revealed the names and addresses of all of those individuals who paid for their utility bills in cash. The final phase involved interpreting and evaluating any results yielded from the data mining. This involved cross checking all of the identified names and addresses by the law enforcement officers against public databases so as to eliminate those individuals not considered to be a member of the RAF. Hilbrans identified that after a trawl of a significant 'number of public and private databases' the application of the RAF *Rasterfahndung* profiling scheme identified only one significant member of the RAF, Rolf Heissler, who was subsequently prosecuted for terrorism offences.[44]

The second *Rasterfahndung* scheme was developed and applied in direct response to the September 11, 2001 terrorist attacks in the US as it became evident that an active cell of the al-Qaeda terrorist organisation had covertly lived and operated in Germany prior to the terrorist attacks. As a result of an active cell of al-Qaeda being able to live and operate covertly within German borders, it rejuvenated a desire amongst law enforcement officers to use *Rasterfahndung* schemes to assist in the identification of other 'sleeper' terrorists that may have remained within Germany after the terrorist attacks.

According to public information, the second *Rasterfahndung* scheme emerged immediately after the September 11 terrorist attacks and involved a knowledge discovery process which also adopted a subject-based data mining approach.[45] This process involved the trawl of approximately 8 million public and private databases affecting almost ten per cent of the national German population which sought to identify the occurrence and pattern of a pre-determined hypothesis.[46] Similar to the RAF *Rasterfahndung* application of terrorist profiling, law enforcement officers started with known information, as it was primarily reactive to the September 11 terrorist attacks. The known information consisted of the following factors/characteristics:

> Male, aged 18 to 40, (ex-)student, Islamic religious affiliation, native country or nationality of certain countries, named in detail, with predominantly Islamic population.[47]

The subject-based data mining approach sought to identify individuals who matched some or most of the known factors/characteristics living within Germany. The factors/characteristics were developed from the actual characteristics of those individuals who were involved in executing the September 11 terrorist attacks.[48] The selection of the factors/characteristics was prepared by a specialist co-ordinated group of law enforcement officers within the 'Federal Criminal Police Office,' the 'Federal Border Security Office' and the 'Federal Office for the Protection of the Constitution.'[49]

The first phase in this *Rasterfahndung* profiling application involved the selection of databases which provided the basis to find the frequency of the known profile. This involved the selection of private and public databases including university registrars, police residential registries and national alien registries so as to identify those individuals who matched some or most of the known information.[50] The second phase involved the pre-processing of the available databases by law enforcement officers seeking so as to eliminate irrelevant information likely to obscure the value of identified patterns. In this case the removal of irrelevant information included any characteristics outside of the known hypothesis from the available database. The removal of the irrelevant information resulted in third phase of 'transformation' which created a data warehouse of searchable datasets likely to find the repetition of the known hypothesis.

The fourth phase involved the performance of the actual data mining and in litigation seeking to challenge the legality of using a knowledge discovery process to identify individuals for greater official scrutiny, it was reported that the searches of these databases resulted in the creation of 31,988 records of individuals from across Germany which were considered by law enforcement officers as being worthy of further investigation in interests of preventing terrorism.[51]

The contents of the yielded results varied from state to state within Germany but common details included the primary source database, the name and address (including previous known addresses) of the 'suspect,' their place of birth, nationality, marital status, gender and their tax history with the German Revenue and Customs.[52] Additionally, the information elicited from university records also indicated their chosen course of study and the duration of their visit to Germany.[53]

Additionally, it was further discovered during the course of the litigation challenging the use of the *Rasterfahndung* profiling scheme that law enforcement officers had inappropriately included information from other databases not originally requested in their judicial *Rasterfahndung* authorisation application to identify 'sleeper' terrorists following the September 11 terrorist attacks. As part of the legal process law enforcement officers seeking to use a *Rasterfahndung* scheme must indicate in their judicial application for authorisation the searchable databases they intend to conduct their searches. It emerged that law enforcement officers had searched databases containing information on new pilot licences and individual applications made for licences for handling radioactive waste in Germany.[54] The inclusion of these two additional databases resulted in subjecting an additional 1,187 individuals to greater levels of official scrutiny who did not actually match any of the identified searchable factors/characteristics.[55] It is evident from the litigation that the inclusion of these databases, as part of the searchable dataset, was part of a zealous attempt by law enforcement officers to purposely widen the search in seeking to identify individuals likely to be engaged in terrorism which was based on previously known information. This demonstrates that in this particular case an additional 1,187 individuals were identified as being individuals likely to be engaged in acts of terrorism or preparatory activities due to the human interference in 'the knowledge discovery process.'

The final phase in the *Rasterfahndung* knowledge discovery process involved interpreting and evaluating any results yielded from the data mining exercise. During the course of the litigation challenging the validity of the *Rasterfahndung* profiling schemes as a basis to identify individuals likely to be engaged in terrorism or terrorism activities, it was identified that the compiled list of suspected terrorists was whittled down from 31,988 individuals to 1,689 individuals.[56] This process involved law enforcement officers identifying individuals that were not considered a terrorist threat. For example, some of the initially identified individuals had already left Germany whilst others were present in Germany on legitimate grounds.[57] However, it is noteworthy that whilst the German law enforcement officers subjected over 1,600 individuals to greater levels of scrutiny, there were no charges brought forward against any identified 'suspect' on grounds of terrorism.[58]

It is evident that the two applications of the *Rasterfahndung* profiling schemes in Germany represent a knowledge discovery process which employed subjected-based data mining approaches. The search of public and private databases identified a number of individuals for greater official scrutiny who were suspected of being involved in terrorist acts or preparatory activities. Both applications of *Rasterfahndung* schemes adopted a reactive methodology in reaction to specific events and known information from specific events and as such can be considered a form of deductive profiling. For example, the first *Rasterfahndung* scheme reacted with known information on RAF members and additionally the second *Rasterfahndung* scheme was also reactionary to the events of the September 11 terrorist attacks. This approach to knowledge discovery demonstrates the ability of subject-based data mining approaches as the basis to identify individuals for further investigation by law enforcement officers.

The effectiveness of knowledge discovery processes and data mining as part of terrorist profiling is explored in detail below after examining the US manifestation of formal terrorist profiling.

4.3.2 *The application of knowledge discovery processes and data mining approaches in the US*

The use of 'knowledge discovery processes' embracing 'data mining' approaches in the US have manifested in at least three different ways: governmental administrative agency knowledge discovery processes, law enforcement knowledge discovery processes and national security knowledge discovery processes.[59] Each of these knowledge discovery processes exist to assist different governmental agencies identify different types of individuals engaged in an array of behaviour depending on the aim of the profiler. The first two manifestations of knowledge discovery processes primarily exist outside of the context of terrorism and are aimed at identifying individuals engaged in criminal activity. For example, in governmental administrative agency knowledge discovery processes, the US Internal Revenue Service utilise knowledge discovery processes to identify individuals underpaying or avoiding their tax obligations.[60] Additionally the use of knowledge discovery processes within law enforcement has been used by the FBI as a basis to investigate serious crime across America.[61] However, in the context of terrorism there has been an array of different knowledge discovery processes which has emerged as a direct consequence of the September 11 terrorist attacks.

Following the September 11 attacks the media,[62] academic commentary[63] and governmental reports[64] all emphasised that law enforcement and security agencies held adequate information to identify the terrorists who committed the September 11 attacks prior to the commission of the attack but their systems fundamentally failed to 'connect the dots in advance of the terrorist attacks.'[65] This raised a significant concern that law enforcement officers and agencies did not have an effective framework to identify patterns in information which could alert law enforcement officers of the likelihood of a terrorist attack. Furthermore, the apparent inability of US law enforcement agencies to proactively manage the threat of terrorism resulted in a profound re-evaluation of the role that law enforcement agencies played in managing the threat of terrorism.[66] Many agencies, such as the FBI and the CIA, shifted focus from prosecuting acts of terrorism and preparatory activities to proactively managing the threat of terrorism by seeking to prevent its occurrence through the development of schemes and frameworks which would assist in identifying likely terrorists.[67] For example, the *New York Times* reported that the US National Security Agency (NSA) were engaged in 'wiretapping telephone and email communications of people in the country in an effort to track individuals affiliated with Al-Qaeda' so as to pre-emptively track likely terrorists.[68] Additionally, in the following year *USA Today* reported that 'the NSA was actively collecting, with the cooperation of major telephone companies, the call records of millions of US citizens and residents in an effort to detect pattern of terrorist behaviour.'[69]

In the aftermath of September 11 three main knowledge discovery processes were developed specifically to assist in managing the threat terrorism. These included knowledge discovery processes to assist in identifying financial transactions likely to be associated with terrorism or preparatory activities, knowledge discovery processes to assist in identifying individuals worthy of further investigation at ports, and general knowledge discovery processes to assist in identifying individuals likely to be engaged in terrorism or preparatory activities. It is important to note that law enforcement officers have employed various knowledge discovery processes at ports before the September 11 attacks, however, it was the September 11 attacks that provided the impetus to further develop and refine the knowledge discovery processes used at US ports.

Although it is possible to categorise these knowledge discovery processes by their area of focus, the 'Homeland Security Act 2002' (HSA) provided a broad framework which encouraged and facilitated the development of knowledge discovery processes to assist in the identification of likely terrorists where section 201(d)(14) provides the 'Undersecretary for Information Analysis and Infrastructure Protection' in 'the Department of Homeland Security' with the specific power to

> ... establish and utilise a secure communications and information technology infrastructure, including data mining and other advanced tools, in order to access, receive and analyse data and information in furtherance of the responsibilities of this section....[70]

Therefore, the terrorist attack on September 11 became the catalyst which resulted in a race to develop new and existing knowledge discovery frameworks and processes capable of identifying patterns and trends in human activity which could indicate terrorism acts or preparatory activities.

Each knowledge discovery process manifestation will be identified and explained individually so as to understand the different ways formal terrorist profiling methods can be applied to identify individuals engaged in terrorism or preparatory activities.

4.3.2.1 Knowledge discovery processes in financial transactions

Knowledge discovery processes assisting in identifying financial transactions likely to be associated with terrorism or preparatory activities have been perceived as holding significant potential to not only frustrate the ability of terrorists to engage in acts of terrorism by freezing terrorist funds but also hold the potential to identify terrorist groups.[71] As terrorists require capital to fund terrorism and inevitably leave a financial trail in the preparation and execution of acts of terrorism, it would appear logical to create the necessary framework to identify financial transactions and activities likely to be associated with terrorism or preparatory activities.

Therefore, the 'United and Strengthening America by Providing Appropriate Tools Required to Intercept and Obstruct Terrorism Act 2001' (US PATRIOT Act) and the subsequent 'USA Freedom Act 2015' (USA FA) facilitates knowledge discovery processes in financial transactions and activities by obligating financial institutions not only to 'monitor and report' on financial transactions but also 'financial institutions are required to' establish a means of discovering patterns in financial activities which may be associated with terrorism or preparatory activities.[72] Additionally, other financial services such as cheque cashing centres, post offices and payment centres such as Western Union are also required to register with the US Department of Treasury so as to ensure the broadest range of financial activities can be monitored to assist in managing the threat of terrorism.[73]

It is significant that the US Department of Treasury has refused to be drawn upon the exact requirements and obligations placed upon the financial institutions but rather has indicated:

> that financial institutions report on certain transactions that are determined to have a high degree of usefulness in criminal, tax, regulatory, intelligence and counter-terrorism matters.[74]

It would appear that 'certain transactions' requires the existence of predetermined criteria for identifying transactions which can be considered 'useful.' The 'Financial Crimes Enforcement Network' (FinCEN) was created by US Department of Treasury to administer information gleaned from financial institutions merit worthy of further investigation by law enforcement officers.

The FinCEN assists, manages and retains information gathered under the US Patriot Act in an attempt to identify individuals engaged in terrorist and general crimes. Furthermore, the FinCEN provides guidance to financial institutions in the information that might lead to the identification of financial activities merit worthy of further investigation.[75]

The process employed by financial institutions can be considered a knowledge discovery-based approach employing data mining approaches to connect information together so as to identify meaningful patterns and trends worthy of further investigation. Financial institutions must issue 'Suspicious Activity Reports' (SAR) to the US Department of Treasury when they detect transactions likely to be associated with criminality or terrorism. In particular, the process of identifying SAR reports depend upon the existence of an infrastructure capable of linking different transactions indicative of terrorism.

In light of the guidance information for financial institutions provided by FinCEN it is possible to discern the knowledge discovery process assisting in identifying financial transactions associated with terrorism or preparatory activities. The guidance framework provided by FinCEN assists in identifying indicators capable of alerting financial institutions of financial activities thought to be associated with criminality or terrorism. For example, FinCEN identify a key characteristic of funds likely to be associated with criminal enterprises or terrorist enterprises are large sums of money with no legitimate explanation of their origin.[76]

Knowledge discovery processes embracing data mining approaches adopt both pattern-based and subject-based approaches in assisting in identifying information. For example, FinCEN recommends that the first stage in identifying a suspicious activity is to identify the background of the company or individual associated with transaction so as to investigate whether the transaction history of their client can be considered of a legitimate origin.[77] Therefore, the first phase in identifying financial activities must begin with a selection of internal databases which will provide the financial institution with a diverse range of information about their client. The second phase will involve pre-processing that information by eliminating those individuals not thought to be associated with either criminality or terrorism.

Financial institutions will inevitably have to conduct an assessment of their client's account and history to determine whether they can be considered 'legitimate.' The third phase will involve transforming the pre-processed information into searchable data which will consist of historical data, raw data and integrated data of their client's activities. These three types of data will be capable of assisting financial institutions determining whether the financial transaction/activities can be considered suspicious on grounds of criminality or terrorism. The fourth phase uses the transformed data by identifying financial activities and transactions which are not considered to be of a legitimate origin. The final phase will involve continually re-evaluating the information contained within their internal databases so as to investigate whether financial transactions can be considered legitimate.

It is clear that knowledge discovery processes employed in financial institutions to detect criminality and terrorism largely depend upon pattern-based data mining approaches to identify patterns and trends in client accounts that merit further investigation firstly by the financial institution and secondly by law enforcement officers. The US Department of Treasury indicated that it has received 1,049,149 SAR reports up to 2007 with a further additional 15,994,484 currency exchange reports which merited closer examination in the interests of terrorism and criminality.[78] According to the US Department of the Treasury, the US Patriot Act provides the mechanism to assist law enforcement officers in identifying the funding of terrorist or terrorist organisation in addition to suspicious financial activity by the co-operation of financial institutions.[79]

4.3.2.2 Knowledge discovery processes at ports

Over the course of the past half century there have been a number of documented knowledge discovery schemes employed in aviation security which have been aimed at identifying individuals who are likely to be engaged in terrorist activities. This knowledge discovery process has existed pre and post the September 11, 2001 attacks. Therefore, the development of knowledge discovery processes at ports has been subjected to developmental progression where each knowledge discovery process has been subsequently developed in an incremental way in an attempt to enhance the ability of law enforcement officers to identify likely terrorists. There have been four attempts to develop a fully integrated and enhanced knowledge discovery process capable of identifying individuals likely to be associated with terrorism or preparatory activities.

The first manifestation of a knowledge discovery process employed at US airports was termed 'the Computer Assisted Passenger Pre-Screening System' (CAPPS) which was aimed at identifying individuals at airports for greater scrutiny by law enforcement officers.[80] The CAPPS knowledge discovery process operated by employing a subject-based data mining approach which required airlines to search databases identified by 'the Federal Aviation Administration' (FAA) for the names of individuals considered 'to be associated with terrorism.'[81] For example, the FAA held databases of key information such as names, date of birth and country of origin of 'suspected' terrorists which was utilised by airlines to cross checking their customer names against the FAA database.

The operation of CAPPS knowledge discovery process existed to assist in identifying known individuals pre-determined as being associated with terrorism so they could be identified by law enforcement officers prior to their security screening at the airport. However, whilst this system may be classified as being a knowledge discovery process, it is more akin to a watch list which was developed solely on the basis of known information on terrorists. The processes applied by this knowledge discovery process did not follow the typical identified phases of knowledge discovery discussed above, but rather only involved airlines searching for known information in predetermined and pre-constructed databases. Therefore, this system suffered from a fundamental weakness as it depended upon highly relevant information from the FAA who relied upon law enforcement information on terrorists.

The CAPPS system was subsequently developed into the CAPPS II knowledge discovery process in the aftermath of September 11 which sought not only to employ subject-based data mining approaches in knowledge discovery but also required pattern-based data mining approaches to enhance security at airports.[82] The fundamental distinction between CAPPS and CAPPS II is the fact that CAPPS II sought to identify patterns and trends in travel which may indicate a risk of terrorism.[83] Additionally, the obligation placed on the airline companies to search databases shifted to the newly created Transport Security Agency (TSA) which undertook a more direct role in managing the threat of terrorism in the aviation industry by administering the information supplied by airlines. This information included passenger records which consisted of 'full name, address, date of birth and phone number.'[84] Therefore, CAPPS II was aimed to 'confirm a passenger's identity and score any potential terrorism-related threat to aviation.'[85]

In considering the knowledge discovery process it is evident that the TSA engaged in the five phases inherent in any knowledge discovery processes identified and discussed above. In particular, the first phase involves the TSA attaining information from the airlines operating in the US and information from one or governmental databases on suspected terrorists. The second phase progresses to eliminating inaccurate information from the commercial databases provided by airlines with the third phase transforming the information into searchable data. At this stage in the knowledge discovery process, the fourth phase involved applying methods and techniques to confirm passengers' identity against their risk of terrorism.

The fourth phase created three tiers of knowledge in categorising the risk of individual likely to be terrorists.[86] Firstly, those individuals who were not considered to be a terrorist risk were placed on a green list to indicate that they did not require additional airport screening. Secondly, those individuals who were identified on foot of a pattern-based data mining search would be placed on a 'yellow' list to indicate that they required some additional security screening at airport. Finally, those individuals who had known links to terrorism or terrorism activities were placed on a 'red' list to indicate that those individuals were at the highest risk of terrorism and should normally be refused permission to travel at airports. The classification of an individual on a green, yellow and red list was highly contingent upon the historical, raw and integrated data contained within the databases at the transformation stage.

The final phase of the CAPPS II system required a continual reassessment of the information at the generated at the third phase so that individuals placed on lists at the fourth phase could be continually reviewed against the threat of terrorism.

Although the CAPPS II knowledge discovery system sought to strengthen the weaknesses of the previous CAPPS system by actively validating the identity of travellers against an individual assessment of the risk of terrorism, it was retired in 2004 in favour of an alternative system called 'Secure Flight.'[87] The rationale underpinning the development of the CAPPS II system into the Secure Flight system rested in a belief that airlines inconsistently collected information in their passenger records. In essence, the development of the Secure Flight system can be considered an attempt to require airlines to collect specific information thought to assist in the identification of individuals likely to be engaged in terrorism or preparatory activities. Secure flight placed a greater requirement on airlines to collect a broader range of information than simply 'name, address, date of birth and phone number' but also required other personal information such as the passenger's gender and their full flight itineraries including:

> (1) departure airport, (2) aircraft operator, (3) departure date, (4) departure time, (5) arrival date, (6) scheduled arrival time, (7) arrival airport code, (8) flight number and (9) the operating carrier.[88]

Similar to the two previous manifestations of aviation security knowledge processes, Secure Flight embraces a 'subject based and pattern based data mining' approaches as it seeks to identify individuals on the basis of pre-existing known information in addition to patterns on the basis of travel.[89] The Secure Flight knowledge discovery process operates a two tiered system for assisting in the identification of likely terrorists. Firstly, passengers intending to fly in to or out of a US airport would be cross-matched against a 'Terrorism No-Fly database' developed by the Department of Homeland Security.[90] Any passenger name appearing on the terrorism database would automatically be prohibited from flying within the US. Secondly, the TSA would also crossmatch passenger names against a 'Selectee' list so as to identify passengers requiring heightened security checks at US airports.[91]

It is the 'Selectee list' that is of most interest as the 'No-Fly database' is directly connected with known information on terrorist gleaned by law enforcement intelligence. The first phase in the knowledge discovery process of Secure Flight is the selection phase where the TSA uses information from commercial airlines in addition to law enforcement databases containing information on terrorists. The second phase in the Secure Flight knowledge discovery process involves the pre-processing of the selected information. This involves removing individuals not likely to be considered terrorists either in light of the full data provided by the commercial airline or alternatively due to information contained within the law enforcement database. The third phase in this knowledge discovery process involves transforming the pre-processed data into a search dataset capable of identifying individuals merit worthy of further investigation prior to their airport security screening. The fourth phase is aimed at conducting the searches on the dataset to identify those individuals for closer scrutiny at the airport. The final phase involves re-evaluating all of the information in the dataset in an attempt to enhance the accuracy of the information.

A more recent attempt to enhance aviation security further by relying upon knowledge discovery processes has been 'the development of the Automated

Targeting System' (ATS) which evaluates the terrorist risk not only of passengers but also of all cargo entering and leaving the US.[92] The ATS knowledge discovery process utilises both 'subject based' and 'pattern based data mining techniques' to identify individuals and/or cargo which is likely to be linked to acts of terrorism or terrorism activities. The process exists by requiring all commercial organisations operating in the movement of goods or people in the US, whether by land, air or sea, to collect the personal information of individuals in addition to cargo information which can be cross checked with various security risk databases within the US by the TSA.[93] The phases involved in the ATS knowledge discovery process involved is very similar to the Secure Flight knowledge discovery process except that it also applies to cargo in addition to individual passengers.

4.3.2.3 General knowledge discovery processes the total information awareness scheme

One of the most known controversial knowledge discovery process employed in the US has been considered the 'Total Information Awareness Scheme' which was renamed as the 'Terrorism Information Awareness' scheme (TIA).[94] The TIA knowledge discovery process was premised upon the ability of searching substantial public and private databases through the use of pattern-based data mining approaches. In essence, the TIA knowledge discovery process was akin to allowing US law enforcement officers to search uncontrollably through an increasing range of public and private databases to identify individuals for greater scrutiny as terrorist suspects. However, it is significant to note that the TIA scheme was not actually used by law enforcement officers as it had not advanced beyond the developmental stage due to Congress withdrawing funding amid concerns about the scheme's potential to collect, store and disseminate vast arrays of citizen information. Although, it was reported in the *New York Times* in 2012 that many aspects of the scheme were used by the 'National Security Agency' (NSA) in the detection of terrorism.[95]

It was proposed that the first phase in the TIA scheme would consist of law enforcement officers identifying vast arrays of public and private information held on individuals in public and private databases.[96] This process was considerably expansive using commercial credit-based agencies such as 'Check Point,' 'Experian' and 'Lexis-Nexis Personal Reports' in addition to publicly held databases to identify individual likely to be associated with terrorism.[97] The second phase involved pre-processing that the information collected from the different databases by removing individuals not suspected of terrorism. It was aimed that law enforcement databases and intelligence could be used as a basis to remove individuals from the database.[98] The third phase was aimed at transforming the data into a number of searchable datasets with key information on individuals likely to be engaged in terrorism. The fourth phase involved identifying individuals matching the criteria established by the Department of Homeland Security which identified individuals likely or suspected as being engaged in terrorism or preparatory activities. The final phase was proposed to be a review phase which would continually review the operation of the databases to ensure that each dataset was accurate and relevant.

The origins of the TIA knowledge discovery process can be traced to the 'Defence Advanced Research Projects Agency' programme which was subsequently rebranded into the TIA programme when Congress has removed its funding due to the privacy concerns raised by collecting and searching a growing number of private and public databases with only a general aim of finding suspicious patterns indicative of terrorism activities. After a further eight months of development the TIA knowledge discovery process was closed down by Congress withdrawing its funding on the basis of the privacy concerns raised by the development of a nationwide 'open' database to facilitate the trawl of vast arrays of personal information.

4.3.2.4 Knowledge discovery processes in the US summary

It is evident that there are a broad range of documented knowledge discovery processes in the US which have emerged in the context of managing the threat of terrorism stemming from the September 11, 2001 terrorist attacks. The US knowledge discovery processes adopt a dissected mix of pattern-based and subject-based data mining approaches to assist law enforcement officers in the identification of individuals likely to be engaged in terrorism acts or preparatory activities. It is also evident that each knowledge discovery scheme has sought to incrementally progress from the previous manifestations of knowledge discovery processes by using a mix of pattern-based and subject-based data mining approaches.

4.4 An evaluation of knowledge discovery processes in the context of terrorism

As discussed above, the use of knowledge discovery processes in counterterrorism involves the use of data mining approaches in two separate ways – either a 'subject based data mining approach' or a 'pattern-based data mining approach.'[99]

'Subject based data mining approaches' typically start with a specific known subject and will seek to search for more meaningful information on that subject. For example, in the German Rasterfahndung profiling schemes, discussed above, the law enforcement officers sought to conduct subject-based enquiries to identify individuals who bore similar known characteristics as those anticipated by law enforcement officers. Additionally, subject-based enquires carry the potential to uncover other links/connections with individuals unknown to law enforcement officers by discovering terrorist associations. This type of knowledge discovery can be considered a form of deductive profiling as it exhibits a number of the key characteristics of scientific deductive profiling methods.

Alternatively, there are pattern-based approaches which involve a predictive model based upon identifying patterns of behaviour which raise the suspicion of terrorism. For example, pattern-based enquiries will allow law enforcement officers to search for individual people, places, terrorist targets etc. by matching information within the dataset with a specific hypothesis of behavioural patterns. For example, the US knowledge discovery process developed for financial transactions seeks to identify trends and patterns based upon patterned behaviour likely to raise the suspicion of financing terrorism. This type of knowledge discovery can be considered a form of inductive profiling as it exhibits a number of the key characteristics of inductive profiling methods.

In either of these knowledge discovery processes data mining is aimed at assisting in the identification of individuals engaged in terrorism or preparatory activities by being the process to identify the trends and patterns which would otherwise remain unknown in the datasets. For example, in the subject-based enquiries data mining is aimed at assisting in the identification of any potential links between individuals by searching the datasets. Additionally, in the pattern-based enquiries data mining can be used as a basis to identify the unknown patterns within the dataset to elicit key behavioural trends.

The study of these methods raises the issue as to whether formal terrorist profiling can be considered 'effective' as an assistive tool for law enforcement officers in identifying individuals likely to be engaged in terrorism or preparatory activities. In the introductory chapter above, a conceptual framework to measure/test the effectiveness of terrorist profiling was developed with a view to applying it to knowledge discovery processes as a formal terrorist profiling method. It can be recalled that there are arguably three core elements in creating an analytical framework capable of measuring/testing the 'effectiveness' of terrorist profiling. These including examining the input processes used to construct profiles, the output processes which assess the use of the profile in the field and thirdly the broader impact of the use of the profile.

4.4.1 *Assessing/measuring the effectiveness of terrorist profiling*

As discussed in the introductory chapter, the 'effectiveness' of terrorist profiling can be assessed/measured by reference to three separate indicators of effectiveness.

Firstly, the input effectiveness involves conducting a utilitarian assessment of the methods used in the construction of terrorist profiles so as to assess whether the methods are capable of identifying likely terrorist characteristics that can be used in the construction of terrorist profiles. For example, in both manifestations of formal terrorist profiling in Germany and US, terrorist profiling can be found in an enabling statute with case law considering its use and application by law enforcement officers. The legal frameworks facilitating formal terrorist profiling in both the German and US manifestations have concentrated in providing law enforcement officers the power to rely upon profiling as an assistive tool in managing the threat of terrorism.

Secondly, the output effectiveness involves conducting an assessment of the application of formal terrorist profiles by law enforcement officers so as to assess whether the methods are capable of identifying individuals likely to be engaged in terrorism or preparatory activities. For example, the German manifestation of formal terrorist profiling only identified one individual associated with terrorism despite identifying over 30,000 suspects. Similarly, in the US financial transaction knowledge process over 1 million records were identified and it remains a mystery as to whether these records actually assisted in identifying individuals likely to be engaged in terrorism or preparatory activities.

Thirdly, it is contended that in order to fully address the assessment of the effectiveness of formal terrorist profiling, it is necessary to go beyond the utilitarian assessment into assessing the broader consequences of terrorist profiling. As noted in chapter one, this involves questioning whether the cost or associated cost of terrorist profiling is so significant that it begins to undermine the very rationale of using terrorist profiling as part of a counterterrorism policy that is aimed at preventing, detecting and prosecuting those likely to be involved in terrorism or its preparatory activities.

4.4.2 The input assessment of the effectiveness of constructing formal terrorist profiles

There were a number of shortcomings identified in chapter three on the use of deductive and inductive profiling methods in the context of terrorism which may be valid in respect of knowledge discovery processes and data mining.

In particular, there were two key criticisms made in chapter three on scientific deductive profiling related to the substantial reliance upon pre-existing information contained in databases as the basis to predict the occurrence of future characteristics and the use of typologies and hypothesis to help the development of profiles. In the context of knowledge discovery approaches relying upon subject-based data mining approaches, it is likely that relying exclusively on pre-existing known information fails to appreciate the capacity of terrorists to adopt their techniques in executing terrorist acts.

For example, the September 11 attacks can be taken as a manifestation of a terrorist attack that clearly illustrated a failure to appreciate the ability of terrorists to turn common items such as planes into lethal weapons capable of inflicting destruction on an unprecedented scale. Furthermore, the use of typologies and hypothesis in the German use of Rasterfahndung knowledge discovery failed to yield positive results in identifying likely members of the RAF and 'sleeper' terrorists. Furthermore, in the US CAPPS knowledge discovery process it was evident that the reliance upon the FAA's known information on terrorists failed in allowing law enforcement officers identify the terrorist attackers who committed the September 11, 2001 attacks.

This may demonstrate that knowledge discovery processes adopting a subject-based approach may be restricted in its capacity to identify individuals likely to be engaged in terrorist acts or preparatory activities.

The shortcomings in the use of inductive profiling methods in the context of terrorism were also identified in chapter two. In particular, it was identified that a common weakness in developing statistical models in terrorism is the fact that acts of terrorism occur relatively infrequently. As a result, it may not be possible to develop adequate models to identify or accurately interpret the results yielded from an application of a knowledge discovery process adopting a pattern-based data mining approach.

Furthermore, Thuraisingham argues that there are at least six challenges in using data mining processes and methods in the context of terrorism.[100]

Firstly, it is not evident 'that the data mining process' can fully manage 'the false positives and false negatives' from the processed data which result from the actual data mining.[101] A false positive is where the application of an algorithm makes an incorrect connection between different information in the dataset which results in identifying an individual who is not connected to terrorism in any way. A false negative is the direct opposite where an algorithm fails to draw together the different information in the dataset to make the connection to identify a terrorist. The occurrence of either is a key challenge for the use of data mining as someone identified from a false positive will become subject to an official suspicion by law enforcement officers with the potential of being stigmatised as being a 'terrorist,' whilst a false negative could result in a terrorist attack occurring undetected. A false negative or positive can occur because the information contained within the datasets may be considered of poor quality due to inaccuracies or incomplete information about specific individuals.[102]

For example, in the second German Rasterfahndung application of knowledge discovery the inclusion of databases on individuals who had acquired an airplane licence directly led to the inclusion of 1,187 who were not considered a risk of terrorism. This can be considered a false positive as the knowledge discovery process had identified individuals likely to be a terrorist threat when the opposite was the case. Furthermore, in considering the US TIA knowledge discovery process it is arguable that the inclusion of mass public and private databases could have created specific difficulties of false positives and negatives simply due to the patterns identifiable from mass availability of personal data.

Secondly, it is not evident that knowledge discovery processes can actually deal with real-time events.[103] Events can occur either in real time or non-real time. Real-time events require an immediate response from law enforcement officers. An example of a real-time threat is the use of chemical weapons without detection or warning by a terrorist group. As it has been identified above, data mining requires vast arrays of available information which is analysed over time to draw out patterns and trends. The fact that real-time events are immediate would appear to challenge the ability of data mining to identify individuals engaged in these acts of terrorism.

For example, the first and second German Rasterfahndung knowledge discovery processes can be considered responsive to particular terrorist events. It is difficult to appreciate how, if at all, this form of terrorist profiling could assist law enforcement officers in the identification of individuals likely to be engaged in terrorist activities where a terrorist attack is live or ongoing. Additionally, the development in the aviation security knowledge discovery processes in the US is evidence of the fact that the changing nature of terrorism threats requires a continual development of data mining techniques in order to take into account new forms and threats of terrorism. This is demonstrated in the weaknesses and deficiencies within the CAPPS system into the CAPPS II system. As terrorism events typically occur in real time, it is arguable that existing knowledge discovery processes may not be capable of identifying new emerging acts of terrorism.

Thirdly, it is evident that knowledge discovery processes using data mining approaches require data to be structured into a pre-processed form so that it is in a useable and searchable state. As social media networks, such as Facebook and/or Twitter, have emerged as a source of potentially valuable data, it seems plausible that existing knowledge discovery processes are unlikely to be able to use these sources given that data tends to be stored in an unstructured way. Previous research on data mining has allowed the development of algorithms to mine structured datasets which contain information in a specific format and structure. However, with the rise of social multimedia there is an increasing vast array of important information continually emerging on social networks which are unstructured databases. The ability of algorithms to process unstructured data is a challenge that grips computer programmers and software developers. The fundamental challenge is the ability to create a programme and algorithm that can turn unstructured data into useful structured data so as to make the information useful for data mining.

Fourthly, a further challenge in data mining in the context of terrorism is actually 'joining all the dots' together to identify important trends and patterns within the datasets. This involves being able to connect the structured data with the unstructured data to identify relevant patterns and trends to make predictions about future terrorist threats. For example, in relation to the development of knowledge discovery processes in the US, it emerged during the National Commission on the September 11 investigation of the terrorist attacks that significant pieces of intelligence and information was available to law enforcement officers in the US which could have allowed the identification of some of the actual al-Qaeda members involved in executing the terrorist attacks. For instance, known individuals suspected of terrorism lived in the US under their real names and undertook flight training lessons over a considerable period prior to the occurrence of the terrorist attacks.

Fifthly, there is still a significant amount of data which may be considered a challenge to not only obtain access to it lawfully but to arrange it into a meaningful and searchable format, given this raw data will almost always be unclassified coming from an array of different jurisdictions across the world. This is data that is contained within databases but remains outside of the reach of data miners due to security or jurisdictional constraints. In the detection and prevention of international terrorism, the jurisdictional boundaries on information is likely to frustrate the ability to fully identify significant databases which may be capable of assisting in the identification of individuals likely to be engaged in acts of terrorism and/or its preparatory activities.

Finally, a further challenge for data mining is the fact that many consider its use a breach of the right to privacy. Throughout much of the early literature, data mining is presented as a dichotomy between security and liberty.[104] The fundamental problem with data mining is the fact that governments are accumulating large qualities of personal information about individuals who may not in fact be engaged in any terrorist activities which may be considered a violation of their right to privacy. The law on privacy differs greatly from jurisdiction to jurisdiction; however, more recently the focus in academic literature has been on the development of systems within technology to ensure the protection of privacy when data mining occurs.[105]

For example, the US TIA knowledge discovery process invoked a thorough investigation by the US Congress which eventually led to its withdrawal due to the refusal of the US Congress to continue to fund this application of knowledge discovery.

In summary it is evident that the discussion in this section cannot conclusively prove that the manifestations of formal terrorist profiling demonstrate input effectiveness. This is largely due to the absence of official information to allow a conclusive evaluation to be made on these manifestations of formal terrorist profiling. The problem with making a conclusive assessment is to do with the methodological limitations of this book which are not necessarily connected with the methods/approaches inherent in manifestations of formal terrorist profiling. As a result, it is contended that for the analytical purposes, the discussion in this chapter shows to a reasonable degree of probability that the profiling methods/approaches analysed in this chapter may be considered as having some degree of input effectiveness. This argument is supported on the basis that profiling by its very nature is an iterative process that improves over time and these profiling manifestations have demonstrated that they are reviewable over time with the potential of being improved.

4.4.3 *The output assessment of the effectiveness of the application of formal terrorist profiles*

The output assessment of the effectiveness of the application of terrorist profiles involves considering the direct and indirect evidence available to demonstrate whether law enforcement officers were able to identify individuals likely to be engaged in terrorism and/or preparatory activities. This involves an evidenced-based assessment of the application of the formal terrorist profiling methods applied in the German and US manifestations.

It is evident in the German manifestation of formal terrorist profiling that this profiling scheme was only capable of actually identifying one individual suspected of terrorism or preparatory activities. In light of the fact that no direct evidence other than one positive identification of a suspected terrorist, it can be concluded that there may be little evidence to support the use of formal terrorist profiling schemes as a basis to identify individuals for arrest and prosecution. Furthermore, in considering the US manifestations of formal terrorist profiling it is not evident how many individuals were actually identified in the detection of terrorism. The DHS website indicates that since 2010 5,700 passengers have been identified through 'pre-departure vetting' as being inadmissible to the US on grounds of being suspected terrorists or being connected with terrorist groups.[106] Furthermore, formal terrorist profiling methods have identified on average 1750 'suspicious' passengers on a yearly basis from around an annual 239 million passengers.[107] Whilst the statistics do not provide information on how many of these individuals were charged or indeed prosecuted with terrorism offences, at minimum it demonstrates the capacity of this manifestation of formal terrorist profiling to assist law enforcement officers identify individuals for enhanced screening. However, considering the absence of the key statistics of arrest and prosecution we cannot conclude whether formal terrorist profiling methods are capable of being of assistance to law enforcement officers in the prevention, detection and prosecution of terrorism. This reveals a complicated picture on the examination of the usefulness of terrorist profiling that may be considered a methodological challenge relating to the application of profiles in the determination of the output effectiveness of formal manifestations of terrorist profiling.

It would appear that in German and US manifestations of formal terrorist profiling there is little actual evidence to support the conclusion that formal terrorist profiling methods can be considered as being effective as an assistive tool for law enforcement officers in the identification of individuals engaged in terrorism or preparatory activities.

4.4.4 The impact of formal terrorist profiling methods

A further measure of effectiveness is to analyse the impact of formal terrorist profiling. This involves questioning whether the discernible impact or likely impact of formal terrorist profiling may be considered as outweighing its usefulness as a counterterrorism tool. Specifically, the assessment of impact is about questioning whether there is any evidence on the individual manifestations of formal terrorist profiling that serves to undermine the input and output effectiveness to the point that the state's moral authority and legitimacy to govern is undermined by law enforcement officer use of this type of terrorist profiling.

4.4.4.1 Germany

A key concern revealed by the discussion on the German Rasterfahndung terrorist profiling scheme was the fact that it required significant amounts of personal data. This effectively meant that the German state had to engage in snooping exercises on its citizens by collecting, storing and analysing vast quantities of personal and public information about its citizens in an attempt to identify those likely to be engaged in terrorism.

In light of the determination of the German Constitutional Court in *B v F*[108] this collection, storing and analysis of personal information was so significant that it represented an infringement of an individual's 'right to informational self-determination.'[109] Although the Court acknowledged that the state's need to protect against the threat of terrorism was a higher ranking constitutional consideration in contrast to the protection of an individual's right to informational self-determination, the concern with the Rasterfahndung scheme related to the sheer array of the private information collected, stored and analysed.[110]

In a subsequent case, *B v R*[111] the German Constitutional Court followed the reasoning adopted in *B v F*. Specifically, the Court concluded that the practice of engaging in a broad collection and analysis of online data belonging to potential suspects which involved the retrieval of information from their social networking profiles so as to identify whether they could be classified as being potential terrorists was contrary to their Constitutional right to informational self-determination.[112]

This manifestation of terrorist profiling questions any determination on usefulness on the basis of whether such levels of state surveillance of its citizens can ever be considered a cost that is worthwhile in the context of the likely usefulness of this manifestation of terrorist profiling. The use of any counterterrorism tool is inevitably going to involve a conflict and tension between the state's right to achieve a minimum level of security and the need to protect fundamental human rights and norms.[113] However, the fact that the state has to descend to the depths of effectively engaging in broad fishing expeditions to make this manifestation work or potentially work goes to the very heart as to whether this manifestation of terrorist profiling can be considered as being potentially harmful by denying citizens their fundamental rights. Therefore, the concern here as identified by the German Constitutional Court is the fact that this level of state surveillance lowers the state to the same level as the terrorists by the denial of fundamental rights.

4.4.4.2 The United States

The discussion on the manifestations of the US examined various terrorist profiling schemes adopted in relation to pre-screening airport passengers and a general terrorist profiling scheme referred to as the TIA profiling scheme. In a similar way to the German terrorist profiling manifestation, these schemes reveal a need for significant quantities of personal information so as to allow the law enforcement officer make sense of the data in the identification of those likely to be terrorists.

The level of concern with these schemes was exposed by the US Congress withdrawing funding of the TIA profiling scheme on the basis of apprehensions it held about the need for the state to effectively engage in mass collection, storing and analysis of private data.[114] However, there has been a report in the *New York Times* which suggests that even though Congress formally withdrew funding of this profiling scheme, the US National Security Agency is allegedly still using a profiling scheme in its covert surveillance operations within the US.[115]

An issue that emerges about these general terrorist profiling schemes, which may be classifiable as being manifestations of formal terrorist profiling, is the fact that significant amounts of personal data is necessary to make them useful or potentially useful to law enforcement officers in the detection, deterrence and prosecution of terrorists. The fact that the US Congress withdrew the funding of the TIA scheme may be evidence of a deeper concern that this type of terrorist profiling is more than likely to outweigh any perceived usefulness in assisting with the prevention, detection or prosecution of likely terrorists. Therefore, it may be the very type of conduct that calls into question the legitimacy of the state, which could compromise the state's ability to engage in any meaningful countering of terrorism.

In the context of the passenger pre-screening profiling schemes including the CAPPS, CAPPS II and Secure Flight schemes, there is some qualitative evidence that reveals some people continuously experience intensive scrutiny without any apparent objective reason for the selection for enhanced examinations. For example, Chadrasekhar identified that since the terrorist attacks on September 11, 2001 there has been an aura of suspicion on passengers who are identifiable from their passenger information as being potentially Muslim.[116] Other research, such as Kleiner also found similar evidence to support the contention that those individuals most likely to be subjected to enhanced scrutiny ports tend to be Muslim which may have been identifiable from their passenger information.[117] However, it has been argued by Cavusoglu *et al* that the Secure Flight profiling programme has the ability to reduce the inconvenience of airport security by ensuring that only those likely to be suspects will be subjected to enhance screening at airports so long as it is continually reviewed for to ensure its accuracy in practice.[118]

Although these qualitative studies are narrow in their focus, they do provide some evidence to at least note a concern with the use of passenger profiling schemes that relate to a potential risk that some passengers may unjustifiably become the focal point of suspicion. It further raises the issue as to whether this type of conduct is something that the state should be engaged in as part of its counterterrorism strategy. The danger posed by such profiling schemes is that the application of these schemes in practice may end up being counterproductive.

4.5 Conclusion

This chapter aimed to identify, explain and evaluate formal terrorist profiling methods so as to investigate to what extent (if at all), and in what ways (if any) terrorist profiling may be useful as part of the law enforcement process of identifying individuals engaged in acts of terrorism and associated preparatory activities.

In considering the formal terrorist profiling methods, it is evident that they provide a basis, at minimum, to identify individuals who may or may not be engaged in terrorism or preparatory activities.

The six challenges identified by Thuraisingham combine to create four fundamental limitations on the use of formal terrorist profiling as being an assistive tool capable of being considered effective in identifying individuals engaged in terrorism or preparatory activities.[119]

Firstly, whilst it can be argued that data mining represents an important tool which may be powerful in identifying trends and patterns inherent in datasets which would otherwise remain unknown, it requires two highly skilled individuals to ensure the smooth running of any data mining activities: a technical specialist capable of writing the computer language necessary to extract the data from the datasets and a skilled data analyst who is capable of interpreting the results for practice.

Secondly, whilst it has been identified above that data mining creates a potential for identifying patterns and trends which would otherwise remain unknown, the results of data mining do not reveal the actual value of the patterns or the trends. Therefore, in some instances the results from data mining may be impossible to interpret as being important or unimportant. The data mining process for counterterrorism must have a system for managing the large data results which emerge from data mining which are not capable of being used for identifying potential terrorist threats.

Thirdly, whilst data mining is capable of making connections between different types of information, it does not automatically always recognise the underlying relationship between individuals and terrorist threats. For example, if an individual is continually buying last-minute flights data mining techniques may be able to reveal the names of the passengers, their destinations and the frequency of their travel but it may fail to provide actual reasons as to why last-minute flights are being purchased. There may be a variety of reasons aside from the obvious terrorist perspective including reasons relating to the individual's work or personal life. Therefore, the effective use of data mining requires that the process and techniques within data mining may sometimes require greater human input so as 'to make sense of the data' results.

Finally, the greatest limitation upon data mining within the context of terrorism is the fact that there is a significant amount of unknown information on terrorists. As information on terrorists can be largely intelligence based, it tends to be national security sensitive which is only released security cleared law enforcement officers within individual countries.

Therefore, it is arguable that formal terrorist profiling may not necessarily be considered ineffective but rather it may be considered limited in its ability to assist in identifying individuals engaged in terrorism or preparatory activities. However, the discussion on impact questioned whether the broader impact of these terrorist profiling schemes eroded the usefulness of the profiling scheme as a counterterrorism tool. The challenge with these manifestations of terrorist profiling is whether the potential effectiveness of the construction and application of profiles is cast in doubt by the broader impact of their use in practice to the point that any discernable usefulness of terrorist profiling is eroded.

It is important to acknowledge that the manifestations of terrorist profiling considered in this chapter were reviewable. This reviewability may partially make them somewhat more acceptable in contrast to other manifestations of terrorist profiling which are examined in chapters five and six. For instance, the German Rasterfahndung scheme was subject to review and control in the German Constitutional Court. Additionally, the criticism of the pre-passenger profiling schemes in the US ultimately led to their reviewability with the aim of improving their application in practice. Specifically, CAPPS to CAPPS II improved by using passenger travel data in combination with public information before selecting individuals for enhanced scrutiny.[120] The further reform of CAPPS II into the Secure Flight programme in 2010 allowed for greater use of known terrorist watch lists as the basis to support the identification of passengers for enhanced screening in addition to relying merely on their passenger data.

As counterterrorism raises a tension between achieving security and human rights, then at minimum manifestations of formal terrorist profiling may provide some basis to allow the protection of human rights to be accommodated within counterterrorism policy given that manifestations of formal terrorist profiling are reviewable. In final conclusion an argument may be made that formal manifestations have the potential to be capable of assisting law enforcement officers identify those likely to be involved in terrorism or its associated preparatory activities. Although the impact of such manifestations of terrorist profiling call into question the legitimacy of a state's counterterrorism policy but nevertheless may be considered as at minimum accommodating human rights within counterterrorism policy.

Notes

1. S. Fienberg, 'Homeland Insecurity: Data Mining, Privacy, Disclosure, Limitation and the Hunt for Terrorists' in H. Chen, E. Reid, J. Sinai, A. Silke and E. Ganor (eds), *Terrorism Informatics: Knowledge Management for Homeland Security* (Springer, 2008), 198–202.
2. N. Memon and H. Larsen, 'Detecting terrorist activity patterns using investigative data mining tools' (2006) 3(1) International Journal of Knowledge and Systems Science 43, 44–45.
3. W. Frawley, G. Piatetsky-Shapiro and C. Matheus, 'Knowledge discovery in databases: an overview' (1992) 14(3) AI Magazine 57, 57.
4. T. Imilienski and H. Mannila, 'A database perspective on knowledge discovery' (1996) 39(11) Communications of the ACM 58, 60.
5. V. Devedzic, 'Knowledge Discovery and Data Mining in Databases' in S. Chang (ed), *Software Engineering and Knowledge Discovery Vol 1 Fundamentals* (World Scientific Publishing Company, 2001), 615–617.
6. P. Adriaans and D. Zanintge, *Data Mining* (Addison-Wesley, 1996), 25–29.
7. R. Roiger and M. Geatz, *Data Mining: A Tutorial based Primer* (Addison Wesley, 2002), 147–174.
8. ibid.
9. U. Fayyad, G. Piatetsky-Shapiro and P. Smyth, 'From data mining to knowledge discovery in databases' (1996) 17(3) Artificial Intelligence Magazine 37, 37. See also: M. De Rosa, *Data Mining and Data Analysis for Counter-Terrorism* (CSIS Press, 2004), 10.
10. W. Inmon, 'Data warehouse and data mining' (1996) 39(11) Communications of the ACM 49, 49.

11. ibid.
12. K. Taipale, 'Data mining and domestic security: connecting the dots to make sense of the data' (2003) 5 The Columbia Science and Technology Law Review 1, 1–4.
13. ibid, 14.
14. B. Thuraisingham, *Data Mining: Technologies, Techniques, Tools and Trends* (CRC Press, 1999), 110–112.
15. S. Vanderlooy, J. Verbeck and J. Van Den Herik, 'Towards privacy preserving data mining in law enforcement' (2007) 2(4) Journal of International Commercial Law and Technology 202, 204.
16. Rosa, 'Data Mining and Data Analysis for Counter-Terrorism' (n9), 3.
17. J. Han and M. Kamber, *Data Mining: Concepts and Techniques* (Morgan Kaufmann, 2001), 8–9.
18. T. Zarksy, 'Governmental data mining and its alternatives' (2011) 116 (2) Penn State Law Review 285, 291.
19. Adriaans and Zantinge, 'Data Mining' (n6), 34–36.
20. 'Machine learning methods' is the use of digital algorithmic programmes which automatically improve the accuracy of a search for information as more and more data is imputed into the programme. For example, the more an individual search is performed on 'Google' the more accurate the search returns will become as 'Google' is able to make more successful connections between the individual and the searchable data.
21. Vanderlooy, Verbeck and van Den Herik, 'Towards privacy preserving data mining in law enforcement' (n15), 203.
22. Han and Kamber, 'Data Mining: Concepts and Techniques' (n17), 8–9.
23. N. Memon, D. Hicks and H. Larsen, 'How investigative data mining can help intelligence agencies to discover dependence of nodes in terrorist networks' (2007) 4632 Lecture Notes in Computer Science 430, 430–435.
24. ibid.
25. Devedzic 'Knowledge Discovery and Data Mining in Databases' (n5), 621.
26. N. Memon, J. Farley, D. Hicks and T. Rosenorn, *Mathematical Methods in Counterterrorism* (Springer Publications, 2009), 2–8.
27. K. Dahbur and T. Muscarello, 'Classification system for serial criminal patterns' (2003) 11(4) Artificial Intelligence and Law Volume 251, 251–255.
28. A. Blokland, D. Nagin and P. Nieuwbeerta, 'Life span offending trajectories of a Dutch conviction cohort' (2005) 43(4) Criminology 919, 919–925. J. De Bruin, T. Cocx, W. Kosters, J. Laros and J. Kok, 'Data Mining Approaches to Criminal Career Analysis' in C. Clifton and N. Zhong (eds), *IEEE International Conference on Data Mining* (IEEE Computer Society, 2006), 171–177.
29. A. Adderley and P. Musgrove 'Data Mining Case Study: Modelling the Behaviour of Offenders who Commit Serious Sexual Assaults' in F. Provost and R. Srikant (eds), *ACM SIGKDD International Conference on Knowledge Discovery and Data Mining* (Association for Computer Machinery, 2001), 215–220.
30. D. Ramierz, J. Hoopes and T. Quinlan, 'Defining racial profiling in a post September 11th world' (2003) 40(3) American Criminal Law Review 1195, 1195–1197.
31. C. Zeugmann, *The Trade-off Between Civil Liberties and Security in the United States and Germany After 9/11/01* (Diplomica Verlag, 2008), 42.
32. S. Aust, *Der Baader-Meinhof-Komplex* (2nd Ed, Goldmann Publishing, 1998), 211. See also: D. Hauser, *Baader und Herold – Beschreibung eines Kampfes* (Alexander Fest Verlag Publishing, 1997).
33. W. Achelpohler and H. Niehaus, 'Data screening as a means of preventing Islamist terrorist attacks on Germany' (2004) 5(5) German Law Journal 495, 496–498.
34. W. Heinz, 'Germany: State Responses to Terrorist Challenges and Human Rights' in A. Brysk (ed), *National Insecurity and Human Rights: Democracies Debate Counterterrorism* (University of California Press, 2007), 162.

35. ibid.
36. BVerfGE, 1 B v F 1/74.
37. O. Lepsius, 'Freiheit, Sicherheit, Terror Die Rechtslage in Deutschland' in T. Jagger, A. Hose and K. Oppermann (eds), *Transatlantische Beziehungen, Sicherheit – Wirtschaft – Offenlichkeit* (VS Verlag fur Sozialwissenschaften, 2005), 322.
38. For example, Gesetz zur Anderung der Strafprozessordnung 1978 and Gesetz zur Bekampfung des Terrorismus 1987 provided law enforcement officers with greater specialist preventative powers to manage the threat of terrorism emanating from rise of the RAF.
39. Lepsius, 'Freiheit, Sicherheit, Terror Die Rechtslage in Deutschland' (n37), 322.
40. For a discussion on the construction of the right to security on the basis of the state's obligation in the Constitution to proactively protect the right to life please see: M. Kutscha, 'Mehr Innere Sicherheit durch weinger Freiheit' in Humanistische Union e. V (ed), *Innere Sicherheit als Gefahr* (Berlin: Humanistische Union, 2003), 32–47. See also for a critique of the decision of the Constitutional Court in *B v F* (1974): M. Kutscha, 'Unerwunschte Hausaufgaben, Die Desetzgeber ignorieren die Vorgaben des Verfassungsgerichts' (2005) 82(3) Burgerrecht und Polizei Clip 16.
41. Heinz, 'Germany: State Responses to Terrorist Challenges and Human Rights' (n34), 165–167.
42. P. Butz, I. Todlicher and W. Willi, *Die Geschichte Der RAF* (Rowohlt Berlin, 2005), 25–29.
43. ibid.
44. S. Hilbrans, 'Neue Grenzen fur die Uberwacher? Zur jungsten Entwicklung der Verfassungsprechung' (2005) 82(3) Burgerrecht und Polizei Clip 24, 24–26.
45. National Research Council, *Protecting Individual Privacy in the Struggle Against Terrorists: A Framework for Programme Assessment* (National Academic Press, 2008), 215–219.
46. T. Berndt and D. Schiffermuller, *Raster Fur Europa – Minister Schily und sein Fahndungsflop*, Panorama, Hamburg, April 8, 2004, available at: http://daserste.ndr.de/panorama/archiv/2004/erste8498.html (accessed 01st July 2020).
47. Bundesverfassungsgericht (BVerfG – Federal Constitutional Court) (2006) Neue Juristische Wochenschrift (NJW) 59: 1939.
48. National Research Council, 'Protecting Individual Privacy in the Struggle Against Terrorists: A Framework for Programme Assessment' (n45), 219.
49. *B v R* 518/02 (*Bundesverfassungsgericht*, 4th April 2006), para 8.
50. ibid.
51. ibid, para 9.
52. ibid, para 13.
53. ibid, para 30.
54. ibid, para 9.
55. ibid.
56. O. Lepsius, 'Liberty, security and terrorism: the legal position in Germany' (2004) 5(5) German Law Journal 435, 437–440.
57. ibid.
58. National Research Council, 'Protecting Individual Privacy in the Struggle Against Terrorists: A Framework for Programme Assessment' (n45), 215–216.
59. F. Cate, 'Governmental data mining: the need for a legal framework' (2008) 43 Harvard Civil Rights-Civil Liberties Law Review 435, 440–450.
60. L. BeVier, 'Information about individuals in the hands of government: some reflections on privacy protection' (1995) 4 William and Mary Bill of Rights Law Journal 455, 456.
61. K. Polanco, 'The Fourth Amendment Challenge to DNA Samples of Arrestees Pursuant to the Justice for All Act of 2004' (2005) 27 University of Arkansas Little Rock Law Review 483, 489–490.

62. For example: CNN, 'US didn't connect 'dots' before 9/11', May 15, 2002, available at: http://articles.cnn.com/2002-05-15/us/inv.fbi.terror_1_memo-dots-osama-bin?_s=PM:US (accessed 01st July 2020). See also: N. Lewis, 'FBI chief admits 9/11 might have been detectable', May 29, 2002, The New York Times, available at: http://www.nytimes.com/2002/05/30/us/traces-of-terror-the-overview-fbi-chief-admits-9-11-might-have-been-detectable.html (accessed 01st July 2020).
63. For example: H. Chen, T. Raghu, R. Ramesh, A. Vince and D. Zeng (eds), *Handbooks in Information Systems: National Security* (Elsevier, 2007). See also: T. Raghu and H. Chen, 'Cyberinfrastructure for homeland security: advances in information sharing, data mining, and collaboration systems' (2007) 43(4) Decision Support Systems 1321.
64. National Commission on Terrorist Attacks Upon the United States, *The Aviation Security System and the 9/11 Attacks* (National Commission on Terrorist Attacks Upon the United States, 2004), available at: http://www.au.af.mil/au/awc/awcgate/911_commission/staff_statement_3.pdf (accessed 01st July 2020). See also: US Select Committee on Intelligence and US House Permanent Select Committee on Intelligence, *Joint Inquiry into the Intelligence Community Activities Before and After the Terrorist Attacks of September 11th* (Government Printing Office, 2002), available at: http://www.gpo.gov/fdsys/pkg/CRPT-107hrpt792/pdf/CRPT-107hrpt792-ERRATA.pdf (accessed 01st July 2020).
65. Taipale, 'Data mining and domestic security: connecting the dots to make sense of the data' (n12), 3.
66. For example: US Department of Justice, 'Fact sheet: shifting from prosecution to prevention: redesigning the justice department to prevent future acts of terrorism' (2002), available at: http://ontario.worldlibrary.net/Members/Government_Library/Collection/2002/05/fbireorganizationfactsheet.pdf (accessed 01st July 2020).
67. ibid.
68. J. Risen and E. Lichtblau, 'Bush lets U.S. spy on callers without courts', The New York Times, December 16, 2005.
69. L. Cauley, 'NSA has massive database of Americans' phone calls', USA Today, May 11, 2006.
70. *Homeland Security Act 2002* (HSA) (Pub.L. 107–296, 116 Stat. 2135, enacted November 25, 2002), §201(d)(14).
71. Cate, 'Governmental data mining: the need for a legal framework' (n59), 444–445.
72. ibid.
73. US Department of Treasury, *A Report to Congress in Accordance with § 357 of the United and Strengthening America by Providing Appropriate Tools Required to Intercept and Obstruct Terrorism Act 2001* (GPO, 2002), available at http://www.fincen.gov/news_room/rp/files/hawalarptfinal11222002.pdf (accessed 01st July 2020), 4.
74. ibid, 6.
75. FinCEN, 'Guidance on preparing a complete and sufficient suspicious activity report narrative', available at: http://www.fincen.gov/statutes_regs/files/sarnarrcompletguidfinal_112003.pdf (accessed 02nd July 2020).
76. ibid, 4.
77. ibid.
78. W. Beaty, *Suspicious Activity and Currency Transaction Reports: Balancing Law Enforcement Utility and Regulation Requirements: Hearings Before Sub Committee on Oversight and Investigation of the Homeland Commission on Financial Services* (GOP, 2007).
79. ibid, 9.
80. National Commission on Terrorist Attacks Upon the United States, *The Aviation Security System and the 9/11 Attacks* (n64).

81. ibid, 6.
82. US General Accounting Office, *Aviation Security: Computer Assisted Passenger Pre-screening System Faces Significant Implementation Challenges* (GAO, 2004), available at: http://www.gao.gov/new.items/d04385.pdf (accessed 02nd July 2020).
83. ibid, 6–7.
84. Taipale, 'Data mining and domestic security: connecting the dots to make sense of the data' (n12), 37.
85. US Department of Homeland Security, *TSA's CAPPS II Gives Equal Weight to Privacy* (GAO, 2003), available at: http://faculty.uml.edu/bleblanc/44.115/pdf/CAPPS%20II.pdf (accessed 02nd July 2020).
86. Electronic Frontier Foundation, *CAPPS II: Governmental Surveillance via Passenger Profiling* (EFF, 2004).
87. J. Seifert, *Data Mining and Homeland Security: An Overview* (Congressional Research Service, 2009), 5–6.
88. Secure Flight Program, 72 Federal Register 48,356 Oct 24, 2007, available at: http://www.gpo.gov/fdsys/pkg/FR-2007-10-24/pdf/07-5254.pdf (accessed 02nd July 2020).
89. ibid.
90. Transport Security Administration, *Secure Flight Program 73* (Department of Homeland Security, 2008).
91. ibid.
92. J. Thai, 'Is data mining ever a search under Justice Steven's Fourth Amendment?' (2006) 74 Fordham Law Review 1731, 1738–1741.
93. D. Solove, 'Data mining and the security-liberty debate' (2008) 75 University of Chicago Law Review 343, 344–345.
94. Thai, 'Is data mining ever a search under Justice Steven's Fourth Amendment?' (n92), 1738–1741.
95. S. Harris, 'Giving in to the surveillance state', New York Times, August 22, 2012, available at: https://www.nytimes.com/2012/08/23/opinion/whos-watching-the-nsa-watchers.html (accessed 12th June 2020).
96. Information Awareness Office, US Department of Defence, *Report to Congress Regarding the Terrorism Information Awareness Program* (US Department of Defence, 2003).
97. ibid.
98. ibid.
99. B. Thuraisingham, 'Data Mining for Counter-terrorism' in H. Kargupta, A. Joshi, K. Sivakumar and Y. Yesha (eds), *Data Mining: Next Generation Challenges and Future Directions* (American Association for Artificial Intelligence, 2004), 179–180.
100. ibid, 158–159.
101. T. Maxwell, 'Information policy, data mining and national security: false positives and unidentified negatives' (2005) HICCSS 1, 4.
102. De Rosa, 'Data Mining and Data Analysis for Counter-Terrorism' (n9), 14.
103. J. Jones and J. Harper, 'Effective counter-terrorism and the limited role of predictive data mining' (2006) 584 Policy Analysis 1, 9–10.
104. H. Tillema, 'A Brief Theory of Terrorism and Technology' in T. Ghosh, M. Prelas and D. Viswanath (eds), *Science and Technology of Terrorism and Counter-terrorism* (Marcel Dekker, 2002), chapter 2.
105. Solove, 'Data Mining and the Security-Liberty Debate' (n91), 355–362.
106. US Department of Homeland Security, 'Preventing terrorism results', available at: http://www.dhs.gov/topic/preventing-terrorism-results (accessed 14th May 2020).
107. US Department of Homeland Security, 'Preventing the next attack: TSA's role in keeping our transportation systems secure', available at: https://www.tsa.gov/news/testimony/2017/11/08/preventing-next-attack-tsas-role-keeping-our-transportation-systems (accessed 14th June 2020).

108. 115 BverfGE 320 (2006).
109. ibid, para 324–331.
110. ibid, para 341–349.
111. 120 BVerfGE 274 (2008).
112. R. Miller, 'Balancing security and liberty in Germany' (2010) 4 Journal of National Security Law and Policy 369, 371–373.
113. F. Teson, 'Liberty Security' in R. Wilson (ed), *Human Rights in the 'War on Terror'* (Cambridge University Press, 2005).
114. Information Awareness Office, US Department of Defence, *Report to Congress Regarding the Terrorism Information Awareness Program* (US Department of Defence, 2003), 22–24.
115. Harris, 'Giving in to the surveillance state' (n93).
116. C. Chandrasekhar, 'Flying while brown: federal civil rights remedies to post 9/11 airline racial profiling of South Asians' (2003) 10 Asian American Law Journal 215, 216–217.
117. Y. Kleiner, 'Racial profiling in the name of national security: protecting minority travelers' civil liberties in the age of terrorism' (2010) 30 Boston College Third World Law Journal 103, 104–105.
118. J. Sweifert, *Data Mining and Homeland Security* (CRS Reports, 2007), 3, available at: http://www.fas.org/sgp/crs/intel/RL31798.pdf (accessed 3rd September 2019).
119. ibid.
120. C. Berrick, *Aviation Security: Secure Flight Development and Testing Under Way, but Risks Should Be Managed as System Is Further Developed* (GAO, 2005), 44–46.

Bibliography

Achelpohler, W. and Niehaus, H., 'Data screening as a means of preventing Islamist terrorist attacks on Germany' (2004) 5(5) *German Law Journal* 495.

Adderley, A. and Musgrove, P., 'Data Mining Case Study: Modelling the Behaviour of Offenders who Commit Serious Sexual Assaults' in F. Provost and R. Srikant (eds), *ACM SIGKDD International Conference on Knowledge Discovery and Data Mining* (Association for Computer Machinery, 2001).

Adriaans, P. and Zanintge, D., *Data Mining* (Addison-Wesley, 1996).

Aust, S., *Der Baader-Meinhof-Komplex* (2nd, Ed, Goldmann Publishing, 1998), 211. See also: D. Hauser, *Baader und Herold Beschreibung eines Kampfes* (Alexander Fest Verlag Publishing, 1997).

B v R, 518/02 (Bundesverfassungsgericht, 4th April 2006) (120 BVerfGE 274 (2008)).

Beaty, W., *Suspicious Activity and Currency Transaction Reports: Balancing Law Enforcement Utility and Regulation Requirements: Hearings Before Sub Committee on Oversight and Investigation of the Homeland Commission on Financial Services* (GOP, 2007).

Berndt, T. and Schiffermuller, D., *Raster Fur Europa Minister Schily und sein Fahndungsflop*, Panorama, Hamburg, April 8, 2004, available at: http://daserste.ndr.de/panorama/archiv/2004/erste8498.html (accessed 01st July 2020).

BeVier, L., 'Information about individuals in the hands of government: some reflections on privacy protection' (1995) 4 *William and Mary Bill of Rights Law Journal* 455.

Blokland, A., Nagin, D. and Nieuwbeerta, P., 'Life span offending trajectories of a Dutch conviction cohort' (2005) 43(4) *Criminology* 919.

Bundesverfassungsgericht (BVerfG Federal Constitutional Court) (2006) *Neue Juristische Wochenschrift (NJW)* 59: 1939.

Butz, P., Todlicher, I. and Willi, W., *Die Geschichte Der RAF* (Rowohlt Berlin, 2005).
BVerfGE, 1 B v F 1/74 (115 BverfGE 320 (2006)).
Cate, F., 'Governmental data mining: the need for a legal framework' (2008) 43 *Harvard Civil Rights-Civil Liberties Law Review* 435.
Cauley, L., 'NSA has massive database of Americans' phone calls', USA Today May 11, 2006.
Chandrasekhar, C., 'Flying while brown: federal civil rights remedies to post 9/11 airline racial profiling of South Asians' (2003) 10 *Asian American Law Journal* 215.
Chen, H., Raghu, T., Ramesh, R., Vince, A. and Zeng, D., (eds) *Handbooks in Information Systems: National Security* (Elsevier, 2007).
CNN, 'US didn't connect 'dots' before 9/11', May 15, 2002, available at: http://articles.cnn.com/2002-05-15/us/inv.fbi.terror_1_memo-dots-osama-bin?_s=PM:US (accessed 01st July 2020).
Dahbur, K. and Muscarello, T., 'Classification system for serial criminal patterns' (2003) 11(4) *Artificial Intelligence and Law Volume* 251.
de Bruin, J., Cocx, T., Kosters, W., Laros, J. and Kok, J., 'Data Mining Approaches to Criminal Career Analysis' in C. Clifton and N. Zhong (eds), *IEEE International Conference on Data Mining* (IEEE Computer Society, 2006).
de Rosa, M., *Data Mining and Data Analysis for Counter-Terrorism* (CSIS Press, 2004).
Devedzic, V., 'Knowledge Discovery and Data Mining in Databases' in S. Chang (ed), *Software Engineering and Knowledge Discovery Vol 1 Fundamentals* (World Scientific Publishing Company, 2001).
Electronic Frontier Foundation, *CAPPS II: Governmental Surveillance via Passenger Profiling* (EFF, 2004).
Fayyad, U., Piatetsky-Shapiro, G. and Smyth, P., 'From data mining to knowledge discovery in databases' (1996) 17(3) *Artificial Intelligence Magazine* 37.
Fienberg, S., 'Homeland Insecurity: Data Mining, Privacy, Disclosure, Limitation and the Hunt for Terrorists' in H. Chen, E. Reid, J. Sinai, A. Silke and E. Ganor (eds), *Terrorism Informatics: Knowledge Management for Homeland Security* (Springer, 2008).
FinCEN, 'Guidance on preparing a complete and sufficient suspicious activity report narrative', available at: http://www.fincen.gov/statutes_regs/files/sarnarrcompletguidfinal_112003.pdf (accessed 02nd July 2020).
Frawley, W., Piatetsky-Shapiro, G. and Matheus, C., 'Knowledge discovery in databases: an overview' (1992) 14(3) *AI Magazine* 57.
Han, J. and Kamber, M., *Data Mining: Concepts and Techniques* (Morgan Kaufmann, 2001).
Harris, S., 'Giving in to the surveillance state', New York Times, August 22, 2012, available at: https://www.nytimes.com/2012/08/23/opinion/whos-watching-the-nsa-watchers.html (accessed 12th June 2020).
Heinz, W., 'Germany: State Responses to Terrorist Challenges and Human Rights' in A. Brysk (ed), *National Insecurity and Human Rights: Democracies Debate Counterterrorism* (University of California Press, 2007).
Hilbrans, S., 'Neue Grenzen fur die Uberwacher? Zur jungsten Entwicklung der Verfassungsprechung' (2005) 82(3) *Burgerrecht und Polizei Clip* 24.
Imilienski, T. and Mannila, H., 'A database perspective on knowledge discovery' (1996) 39(11) *Communications of the ACM* 58.
Information Awareness Office, US Department of Defence, *Report to Congress Regarding the Terrorism Information Awareness Program* (US Department of Defence, 2003).

Inmon, W., 'Data warehouse and data mining' (1996) 39(11) *Communications of the ACM* 49.

Jones, J. and Harper, J., 'Effective counter-terrorism and the limited role of predictive data mining' (2006) 584 *Policy Analysis* 1.

Kleiner, Y., 'Racial profiling in the name of national security: protecting minority travelers' civil liberties in the age of terrorism' (2010) 30 *Boston College Third World Law Journal* 103.

Kutscha, M., 'Mehr Innere Sicherheit durch weinger Freiheit' in Humanistische Union e. V (ed), *Innere Sicherheit als Gefahr*(Berlin: Humanistische Union, 2003).

Kutscha, M., 'Unerwunschte Hausaufgaben, Die Desetzgeber ignorieren Die Vorgaben des Verfassungsgerichts' (2005) 82(3) *Burgerrecht und Polizei Clip* 16.

Lepsius, O., 'Liberty, security and terrorism: the legal position in Germany' (2004) 5(5) *German Law Journal* 435.

Lepsius, O., 'Freiheit, Sicherheit, Terror Die Rechtslage in Deutschland' in T. Jagger, A. Hose and K. Oppermann (eds), *Transatlantische Beziehungen, Sicherheit Wirtschaft Offenlichkeit* (VS Verlag fur Sozialwissenschaften, 2005).

Lewis, N., 'FBI chief admits 9/11 might have been detectable', May 29, 2002, The New York Times, available at: http://www.nytimes.com/2002/05/30/us/traces-of-terror-the-overview-fbi-chief-admits-9-11-might-have-been-detectable.html (accessed 01st July 2020).

Maxwell, T., 'Information policy, data mining and national security: false positives and unidentified negatives' (2005) HICCSS 1.

Memon, N., Farley, J., Hicks, D. and Rosenorn, T., *Mathematical Methods in Counterterrorism* (Springer Publications, 2009).

Memon, N., Hicks, D. and Larsen, H., 'How investigative data mining can help intelligence agencies to discover dependence of nodes in terrorist networks' (2007) 4632 *Lecture Notes in Computer Science* 430.

Memon, N. and Larsen, H., 'Detecting terrorist activity patterns using investigative data mining tools' (2006) 3(1) *International Journal of Knowledge and Systems Science* 43.

Miller, R., 'Balancing security and liberty in Germany' (2010) 4 *Journal of National Security Law and Policy* 369.

National Commission on Terrorist Attacks Upon the United States, *The Aviation Security System and the 9/11 Attacks* (National Commission on Terrorist Attacks Upon the United States, 2004), available at: http://www.au.af.mil/au/awc/awcgate/911_commission/staff_statement_3.pdf (accessed 01st July 2020).

National Research Council, *Protecting Individual Privacy in the Struggle Against Terrorists: A Framework for Programme Assessment* (National Academic Press, 2008).

Polanco, K., 'The Fourth Amendment Challenge to DNA Samples of Arrestees Pursuant to the Justice for All Act of 2004' (2005) 27 *University of Arkansas Little Rock Law Review* 483.

Raghu, T. and Chen, H., 'Cyberinfrastructure for homeland security: advances in information sharing, data mining, and collaboration systems' (2007) 43(4) *Decision Support Systems* 1321.

Ramierz, D., Hoopes, J. and Quinlan, T., 'Defining racial profiling in a post September 11th world' (2003) 40(3) *American Criminal Law Review* 1195.

Risen, J. and Lichtblau, E., 'Bush lets U.S. spy on callers without courts', *The New York Times*, December 16, 2005.

Roiger, R. and Geatz, M., *Data Mining: A Tutorial Based Primer* (Addison Wesley, 2002).

Secure Flight Program, 72 Federal Register 48,356 Oct 24, 2007, available at: http://www.gpo.gov/fdsys/pkg/FR-2007-10-24/pdf/07-5254.pdf (accessed 02nd July 2020).

Seifert, J., *Data Mining and Homeland Security: An Overview* (Congressional Research Service, 2009).

Solove, D., 'Data mining and the security-liberty debate' (2008) 75 *University of Chicago Law Review* 343.

Sweifert, J., *Data Mining and Homeland Security* (CRS Reports, 2007), 3, available at: http://www.fas.org/sgp/crs/intel/RL31798.pdf (accessed 3rd September 2019).

Taipale, K., 'Data mining and domestic security: connecting the dots to make sense of the data' (2003) 5 *The Columbia Science and Technology Law Review* 1.

Teson, F., 'Liberty Security' in R. Wilson (ed), *Human Rights in the 'War on Terror* (Cambridge University Press, 2005).

Thai, J., 'Is data mining ever a search under Justice Steven's fourth amendment?' (2006) 74 *Fordham Law Review* 1731.

Thuraisingham, B., 'Data Mining for Counter-Terrorism' in H. Kargupta, A. Joshi, K. Sivakumar and Y. Yesha (eds), *Data Mining: Next Generation Challenges and Future Directions* (American Association for Artificial Intelligence, 2004).

Thuraisingham, B., *Data Mining: Technologies, Techniques, Tools and Trends* (CRC Press, 1999).

Tillema, H., 'A Brief Theory of Terrorism and Technology' in T. Ghosh, M. Prelas and D. Viswanath (eds), *Science and Technology of Terrorism and Counter-Terrorism* (Marcel Dekker, 2002).

Transport Security Administration, *Secure Flight Program 73* (Department of Homeland Security, 2008).

US Department of Homeland Security, 'Preventing terrorism results,' available at: http://www.dhs.gov/topic/preventing-terrorism-results (accessed 14th May 2020).

US Department of Homeland Security, 'Preventing the next attack: TSA's role in keeping our transportation systems secure', available at: https://www.tsa.gov/news/testimony/2017/11/08/preventing-next-attack-tsas-role-keeping-our-transportation-systems (accessed 14th June 2020).

US Department of Homeland Security, *TSA's CAPPS II Gives Equal Weight to Privacy* (GAO, 2003), available at: http://faculty.uml.edu/bleblanc/44.115/pdf/CAPPS%20II.pdf (accessed 02nd July 2020).

US Department of Justice, 'Fact sheet: shifting from prosecution to prevention: redesigning the justice department to prevent future acts of terrorism' (2002) available at: http://ontario.worldlibrary.net/Members/Government_Library/Collection/2002/05/fbireorganizationfactsheet.pdf (accessed 01st July 2020).

US Department of Treasury,*A Report to Congress in Accordance with § 357 of the United and Strengthening America by Providing Appropriate Tools Required to Intercept and Obstruct Terrorism Act 2001*(GPO, 2002), available at: http://www.fincen.gov/news_room/rp/files/hawalarptfinal11222002.pdf (accessed 01st July 2020).

US General Accounting Office, *Aviation Security: Computer Assisted Passenger Pre-screening System Faces Significant Implementation Challenges* (GAO, 2004), available at: http://www.gao.gov/new.items/d04385.pdf (accessed 02nd July 2020).

US Select Committee on Intelligence and US House Permanent Select Committee on Intelligence, *Joint Inquiry into the Intelligence Community Activities Before and After the Terrorist Attacks of September 11th*(Government Printing Office, 2002), available at: http://www.gpo.gov/fdsys/pkg/CRPT-107hrpt792/pdf/CRPT-107hrpt792-ERRATA.pdf (accessed 01st July 2020).

Vanderlooy, S., Verbeck, J. and van Den Herik, J., 'Towards privacy preserving data mining in law enforcement' (2007) 2(4) *Journal of International Commercial Law and Technology* 202.

Zarksy, T., 'Governmental data mining and its alternatives' (2011) 116 (2) *Penn State Law Review* 285.

Zeugmann, C., *The Trade-off Between Civil Liberties and Security in the United States and Germany After 9/11/01* (Diplomica Verlag, 2008).

5 Behavioural profiling

The construction and application of behavioural profiles in the context of terrorism

5.1 Introduction

As a result of the limitations evident from the discussion on the manifestations of formal terrorist profiling in the previous chapter, a question arises as to whether other profiling methods/approaches can be adopted in combination with formal terrorist profiling so as to minimise or address any of the identified limitations.

Therefore, the primary exploratory aim of this chapter is to analyse behavioural terrorist profiling so as to assess whether this manifestation of profiling can resolve some of the limitations evident in the manifestations of formal terrorist profiling examined in the previous chapter. This exploration will inevitably involve assessing whether behavioural profiling can be considered an independent form of formal profiling or whether it exists purely as a complementary form of profiling to support other forms of profiling.

The definition of behavioural profiling can be considered a contentious issue throughout the literature as there is no international consensus on the formal definition of behavioural profiling in the context of terrorism. From a theoretical perspective, behavioural profiling concentrates on identifying physiological human traits that 'contribute to predicting behaviour'[1] so as to measure 'bodily behaviours such as key-stroke behaviour, gait and facial expressions' as a basis to assist law enforcement officers select individuals for enhanced scrutiny.[2]

The discussion in chapter three did not examine behavioural profiling methods/approaches as it is not classified as being a manifestation of formal profiling in comparable terms with those manifestations of profiling examined in chapters three and four. Behavioural profiling can be distinguished from the other manifestations of profiling methods/approaches analysed in chapters two and three as it does not rely on information about any sensitive characteristics, such as race, ethnicity, gender, religion etc. Specifically, behavioural profiling is reliant on identifying and measuring physical bodily movements that transcend the common sensitive characteristics used in other forms of profiling. Behavioural profiling has some elements of a formalised and systematic process to construct and apply profiles but falls a little short of the systematic processes commonly evident in manifestations of formal terrorist profiling. As a result, it is contended that the manifestation of behavioural terrorist profiling examined in this chapter is on the profiling spectrum set out in chapter one but moves towards the informal end of the profiling spectrum.

For the analytical purposes, behavioural profiling can be defined as being any process aimed at preventing, detecting and managing the threat of terrorism that concentrates exclusively on identifying and measuring human bodily movements as a basis for selecting individuals for further and/or enhanced levels of scrutiny. This definition provides the basis to understand the most likely use of behavioural profiling in the prevention, detection or prosecution of terrorism. However, due to the contentious nature of defining behavioural profiling in the context of terrorism, it will be necessary to revisit the definition attributable to behavioural profiling later in the chapter in light of the discussion and evaluation of behavioural profiling methods/approaches and the examination of the manifestations of behavioural profiling.

The aim of this chapter is explored in three parts below. In the first part, the discussion concentrates on identifying, explaining and evaluating the theory underpinning the methods/approaches used to construct behavioural profiles. The identification and explanation of the behavioural profiling methods/approaches assists in conducting an evaluation of these methods in the context of terrorism prior to examining different manifestations of behavioural profiling. The second part progresses to consider different manifestations of the application of behavioural profiling in two countries so as to assess whether the theory of behavioural profiling is evident in the practical application of behavioural profiling. The countries selected are Israel and the US as both provide a different perspective on the application of behavioural profiling approaches in the context of terrorism. In the final section a conclusion draws on the analysis of the construction of behavioural profiles and the different manifestations of the application of behavioural profiling so as to test whether behavioural profiling can be used as a basis to address the limitations of formal terrorist profiling.

5.2 The construction of behavioural profiles

The primary aim of this section is to identify, explain and evaluate the methods/approaches used to construction of behavioural profiles so that we can analyse the applicability of behavioural profiling methods/approaches in the context of preventing and detecting terrorism.

It is contended that in order to analyse behavioural profiling methods/approaches we need to firstly categorise various behavioural profiling approaches so that we can appreciate the way behavioural profiling can occur. Secondly, we need to progress by examining the various methods/approaches that can be used to profile human behaviour so we can fully analyse the applicability of these profiling methods in the context of terrorism. Finally, in light of the categorisation and explanation of behavioural profiling methods/approaches we need to evaluate their applicability in the context of terrorism.

5.2.1 The categorisation of behavioural profiling

According to the literature profiling methods/approaches used to construct behavioural profiles can be categorised in three different ways including 'biometric profiling,' 'psychometric profiling' and 'sociometric profiling.'[3] Each of these require some explanation and it is also important to note that these individual behavioural profiling approaches can be applied individually or in combination with each other depending on the aim of the profiling exercise.

5.2.1.1 Biometric profiling

The term 'biometric' in the context of behavioural profiling is taken as referring 'to the scientific and technological measurement of either physiological or behavioural human characteristics' so as to make predictions about future behaviour.[4] Biometric behavioural profiling concentrates on identifying and measuring two aspects of an individual's physical features, the physical biometric and the behavioural biometric so as to construct a behavioural profile.[5]

Firstly, the physical biometric involves assessing physical characteristics such as finger prints, iris recognition and facial recognition so as to recognise pre-known physical features.[6] For example, law enforcement officers can use physical biometric profiling where they have physical evidence from a crime scene or previous police records about a known criminal or terrorist so as to identify individuals at sensitive locations such as airports, seaports and land ports. Although the physical biometric can be considered as being relevant only where law enforcement officers have pre-known information about a particular terrorist, the point of interest to this chapter is that this category of behavioural profiling demonstrates that behavioural profiling can be used in connection with other human characteristics to assist in identifying individuals for enhanced investigation. This is important in the context of this chapter as it provides an insight into the ways in which law enforcement officers may be able to rely on behavioural profiling in the context of terrorism.

Secondly, the behavioural biometric involves identifying and measuring other physical characteristics such as emotional recognition, sweating profusely, an elevated pulse rate and irregular respiration patterns which may indicate that an individual is under some form of stress indicative of attempting to conceal something from law enforcement officers.[7] This form of behavioural profiling concentrates on identifying common 'habits of the body' which may be considered as a 'signature' of an automated behaviour performed by the individual unconsciously.[8] For example, if an individual in a security line in an airport or port exhibits characteristics such as sweating uncontrollably and/or breathing irregularly it may indicate to law enforcement officers the necessity to subject that individual to an increased level of security, such as questioning, so as to assess whether they merit an enhanced level of screening. Behavioural biometric profiling relies on identifying body traits rather than known knowledge about an individual as the basis for identification for further scrutiny.[9]

5.2.1.2 Psychometric profiling

Psychometric profiling concentrates on evaluating an individual's physical behaviour such as

> human cognition, emotion, motivation and behavioural tendencies, as well as a plethora of observed traits further describing certain behaviours such as speaking and walking.[10]

Although at first instance it may be considered quite similar in nature to biometric behavioural profiling as it focuses on physical bodily behaviours, this form of profiling involves concentrating on identifying emotions and gestures that demonstrate an individual may be concealing something so that law enforcement officers may subject them to an enhanced level of security.[11]

5.2.1.3 Sociometric profiling

Sociometric profiling concentrates on assessing an individual's social connections including 'interpersonal, intragroup, intraorganisational and intracultural aspects of an individual's biological, psychological and social functioning.'[12] For example, sociometric profiling involves assessing an individual's social connection with known terrorist groups or terrorist networks so that law enforcement officers can make some predictions as to their capacity to commit terrorist or criminal acts.

It is important to emphasise here that sociometric profiling can be distinguished from the previous two forms of behavioural profiling as it adopts a broader concept of 'behaviour' by analysing an individual's social connections and interactions as the basis for predicting future behaviour, whereas the previous two forms concentrates on individual human behavioural traits.

5.2.1.4 Summary

Whilst it may be possible to further categorise and refine behavioural profiling approaches, it is contended that the focus of this chapter is to evaluate whether behavioural profiling may be capable of addressing the limitations of formal terrorist profiling and not to trace the origins and history of behavioural profiling. Hence, the examination of behavioural profiling in this chapter serves a different function in contrast to the examination of the criminal profiling methods examined in chapter three. The discussion in this chapter examines behavioural profiling so as to question whether it can be adopted to minimise the limitations of the manifestations of formal profiling already examined in chapter four. In light of the discussion in this chapter it is evident that behavioural profiling approaches, such as biometric and psychometric approaches, can measure human physical traits so as to assist in the identification of individuals for further investigation. This form of profiling relies on physical bodily movements and expressions as the basis to identify and select individuals for further scrutiny and notably relies less on sensitive characteristics data such as age, race, ethnicity, gender, religion or country of origin.

As noted above each of these behavioural profiling approaches can be employed by law enforcement officers collectively or individually which we will discuss in more detail below when we consider the different manifestation of the application of behavioural profiles by law enforcement officers. However, it is sufficient to identify here that the choice of behavioural profiling approach will largely depend on the aim of the profiling exercise. For example, biometric profiling may assist in identifying known individuals by separating known physical and behavioural characteristics, psychometric profiling may assist by identifying individuals purely on behavioural characteristics, whilst sociometric profiling may assist in identifying an individual based on their social connections.

5.2.2 The behavioural profiling methods/approaches

We can also note that each of the behavioural profiling categories concentrate on identifying and measuring behavioural characteristics as a basis to assist law enforcement officers select individuals for enhanced investigation. According to Yannopoulos *et al*,[13] there are three core human behavioural characteristics including 'emotion,' 'gesture' and 'gait' that are capable of assisting in making predictions about future behaviour and are employed in the behavioural profiling categorises identified above.

5.2.2.1 The assessment of emotion

According to Fasel and Luettin[14] and Scherer,[15] individual human emotion can be identified and measured so as to predict future behaviour by segregating the analysis of human emotion into three distinctive stages.

The first stage involves the profiler identifying and selecting the required human emotion by drawing on the study of human psychology to identify common human emotions.[16] For example anger, fear, worry, etc. are all human emotions that may be identifiable from an individual's facial expressions or body composure or movement.[17] Over recent decades there has been considerable work conducted by various psychologists to identify and explain different human emotions identifiable from human behaviour.[18]

The second stage involves categorising the selected emotion into different classes according to body parts so that individual body movements can become predicative of human emotion.[19] For example, a profiler may classify rapid eye movements with fear or worry, or a profiler could classify frequent 'movements in voice or eyebrow corner motions in face analysis' with anger or worry.[20]

The final stage involves drawing on the previous two stage so as to apply and interpret individual human behaviour to identify individuals by their exhibition of emotion.[21]

The three-stage process of identifying, categorising and applying human emotion so as to identify individuals may assist law enforcement officers to select individuals for enhanced investigation.

5.2.2.2 The assessment of gesture

According to Nespoulous *et al*, 'the notion of gesture is to embrace all kinds of instances where an individual engages in movements whose communicative intent is paramount, manifest and openly acknowledged.'[22] Gestures can be classified into two common manifestations, those gestures that follow communication and those that are unconscious gestures occurring naturally as part of human interaction.[23] In the context of terrorism, both forms of gestures may assist law enforcement officers in making behavioural predictions about specific individuals.

In a similar process to the assessment of human emotion, the recognition of gesture as the basis to predict human behaviour can form a three stage process.[24] The first stage involves identifying and selecting the gesture required by the profiler by drawing on the study of human gesture.[25] The second stage involves classifying different gestures with different body parts so that different gestures can become correlated with different predicative intentions.[26] The final stage involves applying the previous two stages so as to identify individuals for enhanced investigation.

5.2.2.3 The assessment of gait

The assessment of gait involves concentrating on analysing human body and muscle movements so as to make predictions as to an individual's future behaviour.[27] Gait can be assessed in at least two ways, firstly the human body can be reduced to a silhouette where profilers concentrate exclusively on body and muscle movements, or alternatively profilers concentrate on individuals so as to assess their body and muscle movements.[28]

The process of assessing gait can be divided into a two-stage process which firstly concentrates on 'a feature extraction phase … [where] motion information is extracted' from the target audience.[29] Secondly, the assessment of gait becomes a 'matching phase' where particular gait movements are matched to the extracted phase so that individuals can be selected for investigation.[30]

5.2.2.4 Summary

The identification and explanation of the selected behavioural profiling methods/approaches above demonstrate that these methods/approaches seek to identify and measure human behavioural traits as the basis to select individuals for investigation. An important point to emphasise is that these profiling methods/approaches do not depend on information about sensitive characteristics but rather are entirely focused on physical behavioural traits so as to discern whether the individual can be considered as being worthy of an enhanced level of investigation by law enforcement officers. The assessment of emotion, gait and gesture reveals a process that draws substantially on psychology as being an indicator of human behaviour. We shall now proceed to evaluate their applicability in the context of terrorism so as to assess whether these profiling methods/approaches represent a way to address some of the limitations identified in chapters two and three of the other forms profiling.

5.2.3 *An evaluation of behavioural profiling methods/approaches*

We can recall that in categorising behavioural profiling above, a distinction was drawn between biometric, psychometric and sociometric profiling. According to the literature there are two inherent criticisms that can be made of this categorisation.

Firstly, according to Canhoto and Backhouse the characterisation of behavioural profiling as being biometric, psychometric and sociometric may be criticised as being artificial in nature.[31] In particular, this approach arguably tends to over-elaborate the distinction between the different forms of behavioural characteristics. For example, some of the profiling characteristics can be considered as being very similar in nature, for example sweating can be classified as being either psychometric or biometric depending on the perspective of the profiler. It is arguable that any critique of this form of profiling must commence by questioning the validity of the distinctions made between each categorisation of behavioural profiling as it reveals the necessity of considerable discretion on the part of the profiler affecting the construction and consequently the application of behavioural profiling.

However, the compartmentalising of different human traits into 'distinct' categories can assist the profiler to adopt a wide approach so as to consider the broadest range of human characteristics used in the identification and selection of individuals for further investigation. In absence of these distinctions, it may lead profilers to concentrate on a narrow range of physiological characteristics, whereas these distinctions may assist in the separation and analysis of physiological traits making it easier to identify behavioural traits worthy of further investigation by law enforcement officers.

Secondly, according to Petherick and Ferguson[32] 'the reliability and validity' of behavioural profiling is closely connected to two interrelated assumptions, the 'behavioural consistency assumption and the homology assumption.'[33] 'The behavioural consistency assumption assumes that' each individual will replicate the same or similar behaviours when committing the same or similar offence.[34] Additionally, the homology assumption contends that individuals engaging in the same or similar offences will exhibit the same or similar behaviours that are capable of being identifiable.

This would suggest that the reliability of behavioural profiling is contingent on the individual conducting crimes or terrorist offences in the same or similar way so as to exhibit common characteristics capable of being discerned by the law enforcement officer. According to Canter a central premise of all forms of profiling is that 'the way an offender carries out a crime on one occasion will have some characteristic similarities to the way he/she carried out crimes on other occasions.'[35] However, as Canter later acknowledges 'a more conceptual challenge to determining consistency, as in all human activity, is that some variation and change is a nature aspect of human processes.'[36] Furthermore, according to Shoda *et al* any analysis and understanding of the consistency of human behaviour must appreciate 'the importance of considering person-situation interactions which means that' behavioural consistency can be altered by the external physical environment.[37] For example, individuals facing security control barriers at ports and airports may be affected by the physical environment of the airport which may alter their discernible behavioural traits resulting in false positives or false negatives.

Consequently, any profiling approach substantially reliant on individuals exhibiting the same or similar behavioural traits may be flawed as individual human behaviour can be altered by the physical environment, thereby questioning whether individuals will exhibit common characteristics in pressurised environments and the degree an individual's behaviour can be altered by the physical environment.

In the context of terrorism there may be an issue as to whether terrorists share the same or similar behavioural traits discernible by law enforcement officers. Research conducted by Mokros and Alison indicates that there is a common correlation between offender characteristics and criminal offences which means that offenders can be classified or grouped according to specific behavioural traits.[38] For example, Woodhams and Toye identify that offenders who commit the same criminal offences not only frequently share characteristics such as 'age, ethnicity, employment status, criminal history and distance travelled from home to the offence location' but also they frequently shared behavioural traits in the preparation and execution of their offences.[39]

However, in the context of terrorism the correlation between terrorists and terrorist offences may not always be as comparable as criminal offences. In particular, the degree of similarity between terrorists engaged in preparing and executing terrorist acts may not necessarily be of similar nature comparable to criminal offenders in their pursuit of crime. For example, extensive research conducted by Crenshaw[40] and Horgan[41] suggests that terrorists are not readily recognisable by their behavioural traits as they are commonly classifiable as being 'normal' and non-distinctive individuals lacking discernible features or traits.[42] This may mean that terrorists may not exhibit any discernible behavioural traits no more than any 'normal' individual. Furthermore, a study of suicide bombers undertaken by Lester *et al* found that attempting to identify common traits between suicide bombers may not only be inaccurate but may be considered extremely difficult.[43] As a result, substantial research on terrorist characteristics may suggest that it may not be possible to identify common behavioural traits from those individuals engaged in terrorism or preparatory activities. This creates a question as to the suitability of using behavioural profiling methods in the context of terrorism.

Therefore, the approaches used in the construction of behavioural profiles are subject to similar limitations identified in relation to other forms of profiling in chapters three and four above. The discussion throughout this chapter demonstrates that there are at least two key limitations concerning the suitability of behavioural profiling methods/approaches in the construction of terrorist profiles.

Firstly, the identification and explanation of the behavioural profiling methods/approaches above reveals that profilers have considerable discretion in the construction of profiles involving substantial individual judgements relating to the categorisation of particular behavioural traits. A key concern raised by the discussion of behavioural profiling methods is the fact that behavioural profiling requires individual profilers to make determinations as to human emotion, gait and gestures which ultimately involves an interpretation of human behaviour.

Secondly, the examination of the behavioural profiling also reveals considerable issues as to the reliability and relevance of behavioural profiling in the context of terrorism.[44] In considering the issue of reliability, according to Popper the profiler 'can never know if one is dealing with a statistical average or a statistical anomaly' when considering behavioural traits.[45] There may be a problem relying on particular traits in light of a growing body of literature questioning whether terrorists exhibit common characteristics or traits capable of detection through behavioural profiling approaches. In considering the further issue of relevance, terrorists may be capable of subverting known behavioural traits so that they can consciously avoid behavioural detection in sensitive locations such as airports and ports.

Consequently, it is evident that the discussion of the behavioural profiling methods/approaches raises a considerable issue as to whether this form of profiling can be considered capable of being applied in the context of terrorism. While the theory underpinning behavioural profiling asserts that it relies on non-sensitive characteristics in the construction and application of behavioural profiles, it may be contended there is a substantial concern as to whether we can apply these profiling methods/approaches in the context of terrorism as a consequence of the identified limitations.

It can be recalled that a key theme of this research is to conduct an evaluation of the effectiveness of terrorist profiling as being an assistive tool for identifying individuals engaged in terrorism or preparatory activities. The first step in the theoretical framework presented in the introductory chapter above involves assessing/measuring the effectiveness of terrorist profiling by conducting an assessment of the 'input effectiveness' of terrorist profiling which concentrates on the methods/approaches used to construct terrorist profiles. In light of the identified concerns of this form of profiling above, there are substantial limitations evident in the use of behavioural profiling methods/approaches in the context of terrorism which may question the measure of the 'input effectiveness' of behavioural profiling.

5.3 The application of behavioural profiling approaches in the context of terrorism

This section will undertake an examination of the different manifestations of the application of behavioural profiling approaches in Israel and the US so as to assess the application of behavioural profiling approaches in assisting law enforcement officers manage the threat of terrorism. Israel is selected as it is commonly regarded as being one of the first countries to apply behavioural profiling methods/approaches so as to prevent and detect terrorism. The US is selected as it is one of the few countries officially recognising the adoption of behavioural profiling to assist in managing the threat of contemporary terrorism.

5.3.1 The application of behavioural profiling in Israel

Israel has faced a growing 'frequency of terrorist acts and the number of deaths and injuries that result have steadily increased during the past 20 years.'[46] Israel is frequently classified in the literature as being 'the epicentre of terrorist activity.'[47] This has resulted in the development of proactive counter-terrorist strategies that are capable of assisting law enforcement officers manage the threat posed by terrorism. According to Harris, the development and origin of contemporary behavioural profiling as an assistive tool for law enforcement officers to prevent, detect and limit terrorist attacks in aviation can be traced to Israel.[48]

The development and adoption of behavioural profiling in Israel's aviation sector has been lauded in the literature as being the 'most successful aviation safety system in the world' as law enforcement officers have 'successfully defended itself from terrorist attacks.'[49] The apparent 'success' of defending the aviation sector from terrorist attack has been commonly attributed in the literature to its development and application of behavioural profiling.[50] Furthermore, the successful detection of 'an explosive device on an El Al fight from Tel Aviv in 1986' is commonly used by the Israelis in support of their aviation security 'system.'[51]

This initial praise attributed to behavioural profiling in Israel appears to contradict the identified limitations above on the application of behavioural profiling in the context of terrorism. Therefore, this manifestation of behavioural profiling can serve as a good means to assess whether the identified limitations are evident in practice.

According to Hasisi and Weisburd the contemporary development of aviation security can be traced to 1968 'after the hijacking of an El Al aircraft' by terrorists which resulted in 'Israel developing terrorist profiles that have been employed ever since.'[52] It is important to remember that behavioural profiling forms part of a multi-layered counter-terrorist strategy aimed at managing the threat of terrorism.[53] However, aviation security at Israeli airports involve at least 'four circles of security' which centre on employing behavioural profiling approaches as a means to identify individuals worthy of enhanced levels of scrutiny.[54]

Firstly, there is a designated 'airport zone' at the external perimeters of the airport where law enforcement officers commonly rely on psychometric profiling to identify 'suspicious' individuals.[55] This 'circle of security' involves conducting an assessment of vehicles and individuals entering the perimeters of the airport zone where law enforcement officers will use 'technology such as weight sensors, trunk X-rays and undercarriage scans ... to inspect' vehicles while 'face to face interaction between passengers and the airport staff is the most important part of' this 'circle of security.'[56] This reveals that law enforcement officers rely on psychometric profiling as one way to identify individuals for investigation prior to their entry into the airport buildings.

Secondly 'inside the terminal and inside the aircraft' biometric and psychometric profiling aid law enforcement officers to identify individuals' worth of enhanced questioning.[57] In addition to the previous layer of screening conducted at the perimeters of the airport, passengers at the entrance and throughout the airport buildings are continually screened by specialist law enforcement officers for discernible behavioural traits. While it would be extremely useful to know the discernible behavioural traits employed by law enforcement officers, this information is not publicly available as if it was known it may assist terrorists subvert detection techniques.

Thirdly, law enforcement officers examine pre-known passenger information provided by airlines so as to identify potential terrorists. This layer of security is

> mainly based on databases and intelligence sources which create 'watch lists' and is also reliant on 'data mining systems' which 'collect dozens of pre-boarding data items from external sources, mainly airlines and travel agencies, about passengers' flight habits, flight itinerary, travel record, whether a car was rented, whether the passenger is flying alone, meal preferences and other data that can inferred from the ticket.[58]

This demonstrates that this manifestation of behavioural profiling is complemented by other formal terrorist profiling methods such as data mining so as to maximise the potential for behavioural profiling to identify individuals engaged in terrorism or preparatory activities.

Fourthly, the final layer of security involves the use of 'special questioning' techniques at the airport by law enforcement officers who seek to distinguish between legitimate travellers and individuals likely to be engaged in terrorism.[59] Behavioural profiling allegedly assists law enforcement officers to identify individuals for 'special questioning' in addition to assessing the responses to the questions asked by law enforcement officers.

At the centre of behavioural profiling in Israel is the observation of an individual's 'body language' so as to make predictions as to whether they merit 'special questioning.' As distinct from other forms of profiling, this form does not rely on information about any sensitive characteristics but rather concentrates on identifying the individual solely on an individual's physical conduct and interaction. Behavioural profiling, in part, can be considered akin to the traditional policing principle of 'reasonable suspicion' where individuals are not subjected to enhanced levels of security unless they create a reasonable suspicion of criminality or in this case terrorism activities.[60]

Although the information available on the application of behavioural profiling in Israel can be considered limited, in an interview given by Rafi Ron who was the Israeli former Head of Aviation Security at Ben Gurion Airport to the US Congress revealed two significant pieces of information on the application of behavioural profiling in Israel.[61]

Firstly, Ron revealed that behavioural profiling is applied to assist law enforcement officers make 'intelligent decisions' in the identification and selection of individuals for enhanced levels of screening so that passengers can be systematically screened in real time without causing a substantial interference to the operation of Israeli airports.[62] This can be considered significant as we can recall in chapter four we identified that one of the core limitations of formal terrorist profiling methods was its inability to screen passengers in real time. This information may indicate that behavioural profiling may be able to assist in the screening of passengers in real time so that the threat of terrorism may be reduced. We will return to this point in the conclusion below.

Secondly, Ron also revealed that law enforcement officers employed biometric profiling of physical characteristics of known terrorists in addition to behavioural biometric profiling by concentrating on identifying individuals who exhibited physical characteristics such as emotional distortions, sweating profusely, elevated pulse rates and/or irregular breathing patterns.[63] This can be considered significant as it may demonstrate that in this manifestation of behavioural profiling law enforcement officers applied a combination of physical and behavioural biometric profiling so as to identify and select individuals for enhanced screening. This may indicate that the effectiveness of behavioural profiling as an assistive law enforcement tool to identify and select individuals for enhanced screening may be contingent on law enforcement officers having some pre-known biometric information on terrorists.

According to Harris behavioural profiling approaches in Israel are primarily conducted by 'highly trained' individuals who undergo specialist courses to firstly identify behavioural traits worth of investigation and secondly in questioning techniques so as to be able to illicit key information from passengers selected for enhanced screening.[64] It can be recalled that in the previous section we identified a concern that considerable discretion was exercised by the profiler in categorising behavioural traits used in the construction of behaviour profiles. This concern may, in part, be addressed by the existence of an adequate level of training so that behavioural profilers can be trained to minimise any potential distorting effect by human input in the process of constructing behavioural profiles.

However, there is some evidence that questions the quality of the training undertaken by staff engaged in behavioural profiling screening in Israel. For example, Blumenkrantz uncovered that behavioural screening is often undertaken by individuals not specifically trained in behavioural profiling approaches.[65] While this evidence may be considered inconclusive, it demonstrates the potential for deficiencies in the operation of behavioural profiling if the profiling process allows either untrained or poorly trained personnel to engage in behavioural profiling.

Although much remains unknown about the precise operation of behavioural profiling in Israel, it is contended by the authorities that the behavioural profiling approaches used by law enforcement officers assists in managing the threat of terrorism by maintaining a zero-terrorist attack statistic at Israeli airports. However, while the official authorities may advance behavioural profiling as a key assistive tool for law enforcement officers in Israel, we must question the effectiveness of behavioural profiling as being an assistive tool for law enforcement officers in managing the threat of terrorism.

5.3.2 *An assessment of the effectiveness of behavioural terrorist profiling in Israel*

As identified in the introductory chapter above the effectiveness of terrorist profiling can be evaluated by considering (a) the 'input effectiveness' which concentrates on the methods/approaches used in the construction of behavioural profiles, (b) the 'output effectiveness' which concentrates on assessing the application of the behavioural profiles and (c) the 'impact effectiveness' which concentrates on assessing the broader impact of behavioural profiling.

In assessing the input effectiveness of this manifestation of behavioural profiling it is evident that Israel relies on some of the behavioural profiling approaches identified in the previous section. In particular, biometric and psychometric behavioural profiling approaches are employed by law enforcement officers at Israeli airports to assist in identifying and selecting individuals for enhanced levels of screening. The discussion earlier on behavioural profiling approaches highlighted two key concerns regarding the input required from profilers in the construction of behavioural profiles as well as concerns regarding the reliability and relevance of behavioural profiling in the context of terrorism.

In considering the first concern, the discretionary input required from the profiler in the construction of behavioural profiles, there is evidence to demonstrate that Israel contends the existence of an advanced training programme so as to train profilers in the skill of behavioural profiling and in questioning techniques. However, the existence of evidence to demonstrate that some law enforcement officers may be engaging in behavioural profiling without any training can be identified as an issue of concern capable of affecting the assessment of behavioural profiling. Furthermore, the absence of information as to the content of training courses may also be identified as a further issue of concern.

In considering the second concern, the reliability and relevance of behavioural profiling in the context of terrorism, there is little or no evidence to demonstrate the reliability and relevance of this manifestation of behavioural profiling in the context of terrorism. The literature is remarkably silent on providing key statistics on the use of behavioural profiling in Israel. In particular, it may be contended that key evidence capable of demonstrating the reliability and relevance of this manifestation of profiling would be statistics on the number of individuals subjected to enhanced screening in addition to the number of terrorist plots foiled as a consequence of the application of behavioural profiling.

The absence of key information makes it difficult to classify the input effectiveness of this form of behavioural profiling as being effective. Consequently, in order to classify the input effectiveness of this manifestation of behavioural profiling we would need more information on the methods/approaches used by Israel so as to determine whether they are capable of addressing the generic limitations of behavioural profiling identified above.

The assessment of the 'output effectiveness' of behavioural profiling can be undertaken by considering the application of behavioural profiles by law enforcement officers in Israel. It is evident from the discussion above that the literature lends support behavioural profiling by identifying the 'success' of law enforcement officers being able to maintain a zero terrorist attack statistics at Israeli airports since its introduction. In order to conduct an assessment of the output effectiveness of behavioural profiling it is contended that this will involve, in part, an assessment of the statistics to demonstrate its capability to identify potential terrorists.

It is challenging to conclusively assess the 'output effectiveness' of the application of behavioural profiles given the absence of official statistics on law enforcement officer usage of this type of profiling. However, this is a methodological limitation of this book given the lack of information on profiling generally. Nevertheless, it is contended that this limitation does not necessarily take away from the analysis in this chapter. Specifically, even if one example were found to demonstrate that this type of profiling assisted in the identification or detection of those involved in terrorist activities, it would not necessarily support a general conclusion to be drawn that this type of profiling could be considered as capable of working. In chapter three, the discussion identified that profiling by its nature should be an iterative process by being able to review the construction and application of profiles in the field. The strongest form of profiling may be considered those manifestations of profiling that have an open and transparent systematic process so that in each use of a profiling method/approach, there is scope for taking into account any learning from previous constructions and/or applications in the field. The more significant question here relates to why this information is not publicly available. It may be to do with the fact that law enforcement officers feel it is not necessary to publish it, or it could be related to national security risks, or at worst the success rate of this type of profiling may simply be unknown. The absence of this information means that the classification of the 'output effectiveness' may be best considered as moving more towards the informal end of the profiling spectrum. This is due to the fact that it is almost impossible to discern if a systematic process exists and to what extent this form of profiling is reviewable.

In assessing the 'impact effectiveness,' it is necessary to consider the broader evidence of the impact of behavioural profiling in Israel beyond the construction and application of behavioural profiles. This is to determine whether the effect or likely effect and associated cost of this type of profiling can be considered as outweighing any potential usefulness. In recent newspaper reports there has been a growing collection of evidence to demonstrate a negative impact of the use of behavioural profiling at Israeli airports affecting particular ethnic minority communities. For example, in an article appearing in the 'Associated Press' concerning the application of behavioural profiling at Ben Gurion Airport Arabs complained that they were frequently subjected to 'enhanced questioning' without any reasonable justification.[66] Similarly in an article by Donnelly considerable concerns were raised that specific ethnic minority communities were being subjected to disproportionate searches and questioning at Ben Gurion Airport as a result of the creation of 'specialist' search areas within Ben Gurion Airport used by individuals with the appearance of particular ethnic origins.[67] A key concern identified by Derfner was the fact that law enforcement officers at Ben Gurion Airport appeared to allow stereotypes to influence the process of selecting individuals for enhanced questioning and screening.[68] While Blumenkrantz identified that official attempts were undertaken to address any perception that particular ethnic minorities were subject to official suspicion by law enforcement officers at Israeli airports, it remains to be seen as to whether ethnic minority communities continue to be subjected to an unjustifiable distinction in treatment at security control areas.[69]

The potential abuse of behavioural profiling has more recently been condemned by an Israeli diplomat, Ambassador Reda Mansour, who contended that an experience by his family through Ben-Gurion Airport in August 2019 was tantamount to racial profiling where they were subjected to enhanced questioning based on a selection prompted by behavioural profiling.[70] Others, such as Kadah, have identified concerns with the process used to identify those passing through Ben-Gurion Airport which relies on behavioural profiling as a key means to identify suspects for enhanced questioning.[71] According to Kadah, passenger luggage is tagged with a code from 1 to 6 with 1–2 being for those of Jewish origin, 2–3 used for Arabs showing no signs of concern and 4 and above being for those identified as being of concern and worthy of questioning. Although, it is entirely plausible that law enforcement officers rely on a range of techniques to identify those of interest and worthy of enhanced questioning/screening, it seems plausible to suggest that at least part of this process is very likely to draw upon a form of behavioural profiling and the evidence appears to show some concern on who is formally being identified by law enforcement officers for enhanced screening and questioning.

This evidence reveals that some ethnic minorities may be facing 'racist treatment' or at least there is a perception of 'racist treatment' at Israeli airports employed under the guise of behavioural profiling. This is where law enforcement officers only employ behavioural profiling as a means to stop particular individuals on their own individual intuition as opposed to the exhibition of behavioural traits. Alternatively, it may be the case that law enforcement officers are labelling the technique they are adopting, either partially or fully, to identify 'suspects' for enhanced questioning as behavioural profiling without much understanding or knowledge of the process involved in the construction and/or application of behavioural profiles. Although this may be considered evidence of a number of isolated incidents, it can be contended that in the absence of official statistics, it is extremely difficult to conclusively determine the impact of this type of profiling in the detection and prevention of terrorism.

Furthermore, the discussion in the earlier part of this chapter highlighted that a core rationale of behavioural profiling is the fact that it exclusively relies on information about non-sensitive characteristics by focusing on physical behavioural traits. Although the theory and the official support for the use of behavioural profiling asserts that it does not rely on information about sensitive characteristics, this manifestation of behavioural profiling provides evidence that contradicts this core rationale which may serve to demonstrate its unsuitability as a tool to assist law enforcement officers identify individuals engaged in terrorism or preparatory activities. The impact that flows from using behavioural terrorist profiling is such that ethnic minorities either are at worst facing 'racist treatment' or at best have a perception of 'racist treatment.' This supports the questioning of this use of behavioural profiling as to whether its cost is worth paying in the context of counterterrorism. If a counterterrorism policy, such as behavioural terrorist profiling, operates in such a way that ethnic minorities feel under official suspicion then this type of conduct lowers the state to the same level of the terrorists, thereby losing the state's legitimacy and moral authority to govern.

In light of this discussion, the issues related to the construction and application of behavioural profiling in addition to the potential impact of behavioural terrorist profiling means that it is unlikely to be considered a useful tool that is capable of assisting law enforcement officers detect, deter and prosecute those likely to be involved in terrorism and/or its preparatory activities.

5.3.3 The application of behavioural profiling in the US

In the aftermath of September 11, 2001, the US adopted a number of 'new' approaches aimed at assisting law enforcement officers manage the threat of terrorism within the US.[72] One such development has been the adoption of behavioural profiling in sensitive locations such as airports, seaports and landports. The Department of Homeland Security (DHS) introduced behavioural profiling through the development of SPOT 'Screening Passengers by Observation Techniques' where law enforcement officers from the Transport Security Agency (TSA) 'observe travellers' faces for hints that they may be a security risk.'[73] SPOT forms part of a broader counterterrorism strategy referred to as the 'Behavioural Detection and Analysis' (BDA) programme.[74] It is significant to note that this manifestation of behavioural profiling represents only one counter-terrorism strategy which forms part of a multi-layered counter-terrorism strategies all aimed at assisting law enforcement officers to proactively manage the threat of terrorism.

SPOT operates by observing 'passengers for certain physical and physiological characteristics and reactions.'[75] Commonly law enforcement officers 'work in pairs and scan passengers at security checkpoints for signs of specific behaviours listed on the officer's checklists.'[76] As a consequence of the high numbers of passengers travelling through airports, law enforcement officers observe passengers simultaneously so as to identify and select individuals exhibiting the pre-defined traits. Similar to the Israeli scheme, SPOT allegedly does not rely on sensitive characteristics such as race or ethnicity but rather concentrates on singling individuals out for heightened security on the basis of their behaviour.[77]

The central aspect of SPOT concentrates

> on an individual's subtle behaviour and appearance – in particular, facial micro-expressions like raising the inner corners of the eyebrows so that brows slope down from the centre of the forehead, the cheeks become elevated and the corners of the lips slightly dip.[78]
>
> Other signs of visual suspicion can include body language and gestures such as slumped posture or excessive pocket patting.[79]

The existence of these physical traits is thought to reveal key information to law enforcement officers capable of assisting in the identification and selection of individuals for enhanced screening.

SPOT involves law enforcement officers screening passengers by scoring their physical bodily behaviours according to 'some thirty possible suspicious behaviours each with an assigned numerical score.'[80] Therefore, according to Wock SPOT aims to rely on 'objective criteria to determine when individuals are trying to disguise emotion.'[81] When individuals are identified and selected for further scrutiny law enforcement officers typically subject them to an enhanced security screening involving 'intrusive questioning, pat-downs or baggage inspections' with the potential for further subsequent re-examinations which may involve law enforcement officers searching governmental databases so as to identify any other relevant information on the passenger intending to travel.[82] The training provided by the TSA consists of a four day instruction course on 'behaviour observation and analysis' with a further 24 hours of field training at an airport before the law enforcement officer commences observation as a behavioural observation officer.[83]

It is evident from the available information on SPOT that it 'relies on the Facial Action Coding System (FACS).'[84] The FACS system relies on facial emotion recognition first developed by Ekman and Friensen[85] which was aimed at deciphering forms of human deception through understanding facial emotions.[86] 'According to Ekman and Friensen faces manifest each emotion similarly irrespective of race, ethnicity or gender.'[87] Consequently, SPOT can be classified as being a form of psychometric profiling which primarily concentrates on facial expressions as the means to identify individuals for investigation.

In the aftermath of September 11, 2001 the DHS maintained 'a list of indicative behaviours of suicide bombers' on its webpage relating to Al Qaeda terrorists.[88] The list was collated from known information about Al Qaeda suicide bombers which identified loose clothing, 'pale face from recent shaving of beards' and individuals who '[do] not respond to authoritative voice commands or direct salutation from a distance' in addition to 'eyes [appearing] as focused and vigilant' and the 'suspect may be carrying heavy luggage, bag or wearing a backpack' as representing key behavioural traits indicative of suicide bombers.[89] The discussion in the previous section identified a substantial concern from research conducted by Crenshaw[90] and Horgan[91] that there may be no discernible traits indicative of terrorists. This list of characteristics may demonstrate that the US authorities view some behavioural characteristics as being indicative of suicide bombers which questions the validity of the assertions made by Crenshaw and Horgan.

The three-step theoretical effectiveness framework identified in the introductory chapter is now applied to this manifestation of profiling so as to assess/measure its likely effectiveness. This involves (a) assessing the 'input effectiveness' by concentrating on the methods/approaches used in the construction of behavioural profiles, (b) assessing the 'output effectiveness' by concentrating on the application of behavioural profiles and (c) assessing the 'impact effectiveness' by concentrating on the broader impact of the construction and application of behavioural profiling.

However, prior to commencing with an assessment of the effectiveness of this manifestation of behavioural profiling Florence and Friedman identify three generic limitations of the SPOT programme which affect any assessment/measurement of its effectiveness.[92]

Firstly, SPOT concentrates almost exclusively on facial emotions as the key behavioural trait which has been criticised by a number of experts who suggest 'expressions do not reflect the inner feelings of the expresser.'[93] Secondly, SPOT relies heavily on the FACS programme created by Ekman and Friesen[94] which only draws on a pre-determined number of facial expressions. The mere fact that we know there are thirty facial expressions listed on the SPOT programme may tend to suggest that it fails to appreciate 'the total repertoire used by a person during his daily life.'[95] Thirdly, SPOT has been developed in a laboratory environment which leads Florence and Friedman to question whether it can be applied outside of laboratory conditions.[96]

5.3.4 *An assessment of the effectiveness of behavioural terrorist profiling in the US*

Aside from these identifiable limitations it is now appropriate to progress by conducting an assessment of the effectiveness of this manifestation of behavioural profiling in light of the framework identified earlier.

In considering the 'input effectiveness' of this manifestation of behavioural profiling we must consider the methods/approaches used in the construction of behavioural profiles. There were two key concerns identified above in relation to this behavioural profiling method/approach centred on the input required by the profiler in the construction of behaviour profiles and the reliability and relevance of the applicability of behavioural profiling in the context of terrorism.

In light of the discussion above on this manifestation of behavioural profiling, behavioural profilers undergo some training in the construction of behavioural profiles which may address some of the concerns relating to the discretionary input required by the profiler. However, whether this training can be considered adequate is open to question as there is no information available on the content of the training provided by the TSA.

In particular, Kleiner argues that 'a mere four days of classroom training on observation and questioning techniques and three days of field practice' was substantially deficient.[97] According to Kleiner any behavioural profiling training programme requires a fundamental understanding of psychology which cannot be taught in four days and limited field practice. Furthermore, Kleiner argues that longer training 'alone does not seem to be the answer, because human beings, [are] not error proof machines.'[98] This may indicate that the problem of training simply exposes a much bigger problem that as humans apply behavioural profiles the entire behavioural profiling process is subject to human error.

In considering the concerns raised above relating to the reliability and relevance of behavioural profiling in the context of terrorism, the US manifestation suggests that the official view attaches considerable value to behavioural profiling. The DHS watch list of indicative behaviours of suicide bombers developed in response to September 11, 2001 suggests that the official view is contrary to the extensive research conducted by Crenshaw[99] and Horgan.[100] In the absence of any evidence to demonstrate the applicability of behavioural profiling methods/approaches in the context of terrorism, it is difficult to classify the input effectiveness of this manifestation of behavioural profiling.

In considering the 'output effectiveness' we must assess the application of SPOT by law enforcement officers. There has been some conflicting evidence on the usefulness of SPOT as an assistive tool for law enforcement officers. A formal review of SPOT undertaken by the US Government Accountability Office (GAO) in 2013 concluded that the TSA did not have reliable statistics to demonstrate the usefulness of SPOT.[101] In light of this report the TSA undertook a review of its SPOT technique, which resulted in limiting the funding, and scope of the programme by removing it from smaller airports. A further formal review conducted by GAO in 2017 also found that the TSA still had no evidence that SPOT was actually capable of assisting law enforcement officers identify individuals likely to be engaged in terrorism.[102]

However, the US Technical Advisory Committee (TAC) presented an alternative view on the usefulness of SPOT. TAC is an advisory committee composed of industry experts and Government officials that advise the US Department of Commerce, amongst other matters, on technical matters relating to the use of technology. According to TAC, the use of SPOT by law enforcement officers was nine times more capable of identifying those likely to be involved in terrorism in contrast to other identification techniques, such as a purely randomised selection of individuals for enhanced screening.[103]

It is unclear from TAC's report as to how it arrived at this determination, but it seems that the GAO required specific evidence to prove that SPOT was capable of actually identifying terrorists. In light of the GAO's two formal reviews of SPOT, it would seem that the TSA does not have this evidence otherwise they would have presented this to the GAO. However, other statistics on the use of SPOT has been presented by Kaye in the *Washington Post* in 2009 that reveal 98,805 passengers were subjected to enhanced security screening at airports across the US as a consequence of SPOT with 9,854 of these passengers necessitating official interview under caution and a total of 813 resulting in arrest for terrorism and non-terrorism offences in 2009.[104] There are currently no statistics available on the successful prosecution of those individuals arrested and the TSA does not provide specific details revealing the behavioural characteristics meriting the subjection of passengers to enhanced security screening.[105]

From a utilitarian perspective, the evidence of the usefulness of SPOT is hotly contested. The GAO casts doubt on the ability of SPOT to actually identify terrorists. However, the TAC report and the statistics presented by Kaye on SPOT tend to demonstrate that it may be capable of assisting law enforcement officers to identify individuals worthy of enhanced screening at airports. Although the official statistics are silent on the number of prosecutions and the number of likely terrorists identified by the application of SPOT in addition to the silence on the indicative behavioural characteristics for selecting individuals for enhanced screening, the statistics demonstrate SPOT's capacity at a purely utilitarian level to identify individuals for enhanced screening. Consequently, at a minimum level SPOT may be considered 'output effective' as the information available on SPOT demonstrates it is at least partially capable of identifying some individuals at airports across the US.

However, in order to conduct a full assessment of this manifestation of behavioural profiling it is necessary to go beyond the input and output assessment of effectiveness by assessing the 'impact effectiveness.' In a similar manner to the discussion above on Israel, the objective here is to determine whether there is any evidence to suggest that the cost associated with this type of terrorist profiling calls into question its potential usefulness.

A common critique identifiable in the literature of behavioural profiling programmes, such as SPOT, is that they operate as a legitimising guise to facilitate racial profiling either in reality or on the basis of a perception.[106] In light of the list of DHS indicative behaviours of suicide bombers identified above, there may be at least a concern that as DHS has not provided any justification for the contents of this list and in fact may be classified as being 'culturally and racially insensitive' to particular ethnic minority communities.[107] In particular, the pale face taken as indicative shaving beards, the apparent inability to respond to 'authoritative commands' and the presence of heavy luggage at airports does not appear to respect the individual autonomy exercisable by individuals practicing their religious or their cultural heritage who may be travelling through US airports.

Although the list of 30 indicative behavioural characteristics used by the TSA to identify individuals for enhanced screening at US airports remains unknown, according to Meyer and Ravich the TSA's early behavioural indicative characteristics affected particular ethnic minority communities without an appreciation of legitimate motivations may affect the broader impact of using behavioural profiling as a basis for identifying individuals.[108] In particular, it is contended by Meyer the consequences of using this form of terrorist profiling is that particular ethnicities become the focal point for official suspicion by law enforcement officers which is not based on any justification for the selection of individuals.[109] Additionally, Ravich poses the question as to whether behavioural profiling is in fact 'rational or racist' and concludes that the evidence available on SPOT reveals that particular ethnic communities appear to be disproportionately focused on by law enforcement officers.[110]

The problem with this type of terrorist profiling in contrast to the manifestations of formal terrorist profiling examined in chapter four is the fact that there is insufficient information to review its application so as to discern its likely impact. The concerns raised in the academic studies above may point to serious issues that leaves much scope to at least question whether the consequences of using this form of terrorist profiling outweighs its usefulness. Even if some of the evidence above is an accurate snapshot of the impact of the SPOT programme, it may be argued in a similar way to the Israeli manifestation that this is the very type of conduct that is likely to be counterproductive by compromising fundamental human rights. As a result, the likely cost of using this form of profiling as a counterterrorism tool may be considered as being counterproductive in detecting, deterring and prosecuting those likely to be involved in terrorism or its associated preparatory activities. The development of a profiling process must be subject and open to review by collecting sensitive information on those stopped and search by law enforcement officers so as to determine whether particular ethnic minorities are subject to a disproportionate investigation by law enforcement officers. This would at least allow for some of the concerns about its application to be addressed and improved over time similar to manifestations of formal terrorist profiling so as to minimise its impact on particular ethnicities.

The discussion on SPOT reveals a disparity between the theory of behavioural profiling advocating the reliance on non-sensitive characteristics and the reality of the potential for its use against ethnic minority communities. Although there is no evidence to demonstrate an official intention by US authorities to apply the SPOT behavioural profiling programme as a means to single out ethnic minority communities as a source of suspicion for law enforcement officers. The discussion demonstrates the potential for the singling out of ethnic minority communities, which is sufficient to characterise SPOT as being ineffective.

5.4 Conclusion

The primary aim of this chapter was to consider whether behavioural profiling approaches used in the construction of behavioural profiles and their application by law enforcement officers can represent a way to address the limitations identified of formal terrorist profiling in chapter four.

In the first section above various approaches used in the construction of behavioural profiles such as 'biometric profiling,' 'psychometric profiling' and 'sociometric profiling' were examined. The examination of these behavioural profiling methods/approaches revealed that the theory of behavioural profiling is aimed at assisting law enforcement officers to identify individuals for investigation solely premised on discernible physical characteristics such as an assessment of human emotion, gait and gesture. As a result, it may seem at first blush that this form of profiling could represent an important way to counterbalance the concerns raised about profiling generally in chapter three and more specifically in chapter four.

However, the applicability of these profiling approaches in the context of terrorism raised considerable concerns as to whether terrorists or likely terrorists exhibit indicative behavioural characteristics capable of being identified through the behavioural profiling approaches. In particular, the 'reliability and validity' of behavioural profiling approaches assumes that each likely terrorist would exhibit the same or similar behaviour each time they engage in an act or preparatory act of terrorism.

Furthermore, the homology assumption assumes that terrorist behaviour can be considered as being the same or similar across groups of terrorists. The literature examined in this chapter questioned the validity of whether terrorists exhibit any particular behaviour discernible through behavioural profiling. Consequently, the use of behavioural profiling approaches to construct behavioural profiles of likely terrorists will be limited by the notion that terrorists are common 'everyday' individuals who do not exhibit particular or discernible traits.

The second section above progressed to consider two different manifestations of the application of behavioural profiling in Israel and the US. In considering the Israeli manifestation, it was noted that there is insufficient information to characterise this manifestation of behavioural profiling as being capable of assisting law enforcement officers in the detection and prevention of terrorism. Furthermore, there is some evidence to demonstrate a negative impact on ethnic minority communities that raises considerable difficulties as to whether behavioural profiling in the context of terrorism is simply a guise for law enforcement officer to select individuals for enhanced screening without any justifiable reasons or rationale.

The potential negative impact of behavioural profiling questions whether the Israeli manifestation of behavioural profiling can actually be considered as being a form of behavioural profiling in light of our discussion on the generic behavioural methods/approaches above. In particular, it was noted in the introduction that a key dimension of behavioural profiling was the fact that it did not rely on the availability of information about sensitive characteristics. However, in the analysis on the Israeli manifestation, there was some evidence to demonstrate a mismatch between the theory and the practice where racial and ethnic minorities were being disproportionately targeted by law enforcement officers using a process labelled as being 'behavioural profiling.'

A further manifestation of behavioural profiling in the US through the TSA's development of the SPOT programme was also examined. This examination found that there are considerable limitations in using SPOT to identify individuals for enhanced screening. The limitations affecting the input and output assessment/measurement of effectiveness may question whether behavioural profiling can be considered as being an appropriate tool to assist law enforcement officers identify and select individuals for enhanced screening. The only positive aspect of this form of profiling is its apparent ability to screen passengers in real time which was cited as a key limitation of formal terrorist profiling methods in chapter four. However, in light of the concerns raised by the construction and application of behavioural profiling it is contended that the concerns far outweigh the advantage of being able to screen passengers in real time.

The general definition of behavioural profiling provided in the introduction tends to support the notion that behavioural profiling exclusively identifies individuals on the basis of their physical activity and interaction in public. However, the disparity between the theory of behavioural profiling which advocates that behavioural profiling does not rely on sensitive characteristics such as race, age, gender, ethnicity, religion, country of origin etc., and the reality in practice in Israel and to a lesser extent in the US reveals an issue of considerable importance which is unresolved by this chapter. In particular, the apparent application of behavioural profiling disproportionately to ethnic minority communities raises the question as to whether the application of behavioural profiling in the context of terrorism can be considered a form of racial profiling. In particular, the two manifestations of behavioural profiling reveal a considerable contradiction between the theory of behavioural profiling as relying exclusively on information about non-sensitive physical characteristics and the reality in practice of this form of profiling being directed at ethnic minority communities without any specific justification. In light of the discussion on human rights in chapter two, it may be argued that this form of profiling is very close to manifestations of profiling that can be categorised as a form of hard racial profiling given that sensitive characteristics appear to be leading the identification and selection of 'suspects' for enhanced levels of questioning/screening.

In final conclusion, there appears to be considerable concerns related to the suitability of behavioural profiling methods/approaches in the context of terrorism that raises serious questions whether, if at all, this form of profiling could ever assist in the detection, deterrence or prosecution of terrorists.

This concern is supported by the two manifestations of behavioural profiling which seem to highlight additional concerns as to the suitability of behavioural profiling as an assistive tool capable of identifying individuals likely to be engaged in terrorism or preparatory activities. The discussion and analysis of the construction and application of behavioural profiles reveals considerable tension between the methods/approaches used in the construction of behavioural profiling and its application in the context of terrorism which questions whether the identified manifestations of behavioural profiling above can actually be regarded as being behavioural profiling.

Consequently, in light of the analysis of the manifestations of behavioural profiling in the context of terrorism cannot sufficiently address the limitations identified of the formal terrorist profiling methods discussed in chapter four.

Notes

1. L. Herbert, 'Othello error: facial profiling, privacy and the suppression of the dissent' (2007) 5 Ohio State Journal of Criminal Law 79, 80–81.
2. J. Candamo, M. Shreve, D. Goldgof, D. Snapper and R. Kasturi, 'Understanding transit science: a survey on human behavior-recognition algorithms' (2010) 11(1) IEEE Transactions on Intelligent Transportation Systems 206, 206–208.
3. IBPP, 'Biometric, psychometric and sociometric profiling' (2003) 15(8) IBBP Online 1, 1–4.
4. A. Yannopoulos, V. Andronikou and T. Varvarigou, 'Behavioural Biometric Profiling and Ambient Intelligence' in M. Hildebrandt and S. Gutwirth (eds), *Profiling the European Citizen: Cross-Disciplinary Perspectives* (Springer, 2010), 109.
5. A. Canhoto and J. Backhouse, 'General Description of the Process of Behavioural Profiling' in M. Hildebrandt and S. Gutwirth (eds), *Profiling the European Citizen: Cross-Disciplinary Perspectives* (Springer, 2010), 47–49.
6. V. Andronikou, A. Yannopoulos and T. Varvarigou, 'Biometric Profiling: Opportunities and Risks' in M. Hildebrandt and S. Gutwirth (eds), *Profiling the European Citizen: Cross-Disciplinary Perspectives* (Springer, 2010), 131–132.
7. Yannopoulos, Andronikou and Varvarigou, 'Behavioural Biometric Profiling and Ambient Intelligence' (n4), 91–98.
8. B. Fasel and J. Luettin, 'Automatic facial expression analysis: a survey' (2003) 36(1) Pattern Recognition 259, 259–260.
9. S. Lozano and B. Tversky, 'Communicative gestures facilitate problem solving for both communicators and recipients' (2006) 55(1) Journal of Memory and Language 47, 47–52.
10. IBPP, 'Biometric, psychometric and sociometric profiling' (n3), 4.
11. J. Hayfron-Acquah, M. Nixon and J. Carter, 'Automatic gait recognition by symmetry analysis' (2003) 24(13) Pattern Recognition Letters 2175, 2175–2176.
12. IBPP, 'Biometric, psychometric and sociometric profiling' (n3), 6.
13. Yannopoulos, V. Andronikou and T. Varvarigou, 'Behavioural Biometric Profiling and Ambient Intelligence' (n4), 111–115.
14. Fasel and Luettin, 'Automatic facial expression analysis: a survey' (n8), 259–261.
15. K. Scherer, 'On the Nature and Function of Emotion: A Component Process Approach' in K. Scherer and P. Ekman (ed), *Approaches to Emotion* (Erlbaum, 1984), 293–294.
16. Fasel and Luettin, 'Automatic facial expression analysis: a survey' (n8), 263.
17. P. Plutchik, *The Psychology and Biology of Emotion* (Harper Collins College Publishers, 1994), 58–59.
18. For example: K. Scherer, R. Banse and H. Wallbott, 'Emotion inferences from vocal expression correlate across languages and cultures' (2001) 32(1) Journal of Cross-Cultural Psychology 76, see also: K. Scherer, 'Vocal communication of emotion: a review of research paradigms' (2003) 40(1) Speech Communication 227.
19. Fasel and Luettin, 'Automatic facial expression analysis: a survey' (n8), 265.
20. Yannopoulos, V. Andronikou and T. Varvarigou, 'Behavioural Biometric Profiling and Ambient Intelligence' (n4), 111.
21. Fasel and Luettin, 'Automatic facial expression analysis: a survey' (n8), 266.
22. J. Nespoulous, P. Perron and A. Lecours, *The Biological Foundation of Gestures: Motor and Semiotic Aspects* (Lawrence Erlbaum Associates, 1986), 25–26.
23. Lozano and B. Tversky, 'Communicative gestures facilitate problem solving for both communicators and recipients' (n9), 49–51.
24. K. Patwardhan and S. Roy, 'Hand gestures modelling and recognition involving changing shapes and trajectories using a Predictive EigenTracker' (2007) 28(3) Pattern Recognition Letters 329, 330–332.

25. K. Oka, Y. Sato and H. Koike, 'Real-time fingertip tracking and gesture recognition' (2002) 22(6) Computer Graphics and Applications 64, 66–67.
26. D. Demirdjian, T. Ko and T. Darrell, 'Untethered gesture acquisition and recognition for virtual world manipulation' (2005) 8(4) Virtual Reality 222, 225–226.
27. R. Collins, R, Gross and J. Shi, 'Silhouette-based human identification from body shape and gait' (2002) IEEE International Conference on Face and Gesture Recognition 351, 352–354.
28. P. Phillips, S. Sarkar, I. Robledo, P. Grother and K. Bowyer, 'Baseline results for the challenge problem of human ID using gait analysis' (2002) IEEE International Conference on Automatic Face and Gesture Recognition 130, 131–134.
29. Yannopoulos, V. Andronikou and T. Varvarigou, 'Behavioural Biometric Profiling and Ambient Intelligence' (n4), 113.
30. ibid.
31. Canhoto and Backhouse, 'General Description of the Process of Behavioural Profiling' (n5), 55–59.
32. W. Petherick and C. Ferguson, 'Behavioural Consistency, the Homology Assumption and the Problems of Induction' in W. Petherick (ed), *Serial Crime – Theoretical Issues in Behavioural Profiling* (Anderson Publishing, 2013), 37–38.
33. ibid.
34. ibid.
35. D. Canter, 'Psychology of Offender Profiling' in R. Bull and D. Carson (eds), *Handbook of Psychology in Legal Concepts* (Wiley Publishing, 1995), 347.
36. D. Canter, 'Offender profiling and investigative psychology' (2004) 1 Journal of Investigative Psychology and Offender Profiling 1, 4.
37. Y. Shoda, W. Mischel and J. Wright, 'Personality processes and individual differences' (1994) 67(4) Journal of Personality and Social Psychology 674, 674.
38. A. Mokros and L. Alison, 'Is offender profiling possible? Testing the predicted homology of crime scene actions and background characteristics in a sample of rapists' (2002) 7 Legal and Criminological Psychology 25, 25–26.
39. J. Woodhams and K. Toyle, 'An empirical test of the assumptions of case linkage and offender profiling with serial commercial robberies' (2007) 13(1) Psychological, Public Policy and Law 59, 62–65.
40. M. Crenshaw, 'Have Motivations for Terrorism Changed?' in J. Victoroff (ed), *Tangled Roots: Social and Psychological Factors in the Genesis of Terrorism* (ISO Press, 2006), 51–61.
41. J. Horgan, 'The Search for the Terrorist Personality' in A. Silke (ed), *Terrorist, Victims and Society: Psychological Perspectives on Terrorism and its Consequences* (Wiley Publishing, 2003), 3–37.
42. R. Schouten, 'Terrorism and the behavioural sciences' (2010) 18(6) Harvard Review of Psychiatry 369, 374–375.
43. D. Lester, B. Yang and M. Lindsay, 'Suicide bombers: are psychological profiles possible' (2004) 27 Studies in Conflict and Terrorism 283, 283–286.
44. Petherick and C. Ferguson, 'Behavioural Consistency, the Homology Assumption and the Problems of Induction' (n32) 55–57.
45. K. Popper, *The Logic of Scientific Discovery* (Routledge, 2003), 14–15.
46. J. Weiner, 'Terrorism: Israel's legal responses' (1987) 14 Syracuse Journal of International and Comparative Law 183, 183.
47. D. Harris, *Good Cops: The Case for Preventive Policing* (The New Press, 2005), 214–215.
48. ibid, 214.
49. D. Harris, 'New risks, new tactics: an assessment of the re-assessment of racial profiling in the wake of September 11, 2001' (2004) 4 Utah Law Review 913, 941.

50. Harris, 'Good Cops: The Case for Preventive Policing' (n47), 214.
51. R. Whitaker, 'Behavioural Profiling in Israeli Aviation Security as a Tool for Social Control' in E. Zureik, D. Lyon and Y. Abu-Laban (eds), *Surveillance and Control in Israel/Palestine* (Routledge, 2011), 378.
52. B. Hasisi and D. Weisburd, 'Going beyond ascribed identities: the importance of procedural justice in airport security screening in Israel' (2011) (45)(4) Law and Society Review 867, 873.
53. Whitaker, 'Behavioural Profiling in Israeli Aviation Security as a Tool for Social Control' (n51), 377.
54. Hasisi and Weisburd, 'Going beyond ascribed identities: the importance of procedural justice in airport security screening in Israel' (n52), 873.
55. ibid.
56. B. Hasisi, 'Ethnic profiling in airport screening: lessons from Israel, 1968–2010' (2012) 41(2) American Law and Economics Review 517, 532.
57. Hasisi and Weisburd, 'Going beyond ascribed identities: the importance of procedural justice in airport security screening in Israel' (n52), 873.
58. Hasisi, 'Ethnic profiling in airport screening: lessons from Israel, 1968–2010' (n56), 532.
59. Hasisi and Weisburd, 'Going beyond ascribed identities: the importance of procedural justice in airport security screening in Israel' (n52), 873.
60. B. Seymour, 'Behavioural pattern recognition and aviation security' (2005) 1(2/3) Journal of Security Education 69, 75–76.
61. R. Ron, *Remarks to the Aviation Subcommittee on Transportation and Infrastructure* (US Congress, 2002), 2.
62. ibid.
63. ibid, 4–6.
64. Harris, 'Good Cops: The Case for Preventive Policing' (n47), 215–216.
65. Z. Blumenkrantz, 'Haaretz probe: Israel airport security often carried out by untrained employees' Haaretz, January 11, 2010, available at: https://www.haaretz.com/1.5083877 (accessed 12th June 2020).
66. Associated Press, 'Israel's airport security: Arabs complain they face racist treatment when boarding planes', Associated Press, March 19, 2008.
67. S. Donnelly, 'A new tack for airport screening: behave yourself', Time, May 17, 2006.
68. L. Derfner, 'Stereotyping security', Jerusalem Post, March 22, 2007.
69. Z. Blumenkrantz, 'Mazuz moves to limit racial profiling at Ben-Gurion Airport', Haazretz, June 4, 2008.
70. N. Landau, 'Israeli diplomat says humiliated by racial profiling at Ben-Gurion Airport: "makes me sick"', Haazretz, August 4, 2019.
71. Jonas Amir Kadah, 'All aboard the Arab line at Ben Gurion Airport!', The Times of Israel, January 21, 2020.
72. J. Florence and R. Friedman, 'Profiles in terror: a legal framework for the behavioural profiling paradigm' (2010) 17 George Mason Law Review 423, 423.
73. ibid.
74. TSA, TSA behavior and detection analysis program', available at: https://www.tsa.gov/news/testimony/2013/11/14/tsa-behavior-detection-and-analysis-program (accessed 2nd June 2020).
75. T. Frank, 'Body language can blow their cover', USA Today, December 28, 2005.
76. P. Shaukovsky, 'Airport profilers: they're watching you', Seattle Post-Intelligencer, December 25, 2007.
77. Donnelly, 'A new tack for airport screening: behave yourself' (n67).
78. P. Ekman, 'How to spot a terrorist on the fly', Washington Post, October 29, 2006.
79. Florence and Friedman, 'Profiles in terror: a legal framework for the behavioural profiling paradigm' (n72), 426.

80. J. Karp and L. Meckler, 'Which travellers have hostile intent? Biometric device may have the answer', Wall Street Journal, August 14, 2006.
81. T. Wock, 'The TSA's new x-ray vision: the fourth amendment implications of 'body-scan' searches at domestic airport security checkpoints' (2009) 49(1) Santa Clara Law Review 213, 218.
82. ibid.
83. Florence and Friedman, 'Profiles in terror: a legal framework for the behavioural profiling paradigm' (n72), 427.
84. Karp and L. Meckler, 'Which travellers have hostile intent? Biometric device may have the answer' (n80).
85. P. Ekman and W. Friesen, *Unmasking the Face: A Guide to Recognising Emotions from Facial Expressions* (Maler Books, 1975). See also: E. Rosenberg, 'The Study of Spontaneous Facial Expressions in Psychology' in P. Ekman and E. Rosenberg (eds), *The Face Reveals: Basic and Applied Studies of Spontaneous Expressions Using the Facial Action Coding System (FACS)* (Oxford University Press, 2005).
86. Herbert, 'Othello error: facial profiling, privacy and the suppression of the dissent' (n1), 82.
87. ibid.
88. J. Richie and J. Mogul, 'In the shadows of the war on terror: persistent police brutality and abuse of people of color in the United States' (2008) 1 DePaul Journal of Social Justice 175, 217–218.
89. US Department of Homeland Security, *Advisory – Maintaining Awareness Regarding Al Qaeda's Possible Threats to the Homeland* (US Department of Homeland Security, September 4, 2003).
90. Crenshaw, 'Have Motivations for Terrorism Changed?' (n40).
91. Horgan, 'The Search for the Terrorist Personality' (n41).
92. Florence and Friedman, 'Profiles in terror: a legal framework for the behavioural profiling paradigm' (n72), 428–430.
93. ibid, 428. For further critique of facial emotion recognition please see: B. Azar, 'What's in a face?' (2000) 31(1) Monitor on Psychology 1.
94. Ekman and W. Friesen, 'Unmasking the Face: A Guide to Recognising Emotions from Facial Expressions', (n85).
95. M. Heller and V. Haynal, 'Perspectives of Psychopathology and Psychotherapy' in P. Ekman and E. Rosenberg (eds), *The Face Reveals: Basic and Applied Studies of Spontaneous Expressions Using the Facial Action Coding System (FACS)* (Oxford University Press, 2005), 506.
96. Florence and Friedman, 'Profiles in terror: a legal framework for the behavioural profiling paradigm' (n72), 429.
97. Y. Kleiner, 'Racial profiling in the name of national security: protecting minority travelers' civil liberties in the age of terrorism' (2010) 30 Boston College Third World Law Journal 103, 136–137.
98. ibid, 137.
99. Crenshaw, 'Have Motivations for Terrorism Changed?' (n40).
100. Horgan, 'The Search for the Terrorist Personality' (n41).
101. GAO, *Aviation Security: TSA Should Limit Future Funding for Behavior Detection Activities, GAO-14-159* (Government Accountability Office, 2013).
102. GAO, *Aviation Security: TSA Does Not Have Valid Evidence Supporting Most of the Revised Behavioral Indicators Used in Its Behavior Detection Activities* (Government Accountability Office, 2017).
103. Technical Advisory Committee, *SPOT Validation Study Final Results: 2011 Technical Advisory Committee (TAC) Review Report* (TAC, 2011), Executive Summary.
104. K. Kaye, 'TSA screenings more than just carry-on bags: behavior detection officers covertly watch travellers', Washington Post, November 9, 2009.

105. B. Harcourt, 'Behavioural profiling at US airports' (2006), available at: http://www.law.uchicago.edu/files/files/Harcourt%20OpEd%20Behavioral%20Profiling%20Longer%20Version.pdf (accessed 04th June 2020).
106. ibid, 138.
107. D. Meyer, 'The SPOT program: hello racial profiling, goodbye fourth amendment?' (2010) 10 University of Maryland Law Journal of Race, Religion, Gender and Class 289, 290–294.
108. ibid, 295–296. T. Ravich, 'Is airline passenger profiling necessary?' (2007) 62(1) University of Miami Law Review 1, 42–44.
109. Meyer, 'The SPOT program: hello racial profiling, goodbye fourth amendment?' (n107).
110. Ravich, 'Is airline passenger profiling necessary?' (n108), 37–44.

Bibliography

Andronikou, V., Yannopoulos, A. and Varvarigou, T., 'Biometric Profiling: Opportunities and Risks' in M. Hildebrandt and S. Gutwirth (eds), *Profiling the European Citizen: Cross-Disciplinary Perspectives* (Springer, 2010).

Associated Press, 'Israel's airport security: Arabs complain they face racist treatment when boarding planes', *Associated Press*, March 19, 2008.

Azar, B., 'What's in a face?' (2000) 31(1) *Monitor on Psychology* 1.

Blumenkrantz, Z., 'Haaretz probe: Israel airport security often carried out by untrained employees', *Haaretz, January* 11, 2010, available at: https://www.haaretz.com/1.5083877 (accessed 12th June 2020).

Blumenkrantz, Z., 'Mazuz moves to limit racial profiling at Ben-Gurion Airport', *Haazretz*, June 4, 2008.

Candamo, J., Shreve, M., Goldgof, D., Snapper, D. and Kasturi, R., 'Understanding transit science: a survey on human behavior-recognition algorithms' (2010) 11(1) *IEEE Transactions on Intelligent Transportation Systems* 206.

Canhoto, A. and Backhouse, J., 'General Description of the Process of Behavioural Profiling' in M. Hildebrandt and S. Gutwirth (eds), *Profiling the European Citizen: Cross-Disciplinary Perspectives* (Springer, 2010).

Canter, D., 'Offender profiling and investigative psychology' (2004) 1 *Journal of Investigative Psychology and Offender Profiling* 1.

Canter, D., 'Psychology of Offender Profiling' in R. Bull and D. Carson (eds), *Handbook of Psychology in Legal Concepts* (Wiley Publishing, 1995).

Collins, R., Gross, R. and Shi, J., 'Silhouette-based human identification from body shape and gait' (2002) IEEE International Conference on Face and Gesture Recognition 351.

Crenshaw, M., 'Have Motivations for Terrorism Changed?' in J. Victoroff (ed), *Tangled Roots: Social and Psychological Factors in the Genesis of Terrorism* (ISO Press, 2006).

Demirdjian, D., Ko, T. and Darrell, T., 'Untethered gesture acquisition and recognition for virtual world manipulation' (2005) 8(4) *Virtual Reality* 222.

Derfner, L., 'Stereotyping security', *Jerusalem Post*, March 22, 2007.

Donnelly, S., 'A new tack for airport screening: behave yourself', *Time*, May 17, 2006.

Ekman, P. and Friesen, W., *Unmasking the Face: A Guide to Recognising Emotions from Facial Expressions* (Maler Books, 1975).

Ekman, P., 'How to spot a terrorist on the fly', *Washington Post*, October 29, 2006.

Fasel, B. and Luettin, J., 'Automatic facial expression analysis: a survey' (2003) 36(1) *Pattern Recognition* 259.

Florence, J. and Friedman, R., 'Profiles in terror: a legal framework for the behavioural profiling paradigm' (2010) 17 *George Mason Law Review* 423.

Frank, T., 'Body language can blow their cover', *USA Today, December* 28, 2005.

GAO, *Aviation Security: TSA Does Not Have Valid Evidence Supporting Most of the Revised Behavioral Indicators Used in Its Behavior Detection Activities* (Government Accountability Office, 2017).

GAO, *Aviation Security: TSA Should Limit Future Funding for Behavior Detection Activities, GAO-14-159* (Government Accountability Office, 2013).

Harcourt, B., 'Behavioural profiling at US airports' (2006), available at: http://www.law.uchicago.edu/files/files/Harcourt%20OpEd%20Behavioral%20Profiling%20Longer%20Version.pdf (accessed 04th June 2020).

Harris, D., 'New risks, new tactics: an assessment of the re-assessment of racial profiling in the wake of September 11, 2001' (2004) 4 *Utah Law Review* 913.

Harris, D., *Good Cops: The Case for Preventive Policing* (The New Press, 2005).

Hasisi, B. and Weisburd, D., 'Going beyond ascribed identities: the importance of procedural justice in airport security screening in Israel' (2011) (45)(4) *Law and Society Review* 867.

Hasisi, B., 'Ethnic profiling in airport screening: lessons from Israel, 1968-2010' (2012) 41(2) *American Law and Economics Review* 517.

Hayfron-Acquah, J., Nixon, M. and Carter, J., 'Automatic gait recognition by symmetry analysis' (2003) 24(13) *Pattern Recognition Letters* 2175.

Heller, M. and Haynal, V., 'Perspectives of Psychopathology and Psychotherapy' in P. Ekman and E. Rosenberg (eds), *The Face Reveals: Basic and Applied Studies of Spontaneous Expressions Using the Facial Action Coding System (FACS)* (Oxford University Press, 2005).

Herbert, L., 'Othello error: facial profiling, privacy and the suppression of the dissent' (2007) 5 *Ohio State Journal of Criminal Law* 79.

Horgan, J., 'The Search for the Terrorist Personality' in A. Silke (ed), *Terrorist, Victims and Society: Psychological Perspectives on Terrorism and Its Consequences* (Wiley Publishing, 2003).

IBPP, 'Biometric, psychometric and sociometric profiling' (2003) 15(8) *IBBP Online* 1.

Kadah, J.A., 'All aboard the Arab line at Ben Gurion Airport!', *The Times of Israel*, January 21, 2020.

Karp, J. and Meckler, L., 'Which travellers have hostile intent? Biometric device may have the answer', *Wall Street Journal*, August 14, 2006.

Kaye, K., 'TSA screenings more than just carry-on bags: behavior detection officers covertly watch travellers', *Washington Post*, November 9, 2009.

Kleiner, Y., 'Racial profiling in the name of national security: protecting minority travelers' civil liberties in the age of terrorism' (2010) 30 *Boston College Third World Law Journal* 103.

Landau, N., 'Israeli diplomat says humiliated by racial profiling at Ben-Gurion Airport: 'makes me sick'', *Haazretz*, August 4, 2019.

Lester, D., Yang, B. and Lindsay, M., 'Suicide bombers: are psychological profiles possible' (2004) 27 *Studies in Conflict and Terrorism* 283.

Lozano, S. and Tversky, B., 'Communicative gestures facilitate problem solving for both communicators and recipients' (2006) 55(1) *Journal of Memory and Language* 47.

Meyer, D., 'The SPOT program: hello racial profiling, goodbye fourth amendment?' (2010) 10 *University of Maryland Law Journal of Race, Religion, Gender and Class* 289.

Mokros, A. and Alison, L., 'Is offender profiling possible? Testing the predicted homology of crime scene actions and background characteristics in a sample of rapists' (2002) 7 *Legal and Criminological Psychology* 25.

Nespoulous, J., Perron, P. and Lecours, A., *The Biological Foundation of Gestures: Motor and Semiotic Aspects* (Lawrence Erlbaum Associates, 1986).

Oka, K., Sato, Y. and Koike, H., 'Real-time fingertip tracking and gesture recognition' (2002) 22(6) *Computer Graphics and Applications* 64.

Patwardhan, K. and Roy, S., 'Hand gestures modelling and recognition involving changing shapes and trajectories using a Predictive EigenTracker' (2007) 28(3) *Pattern Recognition Letters* 329.

Petherick, W. and Ferguson, C., 'Behavioural Consistency, the Homology Assumption and the Problems of Induction' in W. Petherick (ed), *Serial Crime Theoretical Issues in Behavioural Profiling* (Anderson Publishing, 2013).

Phillips, P., Sarkar, S., Robledo, I., Grother, P. and Bowyer, K., 'Baseline results for the challenge problem of human ID using gait analysis' (2002) IEEE International Conference on Automatic Face and Gesture Recognition 130.

Plutchik, P., *The Psychology and Biology of Emotion* (Harper Collins College Publishers, 1994).

Popper, K., *The Logic of Scientific Discovery* (Routledge, 2003).

Ravich, T., 'Is airline passenger profiling necessary?' (2007) 62(1) *University of Miami Law Review* 1.

Richie, J. and Mogul, J., 'In the shadows of the war on terror: persistent police brutality and abuse of people of color in the United States' (2008) 1 *DePaul Journal of Social Justice* 175.

Ron, R., *Remarks to the Aviation Subcommittee on Transportation and Infrastructure* (US Congress, 2002).

Rosenberg, E., 'The Study of Spontaneous Facial Expressions in Psychology' in P. Ekman and E. Rosenberg (eds), *The Face Reveals: Basic and Applied Studies of Spontaneous Expressions Using the Facial Action Coding System (FACS)* (Oxford University Press, 2005).

Scherer, K., 'On the Nature and Function of Emotion: A Component Process Approach' in K. Scherer and P. Ekman (eds), *Approaches to Emotion* (Erlbaum, 1984).

Scherer, K., 'Vocal communication of emotion: a review of research paradigms' (2003) 40(1) *Speech Communication* 227.

Scherer, K., Banse, R. and Wallbott, H., 'Emotion inferences from vocal expression correlate across languages and cultures' (2001) 32(1) *Journal of Cross-Cultural Psychology* 76.

Schouten, R., 'Terrorism and the behavioural sciences' (2010) 18(6) *Harvard Review of Psychiatry* 369.

Seymour, B., 'Behavioural pattern recognition and aviation security' (2005) 1(2/3) *Journal of Security Education* 69.

Shaukovsky, P., 'Airport profilers: they're watching you', *Seattle Post-Intelligencer*, December 25, 2007.

Shoda, Y., Mischel, W. and Wright, J., 'Personality processes and individual differences' (1994) 67(4) *Journal of Personality and Social Psychology* 674.

Technical Advisory Committee, *SPOT Validation Study Final Results: 2011 Technical Advisory Committee (TAC) Review Report* (TAC, 2011).

TSA, TSA behavior and detection analysis program', available at: https://www.tsa.gov/news/testimony/2013/11/14/tsa-behavior-detection-and-analysis-program (accessed 2nd June 2020).

US Department of Homeland Security, *Advisory – Maintaining Awareness Regarding Al Qaeda's Possible Threats to the Homeland* (US Department of Homeland Security, September 4, 2003).

Weiner, J., 'Terrorism: Israel's legal responses' (1987) 14 *Syracuse Journal of International and Comparative Law* 183.

Whitaker, R., 'Behavioural Profiling in Israeli Aviation Security as a Tool for Social control' in E. Zureik, D. Lyon and Y. Abu-Laban (eds), *Surveillance and Control in Israel/Palestine* (Routledge, 2011).

Wock, T., 'The TSA's new x-ray vision: the fourth amendment implications of 'body-scan' searches at domestic airport security checkpoints' (2009) 49(1) *Santa Clara Law Review* 213.

Woodhams, J. and Toyle, K., 'An empirical test of the assumptions of case linkage and offender profiling with serial commercial robberies' (2007) 13(1) *Psychological, Public Policy and Law* 59.

Yannopoulos, A., Andronikou, V. and Varvarigou, T., 'Behavioural Biometric Profiling and Ambient Intelligence' in M. Hildebrandt and S. Gutwirth (eds), *Profiling the European Citizen: Cross-Disciplinary Perspectives* (Springer, 2010).

6 An examination of manifestations of informal terrorist profiling

6.1 Introduction

This chapter explores manifestations of terrorist profiling that may be classifiable as being closer towards the 'informal' end on the terrorist profiling spectrum. In order to examine manifestations of informal terrorist profiling, this chapter assesses the exercise of police powers, as the basis to demonstrate that some uses of police powers may be capable of being classified as an example of informal terrorist profiling. These police powers include police-initiated stop and searches, the use of powers of arrest and the power to engage in identity checking and the searches of premises.

The argument advanced in this chapter is that certain manifestations of profiling can be classified as being 'informal' where at least two criteria are met.

Firstly, it is common that there is no official or formal acknowledgement that some uses of police powers may be deployed either advertently or inadvertently as part of a wider law enforcement profiling process. Indeed, it is common for the state to refuse to recognise or acknowledge the use of profiling in the exercise of police powers. These police powers appear as part of their available apparatus of tools and mechanisms to assist in detecting, deterring and preventing acts of terrorism or associated preparatory activities.

Secondly, manifestations of informal profiling do not exhibit the same level of a systematic process, approach or structure in contrast with manifestations of formal terrorist profiling such as those manifestations already considered in chapter four.

It is important to acknowledge here that those manifestations of terrorist profiling that move towards the informal end of the profiling spectrum are classified as being informal on the basis of available evidence. As a result, the discussion throughout this chapter draws upon an array of available evidence in different countries so as to demonstrate, to quite a high degree of probability, that some uses of police powers may constitute examples of informal terrorist profiling.

The discussion in this chapter is set out in three parts.

The discussion in the first part begins by examining stop and search powers in England and Wales and argues that there is a high probability some uses of this power may be considered examples of informal terrorist profiling. This argument is advanced on the basis of an examination of both the construction and application of the various counterterrorism statutory provisions authorising the power to stop and search. The focus of the discussion is on England and Wales, given that there is an array of available data on law enforcement officer use of this power. The construction of the power to stop and search is examined so as to discern the permissible types of information/criteria capable of being included when exercising this power and to further consider whether the statutory framework places controls or limits on the use of such information/criteria as the basis for exercising the powers. Additionally, the application of this power is also examined because the evidence demonstrates there is a high probability some exercises of the power may be considered as at least showing the hallmarks of a profiling process, but it falls far short of the sort of systematic 'formal' profiling processes examined in chapter four.

The second part of this chapter examines other evidence of informal terrorist profiling based on the use of a range of police powers including the police power to engage in identity checking, targeted raiding of premises and the use of arrest powers. This discussion draws upon evidence from other jurisdictions including Germany, Italy and France as the basis to support the contention that some uses of police powers may be capable of constituting examples of informal terrorist profiling given that they are not acknowledged as a profiling tool and on the basis of the evidence it seems highly probable that there may be no formalised process at the construction/application stages in contrast to manifestations of formal profiling examined in chapter four.

The third part of the chapter evaluates the usefulness of informal terrorist profiling in assisting law enforcement officers identify, detect or deter acts of terrorism or preparatory activities.

It is acknowledged that not every ordinary or exceptional use of police powers will represent an example or be evidence of informal terrorist profiling. Rather, the discussion throughout this chapter examines the general application and use of discretionary police powers to support the argument that in some instances it would seem highly probable that law enforcement officers may be using their powers to engage in profiling practices tantamount to informal terrorist profiling.

A further issue that arises from the study of informal profiling is whether this type of profiling is classifiable as being a form of deductive or inductive profiling. It is acknowledged that the examples on the use of discretionary police powers considered in this chapter are difficult to classify as being either a form of deductive or inductive profiling. This difficulty relates to the apparent absence of the systematic processes evident in other types of profiling considered in chapter four. As a result, the examples of informal profiling considered in this chapter could be a form of deductive profiling where the law enforcement officers may be using their powers on the basis of past knowledge on terrorism crimes as the basis to identify or select individuals for questioning or screening. Further, it can equally be argued that the examples of informal profiling considered in this chapter may be a form of inductive profiling where law enforcement officers may be identifying their suspects on the basis of a profile constructed using raw sources of data. Consequently, it is best to consider examples of informal profiling as being either deductive or inductive depending on the way this type of profiling is used by individual law enforcement officers.

6.2 Stop and search in England and Wales

It is necessary to examine two aspects of the power to stop and search in order to demonstrate to a high degree of probability that some uses of this power may be classifiable as examples of informal terrorist profiling.

Firstly, it is necessary to examine the construction of the power to stop and search so as to evaluate whether the statutory framework provides a basis to control the types of information/criteria that can be utilised in deciding whether to exercise powers of stop and search in any given situation and further to consider whether there is any data control processes comparable with the processes in manifestations of formal terrorist profiling examined in chapter four.

Secondly, it will also be necessary to consider the use of the stop and search power by law enforcement officers as the basis to examine the output of these powers as a profiling tool/mechanism. This will involve considering the statistical evidence on actual law enforcement use of the power and various studies that have been conducted on this statistical data.

6.2.1 The power to stop and search in England and Wales

Although the power to stop and search has long been the subject of debate, there is no formally agreed definition on what constitutes a stop and search.[1] The decision by a law enforcement officer to issue an instruction to a citizen 'to stop initiates a coercive and intrusive process that is available to law enforcement agencies around the world.'[2]

According to Harris,

> [a] stop is a detention of a person by the police. It differs from a seizure or an arrest in that it is presumed to be temporary. A frisk is a search, but like a stop it is limited type of police action that … can include only a 'pat down' on the suspect's outer clothing. No further search – no reaching into a pocket or under a shirt – can take place.[3]

As a result, a stop and search may be defined as being a temporary detention of a 'suspect' by a law enforcement officer in the pursuit of their policing duty so as to allow the officer to engage in a non-invasive, but nonetheless intrusive, search of a person and/or their property. The decision to exercise this power effectively involves selecting and identifying individuals for enhanced questioning and/or screening with the aim of preventing, detecting or deterring criminality and/or terrorism. This selection 'process' on the part of an individual law enforcement officer involves making a distinction in treatment between those suspects selected versus those not selected for a stop and search. In some instances, the decision to exercise this power may well be guided by a law enforcement officer forming a suspicion about their suspect. However, in other instances as the discussion below will demonstrate, the law enforcement does not necessarily have to hold any suspicion about their suspect. As a result, the very nature of the stop and search power may be considered in some instances as being akin to a profiling process simply on the basis that an individual officer may be selecting and identifying individuals for enhanced questioning and/or screening with the aim of preventing, detecting or deterring or terrorism.

The legal framework providing for the use of stop and search powers can be characterised as being broad due to the extensive array of statutes affording the power to stop and search. A common feature of stop and search powers in England and Wales is that law enforcement officers are given a high degree of discretion as to when they may exercise the power to stop and search. This discretion may be considered as being akin to 'low visibility policing' and as such it can be quite difficult to identify those factors capable of influencing individual law enforcement officers when they exercise their discretion to stop and search. As a result of this difficulty, it is necessary to examine the statutory powers as the basis to work out what factors can lawfully influence a law enforcement officer's decision to exercise a stop and search.

In England and Wales, there are a considerable number of laws which afford law enforcement officers the power to stop and search, but not all of these powers are necessarily relevant to assessment in this chapter.[4] Bowling and Phillips identify

> ...section 1 of the Police and Criminal Evidence Act 1984 (PACE), section 23 of the Misuse of Drugs Act 1971 (MDA), section 60 of the Criminal Justice and Public Order Act 1994 (CJPO), section 47 of the Firearms Act 1968 (FA) and sections...

47A-C of the Terrorism Act 2000 (TA) as being the most popular laws used by law enforcement officers to exercise the power of stop and search.[5] In addition to these powers, section 53 and its Schedule 7 of the TA 2000 also provide a special power of stop and search at border entry points in ports and airports. However, as the primary focus of analysis in this chapter is on terrorist profiling, the discussion will only focus on the counterterrorism stop and search powers.

The legal framework authorising the power to stop and search is commonly constructed in two ways; law enforcement officers will be afforded the power to stop and search so long as they have formed 'reasonable suspicion' about their suspect, *or* in some instances law enforcement officers are not required to have formed any reasonable suspicion. As a result of this distinction it is necessary to separately examine the construction of the power of stop and search with and without reasonable suspicion. The objective here is to discern the permissible types of information and criteria which may be used as a basis for exercising the power. This provides a foundation for examining whether the statutory framework provides a process to manage/control the permissible information/criteria in a similar way to the processes evident to manifestations of formal terrorist profiling examined in chapter four.

6.2.1.1 Stop and search requiring reasonable suspicion

Section 43(1) of the Terrorism Act 2000 (TA) provides law enforcement officers with the power to stop and search

> a person whom [they] reasonably suspects to be a terrorist to discover whether he has in his possession anything which may constitute evidence that he is a terrorist.[6]

Further, Code A of the PACE Code of Practice states:

> [r]easonable grounds for suspicion is the legal test which a police officer must satisfy before they can stop and detain individuals or vehicles to search them under powers such as section 1 of PACE (to find stolen or prohibited articles) and section 23 of the Misuse of Drugs Act 1971 (to find controlled drugs). This test must be applied to the particular circumstances in each case and is in two parts:
>
> i Firstly, the officer must have formed a genuine suspicion in their own mind that they will find the object for which the search power being exercised allows them to search (see Annex A, second column, for examples); and
> ii Secondly, the suspicion that the object will be found must be reasonable. This means that there must be an objective basis for that suspicion based on facts, information and/or intelligence which are relevant to the likelihood that the object in question will be found, so that a reasonable person would be entitled to reach the same conclusion based on the same facts and information and/or intelligence.[7]

The inclusion of reasonable suspicion is to curtail and limit the circumstances in which a law enforcement officer can justifiably stop and search an individual and/their vehicle. From a profiling perspective, the requirement of 'reasonable suspicion' suggests that the law enforcement officer must go through a rational thought process before they decide to exercise their power to stop and search. The law enforcement officer will form their reasonable suspicion about their suspect during this thinking process. It is accepted that in some instances reasonable suspicion may be linked to other factors, such as the suspect being in an area that a terrorist incident has just occurred, or their behaviour may be suspicious to the individual law enforcement officer. It would seem reasonable to suggest that during this thinking process, when forming reasonable suspicion, the individual officer may (in some instances) be engaging in an act of profiling as they are essentially selecting individuals for screening and/or enhanced questioning when there may be other factors to support reasonable suspicion. This may represent examples of profiling in conjunction with other factors such as a suspect's suspicious behaviour.

This process is not officially classified as being a profiling process because this power is formally aimed at allowing a law enforcement officer to allay their suspicions about a potential suspect. However, it seems highly probable that the decision to stop and search a 'suspect' involves a degree of profiling as the decision process to exercise a stop and search by individual law enforcement officer essentially involves making selections between suspects to identify individuals for screening and/or enhanced questioning. This is due to the fact that a law enforcement officer must make a selection about who they are deciding to stop and search. This decision-making process created in statute does not delineate a systematic process in comparable terms with manifestations of formal profiling already discussed in chapter four. Rather the statute merely establishes a standard – 'reasonable suspicion' – but does not specify with precision what this might be, or all the factors which might be relevant to meeting/not meeting the standard.

Indeed, the concept of 'reasonable suspicion' in a law enforcement context may be considered as being ill-defined. For example, Sanders *et al* brand it 'as being somewhat of a slippery concept.'[8] Smith and Grey identify that law enforcement 'officers have long found it difficult to express in words their individual justifications for exercising the power to stop and search.'[9] It is akin to intuition or a 'hunch' on the part of the individual officer as to when a reasonable suspicion is formed about an individual and/or a vehicle.

Although the statutory framework establishes a test that law enforcement officers must use before engaging in a stop and search, it is contended that it remains extremely difficult to pinpoint justifications for stop and search in practice which may create an opportunity for law enforcement officers to engage in informal profiling. This opportunity may in some instances be on an inadvertent basis at best or at worst on an advertent basis. This means that an examination of the statute will not necessarily expose the factors that can influence a law enforcement officer in their decision to stop and search, rather the statute and its supporting Code only exposes the types of factors that cannot be taken into account. This approach is not as systematic as the processes already considered in relation to manifestations of formal profiling in chapter four.

The Code has been continually updated in an attempt to deal with the problems around the exercise of stop and search powers. For instance, in paragraph 2.2B of the Code expressly states:

> [r]easonable suspicion can never be supported on the basis of personal factors. This means that unless the police have information or intelligence which provides a description of a person suspected of carrying an article for which there is a power to stop and search, the following cannot be used, alone or in combination with each other, or in combination with any other

factor, as the reason for stopping and searching any individual, including any vehicle which they are driving or are being carried in:

a A person's physical appearance with regard, for example, to any of the 'relevant protected characteristics' set out in the Equality Act 2010, section 149, which are age, disability, gender reassignment, pregnancy and maternity, race, religion or belief, sex and sexual orientation...., or the fact that the person is known to have a previous conviction; and

b Generalisations or stereotypical images that certain groups or categories of people are more likely to be involved in criminal activity.[10]

Furthermore, paragraph 1.1 of the Code recognises that '[p]owers to stop and search must be used fairly, responsibly with respect for people being searched and without unlawful discrimination.'[11]

Despite these developments, it is evident that the Code may be considered as still lacking a clear, accessible and formalised framework in comparable terms with the types of processes/approaches comparable terms with the types of processes or approaches discussed in respect of manifestations of formal profiling when constructing profiles to identify those suspects to stop and search. Nevertheless, the Code pinpoints the types of characteristics that should not be taken into account when forming reasonable suspicion.

It is accepted that there is no clear answer as to how stop and search requiring reasonable suspicion could become more systematic in comparable terms with manifestation of formal terrorist profiling. The very nature of these powers means that they exist as being discretionary low visibility policing tools that are nearly always going to involve some degree of informal profiling on the part of law enforcement officer, which is only constrained by the requirement of reasonable suspicion. Other powers constrained by reasonable suspicion, such as the power of arrest, have a greater degree of oversight by law enforcement officers having to account for arrests at the police station. Nevertheless, the informal nature of this process stands in direct contrast to the types of processes evident in manifestations of formal profiling already discussed in chapter four.

6.2.1.2 Stop and search without reasonable suspicion

The British statutory framework also affords law enforcement officers the power to exercise a stop and search in some circumstances without the formation of any reasonable suspicion. The argument explored in this section is that the creation of stop and search powers without the need for reasonable suspicion provides an even weaker means to control the types of data that can inform a law enforcement officer's decision-making process when deciding to stop and search their suspect.

The absence of the requirement of reasonable suspicion removes any degree of a formalised thinking process on the part of the individual law enforcement officer who is deciding to conduct a stop and search without reasonable suspicion. The removal of reasonable suspicions slips further into a highly discretionary low visibility use of police powers that creates widespread opportunities for informal profiling with a very limited, if any, formalised process to assist in the identification of suspects.

The counterterrorism power to stop and search without reasonable suspicion exemplifies an apparent *ad hoc* power that appears to have a very weak formalised or systematic process to control data types. It is evident that the statutory framework does not control the types of data that may influence a law enforcement officer decision-making process in contrast to those manifestations of formal profiling considered in chapter three.

The power to stop and search without reasonable suspicion is currently provided in two key statutory provisions, section 47A-C of the TA 2000 and section 53 along with Schedule 7 of the TA 2000. Each of these provisions will now be considered so as to demonstrate the apparent absence of a process in comparable terms with those manifestations of formal profiling already considered in chapter three.

6.2.1.3 Section 47A-C of the TA 2000

The statutory power to stop and search contained in section 47A-C of the TA 2000 creates a two-tiered process that authorises a law enforcement officer to exercise a counterterrorism stop and search of individuals and/or vehicles without having to form any reasonable suspicion.

Firstly, a senior law enforcement officer must designate a geographical area in which a law enforcement officer is permitted to engage in a stop and search without reasonable suspicion under section 47A(1) of the TA 2000. This is akin to the creation of an upper tiered process that aims to control the geographical area as well a defined period of time within which a law enforcement officer at ground level is permitted to exercise a right to stop and search their suspect without having formed any reasonable suspicion. As part of the authorisation process, the senior law enforcement officer must ensure that any authorisation of a geographical area relates to a defined location and it can only be for a maximum of 14 days. In the context of profiling, this upper tier is of little significance as the decision to authorise an area is simply authorising a geographical area in which law enforcement officers *may* use the power to stop and search. The specific point of interest in this chapter is the actual exercise of the power to stop and search by the law enforcement officer at the ground level, it is at this precise point that a law enforcement officer may risk straying into profiling their suspects and this may be on an informal basis.

Secondly, it is at this lower tier after an area has been authorised by the senior officer, section 47A(2) of the TA 2000 allows an individual officer to exercise the power to stop and search without forming any reasonable suspicion. The decision to exercise this power is of significance to this chapter as it allows an examination of the permissible data a law enforcement officer can take into account when deciding to exercise their power to stop and search an individual. It is at this point it may be possible to identify if any formalised process is likely to exist to control the types of data and the use of this data that influences the decision to exercise a stop and search.

The counterterrorist power to stop and search has undergone significant review in recent years prior to its current formulation. This review is due to the decision in *Gillan and Quinton v The United Kingdom*[12] which assessed the compatibility of suspicionless stop search powers with the requirements of the ECHR; namely the right to liberty (article 5 ECHR); and the right to privacy (Article 8 ECHR). Although this review concerned both the upper and lower tiers of the stop and search power, the discussion here is focused on the lower tier so as to assess if a formalised process is likely to exist on the basis of any discernible evidence of control on the types of data that can be taken into account by law enforcement officers when deciding to exercise a stop and search.

Prior to the current formulation of the power to stop and search in section 47A of the TA 2000, the older formulation of this power permitted law enforcement officers to 'stop and search pedestrians and/or vehicles within the geographical area confirmed in an authorisation for any articles of a kind which could be used in connection with terrorism regardless of whether' the individual officer held 'grounds for suspecting the presence of articles of that kind.'[13] The use of this stop and search power by law enforcement officers required that each officer should 'have regard' to Code A of the PACE 1984. The existence of the Code was and continues to be aimed at providing law enforcement officers with guidance on how they should exercise their discretion to stop and search pedestrians and/or vehicles. Therefore, Code A may be considered as being indicative of the factors that may influence an officer when they are deciding to select their suspect for a stop and search.

The *Gillan and Quinton* decision exposed a number of weaknesses with the formulation of the suspicionless power to stop and search. These weaknesses included the absence of direction on how law enforcement officers should use the guidance in the Code in conjunction with the power to stop and search, the statistical evidence on the use of the power to stop and search represented a source of grave concern for the court and the reviewability of the exercise of stop and search power in the domestic courts was weak. These weaknesses led the European Court of Human Rights (ECtHR) to concluded that 'the safeguards within the [TA 2000] was highly inadequate to protect against abuse and misuse, the legislative framework was neither sufficiently circumscribed nor subject to adequate legal safeguards against abuse' which led the Court to conclude that the powers were 'not in accordance with the law' in breach of Article 8 of the ECHR.[14]

Consequently, the *Gillan* case may be taken as evidence to suggest that the legal framework did not adequately control the use of suspicionless stop and search powers by advancing a clear formalised framework to guide the use of the stop and search power. At minimum, the ECtHR appeared less than satisfied with the level of control on the decision-making processes of individual law enforcement officers when exercising the power to stop and search so as to ensure sufficient safeguards from potential abuse or even misuse. The Government's reaction to the *Gillan* decision resulted in a process of review, which led to the introduction the Terrorism Act 2000 (Remedial) Order 2011 that repealed sections 44-47 by inserting sections 47A to C into the TA 2000.

As part of the development of stop and search in the 2011 Order, the Home Secretary issued new guidance in the form of a revised version of the Code of Practice. This guidance essentially removed the use of suspicionless stop and search powers from law enforcement officers. Specifically, this new guidance allowed for stop and search to be authorised if it was 'necessary to prevent acts of terrorism.'[15] Therefore, this temporary reform only related to the upper tier processes of the stop and search power and not to the lower tier processes. As a result, this early reform did not appear to create a more formalised process relating to the decision-making process exercised by law enforcement officers when deciding to engage in a stop and search within an authorised area.

A further review of counterterrorism powers was instigated by the then Home Secretary and this was completed in January 2011.[16] This review identified four core problems with the use of stop and search powers in England and Wales: the 'excessive use of stop and search powers,' the 'disproportionate use of stop and search on ethnic minority communities,' the 'absence of terrorism convictions' as a result of using stop and search powers and the 'errors evident in the process of authorising the use of stop and search powers.'[17] These criticisms can really be considered unsurprising given the *Gillian* case as well as the long-standing concern with the use of stop and search power in England and Wales.

The Home Secretary adopted the 'Terrorism Act 2000 (Remedial) Order 2011' to operate temporarily on the basis of section 10(2) of the HRA 1998 until the 'Protection of Freedoms Bill' was enacted. In response to the period of review, the Home Secretary tampered with the discretion exercised at the upper tiers by senior law enforcement officers by reducing the authorisation period. Furthermore, 'the authorising officer had to reasonably suspect that terrorism would take place within' the particular location and the 'authorisation was necessary to prevent terrorism.' The only development of the lower tiers relating to the discretionary use of the stop and search power was the new guidance offered through a revamp of the Code of Practice A.

The culmination of this review resulted in the enactment of the 'Protection of Freedom Act 2012' (PFA) which meant that the 2011 Order ceased to have effect. However, section 61 of the PFA 2012 effectively copied the provision already in the 2011 Order which placed the content of the 2011 Order provision of stop and search on to a permanent basis by inserting section 47A-C into the TA 2000.

The level of change resulting from this development in the law is debatable. Specifically, the newly reformed law on stop and search continues to permit law enforcement officers to engage in a process that may in some instances be classifiable as being an informal profiling process in light of an apparent absence of a sufficiently systematic process in direct contrast to those processes evident in formal manifestations of profiling. The only significant change related to the upper tier of control on the power to authorise an area for stop and search which is not relevant to this discussion in this chapter.[18] As noted earlier, this upper tier is not of significance as the decision-making process concerning whether to authorise a geographical area is entirely a policing operational matter, which does not necessarily involve any profiling process. Once an area is now authorised, the focus remains on the decision-making powers exercisable by individual law enforcement officers so as to question how the statute allows individual officers to make their selection of suspects for a stop and search.[19]

There is little reform pursued in the context of the lower tier of discretion exercised by individual officers once an area has been authorised. For example, the stop and search power in section 47A of the TA 2000 creates a degree of confusion over the state of mind the law enforcement officers must have to justify a stop and search. As the guidance remains attached to Code A which at best is classifiable as being vague.[20] This potential for confusion leaves open the possibility that this police power can be used in an informal manner to profile suspects given it may be exercisable outside of a formalised process in contrast to those manifestations of formal profiling considered in chapter four. A key concern here is the vagueness of the weight that should be attached to the guidance in Code A.

Under the old law formulation of stop and search a law enforcement officer could only exercise the power to stop and search 'whether or not the constable has grounds for suspecting the presence of articles of that kind.'[21] The current formulation suggests that a law enforcement officer can exercise the stop and search power 'whether or not the constable reasonably suspects that there is such evidence.'[22] The problem with both the old and the new formulation is that the statutory framework does not require the law enforcement to have held a reasonable suspicion before exercising the power to stop and search. Although, it was noted above that 'reasonable suspicions' in itself was a 'slippery concept,' the removal of it moves lower into even murkier waters where it is virtually impossible to discern the thinking process a law enforcement officer engages in prior to the exercise of this type of stop and search.[23] This means it makes it very difficult to understand the types of data the law enforcement officer may be relying upon when deciding to stop and search which is made even more vague by the Code A guidance setting out the types of factors/data the law enforcement officer may not take into account.

As a result, the challenge here with this formulation is that it is difficult to discern the 'state of mind' a law enforcement officer must have before exercising their discretion. It is possible to suggest at least two states of mind, one where the law enforcement officer has formed a subjective suspicion of their target but cannot objectively provide a reasonable ground for the formation of that suspicion.[24] Alternatively, the law enforcement officer may not have any suspicion at all which may be considered akin to simple random searches. The issue with both of these circumstances is that they appear at odds with the legal review undertaken by the House of Lords in *Gillan*.[25] There appears to be no means to control the individual use of the power to stop and search through any process once an area has been authorised.

The Code of Practice provides law enforcement officers with an objective list of factors to assist in 'the selection of individuals or vehicles at random.'[26] According to a former Independent Review of Terrorism Legislation, this part of the Code appears to legitimise the use of randomised searches despite the fact that the House of Lords was quite clear in disapproval of such searches.[27] Other criticism of the inadvertent support of randomised searches was also criticised by the Joint Committee on Human Rights (JCHR).[28] In the view of the JCHR, the inclusion of the word 'random' in the Code which is linked to the guidance on the level of suspicion to justify a stop and search only serves to confuse the state of mind a law enforcement officer should have before deciding to exercise a stop and search.

Therefore, it seems that the juxtaposition of 'without reasonable suspicion' in the statutory provision and 'random' in the objective guidance in the Codes represents a fundamental flaw to control the types of information/criteria that may be relied upon by a law enforcement officer deciding to engage in a stop and search.[29] This absence of control in comparable terms with formal manifestations of profiling may be taken as evidence of the absence, or at least likely absence, of a process surrounding the exercise of a stop and search in comparable terms with the processes already considered in chapter three.

6.2.1.4 Section 53 and Schedule 7 of the TA 2000

Let's turn our discussion now to focus on section 53 and Schedule 7 of the TA 2000 as the basis to further explore the likelihood that the exercise of the power to stop and search without reasonable suspicion may not be as controlled as those manifestations of formal profiling considered in chapter three. Paragraph 7(2) of Schedule 7 of the TA 2000 allows individual law enforcement officer or 'examination officer' as referred to in Schedule 7 of the TA 2000 'at a port or airport to stop and search an individual' so as 'to determine whether they appear to be a person failing within section 40(1)(b) of the TA 2000.' This effectively means that Schedule 7(2) of the TA 2000 affords an individual law enforcement officer the power to stop and search any person within a border area in a port or airport to determine whether they are 'concerned in the commission, preparation of instigation of acts of terrorism.'[30]

As a result of the construction of this statutory power to stop and search, a question arises as to what state of mind the examination officer should have when they are exercising their power to stop and search a suspect. It is clear from Paragraph 7(4) of Schedule 7 of the TA 2000 that the examination officer does not have to form any reasonable suspicion that their suspect falls within section 40(1)(b) of the TA 2000. Paragraph 7(2)(1) of Schedule 7 of the TA 2000 makes it clear that the purpose of the power is to allow an examining officer to 'determine whether [the suspect] appears to be '"involved in the commission, preparation or instigation of acts of terrorism."'[31]

In common with the other statutory provisions on the power to stop and search, there is also a 'Code of Practice for Examining Officers' that offers guidance on how this power to stop and search in Schedule 7 should be applied.[32] In a similar way to the other Code discussed earlier in this chapter, this Code expresses that a law enforcement officer should 'make every reasonable effort to exercise the power in such a way as to minimise causing embarrassment or offence to a person who is being questioned.' This is also replicated in the amended June 2020 Draft Code currently before Parliament awaiting approval.[33] Furthermore, any exercise of the power must be 'used proportionately, reasonably, with respect and without unlawful discrimination.' In the June Draft 2020 Code this is extended where it states that the exercise of the power must be 'proportionate to the legitimate aim and which does not unlawfully discriminate against anyone on the grounds of age, race (including colour, nationality, ethnic or national origin), religion or belief, gender or sexual orientation.'[34] A similar confirmation is found in the June 2020 Draft Code where it states:

> Examining officers must take particular care to ensure that 'protected characteristics' (whether separately or together) are not used as criteria for selection except to the extent that they are used in association with considerations that relate to the threat from terrorism.[35]

Additionally, the 2015 Code suggests that the decision to stop and search a suspect by an examining officer must not be 'solely based on their perceived ethnic background or religion and a person's perceived ethnic background or religion must not be used alone or in combination with each other as the sole reason for selecting the person for examination.'

A key development in the Draft June 2020 Code of Practice is that there appears to be an explicit recognition that 'protected characteristics' (or as chapter two referred to them as 'sensitive characteristics') can be used 'separately or together' where the examining officer is applying the criteria 'with considerations that relate to the threat of terrorism.'[36] This new addition is somewhat concerning as it appears to be legitimatising the use of sensitive characteristics as the basis to select and identify suspects for enhanced questioning under Schedule 7 in the specific realm of terrorism. Although the Draft June 2020 Code makes clear any application of the power to stop and search should not be exercised in a manner that is 'unlawfully discriminat[ing] against anyone,' this new formulation of the Code is proposing to create an exception to this principle if the threat of terrorism so dictates.

As a result of the 2015 review of the Code, there are a number of express factors listed that law enforcement officers may take into account when deciding whether to exercise a stop and search of a suspect. These include

- known and suspected sources of terrorism
- individuals or groups whose current or past involvement in acts or threats of terrorism is known or suspected, and supporters or sponsors of such activity who are known or suspected
- any information on the origins and/or location of terrorist groups
- possible current, emerging and future terrorist activity, the means of travel (and documentation) that a group or individuals involved in terrorist activity

could use emerging local trends or patterns of travel through specific ports or in the wider vicinity that may be linked to terrorist activity
- [and] observation of an individual's behaviour[37]

This list of factors is also amended in the June 2020 Draft Code to include:

- known and suspected sources of terrorism
- persons, organisations or groups whose current or past involvement in acts or threats of terrorism is known or suspected, and supporters or sponsors of such activity who are known or suspected
- any information on the origins and/or location of terrorist groups
- possible current, emerging and future terrorist activity
- the means of travel (and documentation) that a group or persons involved in terrorist activity could use
- patterns of travel through specific ports or in the wider vicinity that may be linked to terrorist activity; or appear unusual for the intended destination
- observation of a person's behaviour and/or
- referrals made to examining officers by other security, transport or enforcement bodies[38]

These factors are not an exhaustive list, but they provide a degree of insight into the types of information/criteria a law enforcement officer may be relying upon when deciding to exercise the power to stop and search. Despite these 2015 reforms and the proposed 2020 reforms, the Code offers only provides guidance in the negative by outlining the ways in which the power cannot be exercised. This approach is not sufficient as it does not provide positive guidance in comparable terms with the guidance offered in manifestations of formal profiling already considered in chapter four.

The construction of this statutory power to stop and search suggests that considerable discretion is given to the examining officer as to how to exercise a stop and search. The problem with this is not the existence of discretion but rather whether there are any controls on the exercise of that discretion. The lack of oversight on the exercise of this discretion may suggest that there is unlikely any formalised process available to the examining officer when they are deciding to exercise a stop and search under this statutory provision.

There has been only one significant case of note, *Beghal v DPP*[39] which provides some insight on the likely existence of a process around the decision to exercise a stop and search. In *Beghal* the High Court confirmed that 'the very purpose [of this power] is to ascertain whether the [suspect] so appeared' to be a terrorist. The Supreme Court accepted that the use of the power to stop and search may involve '[s]ome degree of profiling of potential suspects for questioning …' but the requirement that the use of the power should only be exercised by drawing on 'sources of [a] terrorist threat' and the requirement that ethnicity and religion should either together or separately should be a sole criterion was a sufficient basis to safeguard against the unlawful use of this power. The problem with this acceptance is that there is no demonstrable process in comparable terms with the systematic processes already considered in manifestations of formal terrorist profiling with this type of profiling. Although, the reform of the Code of Practice, which was adopted in response to the problem exposed by this case, may be perceived as progress towards assisting law enforcement officers make better use of their powers in practice, a fundamental weakness is the Code still does not institute a process comparable with the manifestations of formal profiling in chapter four.

As a result, the case law on the use of this power to stop and search has not been helpful by clarifying the types of factors or characteristics that examining officers *could* rely on to justify their decision to stop and search. This may suggest that the process is not as systematic in controlling the types of data and characteristics to be used as part of a profiling process in contrast to those manifestations of formal profiling already considered in chapter four.

It is contended that the statutory framework advancing the power to stop and search under Schedule 7 of the TA 2000 is unlikely to have a sufficiently formalised process to control the data input at the point at which an examining officer is deciding to exercise their power to stop and search. Further, even if the Code provides a limited basis to control the types of data that an examining officer can take into account, there does not appear to be any process to control the use of this data in terms of the influence each data set can have on an examining officer's decision comparable with manifestations of formal terrorist profiling in considered in chapter four.

6.2.1.5 Summary

In light of the discussion on the British counterterrorism statutory framework advancing the power to stop and search, there is a high probability that this statutory framework may have created a profiling process that is informal in contrast to those manifestations of profiling already discussed in previous chapters. The discussion above identifies that the construction of the power to stop and search with and without reasonable suspicion creates a process for law enforcement officers to engage in selecting individuals and/or vehicles for their stop and search.

Although, the exercise of this power is supported with Codes of Practice, the use of these Codes are not legally mandated requirements and can only be considered at best 'guidance' that law enforcement officers *should* follow. As a result, it is difficult to discern the factors that may influence a law enforcement officer in their exercise of a stop and search and the types of data actually used by individual officers exercising a stop and search. Further, it does not appear that the construction of the power that there is no systematic process to control the usage of the permitted information/criteria in comparable terms with those formal manifestations of terrorist profiling examined in chapter four. Consequently, the lack of a process around the types of permitted information/criteria and the control on the use of this information/criteria appears to fall far short of the processes evident in manifestations of formal terrorist profiling.

6.2.2 *The use of stop and search by law enforcement officers in England and Wales*

There are at least two key sources on the use of the power to stop and search by law enforcement officers that can be used as a basis to support the contention that this power may, in some instances, be considered as being very close to existing as an informal profiling process.

Firstly, the statistics on the use of the power to stop and search by law enforcement officers reveals the frequency of this policing mechanism and further who has been the subject of stop and search powers. These statistics reveal that this power appears to be deployed increasingly and frequently in a manner that focuses on particular ethnic minorities without any discernible explanation for why this is happening other than that some form profiling is at play. Since the Code of Practice states this should not happen/is not permitted, it is clear that it is 'informal' in the sense that it lacks any official basis, and is not 'systematic,' and bureaucratised in the way in which those 'formal' profiling systems examined in chapter four were explained.

Secondly, there are a number of studies on people's experiences of police powers that seem to support the statistical evidence that particular ethnicities are a focal point for suspicion without any objective justification.

The continual growth in the disparity rate (discussed below) may be taken as evidence of a very strong likelihood that a weak process, if any, exists around the use of stop and search powers which may be accurately considered tantamount to an imprint of a profiling process, that falls far short of the types of profiling processes adopted in more formalised manifestations of profiling considered in chapter four.

6.2.2.1 The statistical evidence on the use of stop and search

The examination of the exercise of stop and search involves considering who has been the subject of suspicion by law enforcement officers. This focus allows an identification of the types of factors that may be influencing law enforcement officers in their selection of their suspects for stop and search as the basis to question the existence of a profiling process in comparable terms with the profiling processes discussed in chapter four.

6.2.2.2 Limitations of the available statistical evidence

Before considering the disparities evident in those being stopped and searched in England and Wales, it is accepted that there are at least four limitations on the use of statistics in this context.

Firstly, the vast majority of those subjected to terrorism stop and search powers were located in London which has a greater ethnic diversity in contrast to other parts of England and Wales.[40] As a result, the use of stop and search powers in London is likely to involve stopping and searching a greater degree of individuals from a diverse range of ethnicities which is capable of impacting the recorded stop and searches. Further, in research conducted by Fitzgerald and Sibbit, it was found that law enforcement officers were more likely to record stop and searches of non-white ethnicities in contrast to the stop and searches of white ethnicities.[41] The reason for this appeared to be due to a fear held by law enforcement officers that non-whites were more likely to complain and individual law enforcement officers sought to demonstrate they had followed procedure with non-white ethnicities.[42]

Secondly, a further concern is that prior to April 1, 2005 the ethnicity of those subjected to a stop and search was identified and recorded by individual law enforcement officers.[43] This creates the problem as to whether law enforcement officers were accurately equipped to consistently identify ethnicity as it is accepted that the identification of ethnicity is a sensitive and complex issue that is not always discernible visually.[44] Further, the recording requirement for stop and search breaks down ethnicity according to four different types which is primarily based on ethnic appearance: White, Black, Asian and other.

> White is recorded as representing white British, white Irish and other White individuals. Black is recorded as being black Caribbean, black African and mixed white and black African. Other is recorded as being 'Chinese, other mixed and 'other other.''[45]

The recording of ethnicities in this manner has been criticised by some, such as Rowe, on the basis that they do not always accurately reflect the actual ethnicity of those subjected to a stop and search.[46] Specifically, Rowe contends that 'white' is being used an 'omnibus category' that fails to appreciate different white ethnicities and that 'Asian conflates subgroups that have sharply contrasting socio-economic profiles.'[47] As a result, the recording of stop and search according to four discernible ethnicities may be considered as being exceptionally narrow and may not always be capable of recording accurately those ethnicities subjected to a stop and search.

Thirdly, there are some concerns related to police recording of stop and search data where law enforcement officers sometimes either fail to record the occurrence of a stop and search or they fail to adopt a systematic and coherent approach to recording data. For example, in a study conducted by the Home Office by Fitzgearld and Sibbit, it would found that police are not always systematic in their recording of stop and search data.[48] Further, it was identified by Miller *et al* who observed 138 stop and searches that should have been recorded but found that only 37 of these stop and searches were actually recorded.[49] Additionally, the Stephen Lawrence Inquiry recommended improvements in police recording of the stop and search data.[50]

Fourthly, the application of the disproportionality test focuses on identifying any disparities between those who were actually stopped and searched purely on the basis of ethnicity against a majority ethnicity attributed to the general population.[51] As this is a test that focuses on disparities between racial majorities and racial minorities, it may be considered as failing to take into account the ethnicity of the population that is actually available to be stopped and searched. It may be argued that some ethnicities have a higher availability rate than others due to lifestyle whilst other ethnicities may have a lower availability rate.[52] This may impact the validity of any disparities identified. There have been some studies conducted by the Home Office[53] and Waddington *et al*[54] that have sought to explore the impact of identifying disparities between the general versus the available population. These studies have tended to show there is a potential disparity between the available population and the general population, but that disparity is not sufficient to invalidate the conclusions drawn on any identified disparities based on a comparison between general majority population against minority population stopped and searched. Consequently, this is a factor that should be kept in mind as a limiting factor but not an invalidating factor.

Despite these limitations, it is argued that given the evidence of disparity considered below there remains considerable evidence to support the contention that law enforcement officers appear in some instances to using their stop and search power to identify likely suspects for questioning/screening in a manner that may be classifiable as being ad-hoc and likely to lack a process similar to those manifestations of profiling considered in chapter three.

In following the analytical approach adopted in the previous section, the discussion will now examine law enforcement officer use of the counterterrorism powers to stop and search by reference to those requiring and not requiring reasonable suspicion.

6.2.2.3 Stop and search requiring reasonable suspicion

The information published by the Home Office on law enforcement officer use of section 43 of the TA 2000 for England and Wales is obscured by combining the statistics on the exercise of other stop and search powers requiring reasonable suspicion. As a result, it is not possible to solely examine the use made by law enforcement officers of section 43 of the TA 2000 in England and Wales. It is noted that every police force in England and Wales collects and records information on its use of section 43 of the TA 2000 but this information is not shared publicly. The failure to publish statistics of law enforcement officer use of section 43 of the TA 2000 has been criticised previously by the independent reviewer of terrorism legislation but the situation has continued.[55] Nevertheless, there is information published on the use of section 43 of the TA 2000 in respect of the London Metropolitan Police Service (MPS). Therefore, the discussion will concentrate on this published statistical use of section 43 of the TA 2000.

Table 6.1[56] reveals that over the course of the last decade there has been a general theme where section 43 of the TA 2000 has been in considerable fluctuation. Between 2010/11 and 2011/12 there was a dramatic decline in the use of section 43 by 23% which continued into 2012/13 by a further 29%. This decline reversed quite considerably in 2015/16 by rising 32% on the year previous before falling back in 2016/17 by 16%. However, in 2017/18 this rose considerably

Table 6.1 Stop and search statistics requiring reasonable suspicion under Section 43 of the Terrorism Act for the London Metropolitan Police Service

Year	*Stop and Searches Terrorism Specific*	*Average Annual % Movement*
2010–11	1,151	
2011–12	819	-29%
2012–13	582	-29%
2013–14	450	-23%
2014–15	410	-9%
2015–16	541	+32%
2016–17	454	-16%
2017–18	808	+70%
2018–19	685	-15%

78% on the year previous before finally dropping back by 15% in the most recent statistics by 15% in 2018/19.

Table 6.2[57] also provides a greater insight into who has been the subject of these stop and searches. Specifically, Table 6.2 reveals that raw data by reference to the ethnicity breakdown of those stopped and searched by the MPS. This can be considered more significant from a profiling perspective given that it generally reveals who has been subjected to this power in practice.

In order to make sense of this data, Fig. 6.1[58] reveals that in respect of the year 2015 those individuals recorded as being 'Black' were 2.0 times more likely to be stopped and searched in contrast to those recorded as being 'White.' Fig. 6.1 also reveals that those recorded as being Asian were 2.8 times and Chinese or 'Other' were 3.9 times more likely to be stopped and searched than those recorded as being 'White.' This reveals quite a significant disproportionality ratio between those individuals recorded as being 'White' versus those recorded as an ethnic

Table 6.2 Ethnicity breakdown of the use of stop and search requiring reasonable suspicion under Section 43 of the Terrorism Act for the London Metropolitan Police Service

Self-Defined Ethnicity	*2011*	*2012*	*2013*	*2014*	*2015*	*2016*	*2017*	*2018*	*2019*
White	462	296	221	152	165	150	139	227	188
Mixed	24	24	13	17	12	18	17	40	25
Black or Black British	111	75	80	65	46	68	54	121	100
Asian or Asian British	373	302	171	126	103	147	126	213	175
Chinese or Other	95	58	43	42	37	54	47	74	79
Not Stated	86	64	54	48	47	104	71	133	118
Total	**1151**	**819**	**582**	**450**	**410**	**541**	**454**	**808**	**685**

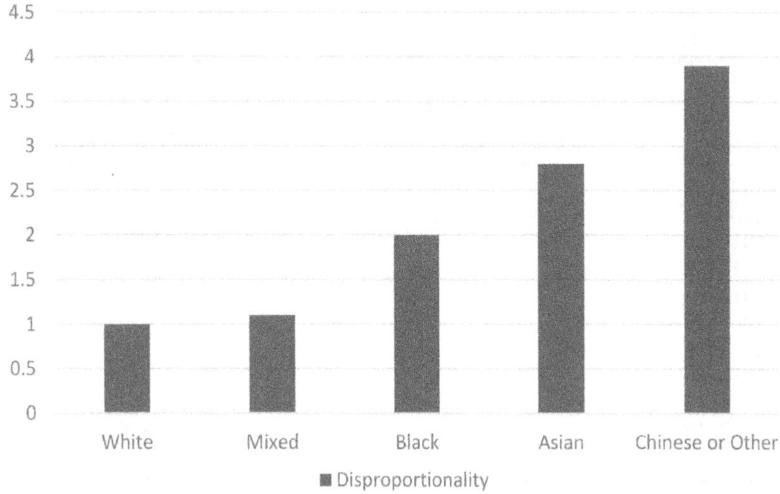

Figure 6.1 Stop and searches in London under Section 43 of The Terrorism Act 2000: the disproportionality ratio between ethnicities

minority. Further, Table 6.2 clearly demonstrates the continuation of this trajectory of greater proportions of ethnic minorities being subject to the stop and search power in contrast to the majoritarian 'white.' We will return to consider the potential significance of these disparities of these stops and searches below.

6.2.2.4 Stop and search not requiring reasonable suspicion

In conducting the examination of the use of section 47A of the TA 2000, the focus here is on firstly examining the fluctuations in the use of suspicionless stop and search power before secondly examining the disparities between those stopped and searched, and those who tend not to be stopped and searched. This approach involves applying a disproportionality test ratio, which engages in a simple comparison between the likelihood of racial minorities being subjected to stop and search powers versus the likelihood of racial majorities being stopped and searched.[59] This comparison is conducted on the basis of identifying any disparities between ethnic and racial minority population against the majority population as determined by national census. The disparity between ethnicities in terms of those being subjected to stop and search provides an insight into who may have been the primary focus of law enforcement officers decision in terms of identifying and selecting 'suspects' in England and Wales.

Table 6.3[60] reveals that there were 210,013 stop and searches under section 44 of the TA 2000 which was the all-time high for the use of this power before continuing to fall to zero in 2011 to 2017 years. In the year 2017–18, Table 6.3 also shows an increase to 149 stop and searches before returning to zero in the following year. These fluctuations in the use of this power to stop and search

Table 6.3 Stop and search statistics not requiring reasonable suspicion under Section 47A and previously Section 44 of the Terrorism Act for England and Wales

Year	*Stop and Searches Terrorism Specific*	*Average Annual % Movement*
2008–09	210,013	
2009–10	108,685	-48%
2010–11	11,787	-89%
2011–12	–	
2012–13	–	
2013–14	–	
2014–15	–	
2015–16	–	
2016–17	–	
2017–18	149	+100%
2018–19	–	-100%

can be considered as being controversial. For example, the former 'Independent Review of Terrorism Legislation' from 2001 to 2011, Lord Carlile, was often vocal about the growth rate of stop and search conducted under section the now obsolete section 44 of the TA 2000.[61] In 2009 Lord Carlile commented '[i]f there is a single issue that can be identified as giving rise to most assertions of excessive and disproportionate police action, it is the use of section 44' of the TA 2000.[62]

In 2009, Lord Carlile was specifically concerned that suspicionless stop and search powers were being used in a manner outside of their statutory intention. For example, Lord Carlile commented that

> [t]he alarming numbers of usages of the power (between 8,000 and 10,000 stops per month as we enter 2009) represent bad news, and I hope for better in a year's time. The figures, and a little analysis of them, show that section 44 is being used as an instrument to aid non-terrorism policing on some occasions, and this is unacceptable.[63]

The United Nations Human Rights Committee also added its concerns about the use of the powers to stop and search by calling for its scope to be urgently reviewed.[64]

Additionally, non-governmental organisations such as Justice[65] and Watch[66] also raised concerns about the use of terrorism stop and search powers by law enforcement officers. The 'Joint Committee on Human Rights' (JCHR) also expressed grave concerns about the statistical evidence demonstrating the use of terrorism stop and search powers by law enforcement officers.[67] The JCHR ultimately concluded 'counterterrorism powers should not be used against peaceful protestors.'[68] Finally, the 'Metropolitan Police Authority' also expressed concerns with the use of stop and search powers.[69]

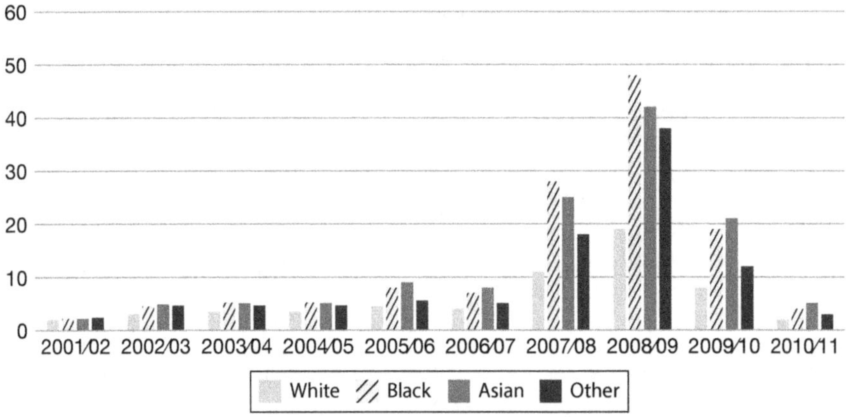

Figure 6.2 The Racial Disparity in Stop and Search

A further concern beyond the use of the suspicionless stop and search power relates to whom this power was used to target. This concern relates to the similar issue with reasonable suspicion stop and search powers where there is a continual subjection of particular ethnic minorities to stop and search without any apparent justification.

Figure 6.2[70] reveals that between 2002 and 2011 there was a significant disparity between those stopped and searched who are recorded as being White and those being recorded as being Black or Asian. The extent of the disparity is highlighted in Table 6.4 which focuses on the ethnicity breakdown of 2008/2009 and 2009/2010 as the basis to highlight the disparity between minority ethnicities versus the majority ethnicity during a peak period in the usage of stop and search under section 44 of the TA 2000. Additionally, the Ministry of Justice from 2007/2008 provided a more detailed breakdown of the recorded ethnicities of those stopped and searched.

Table 6.4 highlights that at the peak of the use of stop and search in 2008/2009 those recorded as being White were stopped and searched at a rate of 2.6 per 1,000 head of population, whereas it was 7.8 for Asians and 10.3 for those recorded as being Black. This meant that those recorded as being Asian were stopped and searched 3.0 times more than their White counterparts. Similarly, those recorded as being Black were 3.9 times more likely to be stopped and searched than their White counterparts. Of particular interest in Table 6.4 is the breakdown within each ethnicity of who was subjected to a stop and search as this helps to demonstrate the likelihood of an absence of a systematic process in comparable terms with those formal manifestations of profiling in chapter four.

Table 6.4[71] reveals that 'there is a general Asian effect,' as classified by Quinlan and Derfoufi, on the basis that those classified as being Asian are significantly 'more likely to be stopped and searched than their White counterparts.'[72]

Table 6.4 Stop and search not requiring reasonable suspicion under Section 44 of the Terrorism Act 2000 in England and Wales

	Rate per 1,000	*Disproportionality Ratios*	*Rate per 1,000*	*Disproportionality Ratios*
White				
British	1.6	1.0	0.7	1.0
Irish	4.1	2.6	1.8	2.6
Other	16.5	10.2	7.5	11.0
Black				
African	10.3	6.3	4.6	6.7
Caribbean	11.4	7.0	4.6	6.8
Other	18.3	11.3	6.9	10.1
Asian				
Bangladeshi	11.7	7.2	5.3	7.7
Indian	6.9	4.3	3.4	4.9
Pakistani	5.1	3.1	2.5	3.7
Other	12.0	7.4	5.8	8.5
Mixed				
African	3.2	2.0	1.2	1.8
Asian	2.4	1.5	1.0	1.4
Caribbean	2.2	1.4	0.9	1.3
Other	7.6	4.7	3.3	4.8
Chinese	8.0	4.9	3.2	4.6
Other	9.9	6.1	4.4	6.4

However, the higher rates of those recorded as being Bangladeshi in contrast to Indian or Pakistani may be explained in part due to where these populations live. For instance, Heath and Martin identify that Bangladeshi ethnicities tend to live in London whilst other Asian ethnicities such as Pakistani tend to live outside of London.[73] This is similar to those recorded as being Black where those recorded as being Black Caribbean or Black Other as being stopped and searched to a higher degree than those recorded as being Black African. On the basis of these statistics, it may be argued they reveal a strong likelihood that the decision to stop and search does not occur in a process comparable to those formal manifestations of formal profiling.

Other suspicionless stop and search powers examined in the previous section were those powers contained in Schedule 7 of the TA 2000. Although, the use of Schedule 7 powers has not been given the same level of focus in the media, the use of these powers shows a similar trend to the use of section 44 of the TA 2000. Table 6.5[74] reveals a similar trend in respect of other suspicionless stop and search powers where there is a general decline in the use of these powers by law enforcement officers. Specifically, Table 6.5 reveals that there was a high

Table 6.5 Schedule 7 examinations to the year ended March 2019

Length of examination, result and ethnicity	2012	2013	2014	2015	2016	2017	2018	2019	Change Number	Change %
Number of Examinations	63902	57621	44118	31769	26167	18103	15391	11154	–4237	–28
Under the hour	61662	55355	42231	29871	24373	16624	13666	9441	–4225	–31
Over the hour	2240	2266	1887	1898	1794	1479	1725	1713	–12	–1
Resultant Detentions	**680**	**667**	**517**	**1311**	**1821**	**1530**	**1776**	**1832**	**56**	**3**
Breakdown by Ethnicity										
Total Examinations										
White	26757	22142	18563	10430	7185	5212	4296	2626	–1670	–39
Mixed	2074	1965	2250	1939	1235	618	633	686	53	8
Black/Black British	5389	5114	3573	2595	1825	1384	1124	825	–299	–27
Asian/Asian British	17254	13303	9173	8007	7779	5186	3869	2811	–1058	–27
Chinese/Other	11190	10300	7525	6363	6065	3737	3000	2753	–247	–8
Not Stated	1238	4794	3034	2435	2078	1966	2469	1453	–1016	–41
Total Detentions										
White	55	58	56	144	214	182	193	213	20	10
Mixed	23	20	37	83	107	100	128	131	3	2
Black/Black British	157	149	93	153	149	148	202	187	–15	–7
Asian/Asian British	237	211	181	464	655	506	454	543	89	20
Chinese/Other	155	145	116	348	481	327	494	510	16	3
Not Stated	53	84	34	119	215	267	305	248	–57	–19

of 63,902 stop and searches in 2012 to a gradual decline to 11,154 in 2019. Table 6.5 also reveals a similar trend in respect of the ethnicities that have been subjected to an examination and a detention where those Black and Asian ethnicities have been continually subjected to the exercise of these powers in contrast to the majority White ethnicity.

Lord Carlile also criticised the use of these powers. For instance, Lord Carlile in 2010 concluded, 'the number of random or intuitive stop and searches could be reduced considerably' without impacting the purpose of the power.[75] Further other reviewers of terrorism laws, such as Anderson also identified concerns about the exercise of this power to stop and search by specific questioning whether the wide construction of the power could be considered 'necessary and subject to sufficient safeguards.'[76]

The ethnicity breakdown of these powers was not publicly available until 2011 and reveals a similar trend to the other stop and search powers already examined in this chapter. However, the disproportionality ratio cannot be utilised here given that there is no collected data on the total number of different ethnicities passing through ports and airports to allow a figure to be identified on the 1,000 per head of population.

Nevertheless, the figures do reveal a similar trend where consistently growing use of the power on Black and Asian ethnicities. This concern was highlighted by Anderson in 2014 where he concluded, 'it is overwhelmingly likely' the application of these powers was being utilised against particular ethnicities, such as Asian ethnicities, which is disproportionately higher than in contrast to individuals of White ethnicity.[77] For instance, Table 6.5 shows that in 2014 9% of all examinations were of Black ethnicity, whilst 13% of detentions in 2014/2015 were of Black ethnicity. Similarly, those of Asian ethnicity comprised 24% of all stop and searches in 2015 and 39% of those detained in 2015.

6.2.2.5 *Evaluation of the statistics*

In light of the discussion in the previous section, it is now pertinent to evaluate the likelihood that stop and search in some instances may be considered as being tantamount as being an example of informal profiling.

The argument that some uses of the power to stop and search can be classified as being an example of informal profiling rests on two central planks.

Firstly, stop and search is not recognised either in the construction or application of the power as being a form of profiling, but it seems plausible to suggest that in some instances the power may be exercised a tool to identify and select suspects. Therefore, a key element in some instances of the exercise of the power to stop and search appear to be about profiling in the sense the power can be exercised to identify suspects, potential suspects or at minimum allay any concerns a law enforcement officer may have about an individual or their property. This is process tantamount to a form of profiling given that the exercise of the power, in some instances, may involve making distinctions between suspects and non-suspects.

Secondly, on the basis of the discussion in the previous section, it seems very unlikely that there is any formalised process in comparable terms with those processes evident in the manifestations of formal profiling examined in chapter four. This is based on the fact that significantly higher levels of minority ethnicities were continually subjected to stop and search without any discernible justification in contrast to the White majority ethnicity. This would stand in complete contrast to the iterative processes inherently part of manifestations of formal profiling examined in chapter four where profiling is meant to be perfected over time. The evidence on the high levels of disparity questions the reason as to why individuals who are recorded as being Black or Asian are significantly more likely to be stopped and searched in contrast to individuals recorded as being White. From the perspective of profiling, the obvious starting point is to focus on the decision-making process that individual law enforcement officers go through whilst determining *when* to exercise the power to stop and search.

There are at least two arguments that are frequently drawn upon to explain the disproportionality ratio evident in the use of stop and search that seeks to avoid evidencing a deficient decision-making process on the part of law enforcement officers.[78]

There is the controversial argument that individuals from Black ethnicities are more likely to be engaged in very types of crimes subject to law enforcement officer attention.[79] This argument may be supported by the fact that in the past arrest rates tended to demonstrate a higher proportion of Black ethnicities in contrast to White ethnicities.[80] However, this is a hotly contested issue where some, such as Smith, contending that higher arrest rates amongst Black ethnicities is simply due to a greater focus on Black communities by law enforcement officers in contrast to White communities.[81] Further, in research conducted by Bowling and Phillips[82] and May *et al*[83] has consistently found that higher offending rates amongst Black communities is very likely due to potential bias in law enforcement officer decision-making. Other studies, such as Thornberry and Krohn, suggest that a better way to analyse disproportionality in law enforcement was to rely on research self-studies as they were more likely to produce an accurate understanding of higher levels of racial disparity in the application of law than official arrest rates.[84] In a sequence of studies complied by Graham and Bowling,[85] Flood-Page *et al*[86] and Sharp and Budd[87] found that individuals from Black ethnicities were either less likely than or comparably similar to White ethnicities to engage in criminality. As a result, it may be argued that any suggestion that individuals from Black ethnicities are more likely to be predisposed to committing crime to justify individual law enforcement officers selecting them for stop and search appear unfounded.

A further argument advanced to defend the higher disproportionate stopping and searching of Black ethnicities is sometimes attributed to the available population. This argument contends that the higher levels of stop and search of Black ethnicities can be explained by reference to the fact there is likely to be greater levels of Black ethnicities available in areas where stop and search is more likely to be carried out by law enforcement officer. According to Shiner and Delsol there is little the evidence to challenge this argument.[88] For example, in studies conducted by MVA and Miller[89] and Waddington *et al*[90] it was found that in a selection of areas where stop and search was frequently deployed, there was a higher proportion of Black ethnicities available in contrast to White ethnicities. However, both of these studies can be challenged. For instance, Sanders *et al* argue that MVA and Miller's study may be distorted given the fact that it was carried out just after the Lawrence Inquiry had published their findings when the use of stop and search was relatively low.[91] Nevertheless, it still does not provide a cogent explanation as to why so many more Black and Asian ethnicities are stopped and searched in comparison to White ethnicities.[92]

As a result, the question comes remains focused on determining why law enforcement officers are engaged in stopping and searching Black and Asian ethnicities at a significantly higher rate in comparison to White ethnicities. In other studies conducted on examining police officer experiences of stop and search, such as HMIC[93] and Shiner,[94] it was found that 'race' is a prominent feature in the decision-making process of some individual law enforcement officers. This may suggest that in some instances the power to stop and search is clouded by visible characteristics over anything connected to the likelihood of the suspect being engaged in crime or terrorism. Although there is some attempt in stop and search powers to control the influence of race and ethnicity, it is contended that these attempts fall far short of the standards expected in manifestations of formal profiling examined in chapter four. This influence is evident in the Codes of Practice where law enforcement officers are guided on the factors that they cannot take into account. However, the extent of the new June 2020 Draft Code of Practice for Schedule 7 powers of stop and search is extremely worrying given it appears to be creating an exception in light of a prevailing threat of terrorism.

The purpose of this discussion is not make the argument that every use of the stop and search power can be considered a form of informal profiling, rather the argument is that given the continual subjection of particular ethnicities to stop and search without any discernible justification, it seems to a high degree of probability that there is either at worst no process or at best a minimal/limited process at play when law enforcement officers are deciding to exercise their stop and search power.

6.2.2.6 People's experiences of stop and search in England and Wales

Beyond the construction and application of the power to stop and search, there have been at least four studies that have focused on law enforcement officer usage of these powers. Each of these studies will be discussed below to further demonstrate that the construction and use of stop and search in England and Wales have long raised concerns about the lack of a process formalising the construction of the power in addition to law enforcement use of the power.

Firstly, the Open Society Institute (OSI) have found branded the 'use of stop and search powers as a form of ethnic profiling' where the consistent disproportionate use of the power to stop and search against those individuals recorded as being Black and Asian ethnicities in contrast to those recorded as being White.[95]

The continual disproportionate use of the power to stop and search over a sustained period of time led the OSI to conclude that the 'stop-and-search practices have targeted persons perceived to be Muslim' without any discernible justification.[96]

Secondly, according to Miller that attempts to reform the stop and search power will do little, if anything, to deal with the disproportionate targeting of ethnicity minority communities thought to be engaged in terrorism or preparatory activities.[97] This suggests that the reforms related to the construction of the power to stop and search may do little to alleviate the focus of suspicion on particular ethnicities. Although in recent years there has been low uses of the counterterrorism power to stop and search, it seems plausible to suggest that when this power is used more frequently in the future, there will likely continue to be a disproportionate focus on particular ethnicities which may in part be attributable to a deficient process regulating the use of the power in practice.

Thirdly, according to Parmer the extent of the disparity in the use of the counterterrorism stop and search in areas such as London appear devoid of a policing function other than to allow for the targeting of particular ethnicities perceived as being involved in terrorism.[98]

Fourthly, Yesufu has found that the continued use of the power to stop and search is simply discriminatory based on the systematic targeting of particular ethnicities such as Asian and Black ethnicities.[99]

Beyond these studies, there have other additional older studies related to police uses of their discretionary powers under older counterterrorism laws such as the Prevention of Terrorism Acts was a cause for concern for the Irish communities living in Britain during the 1980s. For instance, Hillyard found considerable evidence that the police were effectively engaged in using their powers as the basis to select members of the Irish community simply because the threat of terrorism emanated from the Irish community due to the political violence coming from Northern Ireland at the time.[100]

More recent studies undertaken by Hickman *et al*[101] and previously Pantazis and Pemberto[102] suggest that there are some parallels between the experiences of the Irish communities with the current experiences of the Muslim communities being the subject of focus of discretionary police powers because of their ethnicity. This had led academics, such as Breen-Smyth,[103] to conclude that the use of police powers in England and Wales focus on particular ethnicities perceived as being a risk to terrorism. It may be argued that the continual effect of focusing on particular ethnicities creates a strong likelihood that police powers in some instances may be deployed in a manner that is at worst lacking any process to construct/apply profiles or at best a deficient process to ensure sufficient controls is placed on the types of data being used by law enforcement officers. This falls far short of the processes evident in manifestations of formal terrorist profiling examined in chapter four.

6.2.2.7 Stop and search powers as an example of informal terrorist profiling

On the basis of the discussion throughout the previous sections, the argument advanced in this chapter is that some uses of the power to stop and search power may be considered as being an example of informal terrorist profiling for at least two reasons.

Firstly, the evidence considered above on law enforcement officer use of stop and search powers would appear to suggest that the power is being deployed as a basis to identify individuals who are perceived as being a suspect for enhanced questioning/screening in an ad hoc manner based on low visibility discretion exercised by individual law enforcement officers. It is the use of stop and search as the basis to identify individuals perceived as being suspects for enhanced levels of investigation/screening that makes this use of the power tantamount to a profiling method/approach/technique. This is demonstrated consistently to a high degree of probability stemming from the construction of the power to stop and search to the use of this power in practice to target particular ethnicities that are thus far unexplained by law enforcement agencies. The studies on the peoples' experiences of stop and search go further to reinforce the very strong likelihood that individuals from Asian and Black ethnicities appear to be the focal point of these powers in practice which would indicate or at least be the hallmarks of a profiling process likely to be without a systematic process comparable with those manifestations of formal terrorist profiling.

Secondly, there is no formal acknowledgement made by the state that some sort of profiling is being/may be being used as part of the ordinary range of police tools, mechanisms and powers as a profiling method/approach/technique in the detection, deterrence or prevention of crime and/or terrorism. This is in direct contrast to the manifestations of formal terrorist profiling in chapter three. For instance, the discussion in chapter four considered formal terrorist profiling manifestations, such as knowledge discovery processes and data mining. It was clear from this discussion that these formal terrorist profiling manifestations contained an official acknowledgement of their use as a profiling method/approach/technique as law enforcement officers used them to assist in the identification of individuals for enhanced questioning.

6.3 Other evidence indicating informal terrorist profiling

Beyond the power to stop and search in England and Wales, there are other examples from the use of police powers, such as some uses of police power to arrest and detain suspects and powers to engage in identity checking, that can be used as a basis to identify the existence of other manifestations of informal profiling. This argument, which is expanded on below, is based on qualitative studies conducted in various countries such as Germany, France and Italy which identify a strong likelihood that some exercises of police powers is tantamount to a profiling process that is not formally acknowledged by authorities as a profiling process and further there does not appear to be a systematic process to construct/apply profiles in comparable terms with those formal manifestations of terrorist profiling.

There are news reports and academic qualitative studies that have focused on analysing peoples' experience of police powers in numerous countries which suggest law enforcement officers may in some instances be relying on discretionary police powers as the basis to select individuals for enhanced screening/questioning in what appears to be outside of an officially acknowledged scheme of profiling and in the absence of a systematic process in comparable terms with those manifestations of formal profiling examined in chapters four.

These qualitative studies suggest that there are at least three core uses of police powers to profile individuals thought or perceived to be engaged in terrorism or preparatory activities. These include the use of mass identity checks, the use of targeted raids by law enforcement officers and the use of police arrest and imprisonment powers. It is contended that some uses of these police powers, as considered in the examples below, are capable of being classified as being a manifestation of informal profiling.

This contention rests on the argument that these uses of police powers are a recognisable act of profiling because in each of the examples below law enforcement officers appear to use their powers to identify or assist in identifying individuals for enhanced levels of screening or questioning who they perceive as being involved in terrorism or preparatory activities. It is also contended that in each of the examples considered below accurately represent an informal manifestation of profiling on the grounds that they are not officially acknowledged as being a profiling mechanism and they do not appear to have a systematic process in comparable terms with those manifestations of formal terrorist profiling in chapters four and five It is also best to view this type of profiling as being a hybrid type of profiling that is capable of manifesting deductive and inductive elements. Specifically, these uses of police powers are capable of constituting a manifestation of deductive profiling approach if law enforcement officers use these powers on the basis of past investigatory experience of specific terrorist activities to target specific individuals but equally, they may constitute elements inductive profiling if law enforcement officers use past investigatory experience and or intelligence as the basis to predict future likely characteristics of terrorists.

6.3.1 The practice of mass identity checks by law enforcement officers

A mass identity check is where law enforcement officers select individuals in ‘soft’ locations such as churches, train stations, shops or restaurants and compel individuals to provide their identity documentation so that individual officers can review the lawfulness of that individual’s identity documentation.[104] The purpose of these mass identity checks are somewhat unclear, as they do not appear to be recognised officially as a counterterrorism strategy.[105] The use of police powers by law enforcement officers to engage in mass identity checks seems to suggest that some uses is to identify those who may be involved in terrorism and/or crime. This rests on the argument that in the aftermath of the terrorist attacks on September 11, 2001 and the rise in the prevalence of terrorism thereafter, there is a growing array of evidence in numerous European countries, which suggests that law enforcement officers may be relying on mass identity checks as a tool to manage the threat of terrorism.

The evidence on the use of mass identity checks appear to suggest that it has been deployed by law enforcement officers as part of a regularised counterterrorism strategy to target those individuals perceived as being involved, or at risk of being involved, in terrorism so that law enforcement officers can engage in enhanced levels of screening and questioning. It is contended that some exercises/uses of these police powers are best considered as being a manifestation of informal terrorist profiling. This contention rests on the argument that there is no official acknowledgement that law enforcement officers use their police powers to engage in mass identity checks and in contrast to the manifestations of formal terrorist profiling in chapter four, there appears to be an absence of a systematic process to construct/apply profiles.

In the immediate aftermath of the US terrorist attacks, there were widespread reports that German police were effectively targeting their Muslim population in direct response to the fact that a group commonly referred to as the 'Hamburg Cell' were living in Germany in the months prior to the US attacks who were directly involved in the planning of the US terrorist attacks. For instance, according to the Open Society Institute at least 30 mosques have been subjected to continued identity checks that have reported concerns about police targeting.[106] The manner in which the police have conducted these checks have commonly been reported as being hostile where police officers are frequently dressed in riot uniforms and commonly surround the mosques in its entirety.

It was also commonly reported that police would take those individuals without proper identification to the police station for enhanced interrogation that could last up to several hours. This targeted approach also received a surge in the aftermath of the London 2005 terrorist attacks where the OSI reported that:

> hundreds of police officers carr[ying] out identity checks in front of mosques in the cities of Aalen, Balingen, Biberach, Esslingen, Freiburg, Friedrichshafen, Heilbronn, Karlsruhe, Lörrach, Ludwigsburg, Mannheim, Pforzheim, Ravensburg, Reutlingen, Sigmaringen, Stuttgart, Tübingen, Ulm and Waiblingen.[107]

Furthermore, significant identity checks were extended beyond Mosques to the nearby streets in August 2005, which resulted in streets leading up and surrounding mosques being closed to allow 1,260 identities being checked. According to the German Ministry of the Interior, the officially stated purpose of these checks was to:

> obtain further information about Islamic extremists and terrorists in order to react quickly to any Islamist threat and to destroy terrorist structures. … Police need to obtain comprehensive information about Islamists. … It must be made clear to the extremists that we will deal most forcibly with any religiously motivated claims to absolute power, intolerance and disregard for human rights.[108]

However, other evidence collected in interviews conducted by the OSI with law enforcement officers on the ground found that they did

> not really expect to find people who are terrorists or supporters. To reach this goal other methods are used. Preventive identity controls are instead used on top of other methods. The main goal of these controls is to find people who are living in Germany illegally or [engaged in] other related crime. We also want to show that the police are there, that we are doing something about terrorism; this increases pressure on persons involved in terrorist activities.[109]

If this law enforcement officer's explanation of this type of conduct is accurate, then this may not be considered profiling but more likely to be simply an attempt to send a signal to communities that they are being watched by agents of the state. Nevertheless, it seems plausible to suggest at minimum this type of police practice is a crude filter that may in some instances be close to a form of profiling.

More recent activities by the German police was reported on Reuters News that on New Years Eve on December 31, 2016 police in Cologne undertook a significant mass identity check of what appeared to be individuals of North African appearance in light of perceived security concerns.[110]

Some evidence collected in Italy would suggest that law enforcement officers are frequently using their powers to engage in identity checks of individuals whom law enforcement officers perceive as being a risk of terrorism or preparatory activities. For instance, it was reported that in 2005 police were frequently engaged in anti-terrorism sweeps of high areas of Muslim populations.[111] It has been reported that these checks are escalating in Northern and Southern territories in Italy since the 9/11 US terrorists attack.[112]

A similar theme is evident in France where there has been evidence collected on police usage of their powers which suggest that they may be frequently engaging in the practice of mass identity checks of Muslim populated areas as a basis for enhanced levels of screening and questioning. For instance, the OSI has found that in interviews held with Muslims, there were reported instances of the police turning up to Mosques with the apparent sole objective to engage in mass identity checks of those in attendance.[113] In other studies conducted by the International Helsinki Federation for Human Rights, there have been similar results found where police simply turn up at mosques as the basis to check the identity of those in attendance with often very little, if any, arrests being made.[114]

Consequently, it may be argued that in each of these countries, it would seem plausible to suggest that some law enforcement officers in some locations may well be engaged in using their police powers as the basis to identify individuals for enhanced screening or questioning without any justification. These mass identity checks undertaken by the law enforcement officers seem to operate outside any official acknowledgement that these powers may be utilised as a profiling mechanism and they appear quite randomised without a systematic process for constructing/applying profiles in comparable terms with those manifestations of formal terrorist profiling examined in chapter four. Or alternatively, this practice may be an abuse of police powers that represent a flagrant act of harassment and collective punishment on some communities.

6.3.2 The practice of targeted raiding by law enforcement officers

There is also evidence to support the argument that law enforcement officers in numerous European countries appear to be using their discretionary powers as the basis to select individuals for enhanced levels of screening or questioning by engaging in the practice of targeted raids. Although law enforcement officers may engage in the use of raids on the basis of available intelligence, in the context of counterterrorism policing strategy, it would seem that in the aftermath of US terrorist attacks that targeted raids are in part being focused on Muslim communities. In some instances, it would seem possible that law enforcement officers may be using this tactic as a basis to assist in the identification of those likely to terrorists or engaged in preparatory activities. Although, this use police powers may simply be abuse of police powers, it is at least possible to question the potential that some law enforcement officers may be using this power in a very crude manner to identify those who they perceive as being at risk of being a terrorist.

6.3.3 For example, according to the International Helsinki Federation for human rights

> ... since September 11th, thousands of Muslims [in Germany] have been subjected to screening of their personal data, house searches, interrogations and arrests solely because their profiles have marched certain criteria, foremost of which is an affiliation with Islam.[115]

For instance, the OSI have found that Muslim places of worship, business and homes are commonplace as part of a 'tough' stance on counterterrorism.[116] The value of these targeted raids are varied. For example, the BBC reported in 2007 on a targeted raid in Italy which suggested that '[p]olice in central Italy say they have uncovered a bomb school for Islamist militants after raiding a mosque in Perugia and making three arrests.'[117] Similarly, CNN reported on a police raid in London by stating

> British anti-terror police found a mini arsenal of weapons when they raided a London mosque linked to a number of key terrorist suspects.[118]

In the context of Germany, there have been some reported successes such as Patterson who identified that

> an operation involving more than 800 officers, police had raided 50 addresses across Germany and confiscated faked passports, computer data and militant Islamic propaganda.[119]

Although these reports have identified positive outcomes as a result of law enforcement officer use of their powers to engage in targeted raiding, there are numerous other reports that demonstrate the unofficial nature of the use of targeted raids by law enforcement officers. For example, Smolar who was a reporter with *Le Monde* in France identified that law enforcement officers appear to engage in raiding businesses and mosques without any discernible justification.[120]

Smolar suggested that in 2005 upwards of 47 mosques were searched along with 473 businesses and 85 cafes which resulted in the police issuing 276 penalties unrelated to terrorism.[121] Individual interviews conducted by the OSI with those subjected to these targeted raids commonly suggest that

> [i]n practice, the [police] arrive with numerous vehicles. They come at peak business hours. Some officials have uniforms; others wear ordinary clothes. They enter the business—health, customs, fraud, police ... They don't show their badges, they don't identify themselves. If any officials show their badges it is the health and hygiene inspectors.[122]

A cafe manager interviewed by OSI recounted their experience of being subjected to a targeted raid:

> [t]he manager called me when the officials arrived and I came immediately. There were six or eight cars and at least 10 officials. It was around 8:00 p.m., a busy time. I observed the manner that they behaved and I asked them questions. I saw that there were two officials from the intelligence services. I could identify them as they did not respond when I asked where they worked. The telephone rang; the employee wanted to answer the phone. One of the intelligence officials said, 'No, turn off your phone and close down the shop.' I watched him [as] he went to the back of the restaurant. I asked what he was doing there. 'Shut up,' he responded ... The other intelligence official said, 'Now, you keep quiet or we'll shut down your business permanently.' I was torn between [wanting to protest] the illegal nature of their words and [my desire not to endanger] my friend. I said nothing further. The police asked everyone inside the restaurant to produce their identity documents. Those who didn't have their documents with them were handcuffed and taken to the police station.[123]

In other countries, such as Italy, there have been similar concerns expressed by those subjected to individual targeted raids by law enforcement officers. For instance, the OSI found there was an increase in the frequency of targeted raids that after either a terrorist attack or information on how an attack was foiled police in Italy which focused on mosques, businesses owned by Muslims and individual houses in known Muslims areas.[124]

Other similar concerns have been identified in Germany where mosques appear to be the direct target of police raids. For instance, Bernstein from the

New York Times in an interview with a Muslim subjected to a targeted raid concluded that:

> [p]robably at the moment, every Muslim is under suspicion. It is the right of the police to search but not to overdo it in such an aggressive way. Somebody hears something from a child and then the police arrive with 200 men. There were other ways of finding out if some-thing like that was shown or not.[125]

In light of this evidence, it may be argued that in certain instances law enforcement officers appear to be using their police powers to engage in selecting individuals for enhanced levels of questioning/screening through targeted raids without any discernible justification. Although, some of the discussion highlighted some successes by being able to identify individuals of interest to law enforcement, it is contended that other evidence showing the potential misuse of police powers in certain circumstances creates a high degree of probability that these powers may in some instances have been deployed in a manner that is not acknowledged as a profiling process and does not exhibit a systematic process in comparable terms with those manifestations of formal profiling already examined in chapter four.

6.3.4 Law enforcement use of powers of arrest and imprisonment

The power of arrest and imprisonment afforded to law enforcement officers can be considered quite an important police power which allows officers to arrest and imprison those deemed to be at risk of, or engagement in, the commission of criminality or in the context of terrorism, the risk of preparing or committing acts of terrorism. However, a concern with the exercise of this power, in common with the other police powers, is its discretionary nature with the potential that it can be used to target particular individuals or groups of individuals who may be perceived as being a risk of criminality or terrorism. In the context of terrorism, it is common that this power is quite broadly constructed, which frequently allow 'suspects' to be detained without little or any evidence of the individual's involvement in terrorism.[126]

In the aftermath of US terrorist attacks there has been some evidence to suggest that law enforcement officers in numerous jurisdictions may be deploying the power to arrest and imprison to target individuals and/or groups who are perceived as being at risk of involvement in terrorism or preparatory activities.

For example, there has been reports in France which suggest that law enforcement officers may, in certain circumstances, be using the power of arrest and imprisonment as the basis to detain those of Muslim appearance. An OSI's interview with one of the French counterterrorism police reveals the thinking process that police officers go through in deciding when to exercise their powers of arrest:

> [t]he first [consideration] is the babysitter, the next is the baker, the next is a Muslim man – simply an ordinary religious Muslim – and the next is a Muslim who was in Afghanistan. The babysitter and baker will be

> easily eliminated and the Muslim that has also been to Afghanistan will be included. It is with respect to the other Muslim that things become problematic, and where a possibility of discrimination arises. The investigative judge will need to make a decision.[127]

Furthermore, the counterterrorism officer suggested that suspicion may be formed about an individual when:

> [t]he personal history and skills necessary to carry out a terrorist act [or] certain behaviours that differentiate a person from the rest. For example, the fact of going to the mosque every day at 5:00 p.m. This is not so common, so this behaviour can differentiate a person; even within this community, everyone does not go to the mosque every day, not European Muslims. ... Operational logic prevents us from keeping everyone under surveillance.... We look who the person knows... If they know 15 people who are good Muslims, we don't care. But if someone's sister and brother are 'Tabligh,' that is more interesting...We basically watch for criteria that differentiate a person, and these criteria include a person's skills, behaviour (such as trips to certain countries or going to the mosque every day), and judicial history.[128]

The most concerning aspect of the French apparent use of the police power to arrest and imprison is the accounts of those subjected to these powers. For instance, one account by an individual subjected to arrest accounted that:

> [t]hey took me to the station. On the way, when we were on the highway at a turn, they said, 'You know Zorro, we can wipe you out here. We have all the rights, so if you cause us problems, we'll take you down and throw you away. We have unlimited powers.' When we got to the police station, they put me in the interrogation room. They took my photo and my fingerprints. They called me 'Zorro.' They said, 'Zorro, your friends sold you, they told us everything.' They asked me what I did. They brought me my old passports. They said I had been to New York. They spoke rudely. They asked questions about my life, my earnings, my rent. They said that I had been under surveillance for some time. They let me go around 6.00 p.m. the same evening.
>
> In fact, they had my cousin under surveillance. He had taken a trip to Ukraine. They had monitored him upon his return....I rarely see my cousin, but they have to find a network and a link, so they create a relationship from diverse elements that in fact are not related. There had been an armed robbery on high security vehicles. They said that this money had gone to buy arms in the Ukraine and bring them back to Paris to carry out attacks. They had no concrete elements to support this hypothesis. I think the reality is that after 9/11 they wanted to show that they were doing something; they have to carry out some arrests.[129]

It would seem that law enforcement officers had little reason to select this individual for arrest and detection which may be question the use of this power in this manner by law enforcement officers.

There are also reports from other countries which reveal similar patterns of reported abuses of the power of arrest and imprisonment. For instance, in Italy the OSI found that in 2006 upwards of 200 individuals were subjected to arrest and imprisonment but ultimately two of these arrests actually led to prosecution and conviction.[130] Additionally, in the context of the UK there have been reports of excessive uses of arrest and imprisonment powers on Muslim communities since the US terrorist attacks on September 11, 2001. According to Jaggi from 2001 up until 2004 there had been arrests of around 600 individuals on the basis of suspected terrorism offences with only 100 charges leading to only 15 successful prosecutions.[131]

These studies form the basis to argue this this police power may in some instances have been deployed in a manner not recognised as a form of profiling and does not exhibit a systematic process in comparable terms with those formal manifestations of profiling already examined in chapter four.

6.4 The usefulness of informal terrorist profiling

In keeping with the theme established in chapters four and five, it is now appropriate to progress to consider, how if at all, these examples of informal profiling may be considered as being useful in prevention, detection and deterrence of terrorism and its preparatory activities.

As it can be recalled from the introductory chapter, the effectiveness of terrorist profiling may be assessed/measured by reference to three separate indicators of usefulness.

6.4.1 The input effectiveness

The input effectiveness involves conducting a utilitarian assessment of the methods used in the construction and/or application of terrorist profiles so as to assess whether the methods are capable of identifying likely terrorist characteristics that can be used in the construction of terrorist profiles. In each of the examples of informal terrorist profiling considered in this chapter, it is difficult to identify whether any methods/approaches were relied upon by the individual law enforcement officers when they decide to exercise their discretionary police powers. As noted in the introduction above, each of these manifestations of informal terrorist profiling may represent examples of inductive or deductive profiling depending on the context in which the individual law enforcement officer decided to use their police power. As these uses of police powers are not recognised as being a form of profiling, it is not clear that there are any methods used to construct a profile. From a methodological perspective it is argued that the apparent absence of a discernible profiling method/approach calls into question the usefulness or indeed effectiveness of this type of profiling. As it was noted in chapter three, there were a number of weaknesses evident in deductive and inductive profiling methods. As it is not possible to firmly classify informal terrorist profiling as being a deductive or inductive profiling method/approach, it is necessary to consider the limitations of both profiling approaches.

Deductive profiling methods/approaches required a significant array of pre-existing knowledge/data to allow themes and patters to be spotted. The identification of these themes and patters allowed for a high degree of typologies and hypothesis as the basis to construct a profile. If informal terrorist profiling is to be deployed as a means to prevent, detect or deter acts of terrorism or its preparatory activities in a meaningful way, then individual officers on the grounds exercising their discretionary police powers as a profiling method/approach needs to draw upon this array of pre-existing evidence to construct typologies and hypothesis. If there is an absence of a methodological approach, then there is little or no means to manage the risks associated with these limitations of deductive profiling. This may prove fatal to the meaningfulness or potential meaningfulness of informal terrorist profiling.

A limitation of inductive profiling methods/approaches identified in chapter three was a high reliance on statistical models as the basis to predict future likely characteristics. If individual law enforcement officers are effectively using their discretionary police powers in an *ad hoc* informal profiling manner, then there will be no statistical model upon which to predict or guide law enforcement officers on how they should be exercising their discretion to select individuals for enhanced questioning/screening.

Consequently, the high degree of probability surrounding the likely absence of any method/approach to construct profiles would call into question the usefulness or effectiveness of this type of profiling.

6.4.2 The output effectiveness

The output assessment of the effectiveness of the application of terrorist profiles involves considering the direct and indirect evidence available to demonstrate whether law enforcement officers were able to identify individuals likely to be engaged in terrorism or preparatory activities.

It is acknowledged that the output effectiveness is difficult, if not impossible, to identify in respect of the qualitative examples of informal terrorist profiling considered above. This is largely due to the lack of any discernible or creditable evidence that these uses of police powers are capable of identifying those likely to be engaged in terrorism or its preparatory activities. As a result, the discussion will focus here on the quantitative evidence available on law enforcement officer use of stop and search powers in England and Wales.

In the context of measuring the output effectiveness of law enforcement officer use of stop and search powers, the most obvious benchmark to focus on is the arrest rate that follows the exercise of the power to stop and search. The problem with identifying the output effectiveness of stop and search powers is that there is a very low arrest rate associated with police uses of stop and search powers.

For example, the most recent statistics on the use of section 47A of the TA 2000 reveals that out of 149 stopped and searched in 2017/18 there were only 3 specific terrorism related arrests, which represents a 3% success rate.[132] Under the previous law, section 44 of the TA 2000, the arrest rate was also low with 0.5% of all section 44 stop and searches resulting in an arrest in 2009/10.[133] Although, the discussion in the earlier part of this chapter acknowledges that focusing on the arrest rate may be artificial as an arrest is not the principle aim of the use of stop and search. Nevertheless, it is argued that such a low level of arrest following the decision to exercise a stop and search calls into question whether the exercise of this power as a profiling method/approach is capable of assisting law enforcement officers identify those likely to be engaged in terrorism or its preparatory activities.

6.4.3 The impact of informal terrorist profiling

It can also be recalled from the introduction chapter that a further measure of effectiveness is to analyse the impact of formal terrorist profiling so as to determine whether the effect and cost of terrorist profiling can be considered as outweighing any input and output effectiveness.

6.4.4 Stop and search in England and Wales

The discussion examining the stop and search powers in England and Wales highlighted the extent of the disproportionality ratio in the application of stop and search powers between ethnic minorities versus the majority White ethnicity in England and Wales. The application of stop and search powers have long concerned civil liberties groups in England and Wales, given the extent of the disproportionality in stop and search between those individuals recorded as being Black or Asian and White ethnicities.[134] There are also various academic studies that have sought to discern the impact of the excessive application of stop and search powers on ethnic minority communities.[135]

According to Pantazis and Pemberton there are at least three core discernible impacts of the disproportionate application of stop and search on ethnic minority communities in England and Wales that questions the cost associated with the use of the stop and search power.[136]

Firstly, the frequent application of stop and search powers on particular ethnicities, such as the Black and Asian ethnicities, has the net effect of reducing public confidence in the police by individuals from within these communities.[137] This means that the high levels of official suspicion felt by some members in Muslim communities often contribute to these communities having limited or no confidence in the police.[138] Spalek *et al* also found that there is a common 'sense of grievance amongst Muslims' attributable to the use of stop and search powers.[139]

This sense of grievance was also exposed by other research conducted by Choudhury and Fenwick who found that there was considerable resentment building in Muslim communities England.[140] The concern exposed by this research found that at seaports and airports, there was a feeling amongst some Muslims that they are effectively being singled out for a form of official suspicion without any objective evidence to justify such suspicion. For example, in some of their participant surveys expressed the following experiences of stop and search at airports:

> I went to Turkey recently with my uncle, and he always gets stopped. Every single time he comes to the UK he gets stopped. The business that he is in is import and export.' (Muslim, female, Leicester)
>
> The first thing you always ask your friend when they come from travelling is, did they stop you… it's not how was the holiday, it's did you get stopped and what did they ask you. That is the first question people ask each other now.' (Muslim, male, Glasgow).[141]

Further, an airport law enforcement officer who was interviewed as part of this research was able to identify resentment by Muslims travelling through British airports. For example, one officer reported:

> [s]topping at the airport that has caused a lot of resentment, not only the young people but older people, families coming back from India and Pakistan or flights from Dubai, they are singling out either the parent, the father or a brother, and it means the rest of the family is kept waiting for five hours. You are not just alienating that individual; you've got a family and the family go into the community; they then tell their community and before you know it you've got the community saying what's happened to you. (Local police officer).[142]

Other research conducted by Blick *et al* found that the consequence of the erosion of confidence in the police means the continual police suspicion on Muslim communities can

> …drip feed into vulnerable communities and gradually erodes confidence and trust … the impact of this will be that just at the time we need the confidence and trust of these communities, they may retreat within themselves.[143]

This allows Pantazis and Pemberton to conclude that a lack of confidence in the police will inevitably disrupt the 'flow of information' between communities and the police.[144] This lack of information flow is further identified by Lambert who argues that the police in England and Wales depend on intelligence from Muslim communities to understand the tactics and threats from Islamist terrorist groups operating in England.[145] As a result, it can be argued that some uses of stop and search powers has the innate potential to alienate the communities that police actually need co-operation from for intelligence purposes.

Secondly, Pantazis and Pemberton also argue that the continual subjection of Muslim communities to a disproportionate level of stop and search powers carries a high risk of furthering radicalisation within ethnic minority communities.[146] A dominant theme identified by Githens-Maze[147] and Neumann and Kleinmann[148] in counterterrorism policy is for governments to place a significant focus on developing policies that aim to engage with the risk of radicalisation. This theme is evident in England and Wales since the formal adoption of the CONTEST counterterrorism strategy which aims to 'Prevent' terrorism acts from occurring, 'Pursue' those responsible for terrorism, 'Protect' against the threat of terrorism and the 'Prepare' the country for imminent acts of terrorism.[149] The 'Prevent' strand within CONTEST is particularly focused on countering radicalisation by creating opportunities for the state to engage with those most likely to be radicalised into committing acts of terrorism.[150] The concern raised by Pantazis and Pemberton is that the continual subjection of particular communities to official suspicion of terrorism or preparatory activities by disproportionately and unjustifiably stopping and searching them carries a high risk that the very aim underpinning counterterrorism strategies like 'Prevent' may well be undermined.[151]

This is supported by reference to Hillyard's study on the use of suspicion adopted in respect of the Irish conflict during the 1980s which was used by the Irish Republic Army to assist with their recruitment of volunteers.[152] Lambert draws the parallel between the police use of stop and search in contemporary counterterrorism policing and the policing strategies adopted during the Irish troubles as the basis to argue, Islamist terrorist groups can use this official suspicion to radiçalise volunteers to support Islamic fundamentalism.[153] Abbas suggests that the official suspicion on Muslims in England and Wales creates and perpetuates a sense of 'dislocation and alienation' that can be used by Islamist groups to galvanise support.[154]

McGhee suggests that these feelings of disconnection between Muslim communities and mainstream ethnicities in England and Wales creates the atmosphere of 'them and 'us' that can be harvested by Islamists groups to generate a sense of solidarity between Muslims against the common enemy of the police.[155] Choudhury and Fenwick found in some instances not many within Muslim communities had any knowledge of 'Prevent' where one of their participants stated that 'the ordinary Muslim man on the street would not have a clue what Prevent is' (Director, Muslim women's organisation).[156] As a result, it seems arguable that if counterterrorism policy is genuinely aimed on preventing radicalisation, it would need to ensure sufficient controls on the exercise of police powers which may be eroding the very rationale of such counterterrorism policies.

Thirdly, Pantazis and Pemberton also argue that the impact of the continual use of stop and search against Black and Asian communities stirs dissent in community relations.[157] It is contended by Poynting and Mason that the impact of the application of stop and search on Black and Asian ethnic minority communities essentially gives the majority White ethnicity the 'permission to hate' them.[158] This creates a lack of cohesion in society between different ethnicities where those subjected to suspicion feel aggrieved while those not subjected to suspicion begin to distrust and perhaps hate those subject to suspicion based on a perception of guilt.

6.4.5 Summary

In light of the discussion on the input and output effectiveness of informal terrorist profiling, it is difficult to contend that this form of profiling can be considered useful or effective in assisting law enforcement officers identify those likely to be engaged in acts of terrorism or preparatory activities. The apparent lack of a methodological approach in the construction of informal profiles and a further systematic process capable of reviewing the application of these profiles calls into question their assistive value as a profiling tool.

Furthermore, the disproportionate application of these powers on Muslim communities that was evident in the qualitative studies discussed earlier in this chapter is considerable evidence to demonstrate that there may be a very high risk of alienating these communities from the state. This alienation is very likely to come at a high cost that undermines the legitimacy of the state to govern. At the very heart of the state and legitimate governance is the ability for any state to govern on the principles of non-discrimination. As a result, it is contended that even if these manifestations of informal terrorist profiling were capable of been classified as being input and output effective, the impact or likely impact of them is so significant that it is capable of compromising the state's ability to manage the threat of terrorism through counterterrorism policies.

6.4.6 Other qualitative studies on the exercise of police powers

In addition to stop and search, other qualitative studies were examined on the use of police powers including the power to engage in identity checking and the raiding of premises in other European countries such as France and Germany. The Open Society Institute (OSI) examined the impact of the evidence on the use of these powers.[159] This examination found that the apparent subjection of ethnicity minorities to police suspicion served to 'associate Muslims, foreigners, illegal immigrants, extremism, and terrorism' together.[160] In subsequent research, the OSI also found that the subjection of police powers on Muslim communities had the effect of alienating ethnic minority communities within society.[161] Other research undertaken by the European Union Agency for Fundamental Rights (FRA) has found that ethnic minorities had a significant distrust of the police.[162]

These studies combine to demonstrate that some uses of police powers to engage in acts of profiling that may be capable of being classified as manifestations of informal terrorist profiling are very likely to lack any effectiveness in managing the threat of terrorism. It is the cost that is associated with the *impact* of these techniques or measures that calls into question their effectiveness as ever being capable of assisting law enforcement officers in the detection, prevention and prosecution of terrorism. Further, given the very high risk that many of these policing tactics could result in the alienation and stigmatisation of a community, it seems that these policing tactics could have a counterproductive effect.

6.5 Conclusion

The primary aim of the discussion in this chapter was to progress the evaluation of terrorist profiling by identifying, explaining and evaluating evidence of informal terrorist profiling.

The examination of statutory powers advancing the power to stop and search found that it failed to provide a systematic process, in comparable terms with the manifestations of formal terrorism profiling examined in chapter four, capable of controlling the data and processing of data when law enforcement officers decide to exercise a stop and search. A specific concern in this discussion was the advancement of the power to stop and search without the requirement of reasonable suspicion given that the Code of Practice only provided very limited guidance on how this power should be exercised. Further, the proposed reform of the Code of Practice in respect of Schedule 7 TA 2000 powers to stop and search is extremely worrying given it seems to be creating the potential of an exception to use stop and search under this provision in a discriminatory manner so long as that use takes account of the prevailing threat of terrorism. The proposed new draft code appears to be positioning the threat of terrorism above that of the fundamental principle of non-discrimination with a very limited explanation of a process designed to identify, select and question suspects. It is this suspicionless stop and search power that resembles very little identifiable controls which stands in stark contrast to manifestations for formal terrorist profiling examined in chapter four.

Further, the examination of the application of the stop and search power found that there is quantitative evidence on the use of the police power to stop and search which shows to a high degree of probability that law enforcement officers are likely to be using these powers in some instances as the basis to engage in profiling. This is also supported by reference to qualitative studies conducted on peoples' experiences of stop and search powers in England and Wales. Some of the uses of the stop and search power may be classified as being informal as law enforcement appear to be using these powers to identify and select individuals for enhanced levels of questioning and/or enhanced screening outside of an officially recognised and systematic process.

The discussion in the third section progressed further by considering other evidence of the use of police powers including the power to engage in identity checking, targeted raids and the use of arrest powers. This discussion found that there are a number of qualitative studies on police uses of their discretionary powers to suggest that law enforcement officers may be using their discretionary police powers to effectively engage in acts tantamount to profiling that may classifiable as being informal.

The final part of the chapter above considered the effectiveness of these uses of discretionary police powers as the basis to consider would they be likely to assist law enforcement officers identify those engaged in terrorism or its preparatory activities. This discussion found at least three grave concerns related to the input and output assessment on the likely effectiveness of informal terrorist profiling.

Firstly, the mere fact that these uses of powers are not acknowledged as a profiling process creates the difficulty in reviewing the process used to construct and apply profiles. The discussion in chapter three found that the reviewability of individual law enforcement officer applications of profiles is essential to ensure that profiling perfects its application as iterative process.

Secondly, the apparent absence of any formalised process to construct or apply profiles suggests the uses of these police powers as a profiling process cannot minimise the limitations and weaknesses of deductive and inductive profiling processes.

Thirdly, the apparent focus on the application of these police powers on specific ethnicities raises serious concerns related to the impact of each application of these powers. The discussion on impact identified a number of qualitative studies, which seem to suggest that Muslim communities are becoming increasingly disenfranchised from the state. This discussion called into question that even if these manifestations of informal terrorist profiling could be considered remotely useful to law enforcement officers in the identification of likely terrorists, the cost of this type of profiling lowers the state below that of the terrorists by compromising fundamental human rights of ethnic minorities. It may even be argued that the use of this manifestation of profiling may be counterproductive in counterterrorism as a whole.

Further, in light of the discussion on lawfulness in chapter two, it may be argued that the manifestations of informal terrorist profiling considered in this chapter would be not only capable of being classified as being unlawful on the basis of a violation of the principle of non-discrimination but also are harmful by carrying a very high risk of producing a counterproductive effect in policing terrorism.

Notes

1. R. Delsol and M. Shiner, 'Introduction' in R Delsol and M. Shiner (eds), *Stop and Search: The Anatomy of a Police Power* (Springer Publishing, 2015), 1.
2. L. Weber and B. Bowling, 'Introduction: Stop and Search in a Global Context' in L. Weber and B. Bowling (eds), *Stop and Search: Police Power in Global Context* (Routledge, 2012), 1–3.
3. D. Harris, *Profiles in Injustice: Why Racial Profiling Cannot Work* (New Press, 2003), 37.
4. For a general list of police powers to stop and search please see: PACE Code A, Annex A.
5. B. Bowling and C. Phillips, 'Disproportionate and discriminatory: reviewing the evidence on police stops and search' (2007) 70(6) The Modern Law Review 936, 937–938. Section 59 of the Protection of Freedoms Act 2012 repeals section 44–47 of the TA 2000 and section 61 inserts 47A to C into the TA 2000.

6. Ibid, 938. See also the definition of a terrorist in section 40 of the Terrorism Act 2000. Also, please note that section 43A of the Terrorism Act 2000 creates a similar power in respect of stopping and searching vehicles so as to allow a law enforcement officer with reasonable suspicion 'to discover ... [if] ....the vehicle is being used for the purposes of terrorism.'
7. Home Office, *Code of Practice for the Exercise by Police Officers of Statutory Powers of Stop and Search, Code A* (Home Office/TSO, 2014), 2.2.
8. A. Sanders, R. Young and M. Burton, *Criminal Justice* (Oxford University Press, 2010), 74.
9. A. Smith and J. Gray, *Police and People in London* (Avebury, 1985), 8–15.
10. Home Office, *Code of Practice for the Exercise by Police Officers of Statutory Powers of Stop and Search, Code A* (n7), 2.2B.
11. ibid, 1.1B.
12. *Gillan and Quinton v The United Kingdom*, Application No. 4158 (12 January 2010).
13. Terrorism Act 2000, s. 45(1).
14. *Gillan and Quinton v The United Kingdom* (n12), para 87.
15. Home Office, *Police and Criminal Evidence Act 1984, Code A* (Home Office, 2011), para 2.18A.
16. Home Office, *Review of Counterterrorism and Security Powers* (Home Office, 2011).
17. ibid, 16.
18. G. Lennon, 'Stop and search powers in UK terrorism investigations: a limited judicial oversight' (2016) 20 The International Journal of Human Rights 634, 638–639.
19. ibid.
20. J. Ip, 'The reform of counterterrorism stop and search after Gillan v United Kingdom' (2013) 13(4) Human Rights Law Review 729, 740–741.
21. Terrorism Act 2000, s. 45(1).
22. Terrorism Act 2000, s. 47A(5).
23. Ip, 'The reform of counterterrorism stop and search after Gillan v United Kingdom' (n20), 743.
24. M. Zander, 'Tighter controls on stop and search – but will they make any difference?' (2014) 178(37) Criminal Law and Justice Weekly 543, 543.
25. ibid, 544.
26. Home Office, *Police and Criminal Evidence Act 1984, Code A* (n15), para 4.1.1.
27. D. Anderson, *The Terrorism Acts in 2010, Report of the Independent Reviewer of the Operation of the Terrorism Act 2000 and Part 1 of the Terrorism Act 2010* (HMSO, 2011), 8.38–8.39. Note that Lord Bingham concluded it would not be appropriate to stop and search individuals 'who were obviously not terrorist suspects' while Lord Hope concluded that 'purely random' searches were not desired. Finally, Lord Brown's view was that stop and searching 'those regarded as presenting no conceivable threat' would likely represent a misuse of power. *R (Gillan) v Metropolitan Police Commissioner* [2006] UKHL 12, paras 63–64, 30 & 50 and 76.
28. Joint Committee on Human Rights, *The Terrorism Act 2000 (Remedial) Order 2011: Stop and Search without Reasonable Suspicion (Second Report)* (HMSO, 2011), para 34.
29. Ip, 'The reform of counterterrorism stop and search after Gillan v United Kingdom' (n20), 745.
30. Terrorism Act 2000, s. 40(1)(b).
31. Terrorism Act 2000, Schedule 7, Paragraph 7(2)(1).
32. Home Office, *Examining Officers under the Terrorism Act 2000: Code of Practice* (Home Office, 2009). Please note the Code has been reviewed and updated in 2015 with the Home Office, *Examining Officers and Review Officers under Schedule 7 of the Terrorism Act 2000: Code of Practice* (Home Office, 2016). Further,

there is a further draft update that is currently before Parliament for approval in the Home Office, *Examining Officers and Review Officers under Schedule 7 to the Terrorism Act 2000: Draft Code of Practice* (Home Office, 2020).

33. Home Office, *Examining Officers and Review Officers under Schedule 7 to the Terrorism Act 2000: Draft Code of Practice* (Home Office, 2020), 8
34. ibid.
35. ibid.
36. ibid.
37. Home Office, *Examining Officers and Review Officers under Schedule 7 of the Terrorism Act 2000: Code of Practice* (n32), 19. This reform of the Code were developed in response to *Beghal v DPP* [2015] EWHC 2573 decision, which is discussed in more detail later in this chapter.
38. Home Office, 'Examining Officers and Review Officers under Schedule 7 to the Terrorism Act 2000: Draft Code of Practice' (n33), 9–10.
39. [2015] EWHC 2573.
40. P. Waddington, K. Stenson and D. Don, 'In proportion: race and police stop and search' (2004) 44 British Journal of Criminology 889, 889–891.
41. M. Fitzgerald and R. Sibbitt, *Ethnic Monitoring in Police Forces: A Beginning* (Home Office, 1997), 96–97.
42. ibid.
43. R. Delsol and M. Shiner, 'Regulating stop and search: a challenge for police and community relations in England and Wales' (2006) 14 Critical Criminology 241, 249–255.
44. M. Banton, *The International Politics of Race* (Polity Press, 2002), 7–15.
45. Equality and Human Rights Commission, *Stop and Think: A Critical Review of the Use of Stop and Search Powers in England and Wales* (EHRC, 2015), 23.
46. M. Rowe, *Introduction to Policing* (Sage Publishing, 2018), 151–152.
47. ibid, 152.
48. M. Fitzgerald and R. Sibbitt, *Ethnic Monitoring in Police Forces: A Beginning* (Home Office, 1997), 62–65. See also: M. Fitzgerald, *Report into Stop and Search* (Metropolitan Police Service, 1999) and S. Choongh, 'Policing the dross: a social disciplinary model of policing' (1998) 38 British Journal of Criminology 623.
49. J. Miller, N. Bland and P. Quinton, *Upping the PACE? An Evaluation of the Recommendations of the Stephen Lawrence Inquiry on Stops and Searches* (Home Office, 2000), vii–viii.
50. W. Macpherson, *The Stephen Lawrence Inquiry, Report of an Inquiry by Sir William Macpherson of Cluny* (Home Office, 1999), Recommendation 61.
51. Bowling and Phillips, Disproportionate and discriminatory: reviewing the evidence on police stops and search' (n5), 945–946.
52. Fitzgearld and Sibbit, 'Ethnic Monitoring in Police Forces: A Beginning' (n48), 63–64.
53. For example: ibid, MVA and J. Miller, *Profiling Populations Available for Stops and Searches* (Home Office, 2000), 84.
54. Waddington, Stenson and Don, 'In proportion: race and police stop and search' (n40).
55. D. Anderson, *The Terrorism Acts in 2015 Report of the Independent Reviewer on the Operation of the Terrorism Act 2000 and Part 1 of the Terrorism Act 2006* (Home Office, 2015), para 6.2.
56. Please note that these statistics refer to section 43 of the TA 2000 which are solely reported in respect of the London Metropolitan Police Service. This information has been collated from: Home Office, *Operation of Police Powers under the Terrorism Act 2000 and Subsequent Legislation: Arrests, Outcomes and Stops & Searches, financial year ending March 2019* (Home Office, 2019), 20–21. The statistics on 2019/20 for the year ended March 2020 will be reported in October 2020.

57. These statistics relate specifically to section 43 of the TA 2000 which are solely reported in respect of the London Metropolitan Police Service. This information has been collated from: Home Office, *Operation of Police Powers under the Terrorism Act 2000 and Subsequent Legislation: Arrests, Outcomes and Stops & Searches, Financial Year Ending March 2019* (Home Office, 2019), 20–21. The statistics on 2019/20 for the year ended March 2020 will be reported in October 2020.
58. This Figure is based on the year ending 2015 with evidence published in: Home Office, *Operation of Police Powers under the Terrorism Act 2000 and Subsequent Legislation: Arrests, Outcomes and Stops & Searches, Financial Year Ending March 2015* (Home Office, 2015). The calculation of the disproportionality ratio is conducted using the same method explained in the previous section. It is published at: https://www.faith-matters.org/2016/05/18/numbers-counter-terrorism-powers-disproportionately-affectethnic-religious-minorities-britain/ (accessed 01st June 2020).
59. B. Harcourt, 'Rethinking racial profiling: a critique of the economics, civil liberties, and constitutional literature, and of criminal profiling more generally' (2004) 71(4) The University of Chicago Law Review 1329, 1330.
60. The figures quoted in this table relate to the published information on the use of section 44 of the TA 2000 and subsequently section 47A of the TA 2000. This table is taken in part from A. Sanders, R. Young and M. Burton, *Criminal Justice* (Oxford University Press, 2010), 76. It has been updated by reference to information published in: Home Office, *Operation of Police Powers under the Terrorism Act 2000 and Subsequent Legislation: Arrests, Outcomes and Stops & Searches, Financial Year Ending March 2019* (Home Office, 2019), 5.
61. Lord Carlile, *Report on the Operation in 2006 of the Terrorism Act 2000* (HMSO, 2007), paras 113–114.
62. Lord Carlile, *Report on the Operation in 2008 of the Terrorism Act 2000* (HMSO, 2009), 42.
63. ibid, para 147.
64. UN Human Rights Committee, *Concluding Observations of the Human Rights Committee United Kingdom of Great Britain and Northern Ireland* (UN, 2008), para 28.
65. Justice, *Stop and Search Under the Terrorism Act 2000* (Justice, 2012).
66. Human Rights Watch, *Without Suspicion* (Human Rights Watch, 2010), 41–47.
67. Joint Committee on Human Rights, *Demonstrating Respect for Rights? A Human Rights Approach to Policing Protest* (HMSO, 2009), 88–99.
68. ibid.
69. Metropolitan Police Authority, *Counterterrorism: The London Debate* (MPA, 2007), 51–52.
70. This figure is taken from: T. Quinlan and Z. Derfoufi, 'Counter-Terrorism Policing' in R. Desol and M. Shiner (eds), *Stop and Search: The Anatomy of a Police Power* (Palgrave Macmillan, 2015), 134.
71. This table is replicated from Quinlan and Derfoufi, 'Counter-Terrorism Policing' (n70), 136. Please note that this follows the same approach as previously quoted material. The disproportionate ratio is calculated by dividing the minority ethnicity by the majority White ethnicity so as to work out how many more times the minority ethnicity is stopped and searched in comparison to the White ethnicity. The figures used are those published by the Minister of Justice in 2010 and the official census figures used to determine majority ethnicity is the 2011 national census.
72. Quinlan and Derfoufi, 'Counter-Terrorism Policing' (n70), 138–139.
73. A. Heath and J. Martin, 'Can religious affiliation explain "ethnic" inequalities in the labour market' (2013) 36(6) Ethnic and Racial Studies 1005.
74. Home Office, *Operation of Police Powers under the Terrorism Act 2000 and Subsequent Legislation: Arrests, Outcomes and Stops & Searches, Financial Year Ending March 2019* (Home Office, 2019), 22–23.

75. Lord Carlile, *Report on the Operation in 2009 of the Terrorism Act 2000 and Part 1 of the Terrorism Act 2006* (Home Office, 2010), para 192.
76. D. Anderson, *Report on the Operation in 2010 of the Terrorism Act 2000 and Part 1 of the Terrorism Act 2006* (Home Office, 2011), para 7.
77. D. Anderson, *The Terrorism Acts in 2013* (HMSO, 2014), 44.
78. M. Shiner and R. Desol, 'The Politics of the Powers' in R Delsol and M. Shiner (eds), *Stop and Search: The Anatomy of a Police Power* (Springer Publishing, 2015), 52.
79. ibid.
80. R. Reiner, *The Politics of the Police* (Wheatsheaf, 1985), 33–34.
81. D. Smith, 'Ethnic origins, crime, criminal justice in England and Wales' (1997) 21 Ethnicity, Crime and Immigration: Comparative and Cross-National Perspectives 101, 105–109.
82. Bowling and Phillips, 'Disproportionate and discriminatory: reviewing the evidence on police stops and search' (n5), 940–941.
83. T. May, T. Gyateng and M. Hough, *Differential Treatment in the Youth Justice System* (Equality and Human Rights Commission, 2010), 21–29.
84. T. Thornberry and M. Krohn, 'The Self-Report Method for Measuring Delinquency and Crime' in D. Duggee, R. Crutchfield, S. Mastrofski, L. Mazerolle, D. McDowall and B. Ostrom (eds), *Innovations in Measurement and Analysis* (National Institute of Justice, 2000), 33–36.
85. J. Graham and B. Bowling, *Young People and Crime* (Home Office, 1995).
86. C. Flood-Page, S. Campbell, V. Harrington and J. Miller, *Youth Crime: Findings from the 1998/1999 Youth Lifestyles Survey* (Home Office, 2000).
87. C. Sharpe and T. Budd, *Minority Ethnic Groups and Crime: Findings from the Offending, Crime and Justice Survey 2003* (Home Office, 2005).
88. Shiner and Delsol 'The Politics of the Powers' (n78), 53.
89. MVA and Miller, 'Profiling Populations Available for Stops and Searches' (n53).
90. Waddington, Stenson and Don, 'In proportion: race and police stop and search' (n40), 891–893.
91. Sanders, Young and Burton, 'Criminal Justice' (n8), 84.
92. Shiner and Delsol 'The Politics of the Powers' (n78), 55.
93. Her Majesty's Inspectorate of Constabulary (HMIC), *Winning the Race (Revisited): Policing Plural Communities* (Home Office, 1999).
94. M. Shiner, 'Post-Lawrence policing in England and Wales: guilt, innocence and the defence of organisational ego' (2010) 50(5) British Journal of Criminology 935, 940–941.
95. Open Society Institute, *Ethnic Profiling in the European Union: Pervasive, Ineffective and Discriminatory* (OSI, 2009), 116–119.
96. ibid, 60.
97. J. Miller, 'Stop and search in England: a reformed tactic or business as usual' (2010) 50(5) British Journal of Criminology 954.
98. A. Parmer, 'Stop and search in London: counter terrorist or counter productive?' (2011) 21(4) Policing and Society 369.
99. S. Yesufu, 'Discriminatory use of police stop and search powers in London, UK' (2013) 15(4) International Journal of Police Science and Management 281.
100. P. Hillyard, *Suspect Community* (Pluto Press, 1993).
101. M. Hickman, L. Thomas, S. Silvestri and H. Nickels, *A Report for Policy Makers and the General Public July 2011* (London Metropolitan University, 2011).
102. C. Pantazis and S. Pemberton, 'From "old" to "new" suspect community: examining the impact of recent counter-terrorist legislation' (2009) 49(5) British Journal of Criminology 646.
103. M. Breen-Smyth, 'Theorising the "suspect community": counterterrorism, security practices and the public imagination' (2014) 7(2) Critical Studies on Terrorism 223.

104. *Rosalind Williams Lecraft v Spain* Comm No. 1493/2006, July 30, 2009, para 7.2.
105. Open Society Institute, 'Ethnic Profiling in the European Union: Pervasive, Ineffective and Discriminatory' (n95), 60.
106. ibid, 65.
107. ibid.
108. 'Germany: Arbitrary control of persons in front of mosques continue', Muslim Affairs, August 8, 2005, available at http://www.muslim-lawyers.net/news/index.php3?aktion=show&number=289 (accessed 01st August 2020). Also reported in Open Society Institute, 'Ethnic Profiling in the European Union: Pervasive, Ineffective and Discriminatory' (n95), 65–66.
109. ibid, 66.
110. Reuters News, 'Cologne Police slammed for "racial profiling" after mass migrant screening on NYE', available at: https://www.rt.com/news/372501-cologne-police-racial-profiling/ (accessed 15th June 2020).
111. Associated Press, 'Italy arrests 142 in anti-terrorism sweep', Associated Press, July 9, 2005, see also: H. Manges Jones, 'Italian police arrest 142 in post-London anti-terror sweep', Jurist, July 9, 2005.
112. ibid.
113. Open Society Institute, 'Ethnic Profiling in the European Union: Pervasive, Ineffective and Discriminatory' (n95), 68. See also: Islamic Institute for Human Rights, 'Country Profile: The Conditions of Muslims in France' in Open Society Institute (OSI), *Monitoring Minority Protection in EU Member States: Overview* (OSI, 2004).
114. International Helsinki Federation for Human Rights, *Intolerance and Discrimination against Muslims in Selected EU Member States; Report to the OSCE Conference on Tolerance and the Fight against Racism, Xenophobia and Discrimination* (International Helsinki Federation for Human Rights, 2005), 15.
115. International Helsinki Federation of Human Rights, *Intolerance and Discrimination Against Muslims in the EU: Developments Since September 11th* (IFHR, 2007), 78.
116. Open Society Institute, 'Ethnic Profiling in the European Union: Pervasive, Ineffective and Discriminatory' (n95), 9.
117. BBC News, 'Italy police raid, terror school', BBC News (2007), available at: http://news.bbc.co.uk/1/hi/world/europe/6909961.stm (accessed 17th June 2020).
118. CNN, 'Mini-Arsenal find at UK mosque', CNN, January 21, 2003, available at: http://edition.cnn.com/2003/WORLD/europe/01/20/mosque.raid/ (accessed 17th June 2020).
119. T. Patterson, 'Raids on mosques broke terror network, claim German police', The Independent, January 13, 2005, available at: http://www.independent.co.uk/news/world/europe/raids-on-mosques-broke-terrornetwork-claim-german-police-5344647.html (accessed 17th June 2020).
120. P. Smolar, 'Disruption of the locations where radical Islam is spread', Le Monde, April 11, 2006.
121. ibid.
122. Open Society Institute, 'Ethnic Profiling in the European Union: Pervasive, Ineffective and Discriminatory' (n95), 74.
123. ibid.
124. ibid.
125. R. Bernstein, 'Raid on "Holy War" Mosque', New York Times, July 14, 2004.
126. H. Fenwick and G. Phillipson, 'UK Counterterror Law Post-9/11: Initial Acceptance of Extraordinary Measures and the Partial Return to Human Rights Norms' in V. Ramraj, M. Hor, K. Roach and G. Williams (eds), *Global Anti-Terrorism Law and Policy* (Cambridge University Press, 2012), 503–504.
127. Open Society Institute, 'Ethnic Profiling in the European Union: Pervasive, Ineffective and Discriminatory' (n95), 83.

128. ibid.
129. ibid 84–85.
130. ibid, 86.
131. R. Jaggi, 'Police gain extra time to question suspects', The Financial Times, August 9, 2004.
132. Home Office, 'Operation of Police Powers under the Terrorism Act 2000 and Subsequent Legislation: Arrests, Outcomes and Stops & Searches, Financial Year Ending March 2019' (n56), 5.
133. ibid.
134. For example: Equality and Human Rights Commission, *Stop and Think: A Critical Review of the Use of Stop and Search Powers in England and Wales* (Equality & Human Rights, 2010), Commission. and Human Rights Watch, *Without Suspicion: Stop and Search Under the Terrorism Act 2000* (Human Rights Watch, 2010), StopWatch, *StopWatch Submission to the Consultation on Police Powers to Stop and Search* (Stop Watch, 2010).
135. For example: P. Hillyard, *Suspect Community* (Pluto Press, 1993), C. Pantazis and S. Pemberton, 'From "old" to "new" suspect community: examining the impact of recent counter-terrorist legislation' (2009) 49(5) British Journal of Criminology 646, A. Parmer, 'Stop and search in London: counter terrorist or counter productive?' (2011) 21(4) Policing and Society 369, J. Miller, 'Stop and search in England: a reformed tactic or business as usual' (2010) 50(5) British Journal of Criminology 954, S. Yesufu, 'Discriminatory use of police stop and search powers in London, UK' (2013) 15(4) International Journal of Police Science and Management 281, M. Breen-Smyth, 'Theorising the "suspect community": counterterrorism, security practices and the public imagination' (2014) 7(2) Critical Studies on Terrorism 223, T. Choudhury and H. Fenwick, *The Impact of Counter-Terrorism Measures on Muslim Communities* (Equality and Human Rights Commission, 2011).
136. Pantazis and Pemberton, 'From "old" to "new" suspect community: examining the impact of recent counter-terrorist legislation' (n102), 659–660.
137. ibid, 659.
138. N. Chakraborti, 'Policing Muslim Communities' in M. Rowe (ed), *Policing Beyond Macpherson: Issues in Policing, Race and Ethnicity* (Willan, 2007), 109–112.
139. B. Spalek and A. Imtoual, '"Hard" approaches to community engagement in the UK and Australia: Muslim communities and counter-terror responses' (2007) 27 Journal of Muslim Minority Affairs 185, 186.
140. Choudhury and Fenwick, 'The Impact of Counter-Terrorism Measures on Muslim Communities' (n135), 1–2.
141. ibid, 22.
142. ibid, 23.
143. A. Blick, T. Chaudhury and S. Weir, *The Rules of the Game: Terrorism, Community and Human Rights* (Joseph Rowntree Foundation, 2006), 34.
144. Pantazis and Pemberton, 'From "old" to "new" suspect community: examining the impact of recent counter-terrorist legislation' (n102), 659.
145. R. Lambert, 'Salafi and Islamist Londoners: stigmatised minority faith communities countering Al Qaida' (2008) 50 Crime, Law and Social Change 73, 82.
146. Pantazis and Pemberton, 'From "old" to "new" suspect community: examining the impact of recent counter-terrorist legislation' (n102), 660.
147. J. Githens-Mazer, 'The rhetoric and reality: radicalization and political discourse' (2011) 33(5) International Political Science Review 556, 557.
148. P. Neumann and S. Kleinmann, 'How rigorous is radicalization research?' (2013) 9 Democracy and Security 360, 363.
149. J. Gearson and H. Rosemont, '"CONTEST as strategy" Reassessing Britain's counterterrorism approach' (2005) 12 Studies in Conflict and Terrorism 1038, 1038.

150. C. Health-Kelly, 'Counterterrorism and the counterfactual: producing the "radicalisation" discourse and the UK prevent strategy (2012) 15(3) The British Journal of Politics and International Relations 394, 305–396.
151. Pantazis and Pemberton, 'From "old" to "new" suspect community: examining the impact of recent counter-terrorist legislation' (n102), 661.
152. Hillyard, 'Suspect Community' (n135).
153. Lambert 'Salafi and Islamist Londoners: stigmatised minority faith communities countering Al Qaida' (n145), 62.
154. T. Abbas, 'Muslim minorities in Britain: integration, multiculturalism and radicalism in the post 7/7 period' (2007) Journal of Intercultural Studies 287, 295–296.
155. D. McGhee, *The End of Multiculturism? Terrorism, Integration and Human Rights* (Open University Press, 2008), 33–34.
156. Choudhury and Fenwick, 'The Impact of Counter-Terrorism Measures on Muslim Communities' (n135), 47.
157. Pantazis and Pemberton, 'From "old" to "new" suspect community: examining the impact of recent counter-terrorist legislation' (n102), 660.
158. S. Poynting and V. Mason, 'Tolerance, freedom, justice and peace? Britain, Australia and Anti-Muslim Racism since 11 September 2001' (2006) 27 Journal of Intercultural Studies 365, 366.
159. Open Society Institute, 'Ethnic Profiling in the European Union: Pervasive, Ineffective and Discriminatory' (n95).
160. ibid, 109.
161. Open Society Institute, *Reducing Ethnic Profiling in the European Union* (OSI, 2012), 22–24.
162. European Union Agency for Fundamental Rights, *Data in Focus Report: Police Stops and Minorities* (FRA, 2010), 6–7.

Bibliography

Abbas, T., 'Muslim minorities in Britain: integration, multiculturalism and radicalism in the post 7/7 period' (2007) *Journal of Intercultural Studies* 287.

Anderson, D., *Report on the Operation in 2010 of the Terrorism Act 2000 and Part 1 of the Terrorism Act 2006* (Home Office, 2011).

Anderson, D., *The Terrorism Acts in 2010, Report of the Independent Reviewer of the Operation of the Terrorism Act 2000 and Part 1 of the Terrorism Act 2010* (HMSO, 2011).

Anderson, D., *The Terrorism Acts in 2015 Report of the Independent Reviewer on the Operation of the Terrorism Act 2000 and Part 1 of the Terrorism Act 2006* (Home Office, 2015).

Anderson, D., *The Terrorism Acts in 2013* (HMSO, 2014).

Associated Press, *'Italy Arrests 142 in Anti-Terrorism Sweep* (Associated Press, 2005).

Banton, M., *The International Politics of Race* (Polity Press, 2002).

BBC News, 'Italy police raid, terror school', BBC News (2007), available at: http://news.bbc.co.uk/1/hi/world/europe/6909961.stm (accessed 17th June 2020).

Beghal v DPP (2015) EWHC 2573.

Bernstein, R., 'Raid on "Holy War" *Mosque', New York Times, July 14,* 2004.

Blick, A., Chaudhury, T. and Weir, S., *The Rules of the Game: Terrorism, Community and Human Rights* (Joseph Rowntree Foundation, 2006).

Bowling, B. and Phillips, C., 'Disproportionate and discriminatory: reviewing the evidence on police stops and search' (2007) 70(6) *The Modern Law Review 936.*

Breen-Smyth, M., 'Theorising the "suspect community": counterterrorism, security practices and the public imagination' (2014) 7(2) *Critical Studies on Terrorism* 223.

Carlile, L., *Report on the Operation in 2006 of the Terrorism Act 2000* (HMSO, 2007).

Carlile, L., *Report on the Operation in 2008 of the Terrorism Act 2000* (HMSO, 2009).

Carlile, L., *Report on the Operation in 2009 of the Terrorism Act 2000 and Part 1 of the Terrorism Act 2006* (Home Office, 2010).

Chakraborti, N., 'Policing Muslim Communities' in M. Rowe (ed), *Policing Beyond Macpherson: Issues in Policing, Race and Ethnicity* (Willan, 2007).

Choongh, S., 'Policing the dross: a social disciplinary model of policing' (1998) 38 *British Journal of Criminology* 623.

CNN, 'Mini-Arsenal find at UK mosque', CNN, January 21, 2003, available at: http://edition.cnn.com/2003/WORLD/europe/01/20/mosque.raid/ (accessed 17th June 2020).

Delsol, R. and Shiner, M., *'Introduction' in R Delsol and M. Shiner (eds), Stop and Search: The Anatomy of a Police Power* (Springer Publishing, 2015).

Delsol, R. and Shiner, M., 'Regulating stop and search: a challenge for police and community relations in England and Wales' (2006) 14 *Critical Criminology* 241.

European Union Agency for Fundamental Rights, *Data in Focus Report: Police Stops and Minorities* (FRA, 2010).

Equality and Human Rights Commission, *Stop and Think: A Critical Review of the Use of Stop and Search Powers in England and Wales*(EHRC, 2015).

Fenwick, H. and Phillipson, G., 'UK Counterterror Law Post-9/11: Initial Acceptance of Extraordinary Measures and the Partial Return to Human Rights Norms' in V. Ramraj, M. Hor, K. Roach and G. Williams (eds), *Global Anti-Terrorism Law and Policy* (Cambridge University Press, 2012).

Fitzgerald, M., *Report into Stop and Search* (Metropolitan Police Service, 1999).

Fitzgerald, M. and Sibbitt, R., *Ethnic Monitoring in Police Forces: A Beginning* (Home Office, 1997).

Fitzgerald, M. and Sibbitt, R., *Ethnic Monitoring in Police Forces: A Beginning* (Home Office, 1997).

Flood-Page, C., Campbell, S., Harrington, V. and Miller, J., *Youth Crime: Findings from the 1998/1999 Youth Lifestyles Survey* (Home Office, 2000).

Gearson, J. and Rosemont, H., '"CONTEST as strategy" reassessing Britain's counterterrorism approach' (2005) 12 *Studies in Conflict and Terrorism 1038.*

Gillan and Quinton v The United Kingdom, Application No. 4158 (12 January 2010).

Graham, J. and Bowling, B., *Young People and Crime* (Home Office, 1995).

Githens-Mazer, J., 'The rhetoric and reality: radicalization and political discourse' (2011) 33(5) *International Political Science Review* 556.

Harcourt, B., 'Rethinking racial profiling: a critique of the economics, civil liberties, and constitutional literature, and of criminal profiling more generally' (2004) 71(4) *The University of Chicago Law Review 1329.*

Harris, D., *Profiles in Injustice: Why Racial Profiling Cannot Work* (New Press, 2003).

Heath, A. and Martin, J., 'Can religious affiliation explain "ethnic" inequalities in the labour market' (2013) 36(6) *Ethnic and Racial Studies 1005.*

Health-Kelly, C., 'Counterterrorism and the counterfactual: producing the "radicalisation" discourse and the UK prevent strategy (2012) 15(3) *The British Journal of Politics and International Relations 394.*

Her Majesty's Inspectorate of Constabulary (HMIC), *Winning the Race (Revisited): Policing Plural Communities* (Home Office, 1999).

Hickman, M., Thomas, L., Silvestri, S. and Nickels, H., *A Report for Policy Makers and the General Public July 2011* (London Metropolitan University, 2011).

Hillyard, P., *Suspect Community* (Pluto Press, 1993).

Home Office, *Code of Practice for the Exercise by Police Officers of Statutory Powers of Stop and Search, Code A* (Home Office/TSO, 2014).

Home Office, *Examining Officers Under the Terrorism Act 2000: Code of Practice* (Home Office, 2009).

Home Office, *Examining Officers and Review Officers Under Schedule 7 of the Terrorism Act 2000: Code of Practice* (Home Office, 2016).

Home Office, *Examining Officers and Review Officers Under Schedule 7 to the Terrorism Act 2000: Draft Code of Practice* (Home Office, 2020).

Home Office, *Operation of Police Powers Under the Terrorism Act 2000 and Subsequent Legislation: Arrests, Outcomes and Stops & Searches, Financial Year Ending March 2015* (Home Office, 2015).

Home Office, *Operation of Police Powers Under the Terrorism Act 2000 and Subsequent Legislation: Arrests, Outcomes and Stops & Searches, Financial Year Ending March 2019* (Home Office, 2019).

Home Office, *Police and Criminal Evidence Act 1984, Code A* (Home Office, 2011).

Home Office, *Review of Counterterrorism and Security Powers* (Home Office, 2011).

Human Rights Watch, *Without Suspicion: Stop and Search Under the Terrorism Act 2000* (Human Rights Watch, 2010).

International Helsinki Federation for Human Rights, *Intolerance and Discrimination against Muslims in Selected EU Member States; Report to the OSCE Conference on Tolerance and the Fight against Racism, Xenophobia and Discrimination* (International Helsinki Federation for Human Rights, 2005).

International Helsinki Federation of Human Rights, *Intolerance and Discrimination Against Muslims in the EU: Developments Since September 11th* (IFHR, 2007).

Ip, J., 'The reform of counterterrorism stop and search after Gillan v United Kingdom' (2013) 13(4) *Human Rights Law Review* 729.

Islamic Institute for Human Rights, 'Country Profile: The Conditions of Muslims in France' in Open Society Institute (OSI), *Monitoring Minority Protection in EU Member States: Overview*(OSI, 2004).

Jaggi, R., 'Police gain extra time to question suspects', *The Financial Times, August 9*, 2004.

Joint Committee on Human Rights, *Demonstrating Respect for Rights? A Human Rights Approach to Policing Protest* (HMSO, 2009).

Joint Committee on Human rights, *The Terrorism Act 2000 (Remedial) Order 2011: Stop and Search without Reasonable Suspicion (Second Report)* (HMSO, 2011).

Justice, *Stop and Search Under the Terrorism Act 2000* (Justice, 2012).

Lambert, R., 'Salafi and Islamist Londoners: stigmatised minority faith communities countering Al Qaida' (2008) 50 *Crime, Law and Social Change* 73.

Lennon, G., 'Stop and search powers in UK terrorism investigations: a limited judicial oversight' (2016) 20 *The International Journal of Human Rights* 634.

Macpherson, W., *The Stephen Lawrence Inquiry, Report of an Inquiry by Sir William Macpherson of Cluny* (Home Office, 1999).

Manges Jones, H., 'Italian police arrest 142 in post-London anti-terror sweep', *Jurist, July 9*, 2005.

May, T., Gyateng, T. and Hough, M., *Differential Treatment in the Youth Justice System* (Equality and Human Rights Commission, 2010).

McGhee, D., *The End of Multiculturism? Terrorism, Integration and Human Rights* (Open University Press, 2008).

Metropolitan Police Authority, *Counterterrorism: The London Debate* (MPA, 2007).

Miller, J., 'Stop and search in England: a reformed tactic or business as usual' (2010) 50(5) *British Journal of Criminology* 954.

Miller, J., Bland, N. and Quinton, P., *Upping the PACE? An Evaluation of the Recommendations of the Stephen Lawrence Inquiry on Stops and Searches* (Home Office, 2000).

Miller, J., *Profiling Populations Available for Stops and Searches* (Home Office, 2000).

Neumann, P. and Kleinmann, S., 'How rigorous is radicalization research?' (2013) 9 *Democracy and Security* 360.

Open Society Institute, *Ethnic Profiling in the European Union: Pervasive, Ineffective and Discriminatory* (OSI, 2009).

Open Society Institute, *Reducing Ethnic Profiling in the European Union* (OSI, 2012).

Pantazis, C. and Pemberton, S., 'From "old" to "new" suspect community: examining the impact of recent counter-terrorist legislation' (2009) 49(5) *British Journal of Criminology* 646.

Parmer, A., 'Stop and search in London: counter terrorist or counterproductive?' (2011) 21(4) *Policing and Society* 369.

Patterson, T., 'Raids on mosques broke terror network, claim German police', The Independent January 13, 2005, available at: http://www.independent.co.uk/news/world/europe/raids-on-mosques-broke-terrornetwork-claim-german-police-5344647.html (accessed 17th June 2020).

Poynting, S. and Mason, V., 'Tolerance, freedom, justice and peace? Britain, Australia and anti-Muslim racism since 11 September 2001' (2006) 27 *Journal of Intercultural Studies* 365.

UN Human Rights Committee, *Concluding Observations of the Human Rights Committee United Kingdom of Great Britain and Northern Ireland* (UN, 2008).

R (Gillan) v Metropolitan Police Commissioner [2006] UKHL 12.

Reiner, R., *The Politics of the Police* (Wheatsheaf, 1985).

Reuters News, 'Cologne Police slammed for "racial profiling" after mass migrant screening on NYE', available at: https://www.rt.com/news/372501-cologne-police-racial-profiling/ (accessed 15th June 2020).

Rosalind Williams Lecraft v Spain Comm No. 1493/2006, 30 July 2009.

Rowe, M. *Introduction to Policing* (Sage Publishing, 2018).

Sanders, A., Young, R. and Burton, M., *Criminal Justice* (Oxford University Press, 2010).

Sharpe, C. and Budd, T., *Minority Ethnic Groups and Crime: Findings from the Offending, Crime and Justice Survey 2003* (Home Office, 2005).

Shiner, M., 'Post-Lawrence policing in England and Wales: guilt, innocence and the defence of organisational ego' (2010) 50(5) *British Journal of Criminology* 935.

Shiner, M. and Desol, R., *'The Politics of the Powers' in R Delsol and M. Shiner (eds), Stop and Search: The Anatomy of a Police Power* (Springer Publishing, 2015).

Smith, D., 'Ethnic origins, crime, criminal justice in England and Wales' (1997) 21 *Ethnicity, Crime and Immigration: Comparative and Cross-National Perspectives* 101.

Smith, A. and Gray, J., *Police and People in London* (Avebury, 1985).

Smolar, P., 'Disruption of the locations where radical Islam is spread', *Le Monde*, April 11, 2006.

Spalek, B. and Imtoual, A., '"Hard" approaches to community engagement in the UK and Australia: Muslim communities and counter-terror responses' (2007) 27 *Journal of Muslim Minority Affairs* 185.

StopWatch, *StopWatch Submission to the Consultation on Police Powers to Stop and Search* (Stop Watch, 2010).

Thornberry, T. and Krohn, M., 'The Self-Report Method for Measuring Delinquency and Crime' in D. Duggee, R. Crutchfield, S. Mastrofski, L. Mazerolle, D. McDowall and B. Ostrom (eds), *Innovations in Measurement and Analysis* (National Institute of Justice, 2000).

Quinlan, T. and Derfoufi, Z., 'Counter-Terrorism Policing' in R. Desol and M. Shiner (eds), *Stop and Search: The Anatomy of a Police Power* (Palgrave Macmillan, 2015).

Waddington, P., Stenson, K. and Don, D., 'In proportion: race and police stop and search' (2004) 44 *British Journal of Criminology* 889.

Weber, L. and Bowling, B., 'Introduction: Stop and Search in a Global Context' in L. Weber and B. Bowling (eds), *Stop and Search: Police Power in Global Context* (Routledge, 2012).

Yesufu, S., 'Discriminatory use of police stop and search powers in London, UK' (2013) 15(4) *International Journal of Police Science and Management* 281.

Zander, M., 'Tighter controls on stop and search – but will they make any difference?' (2014) 178(37) *Criminal Law and Justice Weekly 543.*

7 Conclusion

The research questioned that this book attempted to address was:

> to what extent (if at all), and in what ways (if any) terrorist profiling may be useful as part of the law enforcement process of identifying individuals engaged in acts of terrorism and associated preparatory activities?

This primary research question was broken down into three subsidiary research questions:

- What is terrorist profiling?
- How should the usefulness of terrorist profiling be examined?
- Can terrorist profiling ever be considered a useful counterterrorism tool?

In addressing the first question, 'what is terrorist profiling' chapter one explained that terrorist profiling exists in variety of different manifestations and it is a phenomenon that is well understood in the literature. As a result, it is best to view terrorist profiling as a label that is not synonymous with any one type of profiling. This book goes beyond previous assessments of terrorist profiling by showing in chapters four to six that a full analysis of terrorist profiling requires an analytical distinction between different manifestations of terrorist profiling. Specifically, chapters four to six analysed terrorist profiling by reference to a profiling spectrum ranging from formal to informal manifestations of terrorist profiling. This adds to the previous examinations of terrorist profiling given that many of these examinations focused on the lawfulness and the impact of terrorist profiling without attempting to understand the very nature of the terrorist profiling process by separately analysing the construction and application of profiles.

In chapter four, it was shown that manifestations of formal terrorist profiling were those that exhibited at least three common features including a systematic and official use of a profiling method/approach to construct/apply profiles, the application of profiles by law enforcement officers and an ability to review the operation and practice of formal terrorist profiling. This chapter examined various manifestations of formal terrorist profiling that adopt a highly systematic and formalised process to construct and apply profiles which draw upon methods, such as 'knowledge discovery processes' and 'data mining' techniques.

In chapter five, it was shown that a further manifestation of terrorist profiling is behavioural profiling which moved towards the informal end of the profiling spectrum. The discussion in this chapter showed that the manifestations of behavioural terrorist profiling in Israel and the US used a greater degree of a formalised and systematic process than in comparison to other more informal manifestations of terrorist profiling.

In chapter six, it was shown to a high degree of probability a further manifestation of terrorist profiling exists that is accurately classified as being informal terrorist profiling. This type of profiling is classified as being 'informal' when at least two criteria are met. Firstly, there is no formal acknowledgement made by the state that some sort of profiling is being/may be used. Indeed, it is common for the state to refuse to recognise or acknowledge the use of profiling as a result of the use of low visibility police powers. These police powers appear as part of their available apparatus of tools and mechanisms to assist in detecting, deterring and preventing acts of terrorism or associated preparatory activities. Secondly, manifestations of informal profiling do not exhibit the same level of a systematic process, approach or structure in contrast with manifestations of formal terrorist profiling such as those manifestations already considered in chapter four.

As a result of these analytical distinctions, it is contended that any analysis of terrorist profiling should be undertaken by reference to the profiling spectrum that ranges from formal to informal manifestations. It is contended that this spectrum provides the basis to conduct a systematic examination of terrorist profiling. It is acknowledged that at various points throughout this book, it has not always been possible to conclusively prove the manifestations of terrorist profiling examined. However, this book has been able to advance an analytical framework to understand and examine the phenomenon of terrorist profiling that can be used in future research to further test its scope as more information on terrorist profiling becomes available. This analytical approach is not undertaken in existing literature and therefore the profiling spectrum provides the basis to move the debate on terrorist profiling further than previous attempts, which represents a contribution to existing knowledge.

In addressing the second research question, 'how should the usefulness of terrorist profiling be examined,' chapter three established an analytical lens that relied upon general profiling methods and approaches as the basis to critique the various manifestations of terrorist profiling examined in chapters four to six. This approach represents an original contribution of knowledge by using criminal profiling methodologies as the basis to critique manifestations of terrorist profiling. Chapter three made a distinction between deductive and inductive profiling so as to analyse the usefulness and potential usefulness of the different manifestations of terrorist profiling examined in chapters four to six. A core argument advanced in chapter three was that only inductive profiling approaches are likely to be capable of assisting law enforcement officers predict likely terrorist characteristics. This was on the basis that deductive profiling methods/approaches tended to only work in the context of pathological crimes where suspects left clues in the form of crime scene evidence that could be interpreted by profilers. Inductive profiling methods/approaches attempted to predict future likely characteristics on the basis of scientific methods/approaches based on an array of different datasets. This inductive/deductive analytical lens provides the basis to identify, explain and evaluate each manifestation of terrorist profiling. Therefore, this approach represents a further contribution to knowledge by extending the reach of criminal profiling methodologies as one basis to evaluate manifestations of terrorist profiling.

Chapter one set out an effectiveness framework capable of addressing the third research question, 'can terrorist profiling ever be considered a useful counter-terrorism tool.' This effectiveness framework adopted a three-tiered evaluative approach by examining the input, output and impact of each manifestation of terrorism profiling. This allowed a full analysis of each constitute part of terrorist profiling from the construction through to the application of terrorist profiles. An input assessment provided the basis to conduct a detailed examination of the construction of terrorist profiles by analysing the likely usefulness of each manifestation of terrorist profiling identified. The output assessment provided the basis to examine the application of terrorist profiles by law enforcement officers in the field separately from the construction of terrorist profiles. This allowed for an evaluation of each of the various manifestations of terrorist profiling so as to determine whether they could be capable of achieving the aim of assisting law enforcement officers identify those likely to be engaged in terrorism or its preparatory activities. These first two assessments, the input and output assessments, essentially conducted a utilitarian assessment of terrorist profiling. However, the effectiveness framework also conducted an impact assessment of each manifestation of terrorist profiling examined. The impact assessment went beyond the utilitarian assessment by asking whether the impact or likely impact of terrorist profiling compromises the very legitimacy of the state's moral authority to govern its citizens.

This three-tiered framework represents a further contribution to knowledge as it provides a new basis to evaluate different manifestations of terrorist profiling so as to determine whether they can be considered as being capable of assisting law enforcement officers identify those likely to be engaged in terrorism or its preparatory activities. It can be considered a new approach as in many of the previous attempts at analysing terrorist profiling, the focus is firmly fixated on the lawfulness and/or the impact of terrorist profiling which fails to engage in an in-depth analysis of the phenomenon of terrorist profiling. It is contended that an input, output and impact assessment provide a basis to help understand whether, if at all, terrorist profiling might be capable of helping law enforcement officers in the managing the threat of terrorism.

In chapter four, it was argued that manifestations of formal terrorist profiling (if properly conducted) may be considered as being capable of assisting law enforcement officers identify those likely to be involved in terrorism by conducting an input and output assessment of various manifestations of terrorist profiling. This argument rested on the contention that a thorough and systematic process used to construct terrorist profiles allows for a careful examination of the types of data needed to construct profiles. Furthermore, an assessment of the application of these profiles provided the basis to review the operation of formal terrorist profiles in the field so as to ensure they are reviewable and controllable.

However, in going beyond the input and output assessment of terrorist profiling, chapter four questioned the impact of formal manifestations of terrorist profiling by querying whether the cost associated with these manifestations of terrorist profiling can be considered as outweighing its capabilities in practice. This was an important assessment given that some manifestations of formal terrorist profiling (if properly conducted) may be considered as being capable of assisting law enforcement officers manage the threat of terrorism. The sheer quantities of personal information required for this type of profiling was a concerning consideration that cast a shadow over whether the state should be involved in profiling exercises that may be considered tantamount to mass snooping exercises on its citizens. These profiling practices may well serve to erode the democratic legitimacy of the state's moral authority to govern its citizens. Nevertheless, manifestations of formal terrorist profiling were at minimum reviewable and could be considered as being capable of accommodating human rights within counterterrorism policy. Furthermore, it is argued that although there are limitations with manifestations of formal terrorist profiling, they are significantly more acceptable than manifestations of informal terrorist profiling examined in chapter six.

The discussion in chapter five examined behavioural terrorist profiling which was classified as being a manifestation of terrorist profiling that moved towards the informal end of the profiling spectrum. The separate analysis of the input and output assessment here allowed for the discussion to identify that this type of profiling was distinguishable from formal manifestations and were unlikely to be considered as being capable of assisting law enforcement officers identify those suspects likely to be involved in terrorism.

The discussion of informal manifestations of terrorist profiling in chapter six concluded that it was highly unlikely that these manifestations could assist law enforcement officers identify those likely to be involved in terrorism given the weaknesses that surrounded the input and output assessments on the construction and application of terrorist profiles.

Chapters five and six also questioned the impact of manifestations of informal terrorist profiling. This discussion found that manifestations of informal terrorist profiling carry a very high risk of alienating ethnic minority communities from the state which carries a high cost that undermines the legitimacy of the state to govern. As a result, it was contended that even if these manifestations of informal terrorist profiling were capable of been classified as being input and output effective, the impact or likely impact of them is so significant that it is capable of compromising the state's ability to manage the threat of terrorism through counterterrorism policies. Therefore, informal manifestations of terrorist profiling are not only unlikely to able to identify those likely to be engaged in terrorism, they pose an extremely high risk of being counterproductive in counterterrorism law and policy.

A further important consideration was the determination of the justification of including sensitive characteristics in terrorist profiling which was conducted in chapter two. The argument advanced in chapter two was there is no single way to address this question. However, in chapter two the justification issue was addressed by reference to firstly considering whether the inclusion of sensitive characteristics could be considered lawful and secondly even if lawful whether there were any other reasons which suggest terrorist profiling should be unlawful and therefore unjustifiable.

The discussion in chapter two concluded that manifestations of formal terrorist profiling were capable of being considered lawful. This argument was advanced with the caveat that these manifestations needed to be properly conducted by having a demonstrable input and output effectiveness. However, chapter two also highlighted that even though manifestations of formal terrorist profiling may be considered lawful, there was a need for this type of profiling to deal with the limitations of its impact in society so as to ensure the state's moral authority and societal values were not eroded by this form of terrorist profiling. The discussion in chapter two also concluded that manifestations of informal terrorist profiling were unlikely to be considered lawful and given the likely harmful effects of this form of profiling, it could never be considered justifiable even in light of a prevailing terrorism threat.

To return to the overall research question, formal manifestations of formal terrorist profiling are at least capable of being considered likely to assist law enforcement officers as part of the process of identifying individuals engaged in acts of terrorism and/or associated preparatory activities. However, formal manifestations of terrorist profiling come with a number of limitations related to its impact which could compromise its ability to assist law enforcement officers. Nevertheless, in contrast to manifestations of informal terrorist profiling, formal terrorist profiling may be considered as being more acceptable. Further, manifestations of informal terrorist profiling are very unlikely to be ever considered capable of assisting law enforcement officers identify individuals engaged in acts of terrorism and/or associated preparatory activities.

To sum up the key conclusions that are drawn in this book are:

Formal terrorist profiling, if properly conducted by having a demonstrable input and output effectiveness, may be capable of assisting law enforcement officers identify those likely to be involved in terrorism and/or its preparatory activities. However, even if these manifestations of terrorist profiling may be considered capable and lawful, there is a further question as to whether the cost of this form of profiling is outweighed by its perceived capabilities by eroding the state's moral authority to govern its citizens.

Informal terrorist profiling (in all forms) is not only likely to be unlawful and unacceptable but this form of profiling is very likely to be harmful by alienating ethnic minority communities which erodes the state's moral authority and legitimacy to govern.

It is acknowledged that the conclusions drawn throughout this book are sometimes tentative which is partly due to available evidence or context. For example, the assessment of lawfulness in chapter two involved a complexity of factual matrixes that required a balance between the interference with rights and a rigorous terrorist profiling scheme. However, despite these limitations, it is contended that the book has managed to develop a methodology capable of assessing terrorist profiling in all of its manifestations. Namely, the use of criminal profiling methods/approaches to evaluate terrorist profiling, the three-tiered evaluative approach and the development of the profiling spectrum. This analytical framework provides the basis to evaluate and test other manifestations of terrorist profiling as more evidence becomes available in the future.

In final conclusion, it is hoped that the discussion in this book moves the debate on terrorist profiling further than previous attempts to examine it. At minimum, this book provides the basis to think about terrorist profiling before dismissing it by being able to analyse its substance within a more balanced and systematic framework.

Bibliography

Book

Adriaans, P. and Zanintge, D., *Data Mining* (Addison-Wesley, 1996).

Ainsworth, P., *Offender Profiling and Crime Analysis* (Willan Publishing, 2001).

American Civil Liberties Union, *Sanctioned Bias: Racial Profiling* (American Civil Liberties Union, 2004).

Anderson, D., *Report on the Operation in 2010 of the Terrorism Act 2000 and Part 1 of the Terrorism Act 2006* (Home Office, 2011).

The Terrorism Acts in 2010, *Report of the Independent Reviewer of the Operation of the Terrorism Act 2000 and Part 1 of the Terrorism Act 2010* (HMSO, 2011).

The Terrorism Acts in 2015, *Report of the Independent Reviewer on the Operation of the Terrorism Act 2000 and Part 1 of the Terrorism Act 2006* (Home Office, 2015).

Aust, S., *Der Baader-Meinhof-Komplex* (2nd Ed, Goldmann Publishing, 1998).

Arnadottir, O., *Equality and Non-Discrimination Under the European Convention on Human Rights* (Martinus Nijhoff, 2012).

Art, R. and Richardson, L., *Democracy and Counter-Terrorism: Lessons from the Past* (United States Institute of Peace Press, 2007).

Banton, M., *The International Politics of Race* (Polity Press, 2002).

Bland, N., Miller, J. and Quinton, P., *Upping the PACE? An Evaluation of the Recommendations of the Stephen Lawrence Inquiry on Stops and Searches* (Home Office, 2000).

Borum, R., *Psychology of Terrorism* (University of South Florida, 2004).

Brussel, J., *Casebook of a Crime Psychiatrist* (Bernard Geis Associates, 1968).

Bumgarner, J., *Profiling and Criminal Justice in America* (ABC-Clio Publications, 2004).

Burch, R., *Study Guide for Hurley's a Concise Introduction into Logic* (Thompson-Wadsworth, 2003).

Burgess, A., Groth, A. and Holmstrom, L., *Sexual Assault of Children and Adolescents* (Lexington Publishing, 1978).

Butz, P., Todlicher, I. and Willi, W., *Die Geschichte Der RAF* (Rowohlt Berlin, 2005).

Canter, D., *Criminal Shadows* (Harper Collins, 1995).

Canter, D. and Alison, L., *Offender Profiling Series II: Profiling in Policy and Practice* (Ashgate Publishing, 1999).

Canter, D. and Youngs, D., *Investigative Psychology: Offender Profiling and the Analysis of Criminal Action* (John Wiley & Sons Publishing, 2009).

Carlile, L., *Report on the Operation in 2006 of the Terrorism Act 2000* (HMSO, 2007).

—— *Report on the Operation in 2008 of the Terrorism Act 2000* (HMSO, 2009).

—— *Report on the Operation in 2009 of the Terrorism Act 2000 and Part 1 of the Terrorism Act 2006* (Home Office, 2010).

Charter, D., *The Deadly Sin of Terrorism: Its Effect on Democracy and Civil Liberty in Six Countries* (Greenwood Press, 1994).

Chen, H., Raghu, T., Ramesh, R., Vince, A. and Zeng, D., (eds), *Handbooks in Information Systems: National Security* (Elsevier, 2007).

Choudhury, T. and Fenwick, H., *The Impact of Counter-Terrorism Measures on Muslim Communities* (Equality and Human Rights Commission, 2011).

Clancey, A., Hough, M., Aust, R. and Kershaw, C., *Crime, Policing and Justice: The Experience of Ethnic Minorities, Findings from the 2000 British Crime Survey* (London, 2001).

Clarke, D., *Bevan and Lidstone's the Investigation of Crime* (Lexis Nexis, 2004).

Coke, T., 'Racial Profiling Post 9/11: Old Story, New Debate' in C. Brown (ed), *Lost Liberties: Ashcroft and the Assault on Personal Freedoms* (New York Press, 2003).

Copson, G., *Coals to Newcastle? Part 1: A Study of Offender Profiling* (Home Office Policy Research Group, 1995).

Cronin, A., *How Terrorism Ends: Understanding the Decline and Demise of Terrorist Campaigns* (Princeton University Press, 2009).

Crown Prosecution Service, *Guidance in Relation to the Prosecution of Offences Relating to Daesh and the Conflict in Syria, Iraq and Libya (revised December 2016)* (Crown Prosecution Service, 2016).

De Rosa, M., *Data Mining and Data Analysis for Counter-Terrorism* (CSIS Press, 2004).

Derfoufi, Z., *The Impact of Elected Police and Crime Commissioners in England and Wales on Police-Black and Ethnic Minority Community Relations, With Specific Reference to Stop and Search* (University of Warwick, 2016).

Desol, R. and Shiner, M., *Stop and Search: The Anatomy of a Police Power* (Palgrave Macmillan, 2015).

Douglas, J., *Mindhunter: Inside the FBI's Elite Serial Crime Unit* (Scriber Publishing, 1995).

Douglas, J., Burgess, A. and Ressler, R., *Crime Classification Manual* (Lexington Publishing, 1992).

Douglas, J. and Olshaker, M., *Unabomber: On the Trail of American's Most Wanted Serial Killer* (Pocket Books, 1996).

Friesen, W., *Unmasking the Face: A Guide to Recognising Emotions from Facial Expressions* (Maler Books, 1975).

Electronic Frontier Foundation, *CAPPS II: Governmental Surveillance via Passenger Profiling* (EFF, 2004).

Equality and Human Rights Commission, *Stop and Think: A Critical Review of the Use of Stop and Search Powers in England and Wales* (EHRC, 2015).

European Union Agency for Fundamental Rights, *Data in Focus Report: Police Stops and Minorities* (FRA, 2010).

Fielding, N., *The Police and Conflict: Rhetoric and Reality* (The Athlone Press, 1991).

Fitzgerald, M., *Report into Stop and Search* (Metropolitan Police Service, 1999).

Fitzgerald, M. and Sibbitt, R., *Ethnic Monitoring in Police Forces: A Beginning* (Home Office, 1997).

Flood-Page, C., Campbell, S., Harrington, V. and Miller, J., *Youth Crime: Findings from the 1998/1999 Youth Lifestyles Survey* (Home Office, 2000).

Friedman, D., *Discrimination Law* (Clarendon Press, 2011).

GAO, *Aviation Security: TSA Should Limit Future Funding for Behavior Detection Activities, GAO-14-159* (Government Accountability Office, 2013).

GAO, *Aviation Security: TSA Does Not Have Valid Evidence Supporting Most of the Revised Behavioral Indicators Used in Its Behavior Detection Activities* (Government Accountability Office, 2017).

Garland, D., *The Culture of Control* (Oxford University Press, 2001).

Goodwin, J., *Murder USA: The Ways We Kill Each Other* (Ballantine Publishing, 1978).

Graham, J. and Bowling, B., *Young People and Crime* (Home Office, 1995).

Gunaratna, R., *Inside al Qaeda: Global Network of Terror* (Columbia University Press, 2002).

Hacker, F., *Crusaders, Criminals, Crazies: Terror and Terrorism in Our Time* (Norton Publishing, 1976).

Han, J. and Kamber, M., *Data Mining: Concepts and Techniques* (Morgan Kaufmann, 2001).

Harcourt, B., *Against Prediction. Profiling, Policing and Punishing in an Actuarial Age* (University of Chicago Press, 2007).

Hargreaves, J., Linehan, C. and McKee, C., *Police Powers and Procedures, England and Wales, Year Ending 31st March 2016* (Home Office, 2016).

Harris, D., *Good Cops: The Case for Preventive Policing* (The New Press, 2005).

—— *Profiles in Injustice* (The New Line Press, 2003).

Hauser, D., *Baader und Herold Beschreibung eines Kampfes* (Alexander Fest Verlag Publishing, 1997).

Hazelwood, R. and Burgess, A., *Practical Aspects of Rape Investigation: A Multi-Disciplinary Approach* (CRC Press, 1987).

Her Majesty's Inspectorate of Constabulary (HMIC), *Winning the Race (Revisited): Policing Plural Communities* (Home Office, 1999).

Hickman, M., Thomas, L., Silvestri, S. and Nickels, H., *A Report for Policy Makers and the General Public July 2011* (London Metropolitan University, 2011).

Hicks, S. and Sales, B., *Criminal Profiling* (American Psychological Association, 2006).

Hillyard, P., *Suspect Community* (Pluto Press, 1993).

Hobbes, T., *Leviathan* (CreateSpace Independent Publishing Platform, 2011).

Holmes, R. and Homes, S., *Profiling Violent Crimes: An Investigative Tool* (Thousand Oaks, 1996).

Home Office, *Code of Practice for the Exercise by Police Officers of Statutory Powers of Stop and Search, Code A* (Home Office/TSO, 2014).

—— *Examining Officers under the Terrorism Act 2000: Code of Practice* (Home Office, 2009).

—— *Examining Officers and Review Officers under Schedule 7 of the Terrorism Act 2000: Code of Practice* (Home Office, 2016).

—— *Operation of Police Powers under the Terrorism Act 2000 and Subsequent Legislation: Arrests, Outcomes and Stops & Searches, Financial Year Ending March 2018* (Home Office, 2018).

—— *Police Powers and Procedures England and Wales 2010 to 2011: Second Edition* (Home Office, 2012).

——*Police and Criminal Evidence Act 1984, Code A* (Home Office, 2011).

——*Review of Counterterrorism and Security Powers* (Home Office, 2011).

Human Rights Watch, *Without Suspicion* (Human Rights Watch, 2010).

Information Awareness Office, US Department of Defence, *Report to Congress Regarding the Terrorism Information Awareness Program* (US Department of Defence, 2003).

International Helsinki Federation for Human Rights, *Intolerance and Discrimination against Muslims in Selected EU Member States; Report to the OSCE Conference on Tolerance and the Fight against Racism, Xenophobia and Discrimination* (International Helsinki Federation for Human Rights, 2004).

——*Against Muslims in the EU: Developments Since September 11th Intolerance and Discrimination* (IFHR, 2007).

Jackson, J., *Offender Profiling; Theory, Research and Practice* (Wiley Publications 1995).

Jackson J. and Bekerian, D., *Offender Profiling: Theory, Research and Practice* (John Wiley & Sons Publishing, 1997).

Joint Committee on Human Rights, *Demonstrating Respect for Rights? A Human Rights Approach to Policing Protest* (HMSO, 2009).

—— *The Terrorism Act 2000 (Remedial) Order 2011: Stop and Search without Reasonable Suspicion (Second Report)* (HMSO, 2011).

Justice, *Stop and Search Under the Terrorism Act 2000* (Justice, 2012).

Kant, I., *The Metaphysical Elements of Justice: Part 1 of the Metaphysical of Morals* (Bobbs-Merrill, 1965).

Kaufmann, M., *Ethnic Profiling and Counter-Terrorism* (Lit Verlag, 2009).

Keeling, P., *No Respect: Young BAME Men, the Police and Stop and Search* (Criminal Justice Alliance, 2017).

Kocsis, R., *Criminal Profiling: Principles and Practice* (Humana Press, 2006).

Lee, H. and Gaensslen, R., *Forensic Science: An Introduction to Criminalistics* (McGraw-Hill, 1983).

Macpherson, W., *The Stephen Lawrence Inquiry, Report of an Inquiry by Sir William Macpherson of Cluny* (Home Office, 1999).

May, T., Gyateng, T. and Hough, M., *Differential Treatment in the Youth Justice System* (Equality and Human Rights Commission, 2010).

Meel, P., *Clinical Versus Statistical Prevention: A Theoretical Analysis and a Review of the Evidence* (Jason Aronson Publishing, 1954).

Memon, N., Farley, J., Hicks, D. and Rosenorn, T., *Mathematical Methods in Counterterrorism* (Springer Publications, 2009).

Metropolitan Police Authority, *Counterterrorism: The London Debate* (MPA, 2007).

Moeckli, D., *Human Rights and Non-Discrimination in the War on Terror* (Oxford University Press, 2008).

Miller, J., *Profiling for Stops and Searches* (Home Office, 2000).

National Research Council, *Protecting Individual Privacy in the Struggle Against Terrorists: A Framework for Programme Assessment* (National Academic Press, 2008).

Nespolous, J., Perron, P. and Lecours, A., *The Biological Foundation of Gestures: Motor and Semiotic Aspects* (Lawrence Erlbaum Associates, 1986).

Neuman, W. and Wiegand, B., *Criminal Justice Research Methods: Qualitative and Quantitative Approaches* (Allyn and Bacon Publishing, 2000).

Open Society Institute, *Ethnic Profiling in the European Union: Pervasive, Ineffective and Discriminatory* (OSI, 2009).

—— *Reducing Ethnic Profiling in the European Union* (OSI, 2012).

Parmar, A., 'Policing and Ethnic Profiling' in K. Pall Sveinsson (ed), *Ethnic Profiling: The Use of Race in UK Law Enforcement* (Runnymede, 2010).

Plaw, A., *Targeting Terrorists: A Licence to Kill?* (Ashgate Publishing, 2008).

Plutchik, P., *The Psychology and Biology of Emotion* (Harper Collins College Publishers, 1994).

Popper, K., *The Logic of Scientific Discovery* (Routledge, 2003).

Ramierz, D., McDevitt, J. and Farrell, A., *A Resource Guide on Racial Profiling Data Collection Systems: Promising Practices and Lessons Learned* (Northeast University, 2000).

Rapoport, D., 'Modern Terror: The Four Waves' in A. Cronin and J. Ludes (eds), *Attacking Terrorism: Elements of a Grand Strategy* (Georgetown University Press, 2004).

Rawls, J., *A Theory of Justice* (Harvard University Press, 1999).
Reiner, R., *The Politics of the Police* (Wheatsheaf, 1985).
Reiner, R., *The Politics of the Police* (Oxford University Press, 2010).
Robertson, J., *Global Issues: Terrorism and Global Security* (Infobase Publishing, 2007).
Roiger, R. and Geatz, M., *Data Mining: A Tutorial based Primer* (Addison Wesley, 2002).
Ron, R., *Remarks to the Aviation Subcommittee on Transportation and Infrastructure* (US Congress, 2002).
Rosen, J., *The Naked Crowd: Reclaiming Security and Freedom in an Anxious Age* (Random House, 2004).
Rowe, M., *Introduction to Policing* (Sage Publishing, 2018).
Sanders, A., Young, R. and Burton, M., *Criminal Justice* (Oxford University Press, 2010).
Schmid, A., and Crelinsten, R., *Western Responses to Terrorism* (Frank Cass Publishers, 1993).
Schmid, A. and Jongman, A., *Political Terrorism: A New Guide to Actors, Authors, Concepts, Data Bases, Theories, and Literatures* (Transaction Publishers, 1988).
Seifert, J., *Data Mining and Homeland Security: An Overview* (Congressional Research Service, 2009).
Sharpe, C. and Budd, T., *Minority Ethnic Groups and Crime: Findings from the Offending, Crime and Justice Survey 2003* (Home Office, 2005).
Smith, A. and Gray, J., *Police and People in London* (Avebury, 1985).
Technical Advisory Committee, *SPOT Validation Study Final Results: 2011 Technical Advisory Committee (TAC) Review Report* (GAO, 2011).
Thuraisingham, B., *Data Mining: Technologies, Techniques, Tools and Trends* (CRC Press, 1999).
Transport Security Administration, *Secure Flight Program 73* (Department of Homeland Security, 2008).
Turvey, B., *Criminal Profiling: An Introduction to Behavioural Evidence Analysis* (Academic Press, 1999).
UN Human Rights Committee, *Concluding Observations of the Human Rights Committee United Kingdom of Great Britain and Northern Ireland* (UN, 2008).
US Department of Homeland Security, *Advisory Maintaining Awareness Regarding Al Qaeda's Possible Threats to the Homeland* (US Department of Homeland Security, September 4th 2003).
Walker, C., *Terrorism and the Law* (Oxford University Press, 2011).
—— *The Anti-Terrorism Legislation* (Oxford University Press, 2009).
Walton, D., *Informal Logic: A Handbook for Critical Argumentation* (Cambridge University Press, 1989).
Zeugmann, C., *The Trade-off Between Civil Liberties and Security in the United States and Germany After 9/11/01* (Diplomica Verlag, 2008).

Contributions to Edited Books

Adderley, A. and Musgrove, P., 'Data Mining Case Study: Modelling the Behaviour of Offenders who Commit Serious Sexual Assaults' in F. Provost and R. Srikant (eds), *ACM SIGKDD International Conference on Knowledge Discovery and Data Mining* (Association for Computer Machinery, 2001).
Andronikou, V., Yannopoulos, A. and Varvarigou, T., 'Biometric Profiling: Opportunities and Risks' in M. Hildebrandt and S. Gutwirth (eds), *Profiling the European Citizen: Cross-Disciplinary Perspectives* (Springer, 2010).

Arai-Takahashi, Y., 'Proportionality' in D. Shelton (ed), *The Oxford Handbook of International Human Rights Law* (Oxford University Press, 2013).

Ashworth, A., 'Security, Terrorism and the Value of Human Rights' in B. Goold and L. Lazarus (eds), *Security and Human Rights* (Hart Publishing, Oxford, 2007).

Boon, J., 'The Contribution of Personality Theories to Psychological Profiling' in J. Jackson and D. Bekarian (eds), *Offender Profiling: Theory, Research and Practice* (John Wiley & Sons Publishing, 1997).

Canhoto, A. and Backhouse, J., 'General Description of the Process of Behavioural Profiling' in M. Hildebrandt and S. Gutwirth (eds), *Profiling the European Citizen: Cross- Disciplinary Perspectives* (Springer, 2010).

Canter, D., 'Psychology of Offender Profiling' in R. Bull and D. Carson (eds), *Handbook of Psychology in Legal Concepts* (Wiley Publishing, 1995).

Choudry, S., 'Protecting Equality in the Face of Terror: Ethnic and Racial Profiling and s. 15 of the Charter' in R. Daniels, P. Macklem and K. Roach (eds), *The Security of Freedom: Essays on Canada's Anti-Terrorism Bill* (University of Toronto Press, 2001).

Crenshaw, M., 'Have Motivations for Terrorism Changed?' in J. Victoroff (ed), *Tangled Roots: Social and Psychological Factors in the Genesis of Terrorism* (ISO Press, 2006).

De Bruin, J., Cocx, T., Kosters, W., Laros, J. and Kok, J., 'Data Mining Approaches to Criminal Career Analysis' in C. Clifton and N. Zhong (eds), *IEEE International Conference on Data Mining* (IEEE Computer Society, 2006).

Dean, G., 'Criminal Profiling in a Terrorism Context' in R. Kocsis (ed), *Criminal Profiling: International Theory, Research and Practice* (Humana Press, 2010).

Delsol, R. and Shiner, M., 'Introduction' in R Delsol and M. Shiner (eds), *Stop and Search: The Anatomy of a Police Power* (Springer Publishing, 2015).

Devedzic, 'Knowledge Discovery and Data Mining in Databases' in S. Chang (ed), *Software Engineering and Knowledge Discovery Vol 1 Fundamentals* (World Scientific Publishing Company, 2001).

Edley, C., 'The New American Dilemma: Racial Profiling Post 9/11' in R. Leone and G. Anrig (eds), *The War on Our Freedoms* (Public Affairs Publishing, 2003).

Farrington, D. and Lambert, S., 'Predicting Offender Profiles from Victim and Witness Descriptions' in *Offender Profiling – Theory, Research and Practice* (John Wiley & Sons Publishing, 2001).

Feldman, D., 'Proportionality and the Human Rights Act 1998' in E. Ellis (ed), *The Principle of Proportionality in the Laws of Europe* (Hart Publishing, 1999).

Fenwick, H. and Phillipson, G., 'UK Counterterror Law Post-9/11: Initial Acceptance of Extraordinary Measures and the Partial Return to Human Rights Norms' in V. Ramraj, M. Hor, K. Roach and G. Williams (eds), *Global Anti-Terrorism Law and Policy* (Cambridge University Press, 2012).

Fienberg, S., 'Homeland Insecurity: Data Mining, Privacy, Disclosure, Limitation and the Hunt for Terrorists' in H. Chen, E. Reid, J. Sinai, A. Silke and E. Ganor (eds), *Terrorism Informatics: Knowledge Management for Homeland Security* (Springer, 2008).

Fitzgerald, M., Hough, M., Joseph, I. and Quereshi, T., *Policing for London* (Willan Publishing, 2002).

Gendreau, P., Goggin, C., Cullen, E. and Paparozzi, M., 'The Common Sense Revolution and Correctional Policy' in J. Maguire (ed), *Offender Rehabilitation and Treatment: Effective Programmes and Policies to Reduce Reoffending* (John Wiley & Sons Publishing, 2002).

Harcourt, 'Muslim Profiles Post 9/11: Is Racial Profiling an Effective Counter-Terrorist Measure and Does It Violate the Right to Be Free from Discrimination?' in B. Goold and L. Lazarus (eds), *Security and Human Rights* (Hart Publishing, 2007).

Heinz, W., 'Germany: State Responses to Terrorist Challenges and Human Rights' in A. Brysk (ed), *National Insecurity and Human Rights: Democracies Debate Counterterrorism* (University of California Press, 2007).

Heller, M. and Haynal, V., 'Perspectives of Psychopathology and Psychotherapy' in P. Ekman and E. Rosenberg (eds), *The Face Reveals: Basic and Applied Studies of Spontaneous Expressions Using the Facial Action Coding System (FACS)* (Oxford University Press, 2005).

Hindman, D. and Cook, P., 'Profiling and Criminal Investigative Analysis of Violent Crimes With Multiple offenders' in H. Hall and L. Whitaker (eds), *Collective Violence: Effective Strategies for Assessing and Intervening in Fatal Group and Institutional Aggression* (CRC Press, 1999).

Horgan, J., 'The Search for the Terrorist Personality' in A. Silke (ed), *Terrorist, Victims and Society: Psychological Perspectives on Terrorism and Its Consequences* (Wiley Publishing, 2003).

Horvath, M., 'Offender Profiling' in S. Tong, R. Bryant and M. Horvath (eds), *Understanding Criminal Investigation* (John Wiley & Sons Publishing, 2009).

Islamic Institute for Human Rights, 'Country Profile: The Conditions of Muslims in France' in Open Society Institute (OSI), *Monitoring Minority Protection in EU Member States: Overview* (OSI, 2004).

Kutscha, M., 'Mehr Innere Sicherheit durch weinger Freiheit' in Humanistische Union e. V (ed), *Innere Sicherheit als Gefahr* (Berlin: Humanistische Union, 2003).

Lai Quinlan, T. and Derfoufi, Z., 'Counterterrorism Policing' in R Delsol and M. Shiner (eds), *Stop and Search: The Anatomy of a Police Power* (Springer Publishing, 2015).

Lepsius, O., 'Freiheit, Sicherheit, Terror Die Rechtslage in Deutschland' in T. Jagger, A. Hose and K. Oppermann (eds), *Transatlantische Beziehungen, Sicherheit Wirtschaft Offenlichkeit* (VS Verlag fur Sozialwissenschaften, 2005).

Luban, D., 'Eight Fallacies About Liberty and Security' in R. Wilson (ed), *Human Rights in the 'War in Terrorism'* (Cambridge University Press, 2005).

Lum, C. and Kennedy, L., 'Evidence-Based Counter-Terrorism Policy' in C. Lum and L. Kennedy (eds), *Evidence-Based Counterterrorism Policy* (Springer Publications, 2012).

Moeckli, D., 'Anti-Terrorism Laws, Terrorist Profiling and the Right to Non- Discrimination' in A. Salinas, De Frias, K. Samuel and N. White (eds), *Counter-Terrorism: International Law and Practice* (Oxford University Press, 2012).

Newburn, T., 'Tough on Crime: Penal Policy in England and Wales' in M. Tonery (ed), *Crime, Punishment and Politics in Comparative Perspectives* (University of Chicago Press, 2007).

Ojanen, T., 'Human Rights Dilemmas in Terrorist Profiling' in M. Scheinin (ed), *Law and Security – Facing the Dilemmas* (EUI Law, 2009).

Partsch, K., 'Discrimination' in R. Macdonald, F. Matscher and H. Petzold (eds), *The European System for the Protection of Human Rights* (Kluwer Law, 2008).

Petherick, W. and Ferguson, C., 'Behavioural Consistency, the Homology Assumption and the Problems of Induction' in W. Petherick (ed), *Serial Crime Theoretical Issues in Behavioural Profiling* (Anderson Publishing, 2013).

Petherick, W. and Turvey, B., 'Behavioural Evidence Analysis: An Ideo-Deductive Method of Criminal Profiling' in B. Turvey (ed), *Criminal Profiling: An Introduction* (Academic Press, 2008).

Quinlan, T. and Derfoufi, Z., 'Counter-Terrorism Policing' in R. Desol and M. Shiner (eds), *Stop and Search: The Anatomy of a Police Power* (Palgrave Macmillan, 2015).

Rosenberg, E., 'The Study of Spontaneous Facial Expressions in Psychology' in P. Ekman and E. Rosenberg (eds), *The Face Reveals: Basic and Applied Studies of Spontaneous Expressions Using the Facial Action Coding System (FACS)* (Oxford University Press, 2005).

Scherer, K., 'On the Nature and Function of Emotion: A Component Process Approach' in K. Scherer and P. Ekman (eds), *Approaches to Emotion* (Erlbaum, 1984).

Schmid, A., 'The Definition of Terrorism' in A. Schmid (ed), *The Routledge Handbook of Terrorism Research* (Routledge, 2011).

Shiner, M. and Desol, R., 'The Politics of the Powers' in R Delsol and M. Shiner (eds), *Stop and Search: The Anatomy of a Police Power* (Springer Publishing, 2015).

Teson, F., 'Liberty Security' in R. Wilson (ed), *Human Rights in the 'War on Terror'* (Cambridge University Press, 2005).

Tillema, H., 'A Brief Theory of Terrorism and Technology' in T. Ghosh, M. Prelas and D. Viswanath (eds), *Science and Technology of Terrorism and Counter-Terrorism* (Marcel Dekker, 2002).

Thornberry, T. and Krohn, M., 'The Self-Report Method for Measuring Delinquency and Crime' in D. Duggee, R. Crutchfield, S. Mastrofski, L. Mazerolle, D. McDowall and B. Ostrom (eds), *Innovations in Measurement and Analysis* (National Institute of Justice, 2000).

Thornton, J., 'The General Assumptions and Rationale of Forensic Identification' in D. Faigman, D. Kaye, M. Saks and J. Sanders (eds), *Modern Scientific Evidence: The Law and Expert Testimony* (West Publications, 2008).

Thuraisingham, B., 'Data Mining for Counter-Terrorism' in H. Kargupta, A. Joshi, K. Sivakumar and Y. Yesha (eds), *Data Mining: Next Generation Challenges and Future Directions* (American Association for Artificial Intelligence, 2004).

Turvey, B., 'Serial Crime' in B. Turvey (ed), *Criminal Profiling: An Introduction to Behavioural Evidence Analysis*(Burlington: Academic Press, 2008).

Weber, L. and Bowling, B., 'Introduction: Stop and Search in a Global Context' in L. Weber and B. Bowling (eds), *Stop and Search: Police Power in Global Context* (Routledge, 2012).

Whitaker, R., 'Behavioural Profiling in Israeli Aviation Security as a Tool for Social Control' in E. Zureik, D. Lyon and Y. Abu-Laban (eds), *Surveillance and Control in Israel/Palestine* (Routledge, 2011).

Yannopoulos, A., Andronikou, V. and Varvarigou, T., 'Behavioural Biometric Profiling and Ambient Intelligence' in M. Hildebrandt and S. Gutwirth (eds), *Profiling the European Citizen: Cross-Disciplinary Perspectives* (Springer, 2010).

Articles

Achelpohler, W. and Niehaus, H., 'Data screening as a means of preventing Islamist terrorist attacks on Germany' (2004) 5(5) *German Law Journal* 495.

Annon, J., 'Investigative profiling: a behavioural analysis of the crime scene' (1995) 13(4) *American Journal of Forensic Psychology* 67.

Banks, R., 'Essay: racial profiling and anti-terrorism efforts' (2004) 89 *Cornell Law Review* 1201.

—— 'Race-based suspect selection and colorblind equal protection doctrine and discourse' (2001) 48 *UCLA Law Review* 1077.

Bartol, C., 'Police psychology: then, now and beyond' (1996) 23 *Criminal Justice and Behaviour* 70.

Bayefsky, A., 'The principle of equality or non-discrimination in international law' (1990) 11 *Human Rights Law Journal* 1.

Benmelech, E., Berrebi, C. and Klor, E., 'Counter-suicide-terrorism: evidence from house demolitions' (2010) NBER Working Paper No 16493.

Bennell, C., Jones, N., Taylor, P. and Snook, B., 'Validities and abilities in criminal profiling: a critique of the studies conducted by Richard Kocsis and his colleagues' (2006) 50(3) *International Journal of Offender Therapy and Comparative Criminology* 344.

BeVier, L., 'Information about individuals in the hands of government: some reflections on privacy protection' (1995) 4 *William and Mary Bill of Rights Law Journal* 455.

Blokland, A., Nagin, D. and Nieuwbeerta, P., 'Life span offending trajectories of a Dutch conviction cohort' (2005) 43(4) *Criminology* 919.

Borden, H., 'Factors for predicting parole success" (1928) 19 *Journal of Criminal Law and Criminology* 328.

Borooah, V., 'Economic analysis of police stops and searches: a reply' (2002) 18 *European Journal of Political Economy* 607.

—— 'Racial bias in police stops and searches: an economic analysis' (2001) 17 *European Journal of Political Economy* 17.

Bowling, B. and Phillips, C., 'Disproportionate and discriminatory: reviewing the evidence on police stops and search' (2007) 70(6) *The Modern Law Review* 936.

Breen-Smyth, M., 'Theorising the "suspect community": counterterrorism, security practices and the public imagination' (2014) 7(2) *Critical Studies on Terrorism* 223.

Brown, L., 'The development of a parolee classification system using discriminate analysis' (1978) 15 *Journal of Research in Crime and Delinquency* 92.

Candamo, J., Shreve, M., Goldgof, D., Snapper, D. and Kasturi, R., 'Understanding transit science: a survey on human behavior-recognition algorithms' (2010) 11(1) *IEEE Transactions on Intelligent Transportation Systems* 206.

Canter, D., 'To catch a rapist' (1988) *New Society* 14.

—— 'Offender profiles' (1989) 2(1) *The Psychologist* 14.

——'Offender profiling and criminal differentiation' (2000) 5 *Legal and Criminological Psychology* 23.

—— 'Offender profiling and investigative psychology' (2004) 1 *Journal of Investigative Psychology and Offender Profiling* 1.

Canter, D. and Wentink, N., 'An empirical test of Holmes and Holmes serial murder typology' (2004) 31 *Criminal Justice Behaviour* 489.

Cate, F., 'Governmental data mining: the need for a legal framework' (2008) 43 *Harvard Civil Rights-Civil Liberties Law Review* 435.

Cauley, J. and Elm, E., 'Intervention policy analysis of skyjackings and other terrorist incidents' (1988) 78(2) *American Economic Review* 27.

Chakravarty, S., 'Economic analysis of police stops and searches: a critique' (2002) 18 *European Journal of Political Economy* 597.

Choongh, S., 'Policing the dross: a social disciplinary model of policing' (1998) 38 *British Journal of Criminology* 623.

Collins, R., Gross, R. and Shi, J., 'Silhouette-based human identification from body shape and gait' (2002) IEEE International Conference on Face and Gesture Recognition 351.

Cook, P. and Hinman, D., 'Criminal profiling: science and art' (1999) 15(3) *Journal of Contemporary Criminal Justice* 230.

Cuellar, M., 'Choosing anti-terror targets by national origin and race' (2003) 6(1) *Harvard Latino Law Review* 9.

Daeid, N., 'Differences in offender profiling in the United States of America and the United Kingdom' (1997) *Forensic Science International* 25.

Dahbur, K. and Muscarello, T., 'Classification system for serial criminal patterns' (2003) 11(4) *Artificial Intelligence and Law Volume* 251.

De Schutter, O. and Ringelheim, J., 'Ethnic profiling: a rising challenge for European human rights law' (2008) 71(3) *Modern Law Review* 358.

Delsol, R. and Shiner, M., 'Regulating stop and search: a challenge for police and community relations in England and Wales' (2006) 14 *Critical Criminology* 241.

Demirdjian, D., Ko, T. and Darrell, T., 'Untethered gesture acquisition and recognition for virtual world manipulation' (2005) 8(4) *Virtual Reality* 222.

Derbyshire, J., 'A (potentially) useful tool' (2002) *Responsive Community* 67.

Doughlas, J. and Burgess, A., 'Criminal profiling: a viable investigative tool against crime' (1986) 55 *FBI Law Enforcement Bulletin* 9.

Douglas, J., Ressler, R., Burgess, A. and Hartman, C., 'Criminal profiling from crime scene analysis' (1986) 4 *Behavioural Science and Law* 401.

Dowden, C., Bennell, C. and Bloomfield, S., 'Advances in offender profiling: a systematic review of the profiling literature published over the past 30 years' (2007) 22 *Journal of Police and Criminal Psychology* 44.

Durgan, L., La Free, G. and Korte, R., 'The impact of British counter-terrorist strategies on political violence in Northern Ireland: comparing deterrence and backlash models' (2009) 47(1) *Criminology* 501.

Egger, S., 'Psychological profiling: past present and future' (1999) 15 *Journal of Contemporary Criminal Justice* 242.

Eilliott, M., 'The "war on terror", UK style: the detention and deportation of suspected terrorists' (2010) 8(1) *International Journal of Constitutional Law* 131.

Ellmann, J., 'Racial profiling and terrorism' (2003) 19 *New York Law School Journal of Human Rights* 305.

Enders, W. and Sandler, T., 'After 9/11: is it all different now?' (2005) 49 *Journal of Conflict Resolution* 259.

—— 'Distribution of transnational terrorism among countries by income, class and geography after 9/11' (2006) *International Studies Quarterly* 367.

—— 'Is transnational terrorism becoming more threatening? A time-series investigation' (2000) 44 *Journal of Conflict Resolution* 307.

—— 'Patterns of transnational terrorism, 1970-1999: alternative time-series estimates' (2002) 46 *International Studies Quarterly* 145.

—— 'The effectiveness of anti-terrorism policies: a vector-autoregression-intervention analysis' (1993) 87(4) *American Political Science Review* 829.

Fasel, B. and Luettin, J., 'Automatic facial expression analysis: a survey' (2003) 36(1) *Pattern Recognition* 259.

Fayyad, U., Piatetsky-Shapiro, G. and Smyth, P., 'From data mining to knowledge discovery in databases' (1996) 17(3) *Artificial Intelligence Magazine* 37.

Fiala, I., 'Anything new? The racial profiling of terrorists' (2003) 16(1) *Criminal Justice Studies* 53.

Florence, J. and Friedman, R., 'Profiles in terror: a legal framework for the behavioural profiling paradigm' (2010) 17 *George Mason Law Review* 423.

Frawley, W., Piatetsky-Shapiro, G. and Matheus, C., 'Knowledge discovery in databases: an overview' (1992) 14(3) *AI Magazine* 57.

Ganor, B. and Conte, A., 'Legal and policy issues in establishing a framework for human rights compliance when countering terrorism' (2005) *International Policy Institute for Countering Terrorism* 1.

Gearson, J. and Rosemont, H., 'CONTEST as strategy reassessing Britain's counterterrorism approach' (2005) 12 *Studies in Conflict and Terrorism* 1038.

Githens-Mazer, J., 'The rhetoric and reality: radicalization and political discourse' (20112) 33(5) *International Political Science Review* 556.

Gross, S. and Livingston, D., 'Racial profiling under attack' (2002) 102 *Columbia Law Review* 1413.

Groth, A., Burgess, A. and Holmstrom, L., 'Rape: power, anger and sexuality' (1977) 134 *American Journal of Psychiatry* 1239.

Grubbin, D., 'Offender profiling' (1995) 6 *Journal of Forensic Psychiatry* 259.

Han, S., 'The long shadow of racial profiling' (2012) 1 *British Journal of American Legal Studies* 77.

Harcourt, B., 'Rethinking racial profiling: a critique of the economics, civil liberties, and constitutional literature, and of criminal profiling more generally' (2004) 71(4) *The University of Chicago Law Review* 1329.

Harris, D., 'Flying while Arab: lessons from the racial profiling controversy' (2002) 6 *Civil Rights Journal* 8.

—— 'New risks, new tactics: an assessment of the re-assessment of racial profiling in the wake of September 11, 2001' (2004) 4 *Utah Law Review* 913.

—— 'Racial profiling revisited: "just common sense" in the fight against terror?' (2002) 17 *Criminal Justice* 36.

—— 'Racial profiling redux' (2003) 22 *Saint Louis University Public Law Review* 73.

Hart, H., 'Predicting parole success' (1923) 41(3) *Journal of American Institute of Criminal Law and Criminology* 405.

Hasisi, B., 'Ethnic profiling in airport screening: lessons from Israel, 1968-2010' (2012) 41(2) *American Law and Economics Review* 517.

Hasisi, B., and Weisburd, D., 'Going beyond ascribed identities: the importance of procedural justice in airport security screening in Israel' (2011) 45(4) *Law and Society Review* 867.

Hayfron-Acquah, J., Nixon, M. and Carter, J., 'Automatic gait recognition by symmetry analysis' (2003) 24(13) *Pattern Recognition Letters* 2175.

Health-Kelly, C., 'Counterterrorism and the counterfactual: producing the "radicalisation" discourse and the UK prevent strategy (2012) 15(3) *The British Journal of Politics and International Relations* 394.

Heath, A. and Martin, J., 'Can religious affiliation explain "ethnic" inequalities in the labour market' (2013) 36(6) *Ethnic and Racial Studies* 1005.

Herbert, L., 'Othello error: facial profiling, privacy and the suppression of the dissent' (2007) 5 *Ohio State Journal of Criminal Law* 79.

Hilbrans, S., 'Neue Grenzen fur die Uberwacher? Zur jungsten Entwicklung der Verfassungsprechung' (2005) 82(3) *Burgerrecht und Polizei Clip* 24.

Holmes, R. and DeBurger, J., 'Profiles in terror: the serial murderer' (1985) 49(3) *Federal Probation* 29.

Holmes, R. and Holmes, S., 'Understanding mass murder: a starting point' (1992) 56(1) *Federal Probation* 53.

Homant, R. and Kennedy, D., 'Psychological aspects of crime scene profiling: validity research' (1998) 25 *Criminal Justice and Behaviour* 319.

Hunt, A., 'Counter-terrorism law' (2017) *Birmingham Law School, Occasional Paper Series* 1.

IBPP, 'Biometric, psychometric and sociometric profiling' (2003) 15(8) *IBBP Online* 1.

Imilienski, T. and Mannila, H., 'A database perspective on knowledge discovery' (1996) 39(11) *Communications of the ACM* 58.

Inmon, W., 'Data warehouse and data mining' (1996) 39(11) *Communications of the ACM* 49.

Ip, J., 'The reform of counterterrorism stop and search after Gillian v United Kingdom' (2013) 13(4) *Human Rights Law Review* 729.

Johnston, D., Brazier, D., Forrest, K., Ketelhut, C., Mason, D. and Mitchell, M., 'Attitudes toward the use of racial/ethnic profiling to prevent crime and terrorism' (2011) 22(4) *Criminal Justice Policy Review* 422.

Jones, A., 'The corrective use of lawsuit data in policing: reconstructing the vocabulary of racial profiling' (2013) 5 *Widener Journal of Law, Economics and Race* 1.

Jones, J. and Harper, J., 'Effective counter-terrorism and the limited role of predictive data mining' (2006) 584 *Policy Analysis* 1.

Jowell, J., 'Beyond the rule of law: towards constitutional judicial review' (2000) *Public Law* 671.

Keppel, R. and Walter, R., 'Profiling killers: a revised classification model for understanding sexual murder' (1999) 43 *International Journal of Offender Therapy and Comparative Criminology* 417.

Kinsley, M., 'Discrimination we're afraid to be against' (2002) *Responsive Community* 64.

Kleiner, Y., 'Racial profiling in the name of national security: protecting minority travelers' civil liberties in the age of terrorism' (2010) 30 *Boston College Third World Law Journal* 103.

Knight, R. and Prently, R., 'The development antecedents and adult adaptations of rapist subject subtypes' (1987) 14 *Criminal Justice and Behaviour* 403.

Kocsis, R., 'An empirical assessment of content in criminal psychological profiles' (2003) 47(1) *International Journal of Offender Therapy and Comparative Criminology* 37.

—— 'Validities and abilities in criminal profiling: the dilemma for David Canter's investigative psychology' (2006) 50(4) *International Journal of Offender Therapy and Comparative Criminology* 458.

Kolko, D. and Kazdin, A., 'The emergence and recurrence of child firesetting: a one-year prospective study' (1992) 20 *Journal of Abnormal Child Psychology* 17.

Kutscha, M., 'Unerwunschte Hausaufgaben, Die Desetzgeber ignorieren Die Vorgaben des Verfassungsgerichts' (2005) 82(3) *Burgerrecht und Polizei Clip* 16.

Landes, W., 'An economic study of US aircraft hijackings, 1961-1976' (1978) 21(1) *Journal of Law and Economics* 1.

Lennon, G., 'Stop and search powers in UK terrorism investigations: a limited judicial oversight' (2016) 20 *The International Journal of Human Rights* 634.

Lepsius, O., 'Liberty, security and terrorism: the legal position in Germany' (2004) 5(5) *German Law Journal* 435.

Lester, D., Yang, B. and Lindsay, M., 'Suicide bombers: are psychological profiles possible' (2004) 27 *Studies in Conflict and Terrorism* 283.

Libert, J., 'Contributions of psychiatric consultation in the investigation of serial murder' (1986) 29 *International Journal of Offender Therapy and Comparative Criminology* 187.

Lozano, S. and Tversky, B., 'Communicative gestures facilitate problem solving for both communicators and recipients' (2006) 55(1) *Journal of Memory and Language* 47.

Lum, C., Kennedy, L. and Sherley, A., 'Are counter-terrorist strategies effective? The results of the Campbell systematic review on counter-terrorism evaluation research' (2006) 2 *Journal of Experimental Criminology* 489.

Madsen, J., 'The rationale of suicide terrorism' (2004) *Review of International Social Questions* 8.

Markovsky, D., 'How to build a fence' (2004) 82(2) *Foreign Affairs* 50.

Maxwell, T., 'Information policy, data mining and national security: false positives and unidentified negatives' (2005) *HICCSS* 1.

McCulloch, J. and Pickering, S., 'Pre-crime and counter-terrorism: impacting future crime in the "war on terror"' (2009) 49(5) *British Journal of Criminology* 628.

McGuirk, N., 'A framework to measure/assess the utility of profiling as a counterterrorism tool' (2019) *Policing: A Journal of Policy and Practice, Advance Access*, paz056, https://doi.org/10.1093/police/paz056 (accessed 2nd July 2020).

McGrath, M., 'Criminal profiling: is there a role for the forensic psychiatrist?' (2000) 28 *Journal of the American Academy of Psychiatry and Law* 319.

Memon, N., Hicks, D. and Larsen, H., 'How investigative data mining can help intelligence agencies to discover dependence of nodes in terrorist networks' (2007) 4632 *Lecture Notes in Computer Science* 430.

Memon, N. and Larsen, H., 'Detecting terrorist activity patterns using investigative data mining tools' (2006) 3(1) *International Journal of Knowledge and Systems Science* 43.

Meyer, D., 'The SPOT program: hello racial profiling, goodbye fourth amendment?' (2010) 10 *University of Maryland Law Journal of Race, Religion, Gender and Class* 289.

Miller, J., 'Stop and search in England: a reformed tactic or business as usual' (2010) 50(5) *British Journal of Criminology* 954.

Miller, R., 'Balancing security and liberty in Germany' (2010) 4 *Journal of National Security Law and Policy* 369.

Moeckli, D., 'Discriminatory profiles: law enforcement after 9/11' (2005) 5 *European Human Rights Law Review* 517.

Mokros, A. and Alison, L., 'Is offender profiling possible? Testing the predicted homology of crime scene actions and background characteristics in a sample of rapists' (2002) 7 *Legal and Criminological Psychology* 25.

Muller, D., 'Criminal profiling. Real science or just wishful thinking?' (2000) 4(3) *Homicide Studies* 234.

Neumann, P. and Kleinmann, S., 'How rigorous is radicalization research?' (2013) 9 *Democracy and Security* 360.

Ojanen, T., 'Terrorist profiling and human rights concerns' (2010) 3(2) *Critical Studies in Terrorism* 295.

Oka, K., Sato, Y. and Koike, H., 'Real-time fingertip tracking and gesture recognition' (2002) 22(6) *Computer Graphics and Applications* 64.

Panaccio, C., 'In defence of two-step balancing and proportionality in rights adjudication' (2011) 24 *CJLJ* 109.

Pantazis, C. and Pemberton, S., 'From "old" to "new" suspect community: examining the impact of recent counter-terrorist legislation' (2009) 49(5) *British Journal of Criminology* 646.

Parmer, A., 'Stop and search in London: counter terrorist or counter productive?' (2011) 21(4) *Policing and Society* 369.

Patwardhan, K. and Roy, S., 'Hand gestures modelling and recognition involving changing shapes and trajectories using a predictive EigenTracker' (2007) 28(3) *Pattern Recognition Letters* 329.

Petherwick, W., 'What is in a name? Comparing applied profiling methodologies' (2003) 5 *Journal of Law and Social Challenges* 173.

Phillips, P., Sarkar, S., Robledo, I., Grother, P. and Bowyer, K., 'Baseline results for the challenge problem of human ID using gait analysis' (2002) IEEE International Conference on Automatic Face and Gesture Recognition 130.

Pinizotto, A., 'Forensic psychology: criminal personality profiling' (1984) 12 *Journal of Police Science and Administration Section* 1.

Polanco, K., 'The Fourth Amendment Challenge to DNA Samples of Arrestees Pursuant to the Justice for All Act of 2004' (2005) 27 *University of Arkansas Little Rock Law Review* 483.

Popper, K., 'On the sources of knowledge and of ignorance' (1960) Proceedings of the British Academy of Sciences 39.

Poythress, N., Otto, R., Darkes, J. and Starr, L., 'APA's expert panel in the congressional review of the USS Iowa incident' (1993) 48 *American Psychologists* 8.

Raghu, T. and Chen, H., 'Cyberinfrastructure for homeland security: advances in information sharing, data mining, and collaboration systems' (2007) 43(4) *Decision Support Systems* 1321.

Ramierz, D., Hoopes, J. and Quinlan, T., 'Defining racial profiling in a post September 11th world' (2003) 40(3) *American Criminal Law Review* 1195.

Ravich, T., 'Is airline passenger profiling necessary?' (2007) 62(1) *University of Miami Law Review* 1.

Reddick, R., 'Point: the case for profiling' (2004) 79 *International Social Science Review* 154.

Richie, J. and Mogul, J., 'In the shadows of the war on terror: persistent police brutality and abuse of people of color in the United States' (2008) 1 *DePaul Journal of Social Justice* 175.

Rider, A., 'The firesetter: a psychological profile (Part 1)' (1980) 49(6) *FBI Law Enforcement Bulletin* 6.

Risse, M., 'Racial profiling: a reply to two critics' (2007) *Criminal Justice Ethics* 4.

Risse, M. and Zeckhauser, R., 'Racial profiling' (2004) 32(2) *Philosophy and Public Affairs* 131.

Roach, K., 'Making progress on understanding and remedying racial profiling' (2004) 41 *Alberta Law Review* 895.

Roberts, D., 'Race, vagueness and the social meaning of order-maintenance policing' (1999) 89 *British Journal of Criminology* 775.

Sakheim, G., Vigdor, M., Gordon, M. and Helprin, L., 'A psychological profile of juvenile firesetters in residential treatment' (1985) 64 *Child Welfare* 453.

Scherer, K., 'Vocal communication of emotion: a review of research paradigms' (2003) 40(1) *Speech Communication* 227.

Scherer, K., Banse, R. and Wallbott, H., 'Emotion inferences from vocal expression correlate across languages and cultures' (2001) 32(1) *Journal of Cross-Cultural Psychology* 76.

Schokkenbroek, J., 'The prohibition of discrimination in article 14 of the convention and the margin of appreciation' (1998) 19 *Human Rights Law Review* 20.

Schouten, R., 'Terrorism and the behavioural sciences' (2010) 18(6) *Harvard Review of Psychiatry* 369.

Seymour, B., 'Behavioural pattern recognition and aviation security' (2005) 1(2/3) *Journal of Security Education* 69.

Shiner, M., 'Post-Lawrence policing in England and Wales: guilt, innocence and the defence of organisational ego' (2010) 50(5) *British Journal of Criminology* 935.

Shoda, Y., Mischel, W. and Wright, J., 'Personality processes and individual differences' (1994) 67(4) *Journal of Personality and Social Psychology* 674.

Smith, D., 'Ethnic origins, crime, criminal justice in England and Wales (1997) 21 *Ethnicity, Crime and Immigration: Comparative and Cross-National Perspectives* 101.

Snook, B., Cullen, R., Bennell, C., Taylor, P. and Gendreau, P., 'The criminal profiling illusion: what's behind the smoke and mirrors?' (2008) 35(10) *Criminal Justice and Behaviour* 1257.

Snook, B., Eastwood, J., Gendreau, P., Goggin, C. and Cullen, R., 'Taking stock of criminal profiling: a narrative review and meta-analysis' (2007) 34(4) *Criminal Science and Behaviour* 437.

Solove, D., 'Data mining and the security-liberty debate' (2008) 75 *University of Chicago Law Review* 343.

Sweet, A. and Mathews, J., 'Proportionality balancing and global constitutionalism' (2008) 47 *Columbia Journal of Transnational Law* 72.

Swiney, C., 'Racial profiling of Arabs and Muslims in the US: historical, empirical and legal analysis applied to the war on terrorism' (2006) 3(1) *Muslim World Journal of Human Rights* 1.

Taipale, K., 'Data mining and domestic security: connecting the dots to make sense of the data' (2003) 5 *The Columbia Science and Technology Law Review* 1.

Testas, A., 'Determinants of terrorism in the Middle East' (2004) 16(2) *Terrorism and Political Violence* 253.

Thai, J., 'Is data mining ever a search under Justice Steven's Fourth Amendment?' (2006) 74 *Fordham Law Review* 1731.

Thomas, P., 'Emergency and anti-terrorist powers 9/11: USA and UK' (2003) 26 *Fordham International Law Journal* 1193.

Turco, R., 'Psychological profiling' (1990) 34 *International Journal of Offender Therapy and Comparative Criminology* 147.

Vanderlooy, S., Verbeck, J. and van Den Herik, J., 'Towards privacy preserving data mining in law enforcement' (2007) 2(4) *Journal of International Commercial Law and Technology* 202.

van Dongen, T., 'Break it down: an alternative approach to measuring effectiveness in counter-terrorism' (2011) 6 *Journal of Applied Security Research* 357.

Waddington, P., Stenson, K. and Don, D., 'In proportion: race and police stop and search' (2004) 44 *British Journal of Criminology* 889.

Weiner, J., 'Terrorism: Israel's legal responses' (1987) 14 *Syracuse Journal of International and Comparative Law* 183.

Westen, P., 'The empty idea of equality' (1982) 95 *Harvard Law Review* 537.

Wilson, P., Lincoln, R. and Kocsis, R., 'Validity, utility and ethics of profiling for serial violent and sexual offenders' (1997) 4 *Psychiatry, Psychology and the Law* 1.

Wock, T., 'The TSA's new x-ray vision: the fourth amendment implications of "body-scan" searches at domestic airport security checkpoints' (2009) 49(1) *Santa Clara Law Review* 213.

Woodhams, J. and Toyle, K., 'An empirical test of the assumptions of case linkage and offender profiling with serial commercial robberies' (2007) 13(1) *Psychological, Public Policy and Law* 59.

Yesufu, S., 'Discriminatory use of police stop and search powers in London, UK' (2013) 15(4) *International Journal of Police Science and Management* 281.

Zander, M., 'Tighter controls on stop and search – but will they make any difference?' (2014) 178(37) *Criminal Law and Justice Weekly* 543.

Zarksy, T., 'Governmental data mining and its alternatives' (2011) 116(2) *Penn State Law Review* 285.

Zussmann, A. and Zussmann, N., 'Assassinations: evaluating the effectiveness of an Israeli counter-terrorism policing using stock market data' (2006) 20(2) *Journal of Economic Perspectives* 193.

Online/Newspapers

Amrar, V., 'Life after 9/11: the golden rule of racial profiling', LA Times, September 22, 2002.

Associated Press, 'Israel's airport security: Arabs complain they face racist treatment when boarding planes', Associated Press, March 19, 2008.

Associated Press, 'Italy arrests 142 in anti-terrorism sweep', Associated Press, July 9, 2005.

Azar, B., 'What's in a face?' (2000) Monitor on Psychology, available at: http://www.apa.org/monitor/jan00/sc1.aspx (accessed 01st May 2020).

Barovick, H., 'Driving while black', Time, June 15, 1998.

BBC News, 'Italy police raid, terror school', BBC News (2007), available at: http://news.bbc.co.uk/1/hi/world/europe/6909961.stm (accessed 17th March 2020).

Berndt, T. and Schiffermuller, D., Raster Fur Europa Minister Schily und sein Fahndungsflop, Panorama, Hamburg, April 8, 2004, available at: http://daserste.ndr.de/panorama/archiv/2004/erste8498.html (accessed 06th January 2020).

Bernstein, R., 'Raid on "Holy War" Mosque', New York Times, July 14, 2004.

Blumenkrantz, Z., 'Haaretz probe: Israel airport security often carried out by untrained employees', Haaretz, January 11, 2010, available at: https://www.haaretz.com/1.5083877 (accessed 12th June 2020).

Blumenkrantz, Z., 'Mazuz moves to limit racial profiling at Ben-Gurion Airport', Haazretz, June 4, 2008.

CNN, 'Mini-Arsenal find at UK mosque', CNN, January 21, 2003, available at: http://edition.cnn.com/2003/WORLD/europe/01/20/mosque.raid/ (accessed 17th March 2020).

CNN, 'US didn't connect "dots" before 9/11', May 15, 2002, available at: http://articles.cnn.com/2002-05-15/us/inv.fbi.terror_1_memo-dots-osama- bin?_s=PM:US (accessed 01st November 2019).

Gold, D., 'The cost of terrorism and the costs of countering terrorism' (2005) International Working Affairs Papers, available at: http://www.gpia.info/files/u1/wp/2005-03.pdf (accessed 03rd January 2020).

Derfner, L., 'Stereotyping security', Jerusalem Post, March 22, 2007.

Dodd, V., 'Asian men targeted in stop and search', The Guardian, August 17, 2005.

Donnelly, S., 'A new tack for airport screening: behave yourself', Time, May 17, 2006.

Ekman, P., 'How to spot a terrorist on the fly', Washington Post, October 29, 2006.

FinCEN, 'Guidance on preparing a complete and sufficient suspicious activity report narrative', available at: http://www.fincen.gov/statutes_regs/files/sarnarrcompletguidfinal_112003.pdf (accessed 2nd November 2019).

Frank, D., 'Body language can blow their cover', USA Today, December 28, 2005.

'Germany: arbitrary control of persons in front of mosques continue', Muslim Affairs, August 8, 2005, available at: http://www.muslim- lawyers.net/news/index.php3?aktion=show&number=289 (accessed 01st January 2020).

Goldson, J., 'Ethnic profiling and counter-terrorism: trends, dangers and alternatives', June 6, 2006, available at: http://www.soros.org/initiatives/justice/articles_publications/articles/counterterrorism_2 0060606/goldston_20060606.pdf (accessed 03rd January 2020).

Harcourt, B., 'Behavioural profiling at US airports' (2006), available at: http://www.law.uchicago.edu/files/files/Harcourt%20OpEd%20Behavioral%20Profiling%20Longer%20Version.pdf (accessed 04th June 2020).

Harris, S., 'Giving in to the surveillance state', New York Times, August 22, 2012, available at: https://www.nytimes.com/2012/08/23/opinion/whos-watching-the-nsa-watchers.html (accessed 12th June 2020).

Jaggi, R., 'Police gain extra time to question suspects', The Financial Times, August 9, 2004.

Karp, J. and Meckler, L., 'Which travellers have hostile intent? Biometric device may have the answer', Wall Street Journal, August 14, 2006.

Kaye, K., 'TSA screenings more than just carry-on bags: behavior detection officers covertly watch travellers', Washington Post, November 9, 2009.

Lewis, N., 'FBI chief admits 9/11 might have been detectable', The New York Times, May 29, 2002, available at: http://www.nytimes.com/2002/05/30/us/traces-of-terror-the-overview-fbi-chief-admits-9-11-might-have-been-detectable.html (accessed 01st November 2019).

Manges Jones, H., 'Italian police arrest 142 in post-London anti-terror sweep', Jurist, July 9, 2005.

National Commission on Terrorist Attacks Upon the United States, *The Aviation Security System and the 9/11 Attacks* (National Commission on Terrorist Attacks Upon the United States, 2004), available at: http://www.au.af.mil/au/awc/awcgate/911_commission/staff_statement_3.pdf (accessed 3rd October 2019).

Patterson, T., 'Raids on mosques broke terror network, claim German police', The Independent, January 13, 2005, available at: http://www.independent.co.uk/news/world/europe/raids-on-mosques-broke-terror- network-claim-german-police-5344647.html (accessed 17th March 2020).

Reuters News, 'Cologne Police slammed for "racial profiling" after mass migrant screening on NYE', available at: https://www.rt.com/news/372501-cologne-police-racial-profiling/ (accessed 15th March 2020).

Rogers, P., 'The war on terrorism: winning or losing' (2003) ORG Briefing Paper, available at: http://www.oxfordresearchgroup.org.uk/publications/briefings/winningorlosing.htm (accessed 03rd January 2018).

Schuck, P., 'Context is everything with racial profiling', LA Times, January 27, 2002.

Shaukovsky, P., 'Airport profilers: they're watching you', Seattle Post-Intelligencer, December 25, 2007.

Secure Flight Program, 72 Federal Register 48,356 Oct 24, 2007, available at: http://www.gpo.gov/fdsys/pkg/FR-2007-10-24/pdf/07-5254.pdf (accessed 04th November 2019).

Smolar, P., 'Disruption of the locations where radical Islam is spread', Le Monde, April 11, 2006.

Sweifert, J., *Data Mining and Homeland Security* (CRS Reports, 2007), 3 available at: http://www.fas.org/sgp/crs/intel/RL31798.pdf (accessed 3rd September 2019).

TSA, 'TSA behavior and detection analysis program', available at: https://www.tsa.gov/news/testimony/2013/11/14/tsa-behavior-detection-and-analysis- program (accessed 2nd June 2020).

Turley, J., 'Use profiling judiciously', LA Times, January 4, 2002.

US Department of Homeland Security, 'Preventing terrorism results', available at: http://www.dhs.gov/topic/preventing-terrorism-results (accessed 14th May 2020).

US Department of Homeland Security, *TSA's CAPPS II Gives Equal Weight to Privacy* (GAO, 2003), available at: http://faculty.uml.edu/bleblanc/44.115/pdf/CAPPS%20II.pdf (accessed 11th November 2019).

US Department of Justice, 'Fact sheet: shifting from prosecution to prevention: redesigning the Justice Department to prevent future acts of terrorism' (2002), available at: http://ontario.worldlibrary.net/Members/Government_Library/Collection/2002/05/fbireor ganizationfactsheet.pdf (accessed 22nd September 2019).

US Department of Treasury, A Report to Congress in Accordance with § 357 of the United and Strengthening, *America by Providing Appropriate Tools Required to Intercept and Obstruct Terrorism Act 2001* (GPO, 2002), available at: http://www.fincen.gov/news_room/rp/files/hawalarptfinal11222002.pdf (accessed 01st November 2019).

US General Accounting Office, *Aviation Security: Computer Assisted Passenger Pre-screening System Faces Significant Implementation Challenges* (GAO, 2004), available at: http://www.gao.gov/new.items/d04385.pdf (accessed 05th November 2019).

US Select Committee on Intelligence and US House Permanent Select Committee on Intelligence, *Joint Inquiry into the Intelligence Community Activities Before and After the Terrorist Attacks of September 11th* (Government Printing Office, 2002), available at: http://www.gpo.gov/fdsys/pkg/CRPT-107hrpt792/pdf/CRPT-107hrpt792-ERRATA.pdf (accessed 12th September 2020).

van Um, E. and Pisoiu, D., 'Effective counterterrorism: what have we learned so far?' (2011) Economics of Security Working Paper 55, available at: http://www.diw.de/documents/publikationen/73/diw_01.c.386651.de/diw_econsec0055. pdf (accessed 03rd January 2020).

Index

Italicized and **bold** pages refer to figures and tables respectively, and page numbers followed by "n" refer to notes.

For Product Safety Concerns and Information please contact our EU representative GPSR@taylorandfrancis.com
Taylor & Francis Verlag GmbH, Kaufingerstraße 24, 80331 München, Germany

www.ingramcontent.com/pod-product-compliance
Lightning Source LLC
LaVergne TN
LVHW011124300926
849160LV00008B/500

* 9 7 8 0 3 6 7 6 9 7 3 4 1 *